The Adjudicator's Toolkit and the Force of International Law

The Adjudicator's Toolkit and the Force of International Law

Comparing Trade and Investment Disputes

By

Nicola Strain

BRILL | NIJHOFF

LEIDEN | BOSTON

Cover illustration: Nicola Claire Strain (generated using the Open AI Dall-E 2 program on February 21, 2024)

Library of Congress Cataloging-in-Publication Data

Names: Strain, Nicola, author.
Title: The adjudicator's toolkit and the force of international law / Nicola Strain.
Description: Leiden ; Boston : Brill/Nijhoff, 2024. | Includes bibliographical references and index. | Summary: "Adjudicators have been placed at the forefront in the search for systemic order within the pluralist international legal order, acting as guardians of the international legal system. Yet, they do so under increasing pressure from the governments. Based on one of the most comprehensive and systematic empirical and doctrinal studies of international trade and investment adjudication, this book asks which tools adjudicators turn to when faced with this dilemma. Dr. Nicola Strain provides new insights on the design choices and normative goals of international economic adjudication, explaining how adjudicators end up consistently inconsistent in their application of international law, even within the more technocratic WTO regime" – Provided by publisher.
Identifiers: LCCN 2024017861 | ISBN 9789004700925 (hardback) | ISBN 9789004700932 (ebook)
Subjects: LCSH: Foreign trade regulation. | International commercial arbitration. | Investments, Foreign (International law) | Jurisdiction (International law)
Classification: LCC K2400 .S77 2024 | DDC 343.08/7–dc23/eng/20240511
LC record available at https://lccn.loc.gov/2024017861

Typeface for the Latin, Greek, and Cyrillic scripts: "Brill". See and download: brill.com/brill-typeface.

ISBN 978-90-04-70092-5 (hardback)
ISBN 978-90-04-70093-2 (e-book)
DOI 10.1163/9789004700932

This book is printed on acid-free paper and produced in a sustainable manner.

Contents

Acknowledgements

International law seems like such a puzzle when you first approach it as a young lawyer – how do its pieces fit together, if at all? Adjudicators are presented with this problem regularly, and on an increasing scale as the number of global concerns continue to reach international courts and tribunals. The intersection of jurisdiction, applicable law and interpretation may seem like dry, technical topics if one is focused on the many challenges facing the legitimacy of international law, topics which we often want to skip over to reach the excitement of the merits of a dispute. But there are necessary to understand the complex workings of international law and its courts and tribunals. This is what I sought to show when I set out on this project.

The process has not been easy, with the stresses on international economic law only continuing to intensify since I began this project. Writing a book on the role of adjudicators in international economic law seems daunting when the "crown jewel" of international economic law, the WTO Appellate Body, becomes redundant. Yet, adjudicators strive on since disputes will not wait for the often-slow process of institutional reform to complete. These points of stress and reform give us an opportunity to rethink how we approach what may seem like technical issues, but nonetheless touch on the legitimacy of international law and its courts and tribunals.

I would like to thank the many supporters of this project, which began as a doctorate at the PluriCourts Centre, University of Oslo. This work was partly supported by the Research Council of Norway through its Centres of Excellence funding scheme (project number 223274 – PluriCourts: The Legitimacy of the International Judiciary) and the Funding Scheme for Independent Projects (FRIPRO) (Young Research Talents) (project number 274946 – State Consent to International Jurisdiction: Conferral, Modification and Termination, Prof. dr. Freya Baetens). I am thankful to my PhD supervisors, Freya Baetens, Mads Andenæs and Johann Ruben Leiss, for their support in carrying out this project. I am also grateful to my PhD adjudication committee, Astrid Iversen, Michael Waibel and Valentina Vadi, whose valuable insights helped develop this publication.

I am indebted to the encouraging interdisciplinary environment at PluriCourts that helped me step beyond my comfort zones and develop new research methodologies and questions. I would like to thank the co-directors of PluriCourts, Geir Ulfstein and Andreas Føllesdal, for developing and nurturing this environment and my research along with it.

I am also appreciative of the many opportunities to travel and present my work, including visiting research stays at the Graduate Institute of

International and Development Studies (IHEID), thanks to Joost Pauwelyn, and the Columbia Law School. Thanks to all those that have taken the time to read my research at seminars, workshops and conferences, all the way from Sydney to New York.

The path from idea to book can be long and arduous so I would like to thank all those friends and colleagues who guided me along the way. A special acknowledgement must be given to my fellow PhDs at PluriCourts, Laura Létourneau-Tremblay and Runar Lie, who shared this entire journey with me, as well as Isuru Devendra who first suggested this path. I would also like to thank Malcolm Langford and Taylor St John for their encouragement and faith in me, as well as the many supportive colleagues at the Faculty of Law and beyond, including Max, Johan, Tarald, Øyvind, Szilard, Antoinette, Silje, Even, Matt, Victoria, Mahalet, Karoline, and Emma.

Last, but certainly not least, I would like to thank my family, whose love and support is never diminished even by the continents between us.

Figures and Tables

Figures

Tables

Selected Abbreviations

BIT	Bilateral Investment Treaty
DSB	Dispute Settlement Body (of the WTO)
DSU	Understanding on Rules and Procedures Governing the Settlement of Disputes (of the WTO)
EC	European Communities (official name of the EU before the WTO until 2009)
ECHR	European Convention on Human Rights
ECtHR	European Court of Human Rights
ECT	Energy Charter Treaty
EU	European Union
FET	Fair and equitable treatment
FTA	Free Trade Agreement
GATT	General Agreement on Tariffs and Trade
GPA	Agreement on Government Procurement
ICA	International Court of Arbitration of the International Chamber of Commerce
ICC	International Criminal Court
ICCPR	International Covenant on Civil and Political Rights
ICJ	International Court of Justice
ICJ Rep	International Court of Justice Reports of Judgments, Advisory Opinions and Orders
ICS	Investment Court System
ICSID	International Centre for the Settlement of Investment Disputes
ICTR	International Criminal Tribunal for Rwanda
ICTY	International Criminal Tribunal for the former Yugoslavia
IIA	International Investment Agreement
ILC	International Law Commission
ILO	International Labour Organization
ISDS	Investor-State Dispute Settlement
ITLOS	International Tribunal for the Law of the Sea
LCIA	London Court of International Arbitration
MERCOSUR	Southern Common Market (Mercado Común del Sur / Mercado Comum do Sul)
MIT	Multilateral Investment Treaty
MPIA	Multi-Party Interim Arrangement
NAFTA	North American Free Trade Agreement
OECD	Organisation for Economic Cooperation and Development

OSPAR	Convention for the Protection of the Marine Environment of the North-East Atlantic
PCA	Permanent Court of Arbitration
PCIJ	Permanent Court of International Justice
PITAD	PluriCourts Investment Treaty and Arbitration Database
SCC	Stockholm Chamber of Commerce
SCM	Subsidies and Countervailing Measures
SPS	Sanitary and Phytosanitary Measures
TIP	Treaty with Investment Provisions
TRIPS	Trade-Related Aspects of Intellectual Property Rights
UN	United Nations
UNCITRAL	United Nations Commission on International Trade Law
UNCLOS	United Nations Convention on the Law of the Sea
UNCTAD	United Nations Conference on Trade and Development
UNRIAA	United Nations Reports of International Arbitral Awards
UDHR	Universal Declaration of Human Rights
UNTS	United Nations Treaty Series
VCLT	Vienna Convention on the Law of Treaties
WTO	World Trade Organization

CHAPTER 1

Introduction

In the wake of the specialization of dispute settlement in international law, adjudicators have been left with a difficult balancing act in interpreting and applying international law beyond the four corners of their specialized regime. Adjudicators as actors of international law have an almost herculean task before them: to "learn how to live in this … complex world" of international law.[1] Despite the state-created pluralist system, concerns of fragmentation at the beginning of the 21st century spurned a earning for a unified and coherent international legal system. Yet, overcoming the boundaries of the individual regimes of the international legal system requires adjudicators to wade through complex and interrelated concepts that may push and pull them in different directions. Indeterminacy plagues defragmentation attempts and the sources of international law. Previous research suggests that adjudicators have managed to avert the concerns of fragmentation through various judicial and procedural tools. However, when we dig deeper into the reasoning of the adjudicators, such solutions are shown to be inadequate, and legitimacy concerns remain prevalent.

This book takes trade and investment adjudicators as its centerpiece to reveal the centripetal force of international law.[2] Trade and investment adjudication exemplifies the struggle for cohesion in international law. The clear regime goals of international economic liberalization are often critiqued for closing the door to the intersection of other regimes, in particular human rights and the environment. At the same time, international economic law, as a creature of public international law, relies on general and customary international law to legitimize it.

Based on one of the most comprehensive and systematic empirical and doctrinal studies of international trade and investment adjudication, this book answers how adjudicators have actually approached the dilemma of the coherence and systemic order of international law. The book analyses the reasoning

1 Rosalyn Higgins, 'A Babel of Judicial Voices? Ruminations from the Bench' (2006) 55 International & Comparative Law Quarterly 791, 804; see, similarly, Judge Simma: Bruno Simma, 'Fragmentation in a Positive Light' (2003) 25 Michigan Journal of International Law 845, 846.

2 Adjudicators (and adjudication) is used as a broad term in this book to refer to those deciding legal and judicial disputes in international law, including arbitrators. Even though the forums in which they operate my differ, the functions arguably remain the same.

 | DOI:10.1163/9789004700932_002

on the interplay between international economic law and "other international law", identifying what tools are available to adjudicators and the challenges faced by them in balancing the different factors influencing the legitimate exercise of their functions.

1 The Toolkit: Opening and Closing the Gateway to Other International Law

The book considers three legal concepts that can be used by adjudicators to "open" these treaty-regimes and dispute settlement mechanisms to broader international law: wide applicable law clauses, general principles of law and systemic integration. These concepts have different functions in dispute settlement: a source of authority (law that may be applied), source of law (general principles) and method of interpretation (systemic integration). However, within their respective functions, the concepts can be used to not only bridge gaps between individual treaties but may also play a role in the harmonization of international law and the creation of a coherent "system of international law". The use of such concepts in the harmonization of international law has become particularly pertinent in combatting the negative perception of the proliferation of international courts and tribunals and the fragmentation of international law, more generally. In this way, wide applicable law clauses, general principles and systemic integration enable international adjudicators to take into account the procedures and substantive judgments of other courts, "coordinating amongst themselves with the aim of reducing fragmentation", even in the absence of a clear hierarchy.[3]

First, the concept of applicable law instructs the international tribunal on which norm it is required to apply in the exercise of its jurisdiction.[4] In this way, applicable law may be a gateway for tribunals to apply "other international law". Yet not all applicable law clauses are created equal. There are significant differences between a wide and a narrow applicable law clause as well as between treaties without an applicable law clause, as is the case in World Trade Organization (WTO) disputes. The way in which a tribunal interacts with

3 Chiara Giorgetti and Mark Pollack, 'Beyond Fragmentation: Cross-Fertilization, Cooperation, and Competition among International Courts and Tribunals' in Chiara Giorgetti and Mark Pollack (eds), *Beyond Fragmentation* (1st edn, Cambridge University Press 2022) 17.

4 Lorand Bartels, 'Jurisdiction and Applicable Law Clauses: Where Does a Tribunal Find the Principal Norms Applicable to the Case before It?' in Tomer Broude and Yuval Shany (eds), *Multi-Sourced Equivalent Norms in International Law* (Hart Publishing 2011) 115.

the terms of the varying applicable law clauses as well as the function of applicable law in general can affect how an adjudicator coordinates and integrates the dispute within international law.

Secondly, general principles of law fulfil important functions in international law as opening tools.[5] General principles play an essential role in filling gaps in international law, thereby avoiding a declaration of *non liquet*. Through their gap-filling role, general principles may also fulfil a broader function of ensuring coherence of international law, thus contributing to a system of international law.[6] In addition, certain general principles, such as *res judicata* and *lis pendens*, serve to avoid jurisdictional collisions, thus replacing the pessimistic view of the proliferation of international courts with a more optimistic outlook, one in which plurality can be viewed as healthy, coordinated and well-managed.[7] In this way, general principles are related to the question of applicable law. To the extent that general principles in fact form part of the applicable law in a given dispute (which may not always be the case if the applicable law is narrowly conceived), they may also play a role in the harmonization of international law and dispute settlement.

Thirdly, systemic integration, a principle of treaty interpretation expressed in Article 31(3)(c) of the Vienna Convention on the Law of Treaties (VCLT), requires a tribunal "to take into account the normative environment more widely".[8] Identified as key principle in the International Law Commission's (ILC) Fragmentation Report, systemic integration extends the law that can be used in interpretation beyond the particular sources of law in the applicable law clause. This principle reflects the fact that treaties are themselves creatures of international law and so must be applied against the background of the general principles of international law, a technique of interpretation that permits reference to other rules of international law, enabling the harmonization of

5 Marcelo Vázquez-Bermúdez, 'Third Report on General Principles of Law by Marcelo Vázquez-Bermúdez, Special Rapporteur' (International Law Commission 2022) A/CN.4/753 14 ff.

6 Hersch Lauterpacht, *The Function of Law in the International Community* (Oxford University Press 2011) ch 3; Patrick Dumberry, *A Guide to General Principles of Law in International Investment Arbitration* (Oxford University Press 2020) 53; see the summary of scholarly discussion in Vázquez-Bermúdez (n 5) 50 ff.

7 Veronika Bílková, 'The Threads (or Threats?) Of a Managerial Approach: Afterword to Laurence Boisson de Chazournes' Foreword' (2017) 28 European Journal of International Law 1259, 1260.

8 Martti Koskenniemi, 'Fragmentation of International Law: Difficulties Arising from the Diversification and Expansion of International Law, Report of the Study Group of the International Law Commission' (International Law Commission 2006) A/CN.4/L.682 paras 414–415.

rules and thereby avoiding conflict of norms.[9] Understood in this way, the principle of systemic integration attempts to partially restore the idea of determinacy within international law.[10]

These opening tools stand behind the limited jurisdiction of the tribunals. While these tools of international law open the door to harmonization of international law, to what extent does the limited jurisdiction of the tribunal close that door? The concept of jurisdiction is intrinsically linked to state sovereignty and voluntarism, which provides for state consent as the sole criterion giving international law its binding force and legitimacy. This view of international law provides the least restrictions on states' freedom, with such rules emanating from the states' own free will, including in relation to the role of international courts.[11] The consequence of exceeding this consent to jurisdiction is to render the international court's decision nullifiable, thereby cementing consent to jurisdiction as the cornerstone principle of international adjudication.[12] Yet, the extent to which jurisdiction "closes the door" to other regimes and general international law is not an easy exercise in practice given the indeterminate nature of the "system of international law".

2 The Puzzle: Normative Goals and Design Choices

The indeterminacy of defragmentation creates space for interpretation and discretion by international adjudicators in using the opening and closing tools.

---

9 Campbell McLachlan, 'The Principle of Systemic Integration and Article 31(3)(c) of the Vienna Convention' (2005) 54 International & Comparative Law Quarterly 279, 280.

10 Gleider I Hernández, 'Interpretation' in Jorg Kammerhofer and Jean D'Aspremont (eds), *International Legal Positivism in a Post-Modern World* (Cambridge University Press 2014) 318.

11 As famously stated in *SS Lotus* (*France v Turkey*), *Judgment* [1927] PCIJ Series A No 10 18; for further discussion, see Stéphane Beaulac, 'The Lotus Case in Context: Sovereignty, Westphalia, Vattel, and Positivism' in Stephen Allen and others (eds), *The Oxford Handbook of Jurisdiction in International Law* (Oxford University Press 2019).

12 As Judge Moore explained, '[t]he requirement of jurisdiction, which is universally recognized in the national sphere, is not less fundamental and peremptory in the international … Ever mindful of the fact that their judgments, if rendered in excess of power, may be treated as null, international tribunals have universally regarded the question of jurisdiction as fundamental': *The Mavrommatis Palestine Concessions* (*Greece v United Kingdom*), *Objection to Jurisdiction* [1924] PCIJ Rep Series A No 2 57–60; see also the discussion in Bin Cheng, *General Principles of Law as Applied by International Courts and Tribunals* (reprint 2006, Steven & Sons 1953) 261. Although the question remains who can ultimately declare the decision null and void, particularly in the absence of any appellate or hierarchical mechanisms within the international legal sphere – a question beyond the scope of this research.

How this discretion is exercised is guided by two contextual factors or elements that intersect and interact in different ways to affect the outcome and legitimacy of the adjudicator's toolkit: normative goals and design choices.[13]

Normative goals address how an international adjudicator construes their own role or function. Are they primarily concerned with "dispute settlement" or "rule development"?[14] On one end of the spectrum, we may have an adjudicator who adheres to an "international judicial function"[15] and promotes the development and coherency of international law, using discrete disputes to clarify the broader legal regime, without fear of criticisms of "judicial lawmaking". On the other extreme, is an adjudicator who more strictly or solely focuses on solving the individual dispute, without concern for the broader development of a consistent and coherent legal regime and may be more deferential to states as the legislators.[16] Normative ideals of a coherent international judicial system may trigger different outcomes on the application and interpretation of other international law. In this way, the formal source-based rules in the individual treaties and the dispute settlement design of each regime could play a much more limited role in understanding a tribunal's approach to other international law than some treaty-drafters may desire or have anticipated.[17]

---

13 See Harlan Grant Cohen and others, 'Legitimacy and International Courts – A Framework' in Andreas Follesdal and others (eds), *Legitimacy and International Courts* (Cambridge University Press 2018) 15 ff.

14 ibid 15; similarly, Fauchald refers to a dispute-oriented tribunal and legislator-oriented tribunal: Ole Kristian Fauchald, 'The Legal Reasoning of ICSID Tribunals – An Empirical Analysis' (2008) 19 European Journal of International Law 301, 307; see also, Relja Radović, 'The Dejudicialization of International Economic Law' in Jelena Bäumler and others (eds), *European Yearbook of International Economic Law 2021* (Springer International Publishing 2022) s 2, who distinguishes between dispute settlement and development of the law functions.

15 This draws on Hersch Lauterpacht's conception of the role of international judges, with some modifications to take account of the development of international law since Lauterpacht's work. See Lauterpacht (n 6); Gleider I Hernández, *The International Court of Justice and the Judicial Function* (Oxford University Press 2014); Martti Koskenniemi, 'The Function of Law in the International Community: 75 Years After' (2009) 79 British Yearbook of International Law 353.

16 According to Fauchald: 'the more a tribunal, when interpreting relevant rules, takes into account factors such as those relating to the interests of third parties, the general functioning of the ICSID system, the potential impact of its reasoning or conclusions for future cases, the general need to clarify issues of law, or the need to prevent future disputes, the closer that tribunal can be placed toward the "legislator-oriented" [or rule development] end of the continuum': Fauchald (n 14) 307.

17 This idea draws on the 'demand-side interpretation space' compared to the 'supply-side interpretation incentives' in the work of Joost Pauwelyn and Manfred Elsig, 'The Politics of Treaty Interpretation: Variations and Explanations Across International Tribunals' in

When we consider the approach of WTO and investor-state adjudicators, will we see similarities in lawmaking or restraint in settling the individual disputes? For the WTO dispute settlement mechanism, adjudicators may end up somewhere in the middle with the member-driven character of the WTO system more likely to limit judicial activism.[18] For investor-state adjudicators, the ambiguity of the substantive obligations combined with attempts at creating a coherent regime of international law, may entail a greater need for judicial lawmaking to ensure the completeness of the investment treaty.

This leads to the next contextual factor: to what extent do these normative goals align with the design choices when implementing the adjudicator's toolkit? No two international dispute settlement mechanisms are the same, yet similar issues of backlash, fragmentation and inconsistency occur across international courts and tribunals. A comparison of international dispute settlement design can teach us not only about the functioning of one regime of international law but also provide further insights into the inconsistency found throughout international law. Dispute settlement design refers to the choices made by states in including (or specifically excluding) certain institutional features in the constitutive treaties of the tribunal, including the type of tribunal (i.e., arbitration or adjudication), the lifespan of a tribunal (i.e., a permanent institution or ad hoc mechanisms), and the existence of appellate mechanisms.[19] Design choices also relate to how states determined that cases will be initiated, who may be parties to a dispute before the tribunal and the effect of the tribunal's decisions.

Disputes before the WTO dispute settlement mechanism and investor-state arbitral tribunals provide a useful point of comparison of the toolkit. Part of the motivation for this comparative study is the fact that the underlying legal sources and design choices of the two regimes are distinct, arguably influencing the normative goals and, ultimately, approach to the adjudicator's toolkit. On the one hand, there is the regime-embedded WTO dispute settlement mechanism.[20] The mechanism is endowed with compulsory and exclusive jurisdiction, with a standing appellate mechanism (albeit currently defunct), that clarifies the existing provisions of a comprehensive set

Jeffrey L Dunoff and Mark Pollack (eds), *Interdisciplinary Perspectives on International Law and International Relations: The State of the Art* (Cambridge University Press 2012).

18 Joost Pauwelyn, *Conflict of Norms in Public International Law: How WTO Law Relates to Other Rules of International Law* (Cambridge University Press 2003) 152.

19 See Cohen and others (n 13) 16 ff.

20 Adopting the design choice language of Cohen of 'regime-embedded' and 'regime-independent' tribunals: ibid 23–4.

of multilateral agreements (referred to as "the WTO Agreements").[21] Yet, the Dispute Settlement Understanding (DSU)[22] of the WTO does not employ such legal terminology as "jurisdiction" or "applicable law" to describe the work of the WTO panels and the Appellate Body,[23] reflecting the mix of political and legal dispute resolution in the DSU.

On the other hand, there is the regime-independent investment tribunals. The tribunals have no unifying dispute settlement mechanism, but rather an array of ad hoc arbitral tribunals draw from the procedures of private international arbitration, in what is collectively termed investor-state dispute settlement (ISDS). The tribunals arbitrate a diverse and heterogeneous network of investment treaties (referred to as International Investment Agreement (IIA) hereafter),[24] traditionally brief treaties setting out limited state obligations to investors.

The divergence in dispute settlement mechanism design and the language of the constitutive treaties founds an assumption that WTO adjudicators are more restrictive in their approach to bringing in other international law than their investor-state counterparts. This assumption suggests that the WTO is more restrained in its incorporation of other international law, being less amenable to other international law, rules and principles as part of its applicable law or laws used in interpretation. Such assumption is usually based on the compulsory jurisdiction of the WTO dispute settlement mechanism, the lack of an applicable law clause and limited reference to applicable international law beyond the customary rules of interpretation.[25] Pursuant to this assumption, WTO adjudicators should be primarily concerned with developing the

21 Marrakesh Agreement Establishing the World Trade Organization (15 April 1994), 1867 UNTS 154.

22 Understanding on Rules and Procedures Governing the Settlement of Disputes, Marrakesh Agreement Establishing the World Trade Organization, Annex 2 (15 April 1994), 1869 UNTS 401.

23 Although these bodies are not properly tribunals in the legal sense of the word, "WTO tribunals" is used as a convenient shorthand for collectively referring to the WTO panels and Appellate Body in other parts of the book.

24 IIAs broadly refers to bilateral investment treaties (BITS), multilateral investment treaties (MITS), treaties with investment provisions (TIPS) and free trade agreements (FTAS) that also include investment chapters.

25 See, for example, Alvarez, who argues that ISDS arbitrators are 'far more likely to consider other international legal rules (including the law of human rights) in the course of adjudicating investment disputes. ISDS tribunals, while charged with enforcing investment law, are not limited to the application of investment treaty law – at least not in the way WTO adjudicators are limited to applying the GATT-covered agreements': José E Alvarez, 'Epilogue: "Convergence" Is a Many-Splendored Thing' in Szilárd Gáspár-Szilágyi, Daniel Behn and Malcolm Langford (eds), *Adjudicating Trade and Investment Disputes: Convergence or Divergence?* (Cambridge University Press 2020) 311.

laws of the trade regime while, as regime-independent tribunals, ISDS adjudicators are more likely to embed investment rules within the broader corpus of international law.[26]

Is this really the state of the matter in trade and investment disputes? Limited comprehensive studies have been taken to test this assumption. However, testing such an assumption allows us to consider the limitations of treaty texts in directing international courts on the place of a regime within international law. Design of the studied dispute settlement mechanisms may weed out some of the relevance of other international law in filling gaps and resolving indeterminacy of the constitutive treaties, as in the case of the comprehensive WTO Agreements compared to the brevity of IIAs. But, does this actually translate to a dispute settlement mechanism more in tune with a consensual approach to its jurisdiction? If the assumption is not representative of the actual practice in

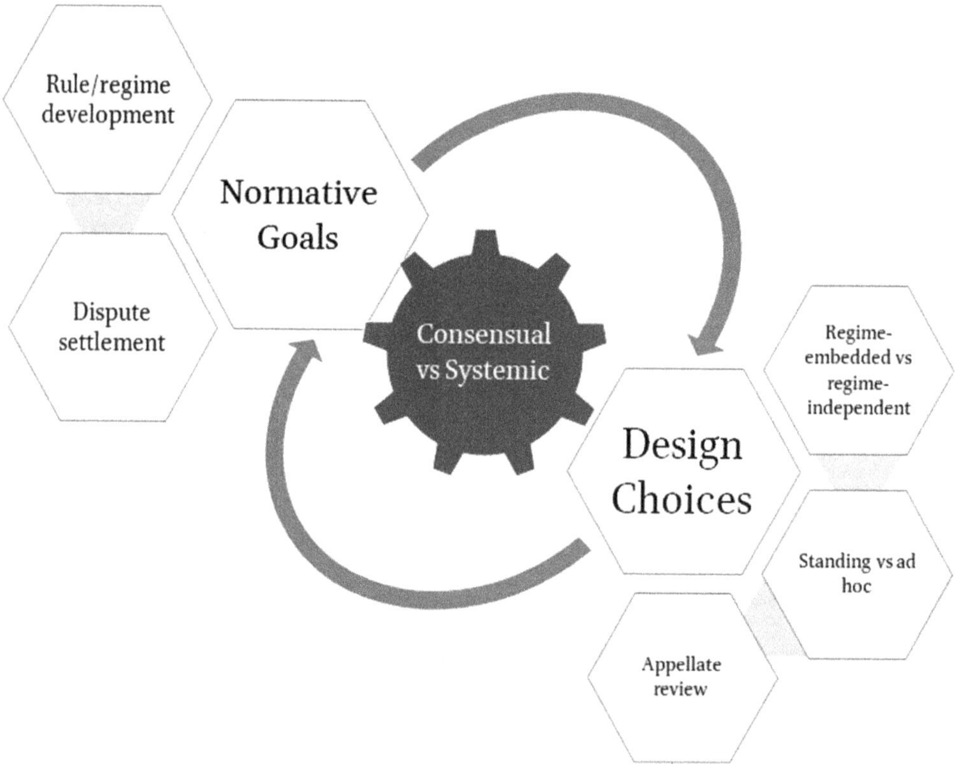

FIGURE 1 The complex interplay of contextual factors

26 See Cohen and others (n 13) 24–5.

these regimes, adjudicators' perception of their role as rule developers within a system of international law may be more aligned than warranted by the design choices and treaty language.

3 Research Approach: Method of the Study

To test the assumption and the implementation of the adjudicators' toolkit, the book analyses over 800 decisions of the dispute settlement mechanisms of the WTO and international investment law. The study includes all publicly available decisions of the WTO panels and Appellate Body and over half of the decisions of treaty-based ISDS tribunals. The study adopts a combination of comparative,[27] empirical and doctrinal methods, which allows:

1. the testing of the assumption that the WTO dispute settlement system is more restrictive in its approach than ISDS to the incorporation of other international law, allowing the identification of similarities and differences between the systems; and
2. the explanation of these similarities by analysing the jurisprudence in relation to the approach to applicable law, general principles and systemic integration.

As such, the method develops a comprehensive and systematic understanding of the interplay between international economic law and both general and other specialized international law in the reasoning of the adjudicators. Previous works on defragmentation often theorize in broad terms about how international courts coordinate to prevent fragmentation or promote convergence,[28] seek to deal with a specific issue of fragmentation[29] or with a

27 On comparative methods in international law, see William Butler, 'Comparative Approaches to International Law' (1985) 190 Collected Courses of the Hague Academy of International Law 9; Anthea Roberts and others, 'Conceptualizing Comparative International Law' in Anthea Roberts and others (eds), *Comparative International Law* (Oxford University Press 2018); Martti Koskenniemi, 'The Case for Comparative International Law' (2009) 20 Finnish Yearbook of International Law 1; Jean d'Aspremont, 'Comparativism and Colonizing Thinking in International Law' (2020) 57 Canadian Yearbook of International Law/Annuaire canadien de droit international 89.

28 For example, Laurence Boisson de Chazournes, 'Plurality in the Fabric of International Courts and Tribunals: The Threads of a Managerial Approach' (2017) 28 European Journal of International Law 13; Anne Peters, 'The Refinement of International Law: From Fragmentation to Regime Interaction and Politicization' (2017) 15 International Journal of Constitutional Law 671.

29 For example, Shany's work on the particular question of the competing jurisdictions of international courts: Yuval Shany, *The Competing Jurisdictions of International Courts and*

particular regime's response to fragmentation.[30] This research bridges the gap through a broader focus on other international law in general in two different regimes, providing both theoretical considerations and empirical results in the process. In this regard, the research adopts a methodology that provides both the specificity and broadness required for sound fragmentation studies.

The use of empirical studies[31] in this book assists in coherently mapping the large number of decisions of international courts and tribunals, thereby contributing to "a better understanding of how, and the conditions under which, international law works".[32] Through the use of data collection, legal scholars not only can test pre-existing theoretical constructs, but also transform the questions we can ask and the theories we can build.[33] In this study, empirical scholarship provides a set of tools to refine our understanding of the design of the dispute settlement mechanisms and the practice of their adjudicators. This enhances our understanding of the legitimacy of the international adjudicators as actors in international law and enables normative arguments on the future of international economic dispute settlement.[34] In addition, empirical studies contribute to the rigour of doctrinal analysis by helping to identify

Tribunals (Oxford University Press 2004); or Zang's work on the specific type of adjudicatory practice among international economic courts, namely judicial engagement among them: Michelle Q Zang, *Judicial Engagement of International Economic Courts and Tribunals* (Edward Elgar Publishing 2020).

30 For example, Pauwelyn's work on the WTO: Pauwelyn (n 18); or, Alvarez on investment and human rights: José E Alvarez, *The Boundaries of Investment Arbitration: The Use of Trade and European Human Rights Law in Investor-State Disputes* (JurisNet 2018).

31 Shaffer and Ginsburg define empirical work as involving the systematic use of qualitative or quantitative methods. They note that scholars often take multimethod approaches to support their claims since each method has its own strengths and deficiencies: Gregory Shaffer and Tom Ginsburg, 'The Empirical Turn in International Legal Scholarship' (2012) 106 American Journal of International Law 1, 3–4.

32 ibid 16 ff. Shaffer and Ginsburg conclude that the new wave of empirical scholarship should lead the way to a better understanding of how, and the conditions under which, international law works, ultimately informing normative projects (at p 46).

33 Elena Baylis, 'The Transformative Potential of Rigorous Empirical Research Empirical Approaches to International Law' (2010) 104 American Society of International Law Proceedings 31, 31: "empirical research can do more than simply provide proof for our preconceived theories. Empirical research can have truly transformative effects by enabling us to develop different kinds of analytic frameworks for understanding international law and to create tools that can be used in producing and engaging with international law in practice".

34 Shaffer and Ginsburg (n 31) 9: "Normative legal arguments depend on assumptions about the state of the world and the likely outcome of alternative legal rules. Empirical scholarship provides a set of tools to refine understandings of institutional design and practice so as to enhance international legal institutions' effectiveness."

and select decisions, without concern of "cherry-picking" case selection.[35] The methodological questions surrounding case selection were identified by Giorgetti and Pollack as one of the elements of the sceptical critique of cross-fertilization by international courts and tribunals,[36] which this comprehensive study addresses.

Even so, it is difficult to turn legal concepts into quantifiable data since it may not accurately capture the realities of the difficult and discretionary task of legal interpretation.[37] Here, empirical research should be complemented with doctrinal or dogmatic studies to grasp the law's complexity.[38] Doctrinal description of the existing law must be a starting point for other methods: empirical analysis "would be impossible without first knowing what the existing law says".[39] As such, the mixed use of empirical and doctrinal techniques in this study recognizes the added value of both methods for understanding law in its totality.[40]

Nonetheless, empirical and doctrinal studies limit the normative, sociological or political perspectives that can be brought within the research. In terms of normative limits of the research, doctrinal analysis has been criticized for concentrating on legal concepts promoting coherence and consistency of a legal system, seemingly filtering out other perspectives on, or dimensions

35 Katerina Linos and Melissa Carlson, 'Qualitative Methods for Law Review Writing Symposium: Developing Best Practices for Legal Analysis' (2017) 84 University of Chicago Law Review 213, 213.

36 Giorgetti and Pollack (n 3) 24.

37 Gabriel M Lentner, 'The Perils of Quantitative Research in International Law' in Rossana Deplano (ed), *Pluralizing International Legal Scholarship* (Edward Elgar 2019) 161–2.

38 As Smits notes, 'doctrine … reflects how subtle the law often can be and why a small change of facts can lead to a wholly different outcome': Jan M Smits, 'What Is Legal Doctrine? On The Aims and Methods of Legal-Dogmatic Research' in Edward L Rubin, Hans-W Micklitz and Rob van Gestel (eds), *Rethinking Legal Scholarship: A Transatlantic Dialogue* (Cambridge University Press 2017) 215.

39 ibid 227, referring to Council of Australian Law Deans, 'Statement on the Nature of Legal Research' 3 <https://cald.asn.au/wp-content/uploads/2017/11/cald-statement-on-the-nature-of-legal-research-20051.pdf> accessed 8 December 2023: "If doctrinal research is a distinctive part of legal research, that distinctiveness permeates every other aspect of legal research for which the identification, analysis and evaluation of legal doctrine is a basis, starting point, platform or underpinning."

40 Holtermann and Madsen refer to three different epistemological understandings of the interface of law and empirical studies, with this research drawing from the synthesis of doctrinal and empirical studies: Jakob vH Holtermann and Mikael Rask Madsen, 'Toleration, Synthesis or Replacement? The "Empirical Turn" and Its Consequences for the Science of International Law' (2016) 29 Leiden Journal of International Law 1001.

of, law, and otherwise suggesting a positivist view of the world.[41] A perspective focussing on consistency and coherence is a choice of the legal doctrinal researcher and bundles the subject and theoretical framework of doctrinal scholarship.[42] In terms of socio-legal research perspectives, doctrinal research helps to establish an understanding of the particular scope of laws and prevent misinterpretations. But research focused on jurisprudence limits the potential understanding of the values of adjudicators. The doctrinal approach only allows us to extrapolate these values based on the reasoning put forward in the decisions. We will not be able to identify the extent to which the arbitrator identities,[43] the appointment process[44] or other factors[45] may affect these values, nor the extent to which the nature of arbitration, requiring compromise in the reasoning of individual adjudicators, affects outcomes.[46] However, studying what adjudicators choose to include in their legal reasoning should still

41 Maurice Adams, Jaakko Husa and Marieke Oderkerk, 'Method and Methodology of Comparative Law: Introductory Remarks' in Maurice Adams, Jaakko Husa and Marieke Oderkerk (eds), *Comparative Law Methodology*, vol 1 (Edward Elgar Publishing 2017) XIII; Terry Hutchinson and Nigel Duncan, 'Defining and Describing What We Do: Doctrinal Legal Research' (2012) 17 Deakin Law Review 83, 116.

42 However, such a perspective is not the only normative perspective of legal doctrinal research. This is Vranken's fourth objection to Westerman's view of legal doctrinal research, that legal doctrinal research does not have to be purely based on the normative perspective of consistency and coherence: JBM Vranken, 'Methodology of Legal Doctrinal Research' in Mark Van Hoecke (ed), *Methodologies of Legal Research: Which Kind of Method for What Kind of Discipline* (Hart Publishing 2011) 118–9.

43 See, for example, Freya Baetens (ed), *Identity and Diversity on the International Bench: Who Is the Judge?* (Oxford University Press 2020).

44 See, for example Joost Pauwelyn, 'The Rule of Law without the Rule of Lawyers? Why Investment Arbitrators Are from Mars, Trade Adjudicators from Venus' (2015) 109 American Journal of International Law 761, which discusses the differences between WTO and ICSID adjudicators.

45 For example, the role of the secretariat or legal clerks in the decision-making process: Joost Pauwelyn and Krzysztof Pelc, 'Who Writes the Rulings of the World Trade Organization? A Critical Assessment of the Role of the Secretariat in WTO Dispute Settlement' (Social Science Research Network 2019); Freya Baetens, 'Unseen Actors in International Courts and Tribunals: Challenging the Legitimacy of International Adjudication' in Freya Baetens (ed), *Legitimacy of Unseen Actors in International Adjudication* (Cambridge University Press 2019); HWA Thirlway, 'The Drafting of ICJ Decisions: Some Personal Recollections and Observations Agora: The International Court of Justice at 60 (Part I)' (2006) 5 Chinese Journal of International Law 15.

46 See, for example, Harry T Edwards, 'The Effects of Collegiality on Judicial Decision Making' (2002) 151 University of Pennsylvania Law Review 1639; to some extent, it also assumes that the tribunal 'thinks the same'. As explained in *9REN Holding S.a.r.l v Kingdom of Spain* (ICSID Case No ARB/15/15), Award, 31 May 2019 [151]: 'whilst the Tribunal has reached a consensus in rejecting Spain's additional objection to jurisdiction, it should not

reflect their shared view of international law, making empirical and doctrinal analysis fruitful for this study.

Empirical studies are only fit-for-purpose if undertaken rigorously and with an understanding of the methodological choices.[47] With that in mind, the following paragraphs set out how the data was gathered. A summary of the design of the data collection is set out in Table 1 below and a complete list of the decisions found to contain references to other international law is

TABLE 1 Summary of data collection

	World Trade Organization	Investor-State Dispute Settlement
Time period[a]	All public decisions from 1995 up to 31 December 2020	All public decisions up to 31 December 2020
Judicial bodies	Panels and Appellate Body of the WTO	– Institutionalized ISDS: including, but not limited to, ICSID, ICA, LCIA, PCA and SCC[b] – Ad-hoc ISDS
Basis of jurisdiction	DSU and WTO covered agreements	Any IIA, including BITS, MITS and TIPS
Total decisions reviewed	402 reports	499 awards[c]

a This refers to all publicly available decisions that were available as of December 2021.
b These abbreviations refer to disputes before the International Center for the Settlement of Investment Disputes (ICSID), the International Court of Arbitration of the International Chamber of Commerce (ICA), the London Court of International Arbitration (LCIA), and the Stockholm Chamber of Commerce (SCC).
c This represents 177 decisions from the five-year collection method and 322 decisions collected through the free-text searches.

be assumed that it's three members share equally the same identical perspective or attach equal importance to the issues raised by the objection'.

47 See Frans L Leeuw, 'Empirical Legal Research: The Gap between Facts and Values and Legal Academic Training' (2015) 11 Utrecht Law Review 19, 22, who notes that methodology addresses how research problems are related to designs of studies, the role of theories, data collection and data analysis, including how to operationalize legal concepts and where to find data; see also Susan D Franck, 'Empirical Modalities: Lessons for the Future of International Investment Empirical Approaches to International Law' (2010) 104 American Society of International Law Proceedings 33, 36.

included in the Appendix. The role of theory in the design of the study is discussed in Chapter 2.

For the WTO disputes, finding the decisions is straightforward: all publicly available panel and Appellate Body reports were collected from the WTO's online database,[48] including all reports from the very first WTO panel report[49] to the last report issued at the end of 2020.[50] This search resulted in 486 documents (excluding addendums). 84 of these documents have then been removed from further analysis as they represent corrigendum or mutually agreed solutions to the disputes. This leaves a total of 402 reports for analysis.

Without a central repository of all ISDS documents, the steps for collecting ISDS decisions is more complex. Given the much larger number of total ISDS tribunal documents, only half of the known decisions were collected and reviewed. However, significant efforts were made to collect all relevant ISDS decisions, being decisions in which the application of public international law was discussed. This was achieved through three data collection steps:

a. free-text searches: search terms informed by the sources of international law and the opening tools were used in free-text searches[51] across all documents issued by tribunals (including, but not limited to, procedural decisions, partial awards, final awards and annulment decisions);[52]
b. subject navigator and article citator tools: research tools incorporated in investor-state dispute databases filter disputes by subject (ranging broadly from "expropriation" to "indigenous peoples") as well as citations to articles of international treaties, beyond the specific IIA;
c. year-sampling: all partial or final awards[53] from five years were collected and reviewed in full. The five-year data set was selected to represent the

48 World Trade Organization, 'WTO Documents Online' <https://docs.wto.org/dol2fe/Pages/FE_Search/FE_S_S005.aspx> accessed 29 March 2021.

49 *United States – Standards for Reformulated and Conventional Gasoline* (Report of the Panel) (29 January 1996), WT/DS2/R.

50 *Korea – Sunset Review of Anti-Dumping Duties on Stainless Steel Bars* (Report of the Panel) (30 November 2020), WT/DS553/R.

51 Free-text searches included systemic integration (and Article 31(3)(c)), general principles of law, necessity (and ILC Article 25), human rights (and indigenous rights), WTO (and GATT), countermeasures (and ILC Article 22), counterclaims. Each of these terms were applied with different Boolean operators to find all variations of the search term.

52 ICSID Annulment Committee decisions are included in the study. However, domestic set-aside and enforcement decisions are not. Although a similar function may be performed through domestic set-aside and ICSID annulment, these domestic decisions no longer involved "international adjudicators" and different standards (and normative goals) apply.

53 The year-sampling was limited to partial or final awards of the tribunals, rather than procedural orders and other smaller interim decisions. As such, the year-sampling identified: Decisions of Annulment Committee, Decisions on Jurisdiction or Preliminary Questions,

more recent approach to other international law in investor-state arbitration (2018 to 2020 decisions) combined with two earlier years to indicate any evolution in dispute settlement. These three sets of years were chosen as providing sufficient segregation between investor-state dispute's early years (1998), its backlash years (2008) and its reform years (2018). In addition, the year-sampling provides confidence that the free-text search methodology identified the major issues in applying other international law. Of the total decisions in the year-sampling, over two-thirds had already been gathered through the free-text searches and only a small fraction of those not collected through free-text searches raised relevant other international law issues.[54] Importantly, the decisions did not identify any sources of other international law that had not been identified through the initial search and citator methodology. While some decisions may not have fallen within the free-text and article citator search methodology, the year-sampling suggests this will have very limited impact on the final results of the analysis.

These steps were repeated across three major databases of ISDS decisions: JusMundi, Investor-State Law Guide and United Nations Conference on Trade and Development's (UNCTAD) Investment Dispute Settlement Navigator.[55] Multilingual technology in these decision databases also made it possible to identify a small number of relevant non-English language decisions.[56]

Data collection for ISDS also encounters the issue of confidential awards. The existence of any confidential awards could affect the representativeness of the results of the study, an issue for any doctrinal, empirical or large-scale analysis of international investment law.[57] As with other empirical or data-driven

---

Final Awards on Jurisdiction, Merits or Damages and Partial Awards or Decisions on the Merits.

54 A total of 177 partial or final awards and decisions on annulment, with jurisdiction based on an IIA, were collected in the year-sampling. Only 15% of those decisions were not already collected using the free-text search methodology.

55 See Investor-State Law Guide: https://www.investorstatelawguide.com/User/Welcome (accessed 30 January 2024); JusMundi: https://jusmundi.com/en/coverage (accessed 30 January 2024); and UNCTAD: https://investmentpolicy.unctad.org/investment-dispute-settlement (accessed 30 January 2024).

56 English is the dominant language in investment law, particularly in ICSID proceedings. In 2020, 68% of cases were held in English with a further 25% in two languages, with English-Spanish as the most frequent combination: International Center for Settlement of Investment Disputes, '2020 ICSID Annual Report' (2020) 28. In the data collection process, 18 decisions were collected where English was not one of the official versions of the award. For some decisions, unofficial translations are provided by the parties.

57 See the discussion of 'missingness' in ISDS in Nicola Strain and others, 'Compliance Politics and International Investment Disputes: A New Dataset' (2024) 27 Journal of International Economic Law 70, app 4; see, also, Malcolm Langford, Daniel Behn and Runar

studies, this research must limit itself to public awards, including those awards that have been redacted.[58] However, this is not overly problematic and does not affect the relevance of the empirical results for two reasons. First, the number of confidential decisions is likely to be significantly smaller than publicly available decisions. Results from the PluriCourts Investment Treaty and Arbitration Database (PITAD) indicate that only 26.9% of the known decided cases do not have a publicly available final award.[59] Secondly, if these confidential awards do not in fact follow the pattern identified in the empirical results, this would not affect the development of investor-state dispute settlement or international law as a whole, either as a matter of public law principle or as a matter of practicality. Any patterns or preferred approaches identified in the public awards would continue to influence later awards[60] in the absence of such confidential awards being made public. Adjudicators or parties relying on confidential awards to support their reasoning would be problematic from a rule of law perspective. This attitude is also supported by the fact that ISDS tribunals primarily deal with issues of public law and state decision-making, presenting strong arguments for transparency.[61]

While the data collection method resulted in a relatively similar number of decisions to the WTO total decisions, the free-text search methodology generated a higher prevalence of other international law within the investor-state data. In addition, some ISDS disputes result in multiple decisions, which can

Hilleren Lie, 'The Revolving Door in International Investment Arbitration' (2017) 20 Journal of International Economic Law 301, 306–7.

58 See, for example, Damien Charlotin, 'The Place of Investment Awards and WTO Decisions in International Law: A Citation Analysis' (2017) 20 Journal of International Economic Law 279, n 44; Niccolò Ridi, 'Approaches to External Precedent: The Invocation of International Jurisprudence in Investment Arbitration and WTO Dispute Settlement' in Daniel Behn, Malcolm Langford and Szilárd Gáspár-Szilágyi (eds), *Adjudicating Trade and Investment Disputes: Convergence or Divergence?* (Cambridge University Press 2020).

59 Daniel Behn, Malcolm Langford and Laura Létourneau-Tremblay, 'Empirical Perspectives on Investment Arbitration: What Do We Know? Does It Matter?' (2020) 21 The Journal of World Investment & Trade 188, 192; see also, Sebastian Puerta and Tim R Samples, 'Investment Law's Transparency Gap' (2022) 55 Cornell International Law Journal 9, who estimate the claim amounts of the missing disputes.

60 In the sense of potential doctrinal force of ISDS decisions: *Eskosol S.pA in liquidazione v Italian Republic* (ICSID Case No ARB/15/50), Decision on Respondent's Application Under Rule 41(5), 20 March 2017 [98], discussed in Chapter 2, section 2 below.

61 Langford, Behn and Lie (n 57) 307; José E Alvarez, *The Public International Law Regime Governing International Investment* (Brill Nijhoff 2011) 394 ff; the increasing transparency of decisions under ICSID and NAFTA also support a focus on public awards: Wolfgang Alschner, 'The Impact of Investment Arbitration on Investment Treaty Design: Myths versus Reality' (2017) 42 Yale Journal of International Law 1, 60 ff.

lead to the over-representation of the approaches of adjudicators who split their cases into several decisions.[62] Consequently, empirical comparison of the two regimes will primarily be presented in percentages and focus on the instances of other international law within the decisions to overcome the different data collection process.

In order to answer the research question on the role of dispute settlement design, a number of interrogations are made in reviewing the decisions of the WTO and investor-state dispute settlement mechanisms. Such questions help to uncover the similarities of the approach to the opening tools of international law and the role of international adjudicators. The following questions seek to highlight how normative ideals of a coherent international judicial system compared to a voluntarist and pluralist international law may trigger different outcomes on the application and interpretation of other international law[63] as well as how the assumption of WTO-restrictiveness plays out. The first interrogation is, unsurprisingly, whether other international law is raised in the decisions of the tribunals. The decisions will then be considered from the following angles and hypotheses:

1. What is the source of the other law? Identifying the source of law is relevant to understanding fragmentation, as we would expect general international law to permeate through these regimes, reflecting that there is no "self-contained regime" in international law. Comparatively, invocation of specific treaty-based law could be more subjective, based on the particular circumstances of that dispute and the international law raised.

---

62 Fauchald noted a potential weakness in studies limited to decisions in ISDS as it could lead to the over-representation of the approaches of tribunals that split their cases into several decisions. Fauchald argued that ICSID dispute resolution is organized in a way that generally contributes to the likelihood that certain perspectives may be over-represented and such a study may in fact shed some light on the extent to which such over-representation of certain views constitutes a problem for ICSID: Fauchald (n 14) 355–6. However, as will be clear from the doctrinal and empirical analysis in the proceeding Chapters, the research focuses on the instances of other international law, rather than number of decisions. As such, the breaking up of ISDS cases into multiple decisions should not impact the analysis of instances of other international law.

63 Drawing on the words of Hernández, '[are] international judges, when interpreting and applying international law, making a claim to normative (or semantic) authority? Are they more modest "agents" in the international legal process? More ominously, are they cloaking themselves in the formalism of classical legal positivism so as to abdicate political responsibility for the constitutive role of their interpretations?': Gleider I Hernández, 'Interpretative Authority and the International Judiciary' in Andrea Bianchi and Matthew Windsor (eds), *Interpretation in International Law* (Oxford University Press 2015) 168.

2. What was the tribunal's basis for including (or excluding) the other international law? For example, did the tribunal refer to the applicable law clause or its limited jurisdiction in the dispute? This question illustrates whether the tribunal refers to formal consent-based sources of authority to incorporate other international law or other non-formal bases. This is significant to whether legal reasoning meets a conscious and transparent standard, regardless of whether that reasoning is based on normative values or legal sources.[64] A working hypothesis based on the dispute settlement differences between the mechanisms and their formal sources is that we would also expect divergence between the WTO and investor-state tribunals on this question.
3. How was the other international law used by the tribunal? For example, did the tribunal use the other law in an exercise to fill gaps or lacunae in the treaty-text? This question is pertinent to the international judicial function and whether a more lawmaking role was performed by the tribunal. Where the tribunal employs gap-filling language, this may suggest a more lawmaking role and avoidance of indeterminacy in international law.[65]

4 Findings

Based on the systematic empirical and doctrinal study of the practice of the adjudicators, the book makes three important contributions to our understanding of these dispute settlement mechanisms and international law, more broadly. First, the comparison of the WTO and investor-state dispute settlement mechanisms reveals the irrelevance of the design of a dispute settlement system in how the dilemma of applying opening or closing tools is approached. Given the divergent text of their constitutive treaties, as well as important institutional and procedural differences, we would expect that the WTO and investor-state regimes approach the openness of their respective regime to international law in vastly different ways. The WTO dispute

64 This draws from Paulus' theories on the methodology of international adjudication, which seeks to reconcile a positivist and postmodernist approach to international law: Andreas Paulus, 'International Adjudication' in Samantha Besson and John Tasioulas (eds), *The Philosophy of International Law* (Oxford University Press 2010) 223.

65 See, similar approach of Fauchald: Fauchald (n 14); as well as Pauwelyn and Elsig, who refer to the 'work-to-rule' compared to the 'gap-filling' approach, where the tribunal may 'push the envelope and complete the contract where appropriate or fill gaps in the treaty as they are discovered in the judicial process': Pauwelyn and Elsig (n 17) 454–5.

settlement mechanism is often regarded as more restrictive when it comes to application of law not contained within the trade agreements than its more “flexible” investor-state counterparts. Yet, the book shows that the WTO dispute settlement mechanism is more restrictive only in regard to the initial process of integrating other international law, namely the parties bringing forward relevant other law. Due to more comprehensive agreements and more limited applicable law, less decisions of the WTO dispute settlement mechanism are faced with questions of other international law. However, once such law is before the WTO panel or Appellate Body, there is little difference in how the adjudicator’s toolkit is utilized: the reasoning on how such other international law is included or excluded as well as the role that such law plays in the resolution of the dispute is surprisingly aligned with ISDS adjudicators.

Secondly, the book reveals the inadequacies of the toolkit available to adjudicators to resolve the defragmentation dilemma. The empirical results of the study indicate the significant incorporation of public international law within these specialized regimes and what reasoning has been used by adjudicators in doing so. However, in-depth case analysis reveals the inconsistency of adjudicators in utilizing the tools provided by States in integrating these specialized economic regimes in international law. The opening toolkit (wide applicable law, general principles, and systemic integration) enables adjudicators to go some way in incorporating international law. But the book shows that the use and limits of these tools is not clear and is contested from one adjudicator to another. Rather than providing coherent and predictable outcomes on the application of public international law, these tools are themselves blurry. Adjudicators find themselves on different sides of the aisle depending on their perception of the normative goals of the regimes and whether deference is to be given to state consent or the international legal system.

Consequently, the book reveals the “consistent inconsistency” in the application of international law by these specialized dispute settlement bodies. This phenomenon describes different forms of inconsistency within the reasoning of the tribunals, yet also a consistency or similarity between the approach of the two specialized regimes in important respects. The first form of inconsistency identified refers to the differences between the WTO, on the one hand, and investor-state tribunals, on the other. Due to the different treaty texts at play, the extensive multilateral WTO agreements compared to the traditionally brief bilateral investment agreements, this inconsistency is expected and unproblematic. However, surprisingly, this inconsistency is much less pronounced than would be expected based on the design of the dispute settlement mechanisms. The second form of inconsistency refers to intra-ISDS and intra-WTO inconsistency. Both of the regimes exhibit chaos when we try to identify how and why international law has been incorporated using the tools available to adjudicators, resulting from the varying weight that adjudicators may place on State consent or coherence of international law. While some departure in reasoning from one tribunal to the next is to be expected,[66] the level of inconsistency found in both the regimes is highly troubling from a legitimacy point of view and an issue that is not explained by the differing designs of the two dispute settlement mechanisms.

A third important finding of the study is the consistent application of international law by adjudicators without relying on any particular rule or legal tool. The empirical analysis of the adjudicators' reasoning identifies the most common basis relied upon for the inclusion of international law is actually none at all: the tribunals provide no clear legal authority for their decision to include international law. This result could be a promising reflection of the implicit legitimacy of international law, in line with a unified international legal order. Yet, in the face of tools being available to adjudicators to resolve this dilemma, the lack of clear reasoning fails to provide conscious and transparent standards of judgment. Such gaps in reasoning, while also illustrating the conflict with a consent-based international law, create further avenues for inconsistency within and between specialized regimes.

These findings illustrate that adjudicators acting alone cannot provide a predictable outcome on the legal process for the universalization and systemization of international law, whilst also taking into account the limits of State consent. While there is some level of implicit consent to a coherent international legal order, calls to resolve this tension, through the adoption of an international judicial function that draws from general principles and systemic integration, fail to overcome the indeterminacy of the legal rules and provide insufficient framework for a more consistent exercise of the adjudicators' discretion. This also has flow-on consequence for the legitimacy of the dispute settlement mechanism, both normatively and from a sociological perspective.

To adequately cross the tightrope of the legitimacy dilemma, reform of the dispute settlement mechanisms may be helpful and even necessary. This is an important and timely finding for these specialized adjudication mechanisms that are currently facing legitimacy crises and reform efforts. The book builds on these findings and assesses the potential for reform proposals to address the legitimacy dilemma, from incremental reforms on the rules on applicable

66 See the discussion in 'Possible Reform of Investor-State Dispute Settlement (ISDS): Consistency and Related Matters' (United Nations Commission on International Trade Law 2018) A/CN.9/WG.III/WP.150.

law, to systemic reforms introducing more judicialized standing mechanisms as avenues to elaborate the interactions between fields of international law. Ultimately, further clarification of the function and limits of the adjudicator's toolkit within international law more broadly will also be required, rather than regime-specific reforms. Accordingly, the findings develop not only our understanding of how international economic adjudicators approach the integration of public international law but also the role played by the underlying design of the dispute settlement mechanisms, enabling transposition of findings in reform efforts and resolution of the dilemma to other areas of international law.

5 Structure of the Book

Chapter 2 sets the scene for the empirical and doctrinal study. The Chapter discusses the theoretical concepts and methodological choices supporting the research, including how different perceptions of defragmentation and adjudicative functions are taken into account. The Chapter reveals the tension between the state-created pluralist system and a coherent system of public international law The Chapter also outlines three important concepts for understanding the adjudicator's toolkit: jurisdiction, applicable law and interpretation. The particular rules governing the WTO and ISDS adjudicator under their constitutive treaties are examined to identify the areas of indeterminacy and potential conflict.

Chapter 3 empirically compares the decisions of the WTO and investor-state dispute settlement mechanisms in relation to the utilization and force of public international law in these dispute settlement systems. With this empirical assessment, the Chapter analyses the role of dispute settlement design in the incorporation of other international law, including analysis of the source of law and the legal (or other) basis for including the other international law. In doing so, the Chapter addresses the relevance of dispute settlement design and proves that the assumption of restrictiveness in WTO dispute settlement mechanism to be overstated. Rather, the empirical results suggest a relevant homogeneity between the mechanisms and their receptiveness to other international law. The Chapter illustrates that the tribunals do in fact incorporate other international law within the framework of defragmentation efforts. However, their reasoning when doing so differs dramatically. An important finding of this Chapter is the implicit legitimacy of public international law within the WTO and investor-state dispute settlement regimes that is developed through the empirical analysis of the legal reasoning of the tribunals.

The second half of Chapter 3 digs deeper into these empirical results, providing a deeper analytical assessment of the legal reasoning. When going beyond the numbers, the Chapter uncovers a "consistent inconsistency" in the decisions: the tribunals share similar levels of substantive fragmentation within their own individual regimes. The Chapter does so by focusing on three particular areas of interaction: human rights, environment and customary international law.

Chapters 4 and 5 examine in detail how the adjudicator's toolkit is applied to resolve the tension between the state-created pluralist system and a coherent system of public international law. In different ways, these perspectives attempt to resolve the indeterminate rules on incorporation of international law outlined in Chapter 2, yet ultimately bring about the "consistent inconsistency" substantiated in Chapter 3. Chapter 4 examines how the opening tools are being used to assist in filling lacunae in the dispute settlement regimes and contribute to coherence of the international legal system. The Chapter examines how these tools have been utilized in adjudicators' attempts to overcome fragmentation problems and the ability of the toolkit to explain the adjudicators' behavior. Chapter 5 turns to the closing tool: limited jurisdiction. The Chapter considers to what extent the opening tools are limited by the jurisdictional authority granted by States to the adjudicators. To what extent does the application of the toolkit fit with a normative understanding based on State consent?

Chapter 6 then attempts to unpack the inconsistency and problems identified in the previous Chapters in the application of the adjudicator's toolkit. In doing so, the Chapter illustrates the tension between the international judicial function and State consent and how the different answers to this question can illuminate whether consent/dispute-oriented or coherence/rule development are favored by individual adjudicators. The results illustrate the areas of tension between the desire for a system of international law and a consensual approach to jurisdiction. As such, neither of these two perspectives provide an adequate answer to how an adjudicator utilizes their toolkit in applying public international law. The analysis of the legal reasoning in the case law throughout these three chapters indicates the insufficiency of such reasoning to engage with the indeterminacy and tension involved in these questions of public international law, resulting in the failure to meet a conscious and transparent standard of judicial decision-making. Consequently, the Chapters demonstrate that the puzzle of international law is not being harmoniously put back together by adjudicators.[67]

67 A summary of these results is reproduced in Nicola Strain, 'Invoking Systemic Ideals or Systemic Rules? Jurisdiction in WTO and Investor-State Dispute Settlement' (2022) 82

The remaining chapter of the book summarizes the implications of this result for the functioning of the WTO and investor-state dispute settlement mechanisms. Chapter 7 begins by adopting the concept of legitimacy as a lens to critique the use of the adjudicator's toolkit. The Chapter reviews the impact of the inconsistency on the legitimacy of the tribunals, from both a normative and sociological perspective. From a normative perspective, the Chapter reviews whether the utilization of the adjudicator's toolkit meets performance and justice standards. As part of sociological legitimacy, the Chapter reviews the divergent views of states on the jurisprudence of these tribunals and the inability of such party intentions to indicate the rational choices to be made by tribunals. The Chapter then considers how the problems arising from the use of toolkit could be addressed through reform efforts, with a particular focus on the ongoing reform negotiations at the United Nations Commission on International Trade Law (UNCITRAL).

Zeitschrift für ausländisches öffentliches Recht und Völkerrecht / Heidelberg Journal of International Law 401.

CHAPTER 2

Setting the Scene

What theories or understandings of the working of international law influence the reasoning of international adjudicators when attempting to resolve trade and investment disputes? This Chapter begins by setting out how defragmentation and the quest for a coherent system of international law have dominated the scholarly debate in recent years. The Chapter then considers the role of adjudicators in this quest and how different values or understandings of international law may affect the normative goals of, and functions of, international adjudication. In addition, the Chapter sets out how the legal concepts of jurisdiction, applicable law and interpretation are dealt with in the constitutive treaties of the WTO and investor-state dispute settlement mechanisms. In this way, the Chapter sets out the extent to which the adjudicator's toolkit is covered by the provisions of the constitutive treaties of the dispute settlement mechanisms and what areas of discretion arise that can be influenced by different conceptions of an adjudicator's role.

1 Defragmentation and the System of International Law

Fragmentation denotes both a process and the result of that process.[1] As a term, it tends to have a negative connotation,[2] but the result itself may not necessarily be problematic.[3] How actors and scholars view the emergence

1 Anne Peters, 'Fragmentation and Constitutionalization' in Anne Orford and Florian Hoffmann (eds), *The Oxford Handbook of the Theory of International Law* (Oxford University Press 2016) 1012.

2 Anne Peters, 'The Refinement of International Law: From Fragmentation to Regime Interaction and Politicization' (2017) 15 International Journal of Constitutional Law 671, 672; Alain Pellet, 'Should We (Still) Worry about Fragmentation?' in Andreas Follesdal and Geir Ulfstein (eds), *The Judicialization of International Law: A Mixed Blessing?* (Oxford University Press 2018) 228, referring more specifically to proliferation as not neutral: reflecting a fast, excessive and uncontrolled growth, almost overshadowing its virtues.

3 As Kingsbury remarked: '[T]he initial question ... is whether the proliferation of international courts and tribunals, in a horizontal legal arrangement lacking in hierarchy and sparse in any formal structure of relations among these bodies, is fragmenting or system-building in its effects on international law. Or to put it more succinctly, is proliferation a problem?' in Benedict Kingsbury, 'Foreword: Is the Proliferation of International Courts and Tribunals a Systemic Problem Symposium Issue: The Proliferation of International Tribunals: Piecing

 | DOI:10.1163/9789004700932_003

of fragmentation may impact their perception of the risks (or lack thereof) of fragmentation and the proliferation of international courts and tribunals. For example, neoliberal international legal theorists view fragmentation as a gradually evolving solution to responding to the challenges of the international community[4] while postmodern theorists welcome the alternative to formal, hierarchical international law.[5] Fragmentation becomes problematic when several institutions are faced with the same problem but deal with it differently.[6] Most poignantly, fragmentation is seen as challenging the "system" of international law. In proposing fragmentation as an area of work for the ILC, Hafner noted that the potential for diversity of solutions in relation to secondary rules "tends to maintain, if not strengthen, the disintegrated nature of international law and the international system as a whole."[7] Ultimately, amongst the various views on fragmentation and its risks, a concern for a loss of legitimacy of international law lies at the heart of this debate, a loss which could "ultimately threaten that law's very existence".[8]

Together the Puzzle' (1998) 31 New York University Journal of International Law and Politics 679, 680.

4 See, for example, Charney who argues that different solutions can represent a level of experimentation in a collective effort to find the best solution. Charney dismisses potential concerns of plurality of courts: '[i]t may not be an unreasonable fear that these variations and innovations could undermine the coherence of international law. Based on the information available at this time, however, a serious problem does not appear to exist': Jonathan Charney, 'Is International Law Threatened by Multiple International Tribunals?' (1998) 271 Collected Courses of the Hague Academy of International Law 101, 351 ff.

5 See, for example, Martti Koskenniemi and Päivi Leino, 'Fragmentation of International Law? Postmodern Anxieties' (2002) 15 Leiden Journal of International Law 553 who argue that excessive worries over fragmentation are not warranted: 'it is an institutional expression of political pluralism internationally'.

6 See, for example, Yuval Shany, *The Competing Jurisdictions of International Courts and Tribunals* (Oxford University Press 2004); James Crawford and Penelope Nevill, 'Relations between International Courts and Tribunals: The "Regime Problem"' in Margaret A Young (ed), *Regime Interaction in International Law: Facing Fragmentation* (Cambridge University Press 2012); Martti Koskenniemi, 'The Fate of Public International Law: Between Technique and Politics' (2007) 70 The Modern Law Review 1; Martti Koskenniemi, 'Fragmentation of International Law: Difficulties Arising from the Diversification and Expansion of International Law, Report of the Study Group of the International Law Commission' (International Law Commission 2006) A/CN.4/L.682.

7 Gerhard Hafner, 'Risks Ensuing from Fragmentation of International Law' (International Law Commission 2000) ILC (LII)/WG/LT.1/Add.1 36.

8 Following a summary of concerns of fragmentation, Peters concludes that 'what is at stake in fragmentation is unity, harmony, cohesion, order and – concomitantly – the quality of international law as a truly normative order ... at the bottom of the fragmentation debate lies a concern for a loss of legitimacy of international law, a loss which will ultimately threaten that law's very existence': Peters (n 2) 680, see also references therein.

Despite the new self-awareness that fragmentation provoked, fragmentation has been viewed by many as largely unavoidable.[9] The historical development of international law has left us with different conceptions or types of fragmentation. Andenas identifies three types of fragmentation: substantive fragmentation, being the creation of different "self-contained" regimes; institutional fragmentation, including the proliferation of courts and tribunals; and, methodological fragmentation resulting in new rules of treaty interpretation applicable in specific fields.[10] Proliferation of international courts and tribunals is expressly characterized as part of institutional fragmentation but also contributes to both substantive and methodological fragmentation, due to the international courts' role in the development of the specialized area of law and its interpretation.

The perceived negative consequence of the proliferation of international courts and tribunals is primarily concerned with the potential for substantive fragmentation and jurisdictional collision.[11] In relation to jurisdictional

9 ibid 702; similarly, Koskenniemi, 'The Fate of Public International Law' (n 6) 2 refers to the problems of international law today as a result of the strategy of 'becoming technical' developed by McNair and Lauterpacht; see also Eyal Benvenisti and George W Downs, 'The Empire's New Clothes: Political Economy and the Fragmentation of International Law' (2007) 60 Stanford Law Review 595 who argue that the narrow and functionalist design following the aftermath of WWII resulted in the piecemeal approach of international law but has also enabled powerful states to maintain their dominance; see also Eyal Benvenisti and George W Downs, *Between Fragmentation and Democracy: The Role of National and International Courts* (Cambridge University Press 2017) 14 ff.

10 Mads Andenas, 'Reassertion and Transformation: From Fragmentation to Convergence in International Law' (2014) 46 Georgetown Journal of International Law 685, 694 ff; see also Mads Andenas and Eirik Bjorge, 'Introduction: From Fragmentation to Convergence in International Law' in Eirik Bjorge and Mads Andenas (eds), *A Farewell to Fragmentation: Reassertion and Convergence in International Law* (Cambridge University Press 2015) 4 ff; in a slightly different vein, Peters identifies two relevant facets of fragmentation: institutional fragmentation (different treaties, organizations etc) and ideational fragmentation (different objectives and values): Peters (n 2) 675.

11 See, for example, President Guillaume's speech to the UN General Assembly in 2000, which warned of the long-term consequences of this proliferation: 'The Proliferation of International Judicial Bodies: The Outlook for the International Legal Order, Speech by H.E Judge Gilbert Guillaume, President of the International Court of Justice, to the Sixth Committee of the General Assembly of the United Nations, 27 October 2000' <https://www.icj-cij.org/public/files/press-releases/1/3001.pdf> accessed 10 December 2020; President Higgins, while noting the generally healthy development of international courts, considered that there was potential for real divergent jurisprudence: 'This is because, in these various judicial bodies, in the varying and different ways I have tried to describe, the very same legal question can come up before them in the application and interpretation of international law' in Rosalyn Higgins, 'The ICJ, the ECJ, and the Integrity of International Law' (2003) 52 International and Comparative Law Quarterly 1, 18; see,

collision, or the uncertainty surrounding jurisdictional competences, the example of the MOX *Plant* litigation[12] and the *Southern Bluefin Tuna* case[13] are frequently cited. Comparatively, substantive fragmentation is often linked to the divergent approaches to the test for control of irregular forces for the purposes of state responsibility. The International Court of Justice (ICJ) adopted an "effective control" test in its decision in *Nicaragua*,[14] which the Appeals Chamber of the International Criminal Tribunal for the former Yugoslavia (ICTY) in *Tadić* decided not to follow and instead adopted its own "overall control test".[15] The ILC's Fragmentation Report described these decisions as an example of a normative conflict in the interpretation of a rule of general international law.[16] This substantive fragmentation problem has come to dominate the discussion as the greater fears of jurisdictional collision, forum shopping and parallel litigation slowly eased. Despite receiving significant attention from both the ILC Fragmentation Report and various other studies, there remains very little systematic and consistent analysis of substantive fragmentation of international law.[17]

"Defragmentation" is a normative preference for coherence and systemic order over fragmentation and plurality,[18] described in the ILC's Fragmentation Report as a combination of complex and interrelated concepts that may push

further Shany (n 6) 10; Mónika Ambrus, 'Constitutionalization through Fragmented Adjudication?' in Andrzej Jakubowski and Karolina Wierczyńska (eds), *Fragmentation vs the Constitutionalization of International Law: A Practical Inquiry* (Routledge 2016) 204.

12 *The* MOX *Plant Case* (*Ireland v United Kingdom*), Provisional Measures, Order of 3 December 2001, ITLOS Reports 95.

13 *Southern Bluefin Tuna* (*New Zealand v Japan, Australia v Japan*), Award on Jurisdiction and Admissibility, 4 August 2000, XXIII UNRIAA 1.

14 *Military and Paramilitary Activities in and Against Nicaragua* (*Nicaragua v United States of America*), Judgment [1986] ICJ Reports 14 [115].

15 *Prosecutor v Tadić* (ICTY Case No IT-94–1-A), Judgment of the Appeals Chamber, 15 July 1999 [137].

16 Koskenniemi, 'Fragmentation of International Law: Difficulties Arising from the Diversification and Expansion of International Law, Report of the Study Group of the International Law Commission' (n 6) para 50; President Higgins views the example in a slightly different way, rather whether 'special regimes' are to be distinct from general international law: Rosalyn Higgins, 'A Babel of Judicial Voices? Ruminations from the Bench' (2006) 55 International & Comparative Law Quarterly 791, 794.

17 Ambrus (n 11) 204.

18 Luca Pasquet, 'De-Fragmentation Techniques', *Max Planck Encyclopedia of International Procedural Law* (Oxford University Press 2018) para 68; Ralf Michaels and Joost Pauwelyn, 'Conflict of Norms and Conflict of Laws? Different Techniques in the Fragmentation of International Law' in Tomer Broude and Yuval Shany (eds), *Multi-Sourced Equivalent Norms in International Law* (Hart Publishing 2011) 20.

and pull the tribunals in different directions.[19] In this way, defragmentation is an indeterminate concept, based on moral considerations: there is no single legal basis or authority for defragmentation, or more generally the harmonization of the regimes with international law. As such, the proliferation of international courts has spurned significant academic debate on how to respond to, and address, fragmentation. These approaches differ both in relation to their perception of the risk of fragmentation and perceived intent behind proliferation, as well as how such risks can be surmounted. Constitutional and hierarchical approaches focus on the unity of international law, based on the primacy of peremptory norms, the UN Charter[20] and the ICJ.[21] Similarly, a systemic approach advocates coherence in international law through the requirement to consider the wider normative environment of international law.[22] Comparatively, a managerial approach perceives fragmentation as less of a risk but, like systemic integration, views international courts and tribunals as key actors in eradicating the risks.[23] The common theme among these approaches appears to be an optimistic view of international law[24] and the

19 The Report sought to 'seek relationships' within the system of international law, through conflict rules, relations of importance and systemic integration to address the 'endemic normative conflicts' in international law in a formal and open-ended way: Koskenniemi, 'Fragmentation of International Law: Difficulties Arising from the Diversification and Expansion of International Law, Report of the Study Group of the International Law Commission' (n 6).

20 See, for example, Andrea Bianchi, *Constitutionalism and Global Governance* (Oxford University Press 2016); Erika De Wet, 'Sources and the Hierarchy of International Law: The Place of Peremptory Norms and Article 103 of the UN Charter within the Sources of International Law' in Samantha Besson and Jean D'Aspremont (eds), *The Oxford Handbook on the Sources of International Law* (Oxford University Press 2017); referring to Article 103 of the Charter of the United Nations (San Francisco, 24 October 1945), 1 UNTS XVI.

21 See discussion in Charney (n 4); Andrew Lang, 'The Role of the International Court of Justice in a Context of Fragmentation' (2013) 62 International and Comparative Law Quarterly 777; Andenas and Bjorge (n 10).

22 Koskenniemi, 'Fragmentation of International Law: Difficulties Arising from the Diversification and Expansion of International Law, Report of the Study Group of the International Law Commission' (n 6) paras 414–5.

23 Laurence Boisson de Chazournes, 'Plurality in the Fabric of International Courts and Tribunals: The Threads of a Managerial Approach' (2017) 28 European Journal of International Law 13; Veronika Bílková, 'The Threads (or Threats?) Of a Managerial Approach: Afterword to Laurence Boisson de Chazournes' Foreword' (2017) 28 European Journal of International Law 1259.

24 For example, Andenas and Bjorge regard fragmentation as part of a dynamic legal system, with fragmentation as a fruitful perspective by which to study almost any legal system or sub-system: Andenas and Bjorge (n 10) 1; Peters notes the potential for fragmentation to

opportunities for convergence or coherence created by international courts, whether through judicial interpretations of substantive[25] or procedural law.[26]

Thus, international courts and tribunals are seen as playing an integral role in the defragmentation and systemic effort[27] in the absence of a single unifying rule of defragmentation. The push for defragmentation through international dispute settlement requires a particular mind-set among international adjudicators. President Higgins made an early call that judges need to "learn how to live in this new, complex world" and should regard it as an opportunity to read each other's judgments, respect other's judicial work and preserve unity unless prevented by the context of the dispute.[28] The recent approaches to defragmentation also presuppose that international adjudicators conceive of international law as a system, with themselves as part of the system.[29] For example, Boisson de Chazournes' managerial approach endorses the view that international judges and arbitrators ought to be tasked with ensuring the legitimacy of the international judicial system, an interpretation of the judicial function that resonates with Lauterpacht's view of international judges.[30]

---

enhance both the effectiveness and the legitimacy of international law and its application, when it is channelled by constitutional principles and procedures: Peters (n 1) 1014.

25 For example, Webb examines the extent of fragmentation of judicial decisions in genocide, immunities and use of force, finding a picture of genuine integration among the four courts studied (ICJ, ICTY, ICTR and ICC): Philippa Webb, *International Judicial Integration and Fragmentation* (Oxford University Press 2013).

26 For example, Brown argues that there is an increasing commonality in the practice of international courts to the application of rules concerning procedure and remedies: Chester Brown, *A Common Law of International Adjudication* (Oxford University Press 2007).

27 Mads Andenas and Johann Ruben Leiss, 'The Systemic Relevance of "Judicial Decisions" in Article 38 of the ICJ Statute' (2017) 77 Heidelberg Journal of International Law 907, 908. Andenas and Leiss argue that Article 38(1)(d) of the ICJ Statute provides a means of institutional integration, a naturally corollary to the principle of systemic integration. Similarly, Boisson de Chazournes's managerial approach to plurality endorses the view that international judges and arbitrators ought to be tasked with ensuring the legitimacy of the international judicial system: Boisson de Chazournes (n 23) 15. For a summary of the processes and tools being used by international adjudicators, see Chiara Giorgetti and Mark Pollack, 'Beyond Fragmentation: Cross-Fertilization, Cooperation, and Competition among International Courts and Tribunals' in Chiara Giorgetti and Mark Pollack (eds), *Beyond Fragmentation* (1st edn, Cambridge University Press 2022).

28 Higgins (n 16) 804; see, similarly, Judge Simma: Bruno Simma, 'Fragmentation in a Positive Light' (2003) 25 Michigan Journal of International Law 845, 846.

29 Pasquet (n 18) para 52.

30 Boisson de Chazournes (n 23) 15 citing; Hersch Lauterpacht, *International Law: Being the Collected Papers of Hersch Lauterpacht*, vol 2: The Law of Peace (Elihu Lauterpacht ed,

2 The Role of Adjudicators: Normative Goals and Judicial Functions

As the previous section illustrated, the indeterminate sources and tools of defragmentation require interpretation by the relevant stakeholders. For this book, the relevant interpretation is undertaken by international adjudicators. However, answering the call for determinacy depends on the normative goals of stakeholders, ranging from international lawmaking being left in the hands of states[31] to dynamic interpretations of law in the hands of the judiciary, as outlined in the Introduction (Chapter 1, section 2). For the cooperation between courts response to fragmentation that is currently the dominant scholarly approach,[32] judicial lawmaking is necessary in systemizing international law. These approaches to adjudication raise competing views of the source of legitimacy of jurisdiction and the limits of judicial authority: state consent or systemic concerns. At the heart of the divergence of the consensualist and systemic approaches is the question: to what extent should there be restrictions on what a court can and should do when faced with uncertainty in international law?

Both to ground the methodology of the study and understand the different normative goals of adjudicators, a necessary first step is to understand the effect of jurisprudence: was a design choice made that decisions were to have binding or precedential effect? And how is this design choice reflected in the adjudicator's understanding of their role as regime/rule developers or dispute settlers?[33] While the specific weight and authority of judicial decisions

---

Cambridge University Press 1975); Hersch Lauterpacht, *The Function of Law in the International Community* (Oxford University Press 1933).

31 For example, Fitzmaurice notes that there may be a somewhat greater role of lawmaking for the international judiciary permissible, and even desirable for international tribunals, but there should not be any lack of predictability as to the law the Court will apply. The requisite degree of certainty to the law should be imparted by states: Gerald Fitzmaurice, 'The Future of Public International Law and of the International Legal System in the Circumstances of Today: Second and Final Part of an Abstract (Prepared by the Author) of a Special Report' (1976) 5 International Relations 949, 964.

32 Cooperation approaches broadly refer to international courts being open to the substantive judgments of other courts and coordinating amongst themselves to reduce fragmentation and increase coherence of international law and the judicial system: Giorgetti and Pollack (n 27) 16–17; see, for example, Andenas and Bjorge (n 10) 2–3; the management approach, whereby international judges have sought to organize proliferation in a 'managerial fashion' also falls within this cooperation approach: Boisson de Chazournes (n 23).

33 See Harlan Grant Cohen and others, 'Legitimacy and International Courts – A Framework' in Andreas Follesdal and others (eds), *Legitimacy and International Courts* (Cambridge University Press 2018) 17, 21 on the design choices and models of interaction between such design choices and normative goals.

is not agreed, the practical reality is that there is a generally accepted role for judicial decisions under international law,[34] resulting in a quasi-acceptance of a *jurisprudence constante* to ensure the consistency and coherence of international dispute settlement.[35]

This turn to ensuring consistency and coherence is true for both WTO and ISDS tribunal decisions. While there is no formal authoritative value of a decision of a WTO panel or an investor-state tribunal beyond the parties to the dispute, the internal consistency and coherence of these dispute settlement systems has led to the informal acceptance of a "light" version of precedent.[36] Early in its development, the WTO Appellate Body recognized that panel decisions did not constitute binding precedent, either under the GATT or the WTO agreements.[37] However, the WTO Appellate Body went on to develop a "cogent reasons" approach to precedent:

> Dispute settlement practice demonstrates that WTO Members attach significance to reasoning provided in previous panel and Appellate Body reports. Adopted panel and Appellate Body reports are often cited by

---

34 See, for example, discussion in Nienke Grossman, 'The Normative Legitimacy of International Courts' (2013) 86 Temple Law Review 61, 69; von Bogdandy and Venzke even go so far as to refer to the effect of judicial precedents being 'concealed' by the doctrinal ordering in Article 38: Armin von Bogdandy and Ingo Venzke, 'In Whose Name? An Investigation of International Courts' Public Authority and Its Democratic Justification' (2012) 23 European Journal of International Law 7, 19.

35 For example, Lauterpacht notes that adherence to legal decisions is 'imperative if the law is to fulfil one of its primary functions, i.e. the maintenance of security and stability': Hersch Lauterpacht, 'The So-Called Anglo-American and Continental Schools of Thought in International Law' (1931) 12 British Year Book of International Law 31, 53; Judge Greenwood emphatically argues for referring to jurisprudence of courts and tribunals: '[i]nternational law is not a series of fragmented specialist and self-contained bodies of law, each of which functions in isolation from the others. It is a single unified system of law and each international court can, and should, draw on the jurisprudence of other international courts and tribunals, even though it is not bound necessarily to come to the same conclusions': *Ahmadou Sadio Diallo (Republic Guinea v Democratic Republic of the Congo), Judgment* [2012] ICJ Reports 324, 8 (Declaration of Judge Greenwood).

36 Cohen refers to a weak form of precedent as supplying an argument that one must respond to: one cannot make an argument about the rule's meaning without some reference to why the prior decision is right, wrong or distinguishable. Comparatively, 'in its strongest form, precedent creates a strong presumption that the prior interpretation of the rule is in fact the rule:' Harlan Grant Cohen, 'Theorizing Precedent in International Law' in Andrea Bianchi and Matthew Windsor (eds), *Interpretation in International Law* (Oxford University Press 2015) 275.

37 *Japan – Taxes on Alcoholic Beverages* (*Report of the Appellate Body*) (4 October 1996), WT/DS8/AB/R; WT/DS10/AB/R; WT/DS11/AB/R 14.

> parties in support of legal arguments in dispute settlement proceedings, and are relied upon by panels and the Appellate Body in subsequent disputes. In addition, when enacting or modifying laws and national regulations pertaining to international trade matters, WTO Members take into account the legal interpretation of the covered agreements developed in adopted panel and Appellate Body reports. Thus, the legal interpretation embodied in adopted panel and Appellate Body reports becomes part and parcel of the acquis of the WTO dispute settlement system. Ensuring "security and predictability" in the dispute settlement system, as contemplated in Article 3.2 of the DSU, implies that, absent cogent reasons, an adjudicatory body will resolve the same legal question in the same way in a subsequent case.[38]

This "cogent reasons approach" has been predominantly followed in subsequent panels and Appellate Body reasoning[39] and has been praised for bringing predictability and stability to the system.[40] Nonetheless, it is not universally accepted by the stakeholders of the WTO dispute settlement system. In the justifications for blocking of Appellate Body members, the US has argued that the Appellate Body's claims that its reports were entitled to be treated as precedent is inconsistent with WTO rules.[41] While representing a minority

38 *United States – Final Anti-Dumping Measures on Stainless Steel from Mexico* (*Report of the Appellate Body*) (30 April 2008), WT/DS344/AB/R [160].

39 In *United States – Countervailing and Anti-Dumping Measures on Certain Products from China* (*Report of the Panel*) (27 March 2014), WT/DS449/R [7.317], the Panel elaborated on what it considered to be 'cogent reasons' for departing from Appellate Body jurisprudence, including (i) multilateral interpretation of covered agreements, (II) a demonstration that prior interpretation proved to be unworkable or (III) prior interpretation leads to conflict with another provision; see Cook for a discussion of WTO reports dealing with precedents of WTO panels and Appellate Body: Graham Cook, *A Digest of WTO Jurisprudence on Public International Law Concepts and Principles* (Cambridge University Press 2015) 248 ff.

40 See, for example, Reto Malacrida and Gabrielle Marceau, 'The WTO Adjudicating Bodies' in Robert Howse and others (eds), *The Legitimacy of International Trade Courts and Tribunals* (1st edn, Cambridge University Press 2018) 51–53.

41 The US argues that Members have the exclusive authority to adopt interpretations of the WTO Agreements, pursuant to Article IX:2 of the WTO Agreement: '2018 Trade Policy Agenda and 2017 Annual Report of the President of the United States on the Trade Agreements Program' (United States Trade Representative 2018) 28; 'Report on the Appellate Body of the World Trade Organization' (United States Trade Representative 2020) 55 ff; see further Sebastian Beckerle, 'Stare Decisis in the WTO Dispute Settlement Procedure: A Response to the Trump Administration's Criticism' (2019) 14 Global Trade and Customs Journal 513; Giorgio Sacerdoti, 'The Authority of "Precedent" in International

view and one that the Appellate Body has yet to adopt (while it was still functional), the US arguments illustrate the conflicting views on precedent and the weight of prior judicial decisions in international law.

In international investment law, there is a less clear and more varied arbitral jurisprudence on the weight and authority of earlier tribunal decisions. ISDS is riddled with examples of inconsistent decisions on jurisdictional issues, treaty obligations and respondent state liability that are not explainable by the differences in the treaty-texts.[42] The public international law component of international investment law led some arbitrators to call for consistency and a harmonious development of international investment law:

> The Tribunal considers that it is not bound by previous decisions. At the same time, it is of the opinion that it must pay due consideration to earlier decisions of international tribunals. It believes that, subject to compelling contrary grounds, it has a duty to adopt solutions established in a

Adjudication: The Contentious Case of the WTO Appellate Body's Practice' (2020) 19 The Law & Practice of International Courts and Tribunals 497.

42 For example, the inconsistent decisions in the Argentine financial crises cases in relation to the defence of necessity: *Enron Creditors Recovery Corp and Ponderosa Assets, LP v Argentine Republic* (ICSID Case No ARB/01/3), Award, 22 May 2007; *Mobil Exploration and Development v Argentine Republic* (ICSID Case No ARB/04/16), Decision on Annulment, 8 May 2019; *LG&E v Argentine Republic* (ICSID Case No ARB/02/1), Decision on Liability, 3 October 2006; *CMS Gas Transmission v Argentina* (ICSID Case No ARB/01/8), Award, 12 May 2005; *Continental Casualty v Argentina* (ICSID Case No ARB/03/9), Award, 5 September 2008; see further, Jürgen Kurtz, 'The Paradoxical Treatment of the ILC Articles on State Responsibility in Investor-State Arbitration' (2010) 25 ICSID Review 200; Working Group III noted a number of examples of inconsistent decisions, ranging from the definition of "investment"; the application of the most-favored nation (MFN) clause to dispute settlement; the notion of indirect expropriation; the interpretation of the scope and effect of the umbrella clause; the identification and application of principles of customary international law; procedural decisions on security in annulment proceedings; treatment of awards in terms of enforcement; ability of States and investors to contract out of ISDS provisions (see A/CN.9/935, paras. 31 and 32); situations of concurrent or multiple proceedings (see also A/CN.9/915, paras. 5 and 6); general rules of customary international law involving the state of necessity/emergency, the law of attribution, and the legal principles regarding damages: 'Possible Reform of Investor-State Dispute Settlement (ISDS): Consistency and Related Matters' (United Nations Commission on International Trade Law 2018) A/CN.9/WG.III/WP.150 paras 14–15; in a recent review of empirical approaches to studying inconsistency in investor-state disputes, Behn et al note that there is a mixed picture, but unjustified inconsistency is present: Daniel Behn, Malcolm Langford and Laura Létourneau-Tremblay, 'Empirical Perspectives on Investment Arbitration: What Do We Know? Does It Matter?' (2020) 21 The Journal of World Investment & Trade 188, 222–223.

> series of consistent cases. It also believes that, subject to the specifics of a given treaty and the circumstances of the actual case, it has a duty to contribute to the harmonious development of investment law and thereby to meet the legitimate expectations of the community of States and investors towards certainty of the rule of law.[43]

Some tribunals even acknowledge a *jurisprudence constante* of prior decisions.[44] Other ISDS adjudicators do not go so far as to recognize their contribution to the harmonious development of investment law but acknowledge the importance of consistency between tribunals.[45] However, this is not a universal view of the role of prior decisions. In response to the same statement on consistency and harmonious development of international investment law set out above, Arbitrator Stern considered it her "duty to decide each case on its own merits, independently of any apparent jurisprudential trend" and did not analyse her role as arbitrator in the same manner as the majority.[46] One of the

---

43 *Saipem S.pA v The People's Republic of Bangladesh* (ICSID Case No ARB/05/07), Decision on Jurisdiction and Provisional Measures, 21 March 2007 [67]; see also, Kurtz who argues that there is a compelling case for hard consistency like the WTO, but this is a delicate normative balance: Jürgen Kurtz, 'Building Legitimacy Through Interpretation in Investor-State Arbitration: On Consistency, Coherence, and the Identification of Applicable Law' in Zachary Douglas, Joost Pauwelyn and Jorge Vinuales (eds), *The Foundations of International Investment Law: Bringing Theory Into Practice* (Oxford University Press 2014); Bungenberg and Titi similarly argue that there may be a general development of jurisprudence constante but there should be caution in adopting binding precedent: Marc Bungenberg and Catharine Titi, 'Precedents in International Investment Law' in Marc Bungenberg and others (eds), *International Investment Law: A Handbook* (Hart Publishing 2015) 1512 ff.

44 For example, *InfraRed Environmental Infrastructure v Spain* (ICSID Case No ARB/14/12), Award, 2 August 2019 [260] in which the tribunal states it could not 'overstate the importance of the long record of recent arbitral awards or partial awards which disposed of the intra-EU jurisdictional objections and maintained the jurisdiction of the respective ECT tribunals. In the Tribunal's view, these form an arbitral jurisprudence constante which, short of binding this Tribunal, provides nonetheless a persuasive, reasoned and documented analytical framework that the Tribunal endorses and adopts without the need to spell it out in detail below'.

45 See, for example, SGS *v Philippines* in which the tribunal noted that it should 'in general seek to act consistently' but this does not reflect the development of a common legal opinion or jurisprudence constante: *SGS Société Générale de Surveillance SA v Republic of the Philippines* (ICSID Case No ARB/02/6), Decision of the Tribunal on Objections to Jurisdiction, 29 January 2004 [97]; the tribunal in Glamis Gold noted the need to consider the 'systemic implications' of decisions: *Glamis Gold Ltd v United States of America* (ad hoc, UNCITRAL), Final Award, 9 June 2009 [6–7].

46 *Burlington Resources Inc v Republic of Ecuador* (ICSID Case No ARB/08/5), Decision on Jurisdiction, 2 June 2010 [100].

reasons underlying not following "jurisprudential trends" (other than obvious differences in IIAs in each dispute) is the ability of such trends to be influenced by only a handful of private actors or arbitrators.[47] Similarly, the decentralized nature of the international investment regime[48] and the mandate of tribunals to interpret in accordance with the VCLT[49] may also counter any persuasive force of decisions. Nevertheless, the dominant practice seems to result in doctrinal consequences for future decisions.[50]

Even if we do not accept the precedential effect of decisions, studying what the adjudicators actually say informs us about their shared view of international law.[51] As Thirlway points out, "law is a matter of words; and it may be said that the choice of words to convey a legal point is in itself the decision of, or a decision on, that point."[52] These insights have value in ascertaining the balance between state consent and the international judicial function, even

---

47 For example, Stern discusses the precedential weight of the decisions on MFN clauses and jurisdiction, following Maffezini, noting that they only appear balanced because of the repeated involvement of some of the arbitrators: *Impregilo v Argentine Republic (I)* (ICSID Case No ARB/07/17), Award, 21 June 2011 [5] (Concurring and Dissenting Opinion of Professor Stern); see, also the discussion in M Sornarajah, *Resistance and Change in the International Law on Foreign Investment* (Cambridge University Press 2015) 183 ff.

48 See, for example, *Perenco Ecuador Ltd v Republic of Ecuador and Empresa Estatal Petróleos del Ecuador* (ICSID Case No ARB/08/6), Award, 27 September 2019 [496], in which the tribunal referred to investment law as 'a de-centralized international legal regime in which investment treaties confer jurisdiction over ad hoc tribunals which in turn have jurisdiction only over the parties to the disputes brought before them, and where it is accepted that different tribunals considering similar matters can arrive at different conclusions' as a reason to reject a *res judicata* effect of the Burlington decision; *Burlington Resources Inc v Republic of Ecuador* (ICSID Case No ARB/08/5), Decision on Ecuador's Counterclaims, 7 February 2017.

49 See, for example, *B-Mex, LLC and Others v United Mexican States* (ICSID Case No ARB(AF)/16/3), Partial Award, 19 July 2019 [119]: 'the Tribunal's mandate is to find the terms of the Treaty as they are and to interpret them in accordance with the VCLT. If other tribunals have arrived at a different interpretation of the same provision, that does not change that mandate'.

50 '[A]ll interpretations of arguably ambiguous treaty language have potential doctrinal consequences for future cases that should not be lightly ignored': *Eskosol S.pA in liquidazione v Italian Republic* (ICSID Case No ARB/15/50), Decision on Respondent's Application Under Rule 41(5), 20 March 2017 [98].

51 Crawford and Nevill make a similarly modest claim that we can still learn a lot about international law "reflecting on the practice of lawyers and what tribunals and courts actually do, even if it does not lead us to theoretical closure": Crawford and Nevill (n 6) 251.

52 HWA Thirlway, 'The Drafting of ICJ Decisions: Some Personal Recollections and Observations Agora: The International Court of Justice at 60 (Part I)' (2006) 5 Chinese Journal of International Law 15, 21.

if we bear in mind the limits of responsibility that we can place on a tribunal to resolve metaphysical and constitutional questions of the international legal system.[53] Considering the particular response of adjudicators themselves to issues of other international law enables the gathering of the approach to issues of consent, fragmentation and whether overarching ideas of judicial functions permeate these "self-contained" dispute chambers.

2.1 *Consensual Approach: the Limits of Jurisdictional Authority*

This section now turns to two relevant diverging views of an adjudicator's role. On the one hand, state consent to jurisdiction is the traditional approach to the normative legitimacy of international courts and tribunals.[54] At the First Hague Peace Conference of 1899, which set up the Permanent Court of Arbitration (PCA), the rationale for the basis of consent to jurisdiction was explained:

> A voluntary system of jurisprudence in origin as well as in jurisdiction, it agrees with the just demands of sovereignty, of which it is only an enlightened exercise. For, if there is no power superior to the States which can force a judge upon them, there is nothing to oppose their selection of an arbitrator by common agreement to settle their disputes, thus preferring a less imperfect means of securing justice to a method more problematical and more burdensome.[55]

State consent to jurisdiction has remained as a fundamental principle of international law, with the ICJ in *Application of the International Convention on the Elimination of All Forms of Racial Discrimination* (*Georgia v Russian Federation*) continuing to stress this point.[56] This conception of the source

53 Crawford and Nevill refer to the limitations that law as a trade and profession imposes: 'it informs how we read individual decisions and limits how much we can read into them; and it limits how much responsibility we might place on a tribunal or court for failing to satisfactorily resolve metaphysical and constitutional questions': Crawford and Nevill (n 6) 249.

54 Cohen and others (n 33) 5. The factors and grounds of normative legitimacy are further discussed in Chapter 7.

55 Baron Descamps at the First Hague Peace Conference on Convention No. I of 1899 on the Pacific Settlement of International Disputes, cited in Malcolm N Shaw, *Rosenne's Law and Practice of the International Court: 1920–2015*, vol II (5th edn, Brill Nijhoff 2016) para 154; see also CF Amerasinghe, *International Arbitral Jurisdiction* (Brill Nijhoff 2011) 49.

56 *Application of the International Convention on the Elimination of All Forms of Racial Discrimination* (*Georgia v Russian Federation*), Preliminary Objections, Judgment of 1 April 2011 [2011] ICJ Reports 70, 125; see also, the PCIJ in *Status of Eastern Carelia, Advisory Opinion* [1923] PCIJ Report Series B No 5 [33]: 'This rule, moreover, only accepts and applies

of an international court or tribunal's authority refers to the fact that when states create courts and submit to their jurisdiction, they do so under specific conditions and expectations of how that power will be exercised. As the PCIJ famously stated in the *Lotus* case, restrictions upon the independence of States cannot be presumed.[57] For example, states can prescribe the sources of law to be relied upon (being the applicable law, discussed in section 3.2 below), and if any other law is applied, it would "disrespect the boundaries prescribed by state consent" and the court's authority would lack legitimacy and justification.[58] As such, for the consensual or state-centric approach to adjudication, it is important to understand the limits of the authority that has been granted to courts through the treaties under which states submit to a court's jurisdiction. While international law does form some sort of a "system",[59] such view being largely accepted in legal scholarship (although the extent of such systemization is controversial),[60] techniques of defragmentation and application of other law may strain the limits of jurisdiction with its focus on consent as set out in formal sources.

Based on the principle that states are the principal lawmakers of international law, a consensualist approach to adjudication promotes the normative

---

a principle which is a fundamental principle of international law, namely, the principle of the independence of States. It is well established in international law that no State can, without its consent, be compelled to submit its disputes with other States either to mediation or to arbitration, or to any other kind of pacific settlement.'

57 *SS Lotus* (*France v Turkey*), Judgment [1927] PCIJ Series A No 10 18.

58 Grossman (n 34) 66, who goes on: 'a court that evades or ignores the limitations placed upon its authority threatens its legitimacy'.

59 In this way, international legal scholarship departs from Hart's conception of international law as a 'simple set', rather than a system: HLA Hart, *The Concept of Law* (3rd edn, with a postscript edited by Penelope A Bullock and Joseph Raz, and an introduction and notes by Leslie Green, Oxford University Press 2012) 234.

60 See, for example, Koskenniemi who notes this his book "starts from the uncontroversial assumption that international law is not just some haphazard collection of rules and principles ... The sense that international law forms a "system" is so deeply embedded in legal thinking': Martti Koskenniemi, *From Apology to Utopia: The Structure of International Legal Argument* (Cambridge University Press 2005) 567; see, further, Andenas and Bjorge who subscribe to the view of international law as a legal system, but to be an effective legal system, the bodies of international law must take account of one another: Andenas and Bjorge (n 10) 2; Shany considers that the international legal system has sufficient coherence, even if the international judiciary may be deharmonizing: Shany (n 6) 93 ff; see also, Simma and Pulkowski, while noting that analogizing strong conceptions of legal systems developed in a domestic context may not be appropriate on the international level, there is at least a minimal conception of the systemic character of international law: Bruno Simma and Dirk Pulkowski, 'Of Planets and the Universe: Self-Contained Regimes in International Law' (2006) 17 European Journal of International Law 483, 495 ff.

goal of dispute settlement, above rule or regime development. For example, the tribunal in *Romak v Uzbekistan* described its function in the following way:

> … the Arbitral Tribunal has not been entrusted, by the Parties or otherwise, with a mission to ensure the coherence or development of "arbitral jurisprudence." The Arbitral Tribunal's mission is more mundane, but no less important: to resolve the present dispute between the Parties in a reasoned and persuasive manner, irrespective of the unintended consequences that this Arbitral Tribunal's analysis might have on future disputes in general. It is for the legal doctrine as reflected in articles and books, and not for arbitrators in their awards, to set forth, promote or criticize general views regarding trends in, and the desired evolution of, investment law.[61]

Similarly, the Appellate Body noted in *US – Wool Shirts and Blouses* that Article 3.2 of the DSU set out the aim of dispute settlement as one that does not "encourage either panels or the Appellate Body to 'make law' … A panel need only address those claims which must be addressed in order to resolve the matter in issue in the dispute".[62]

2.2 *Systemic Approach: the International Judicial Function*

On the other hand, within the international judicial function there is an optimistic view of what international courts could and should do: building the rule of law in the international legal system.[63] The international judicial function represents a step away from a strict view of state consent, by enabling the exercise of an independent role for international judges. Judges are crucial actors in the design and repair of international dispute settlement in

61 *Romak SA v The Republic of Uzbekistan* (PCA Case No 2007–07/AA280), Award, 26 November 2009 [171]. This decision did not fall within the empirical study. While international law was raised by the parties, it was only in relation to the merits and the tribunal dismissed the dispute on jurisdictional grounds, namely the lack of an investment (at [242–3]). No relevant other international law was considered by the tribunal.

62 *United States – Wool Shirts and Blouses* (*Report of the Appellate Body*) (25 April 1997), WT/DS33/AB/R 19.

63 In one passage, Lauterpacht notes that 'judicial activity is essentially the last link in the chain of the crystallization of the rule of law … it is the bridge between the necessarily abstract legal rule and the necessarily individual nature of the particular case': Hersch Lauterpacht, *The Function of Law in the International Community* (Oxford University Press 2011) 110; see recently also, Sarah Thin, 'Guardians of Legality? The International Judicial Function in an Era of Community Interest' (2023) 92 Nordic Journal of International Law 499, who considers the role of adjudicators in compliance and the rule of law.

the current defragmentation techniques, resonating with Lauterpacht's view of the creative activity of judges in taking into consideration the "entirety of international law and the necessities of the international community".[64] The international judicial function and the creativity of judges is central to resolving the indeterminacy of international law. The international judicial function recognizes a role for international tribunals beyond merely settling disputes between states. Rather, the international judicial function "fulfils an important role in safeguarding the coherence of the international legal system".[65] Law has normative objectivity, and the role of the international judge was to expound the general law, while deciding the individual case. In this way, judges were required to be creative in filling material gaps in the law to avoid declarations of *non liquet*.[66]

Judicial lawmaking,[67] as conceived in the international judicial function (also sometimes referred to as judicial legislation),[68] refers to the process of changing the existing (state-made) law.[69] Judicial lawmaking may find expression through the application of general principles of law, drawing from principles from parallel developments in other spheres of international law, defining new principles of law and regulating the various interests involved in the dispute in a manner going beyond interpretation of the existing law.[70] In this way,

---

64 Boisson de Chazournes (n 23) 15 citing; Lauterpacht, *The Function of Law in the International Community* (n 30) 319–320.

65 Gleider I Hernández, *The International Court of Justice and the Judicial Function* (Oxford University Press 2014) 1.

66 Lauterpacht, *The Function of Law in the International Community* (n 63); see also, Iain GM Scobbie, 'The Theorist as Judge: Hersch Lauterpacht's Concept of the International Judicial Function' (1997) 8 European Journal of International Law 264; Martti Koskenniemi, 'The Function of Law in the International Community: 75 Years After' (2009) 79 British Yearbook of International Law 353.

67 In referring to the term, 'judicial lawmaking', the research does not adopt this as an aspect of positive law, but rather the scholarly concept: Armin von Bogdandy and Ingo Venzke, 'Beyond Dispute: International Judicial Institutions as Lawmakers' in Armin von Bogdandy and Ingo Venzke (eds), *International Judicial Lawmaking: On Public Authority and Democratic Legitimation in Global Governance* (Springer 2012). In this way, the research does not promote judicial lawmaking but considers how different theoretical perspectives on international law view such lawmaking as well as the extent to which this may be occurring in WTO and investor-state disputes.

68 Judicial lawmaking is perhaps the more commonly used term in the international legal scholarship, being 'less precarious' than using the term legislation for the activity of courts: ibid 15. Lauterpacht himself also seems to refer to the terms 'judicial legislation' and 'judicial lawmaking' interchangeably.

69 Hersch Lauterpacht, *The Development of International Law by the International Court* (Cambridge University Press 1982) 155.

70 ibid 156–7.

judicial lawmaking and the international judicial function go hand-in-hand with the normative goal of rule/regime development.

Since judicial lawmaking is not a concept of positive law, but arguably a scholarly concept,[71] this process of lawmaking draws out concerns of judicial activism.[72] Judicial activism taps into the balance between law and politics and the proper conduct of judicial business,[73] thereby possibly detracting from the sociological legitimacy of the tribunal, discussed in Chapter 7. "Judicial lawmaking", and consequently, judicial activism, can have both a positive and a negative perception based on the perspective taken on the formalism of law and the role and function of the judiciary.[74] For this book, the pertinent question is whether seeking coherence of international law is an appropriate or desired outcome of judicial lawmaking where such coherence is indeterminate in the formal sources.[75]

71 von Bogdandy and Venzke (n 67) 14; Howse and Teitel similarly refer to a 'judicial philosophy': Robert Howse and Ruti Teitel, 'Global Judicial Activism, Fragmentation, and the Limits of Constitutionalism in International Law' in Ulrich Fastenrath and others (eds), *From Bilateralism to Community Interest: Essays in Honour of Bruno Simma* (Oxford University Press 2011) 962.

72 'However extensive the scope of law-creating judicial interpretation may be, it is always limited, although not totally determined, by existing legal materials. The undeniable freedom of judicial decision is one within the law': Lauterpacht, *The Function of Law in the International Community* (n 63) 110–1; Paulus makes a similar argument that international adjudication cannot and should not disregard the legal sources from which it derives its authority: Andreas Paulus, 'International Adjudication' in Samantha Besson and John Tasioulas (eds), *The Philosophy of International Law* (Oxford University Press 2010) 219.

73 Fuad Zarbiyev, 'Judicial Activism in International Law – A Conceptual Framework for Analysis' (2012) 3 Journal of International Dispute Settlement 247, 250. Zarbiyev notes some of the attempts at systematizing the various meanings attributed to judicial activism and attempts to draw out the two major traits of these efforts: definition by reference to a certain implicit conception of the relationship between judicial and political branches, and a certain conception of the manner in which the judiciary should conduct what is indisputably conceived to be its own 'business'. In a similar vein, on defining Judge Simma's 'judicial maximalism', Howse and Teitel refer to an institutional vision of activism which would see the international judiciary as an institution analogous to a constitutional court: Howse and Teitel (n 71) 961; Hernández refers to the range within which a judicial institution may operate and where its conduct is regarded as being appropriate to its function: 'the very definition of that range sets limits that a judiciary may not legitimately transgress, lest it risk being tarred with the epithet of "judicial activism"': Hernández, *The International Court of Justice and the Judicial Function* (n 65) 1–2.

74 Zarbiyev (n 73) 250 ff.

75 Howse and Teitel refer to this as substantive or functional view of activism, whereby the integrity of international legal order is achieved through interpretation under conditions of fragmentation: Howse and Teitel (n 71) 962. However, in this author's view it is more

A tension between the international judicial function and the traditional positivist approach is the recognition of indeterminacy of international law. A central aspect in defining and understanding the international judicial function is this indeterminacy. Indeterminacy opens the potential for a normative function for a court.[76] For the international judicial function, the creativity of judges is central to resolving the indeterminacy of international law. General principles of law play a central role in filling lacunae in international law, enabling judicial legislation and avoiding *non liquet*. For Lauterpacht, it is both a duty of, and an obligation on, international adjudicators to apply general principles to avoid *non liquet,* thereby ensuring the completeness of the rule of law.[77] In this way, general principles draw from natural law to ensure the completeness of international law:[78]

> If the international judicial function is normative and plays a systemic role, it would seem that the [ICJ] has also a public function going beyond the settlement of the dispute: it contributes to the positive creation of norms, which carry with them authority and generate compliance with those norms.[79]

This systemic role of the international judicial system challenges the voluntarist view of international law and continuing justifications for this general principle of consent. For example, Elihu Lauterpacht argued that the requirement of consent was based on the prevailing positivist view of law at the time of the Hague Peace Conferences. In this way, the principle is the relic of habit, reflecting an obsolete state practice, which international tribunals may apply

appropriate to fit this within the function of lawmaking, rather than the generally negative conception of activism.

76 Gleider I Hernández, 'Interpretative Authority and the International Judiciary' in Andrea Bianchi and Matthew Windsor (eds), *Interpretation in International Law* (Oxford University Press 2015) 172.

77 Lauterpacht, *The Function of Law in the International Community* (n 63) 71 ff.

78 Similarly, Fitzmaurice considers the general principles of law comprising those of natural law and justice, constituting a separate source of international law independent of the specific consent of states: Fitzmaurice (n 31) 993–4.

79 Hernández, *The International Court of Justice and the Judicial Function* (n 65) 93. In more recent research on the ICJ and the judicial function, Hernández argues that it may be premature to argue for a robust international judicial function, but it is not "unreasonable to claim that law-making is an intrinsic element of adjudication" (p 89). See also Thin (n 63) who concludes that although international law's bilateralist, private law foundations have an enduring effect, theoretical contours of a new international judicial function on community and rule of law approaches is taking shape.

less rigorously and at a lower threshold.[80] Andenas similarly notes that the transformation of public international law includes a relaxation of the restrictions of state consent, so that the ICJ is no longer predominantly concerned with jurisdictional issues, but rather with issues of substance.[81]

Defragmentation and the international judicial function may construct a narrative that is often incommensurable with positive law and the limited confines of consent to jurisdiction,[82] raising the conflict with the consensual approach. Yet, the limited jurisdiction approach assumes that there is an identifiable consent, which may not be apparent from either the treaty provisions discussed in the next section or from the current views of states on the functioning of these dispute settlement mechanisms.[83]

3 Legal Concepts and Provisions

The remainder of the Chapter examines three fundamental concepts of judicial dispute settlement and the relevant provisions of the WTO and investor-state treaties. The aim of this section is two-fold. First, the section sets out the content of the formal (consent-based) sources of authority in relation to jurisdiction, applicable law and interpretation of each of the dispute settlement mechanisms. Sketching the boundaries of the concepts is the essential first step in examining the tribunals' approach to other international law as these concepts delineate the formal powers and functions of the tribunals to do so. The second aim of this section is to identify any areas of indeterminacy, thereby potential areas of tribunal discretion, that are embedded in these concepts and the relevant provisions of the treaty texts when it comes to questions of other international law. Framing the indeterminacy of these concepts enables the examination of how such indeterminacy is dealt with by tribunals in the exercise of their discretion in the following Chapters.

80 Elihu Lauterpacht, 'Principles of Procedure in International Litigation' (2011) 345 Collected Courses of the Hague Academy of International Law 1, 449.

81 Andenas (n 10) 733.

82 This builds on legal methodology and international legal positivist theories of Paulus (n 72); and Jörg Kammerhofer, *International Investment Law and Legal Theory: Expropriation and the Fragmentation of Sources* (Cambridge University Press 2021).

83 See also Laurence Boisson de Chazournes, 'Variations around the Notion of Consent in Investment Arbitration' in Samantha Besson (ed), *Consenting to International Law* (1st edn, Cambridge University Press 2023) 224, who refers to the uncertainties surrounding the notion of consent, asking whether we really know what this inherently indeterminate concept means.

Before this exercise, a short review of the negotiations of the WTO and investor-state dispute settlement mechanisms is useful to indicate whether such general concepts of judicial dispute settlement were considered in the design choices. For investor-state disputes, the development of the Convention on the Settlement of Investment Disputes (the ICSID Convention), which created the International Center for the Settlement of Investment Disputes (ICSID),[84] suggests a more traditional legal approach to settling investment disputes. While the WTO negotiation process was undertaken through diplomatic channels and negotiating groups comprising solely of states represented by their ambassadors to the GATT,[85] the drafting of the ICSID Convention arguably took a much less political approach. In the drafting of the ICSID Convention, officials of the World Bank took the primary role and drew on their prior experience in mediating investment disputes.[86] The procedure adopted therefore appears to draw largely from concepts of international arbitration, including similar language from inter-state dispute settlement before the PCA in the 1899 and 1907 Hague Conventions.

The drafting history of the DSU indicates that general concepts of legal dispute settlement were not at the forefront of drafters' agendas. Rather, the focus was on improving the existing GATT dispute settlement procedures[87] in which GATT panels acted in a "semi-judicial" way,[88] and the purpose of dispute settlement was "not, strictly speaking to ensure compliance with the law but to arrive at a settlement acceptable to the parties concerned."[89] The continuation

84 Convention on the Settlement of Investment Disputes Between States and Nationals of Other States (Washington, 18 March 1965), 575 UNTS 159, Article 1.

85 The Dispute Settlement Negotiating Group (NG13) was responsible for negotiations on the dispute settlement mechanism and the Ambassadors of Uruguay and the United States were appointed as the first chairmen of the group: Terence P Stewart, *The GATT Uruguay Round: A Negotiating History (1986–1992)*, vol 2 (Kluwer Law and Taxation Publishers 1993) 2726.

86 Taylor St John, *The Rise of Investor-State Arbitration: Politics, Law, and Unintended Consequences* (Oxford University Press 2018) 125.

87 The Dispute Settlement Negotiation Group's negotiating structure was divided into two phases, the first of which included a review of the current dispute settlement procedures to identify areas for negotiation: Stewart (n 85) 2725.

88 ibid 2706; prior to the Uruguay Round, the customary practice of GATT panels was codified in the 'Understanding Regarding Notification, Consultation, Dispute Settlement and Surveillance: Adopted on 28 November 1979, GATT Doc No. L/4907.' <https://exhibits.stanford.edu/gatt/catalog/kb635pf3561> accessed 15 October 2019.

89 'The Settlement of Disputes Between Contracting Parties to the General Agreement' by Guy Ladreit de Lacharriere in Fritz Leutwiler (ed), *Trade Policies for a Better Future: The 'Leutwiler Report', the GATT and the Uruguay Round* (Martinus Nijhoff Publishers 1987) 120.

of the language used in the customary practice of GATT panels could suggest that a truly judicial body was not being created by the drafters of the DSU. The continued usage of "terms of reference" and other more political, rather than legal, terminology may allow for an inference that the WTO DSU drafters did not think that the next generation of panels and the new Appellate Body would be strictly bound by international legal conceptions of judicial terms and practice. However, the inclusion of the reverse consensus requirement to adopt panel and Appellate Body reports made significant steps in the "quasi-judicialization" of the dispute settlement process.[90]

3.1 *Jurisdiction*

In international law, there is a wide variety of jurisdictional clauses and ways in which jurisdiction can be conferred on an international tribunal. "Jurisdiction" relates to the concepts of sovereignty and power, delimiting the scope of the issues that a court or tribunal may decide. However, these constitutive instruments generally refer to the term "jurisdiction" without definition of the concept and the specific powers that are involved.[91]

3.1.1 WTO

The DSU does not explicitly refer to the term "jurisdiction", however, a number of articles deal with what are largely "jurisdictional" issues for both panels and the Appellate Body.[92] Article 1 deals with the coverage and application of the DSU. Article 2 establishes the Dispute Settlement Body (DSB) to administer the DSU while Article 6 provides for the establishment of panels. Under Article 3.1, Members affirm their adherence to the principles for the management of disputes that previously applied under Articles XXII and XXIII of the GATT. Article 7 provides the standard terms of reference for panels, unless parties otherwise agree, while Article 17.6 limits appeals to the Appellate Body to issues of law only. Finally, Article 17.13 authorizes the Appellate Body to uphold, modify or reverse legal findings and conclusions of panels. The dispute settlement mechanism of the WTO is also compulsory and exclusive. As the Appellate Body made clear in *US – Section 301 Trade Act*, this means:

> [Article 23.1 of the DSU] imposes on all Members to "have recourse to" the multilateral process set out in the DSU when they seek the redress

---

90 Ernst-Ulrich Petersmann, *The GATT/WTO Dispute Settlement System: International Law, International Organizations and Dispute Settlement* (Kluwer Law International 1997) 186.

91 The indeterminacy of jurisdiction as a concept is further examined in Chapter 5.

92 David Palmeter and Petros C Mavroidis, *Dispute Settlement in the World Trade Organization: Practice and Procedure* (2nd edn, Cambridge University Press 2004) 17.

> of a WTO inconsistency. In these circumstances, members have to have recourse to the DSU dispute settlement system to the exclusion of any other system, in particular a system of unilateral enforcement of WTO rights and obligations. This, what one could call "exclusive dispute resolution clause", is an important new element of members' rights and obligations under the DSU.[93]

The consequence of such compulsory and exclusive jurisdiction is that there is no separate consent requirement to invoke the provisions of the DSU,[94] unlike investor-state tribunals.

Very little needs to be said of the jurisdiction *ratione materiae* of WTO panels and the Appellate Body, given its clear and finite nature. Quite simply, panels and the Appellate Body only have jurisdiction over disputes arising out of the "covered agreements", which are set out in Appendix 1 to the DSU.[95] Panels are established on an ad hoc basis to hear specific complaints relating to "measures affecting the operation of any covered agreement taken within the territory" of a WTO member.[96] Each panel has jurisdiction to decide both factual and legal issues. Article 7.1 of the DSU establishes the jurisdiction of a panel in a particular dispute by setting out the standard terms of reference for each complaint, namely:

> To examine, in the light of the relevant provisions in (name of the covered agreements (s) cited by the parties to the dispute), the matter referred to the DSB by (name of party) in document ... and to make such findings as will assist the DSB in making the recommendations or in giving the rulings provided for in that/those agreement(s).

In combination, these Articles clearly restrict each panel's jurisdiction *ratione materiae* to claims based on covered agreements. As such, a particular panel

93 *United States – Sections 301–310 of the Trade Act of 1974* (*Report of the Panel*) (22 December 1999), WT/DS152/R [7.43].

94 CF Amerasinghe, *Jurisdiction of Specific International Tribunals* (Martinus Nijhoff 2008) 511–2; Frieder Roessler, 'Dispute Settlement in the WTO: From a Deliberately Designed to a Spontaneously Grown Order' in Bernard Hoekman, Joost Pauwelyn and Manfred Elsig (eds), *Assessing the World Trade Organization: Fit for Purpose?* (Cambridge University Press 2017) 99 ff.

95 Article 1.1 of the Understanding on Rules and Procedures Governing the Settlement of Disputes, Marrakesh Agreement Establishing the World Trade Organization, Annex 2 (15 April 1994), 1869 UNTS 401; see further, Amerasinghe (n 94) 535; Palmeter and Mavroidis (n 92) 21–22.

96 Article 4.2 of the DSU.

may only be able to consider other claims if non-standard terms of reference are adopted.[97] The Appellate Body may uphold, modify or reverse the legal findings and conclusions of a panel.[98] The jurisdiction *ratione materiae* of the Appellate Body is a subset of the particular panel's subject-matter jurisdiction.[99] However, the Appellate Body can only be seized of legal issues pursuant to Article 17.6 of the DSU.

3.1.2 ISDS

It is not possible to set out all the jurisdictional clauses in use in investor-state dispute settlement. Generally speaking, the jurisdictional clauses often go further than merely setting out the scope of the four dimensions of jurisdiction but also include the proper forum for dispute settlement, how consent to investor-state arbitration is to be established and any other conditions for the exercise of the tribunal's jurisdiction (such as exhaustion of local remedies or waiting periods). The particular IIA, together with the rules of the forum, will greatly affect the jurisdictional limits of each dispute.

To illustrate, two examples are provided, one multilateral and the other bilateral, both of which are the subject of tribunal decisions discussed in the later Chapters: Article 26 of the Energy Charter Treaty (ECT)[100] and Article VII of the US – Argentina BIT.[101] As the research is most concerned with jurisdiction *ratione materiae*, the examples will be limited to the definition of the dispute in each of the treaties.

For each of these provisions, the jurisdiction *ratione materiae* of the tribunal is a "dispute" between an investor and the host state over the alleged breach of, *inter alia*, the provisions of the IIA. In this way, the jurisdiction *ratione materiae* of tribunals is limited in its subject-matter to rights and obligations explicitly contained in the IIA, in a similar way to which the DSU limits jurisdiction to disputes under the WTO covered agreements.

The uniting feature of the disparate range of jurisdictional clauses is that consent to arbitration remains a primary step in establishing jurisdiction for any arbitral forum for determining investor-state disputes. Most often, investment treaty arbitration is founded in general offers to arbitrate contained in

---

97 Andrew Mitchell, *Legal Principles in WTO Disputes* (Cambridge University Press 2008) 90.
98 Article 17.13 of the DSU.
99 Mitchell (n 97) 92.
100 The Energy Charter Treaty (Lisbon, 17 December 1994), 2080 UNTS 95.
101 Treaty between United States of America and The Argentine Republic concerning the Reciprocal Encouragement and Protection of Investment (Washington, 14 November 1991).

TABLE 2 Example jurisdictional clauses

Energy Charter Treaty	US – Argentina BIT
(1) Disputes between a Contracting Party and an Investor of another Contracting Party relating to an Investment of the latter in the Area of the former, which concern an alleged breach of an obligation of the former under Part III [Investment Promotion and Protection] shall, if possible, be settled amicably.	(1) For purposes of this Article, an investment dispute is a dispute between a Party and a national or company of the other Party arising out of or relating to (a) an investment agreement between that Party and such national or company; (b) an investment authorization granted by that Party's foreign investment authority (if any such authorization exists) to such national or company; or (c) an alleged breach of any right conferred or created by this Treaty with respect to an investment.

investment treaties.[102] In this respect, the investment treaty represents an offer to arbitrate by the host State which the investor will accept by submitting the dispute to arbitration. As such, this offer by the host State can be considered similar to the optional clause declarations in dispute settlement before the ICJ.[103] Once the investor has accepted the offer to arbitrate, the host State's offer to consent is irrevocable, essentially establishing "bilateral islands of quasi-compulsory jurisdiction".[104]

3.1.3 Conclusion on Jurisdiction

The jurisdiction *ratione materiae* of the WTO and investor-state dispute settlement mechanisms appear similarly limited to disputes arising from the application of the constitutive treaties. The jurisdiction is limited in this way, although specific treaty language and the method of consent to jurisdiction may be different. However, "jurisdiction" itself is not an easily defined concept. The particular scope of their jurisdictional powers remains at the mercy of this

102 Michael Waibel, 'Investment Arbitration: Jurisdiction and Admissibility' in Marc Bungenberg and others (eds), *International Investment Law* (Beck Nomos Hart 2015) 1215; on the four general trends of offers to consent to arbitration, see 'Bilateral Investment Treaties 1995–2006: Trends in Investment Rulemaking' (United Nations Conference on Trade and Development 2007) UNCTAD/ITE/IIT/2006/5 105–6; and Zachary Douglas, *The International Law of Investment Claims* (Cambridge University Press 2009) 234 ff.

103 Waibel (n 102) 1215.

104 ibid 1216.

elusive definition. To describe this as merely an academic problem or technicality would be unjust. The terminological clarity (or lack thereof) of jurisdiction has consequences for our understanding of the judicial function and responses to fragmentation. Jurisdiction as a concept is innately linked to the judicial function and so how an adjudicator approaches this concept could be influenced by their view of the international judicial function. Further, consistent responses to fragmentation could be hindered by the lack of understanding of the boundary of "jurisdiction" as a term and its relationship to other dispute settlement concepts. Both of these issues are explored in Chapter 5 when analysing the impact of jurisdiction as a closing tool.

3.2 *Applicable Law*

The concept of applicable law instructs the international tribunal on which norm it is required to apply in the exercise of its jurisdiction.[105] Compared to jurisdiction, applicable law is used to "incidental ends" which enables the content of applicable law to be fixed very liberally.[106] However, this should not suggest a less important role for applicable law. Rather, the question of the applicable law can be a crucial phase of many international disputes, given the relative nature of applicable law:

> international tribunals are never the judges of "the" international law; they are only the judges of "an" international law, the one applicable to the dispute as defined according to the particular concept of applicable law encapsulated in the statute of each tribunal and by the parties.[107]

For some of the permanent international courts and tribunals, the applicable law is set out in a treaty.[108] Article 38(1) of the ICJ Statute is frequently cited as an example of a broad applicable law clause. Much scholarly discussion of

105 Lorand Bartels, 'Jurisdiction and Applicable Law Clauses: Where Does a Tribunal Find the Principal Norms Applicable to the Case before It?' in Tomer Broude and Yuval Shany (eds), *Multi-Sourced Equivalent Norms in International Law* (Hart Publishing 2011) 116.

106 Mathias Forteau, 'The Diversity of Applicable Law Before International Tribunals as a Source of Forum Shopping and Fragmentation of International Law: An Assessment' in Rüdiger Wolfrum and Ina Gätzschmann (eds), *International Dispute Settlement: Room for Innovations?* (Springer Berlin Heidelberg 2013) 439.

107 ibid 423.

108 For example, United Nations Convention on the Law of the Sea (Montego Bay, 10 December 1982), 1833 UNTS 397, Article 293; Rome Statute of the International Criminal Court (adopted 17 July 1998), 2187 UNTS 90, Article 21.

Article 38(1) surrounds what qualifies as a source of international law,[109] however, this section is concerned with the concept of applicable law itself and its function within international dispute settlement. Article 38(1) is not merely an applicable law clause, but rather has a "triple duty", setting out the functions of the ICJ, its means and its limits.[110] The text of the provision states that the ICJ "shall apply", which involves identifying, interpreting and applying the applicable rules of law on the basis of the sources listed in paragraphs (a) to (d).[111] As the ICJ stated in the *Nuclear Weapons* Advisory Opinion:

> The question put to the Court by the General Assembly is indeed a legal one, since the Court is asked to rule on the compatibility of the threat or use of nuclear weapons with the relevant principles and rules of international law. To do this, the Court must identify the existing principles and rules, interpret them and apply them to the threat or use of nuclear weapons, thus offering a reply to the question posed based on law.[112]

Although Article 38(1) directs the ICJ to apply certain sources of international law, it is a relative provision. The applicable law can be different from case to case, depending on the cause of action and the treaties entered into by the parties to the dispute.[113] Further, states may also extend or limit the applicable law within or beyond the scope of Article 38.[114] While applicable law provisions in treaties may differ in wording, scholars have argued that this does not necessarily mean that they embody radically different concepts of international law.[115] According to Forteau, applicable law provisions generally do not depart from the general framework of Article 38 of the ICJ Statute.[116]

---

109 See, for example, Alain Pellet and Daniel Müller, 'Article 38' in Andreas Zimmermann and others (eds), *The Statute of the International Court of Justice: a commentary* (3rd edn, Oxford University Press 2019); Samantha Besson and Jean d'Aspremont, 'The Sources of International Law. An Introduction' in Samantha Besson and Jean d'Aspremont (eds), *The Oxford Handbook on the Sources of International Law* (Oxford University Press 2017); Andenas and Leiss (n 27).

110 Pellet and Müller (n 109) 822.

111 Sienho Yee, 'Article 38 of the ICJ Statute and Applicable Law: Selected Issues in Recent Cases' (2016) 7 Journal of International Dispute Settlement 472, 475.

112 *Legality of the Threat or Use of Nuclear Weapons*, Advisory Opinion [1996] ICJ Reports 226, 234.

113 Forteau (n 106) 421.

114 ibid 422.

115 ibid 429.

116 ibid; see also, Yee (n 111) 475, in which Yee refers to the 'impressive progeny' that has been spawned by Article 38.

3.2.1 WTO

Like the term "jurisdiction", the term "applicable law" is not found within the DSU. The concept of applicable law is covered by several provisions but there is no separate provision of the applicable law, unlike Article 38(1) of the ICJ Statute.[117] The provisions of the DSU commonly referred to in the context of applicable law include Article 3.2, Article 7 and Article 11,[118] which have already been mentioned in relation to jurisdiction above. These provisions clearly show that WTO covered agreements apply as applicable law to disputes.[119] However, the interpretation of these articles provokes significant debate on whether the articles have the effect of bringing in all sources of international law and the terms of Article 38(1) of the ICJ Statute or have the effect of excluding the application of international law.[120] The interpretation primarily hinges on the extent to which the last sentence of Article 3.2 and 19.2 of the DSU ("cannot add to or diminish the rights and obligations under the covered agreements"), as well as the extent to which the WTO treaty language itself, encapsulates general international law.[121] This debate is particularly pertinent

---

117 Isabelle Van Damme, 'Jurisdiction, Applicable Law, and Interpretation' in Daniel Bethlehem and others (eds), *The Oxford Handbook of International Trade Law* (Oxford University Press 2012) 315; Joost Pauwelyn, *Conflict of Norms in Public International Law: How WTO Law Relates to Other Rules of International Law* (Cambridge University Press 2003) 465; Palmeter and Mavroidis (n 92) 50.

118 Joel Trachtman, 'The Domain of WTO Dispute Resolution' (1999) 40 Harvard International Law Journal 333, 342; Pauwelyn, Conflict of Norms in Public International Law: How WTO Law Relates to Other Rules of International Law (n 117) 465–466, although for Pauwelyn Article 7 is most directed at applicable law while Article 3.2 and Article 11 relate to the jurisdictional mandate of the panels; see also, Lorand Bartels, 'Applicable Law in WTO Dispute Settlement Proceedings' (2001) 35 Journal of World Trade 499, 504.

119 Van Damme (n 117) 315; Rupert Reece, Alexis Massot and Marie-Hélène Bartoli, 'Searching for the Applicable Law in WTO Litigation, Investment and Commercial Arbitration' in Jorge Huerta-Goldman, Antoine Romanetti and Franz Xaver Stinimann Fuentes (eds), *WTO Litigation, Investment Arbitration and Commercial Arbitration* (Kluwer Law International 2013) 214.

120 Bartels, 'Applicable Law in WTO Dispute Settlement Proceedings' (n 118) 504; on the argument that Article 7 acts as a substitute for Article 38(1) of the ICJ Statute see: Palmeter and Mavroidis (n 92) 50, who argue that all of the sub-paragraphs in Article 38(1) of the ICJ Statute are potential sources of law to be used in WTO dispute settlement, with the terms of Article 38(1) being effectively brought in through the provisions of Article 3.2 and 7 of the DSU; see, also Meinhard Hilf and Goetz Goettsche, 'The Relation of Economic and Non-Economic Principles in International Law' in Stefan Griller (ed), *International Economic Governance and Non-Economic Concerns: New Challenges for the International Legal Order* (Springer-Verlag Wien 2003) 14; on the alternative argument that Article 7 does not incorporate the sources of law in Article 38(1), see Trachtman (n 118) 342.

121 Van Damme (n 117) 315.

in a system with compulsory jurisdiction as a broad definition of the applicable law could evolve toward a more general jurisdiction of the WTO dispute settlement mechanism.[122]

A narrow interpretation of the applicable law provisions of the DSU proposes that panels and the Appellate Body are only permitted to apply WTO law. This interpretation does not divorce the WTO system from public international law entirely: panels and the Appellate Body may refer to non-WTO law for interpretation, in accordance with the customary principles of interpretation, and where non-WTO law is incorporated by reference in WTO law, either by express treaty language or by waiver.[123] This narrow interpretation could be supported by general international law and an *a contrario* reading of the ICJ's observation in *Kasikili/Sedudu Island*, on the basis that the WTO DSU only mentions the covered agreements.[124] It has also been argued that only a complete limitation against non-WTO law is sufficient to meet the restriction that WTO dispute settlement does not "add to or diminish the rights and obligations".[125] This narrow interpretation also accords with some views of DSU negotiators and WTO member states. For example, the US and Chile have expressed concern about the approach of panels and the Appellate Body and suggested additional guidance be provided on the constructive ambiguity of

122 See, for example, Gabrielle Marceau, 'A Call for Coherence in International Law: Praises for the Prohibition Against "Clinical Isolation" in WTO Dispute Settlement' (1999) 33 Journal of World Trade 87, 109 ff where Marceau notes the 'sound policy' mitigating against permitting WTO panels and the Appellate Body to enforce outside obligations, including overloading the multilateral trading system and averting focus from improving dispute resolution and enforcement in other sub-systems of international law (p 111).

123 Trachtman (n 118) 343: Trachtman refers to the incorporation of non-WTO law within WTO law through treaty language in TRIPS and the Lomé waiver; see also Reece, Massot and Bartoli (n 119) 213 ff; Marceau (n 122) 112–3.

124 The ICJ stated: 'It can therefore be assumed that the reference expressly made, in this provision, to the "rules and principles of international law", if it is to be meaningful, signifies something else. In fact, the Court observes that the expression in question is very general and, if interpreted in its normal sense, could not refer solely to the rules and principles of treaty interpretation. [...] This wording shows that the Parties had no intention of confining the rules and principles of law applicable in this case solely to the rules and principles of international law relating to treaty interpretation': *Kasikili/Sedudu Island* (*Botswana v Namibia*), *Judgment* [1999] ICJ Reports 1045, 1102; see Van Damme (n 117) 316.

125 Debra Steger, 'The Jurisdiction of the WTO' (2004) 98 American Society of International Law Proceedings 142, 144; cf. Bartels who argues that if there is no place for non-WTO law in proceedings, then this sentence of Article 3.2 and 19.2 has no role to play: Lorand Bartels, 'The Appellate Body and Public International Law' in Federico Ortino and Sergey Ripinsky (eds), *WTO Law and Process: The Proceedings of the 2005 and 2006 Annual WTO Conferences* (British Institute of International and Comparative Law 2007) 59.

the WTO agreements and the unacceptable methods of gap-filling.[126] In this respect, Kuijper has argued that negotiators may not have fully considered the potential implications of the language of the DSU and it is only a "natural phenomenon that negotiators are surprised when neutral 'judges' who were not involved in the negotiations start interpreting a text outside of the context of negotiations".[127]

The other side of the debate suggests a much wider interpretation and relevance of non-WTO law to disputes. This interpretation relies on the silence of the DSU on applicable law: there is no express limitation on the applicable law.[128] In the absence of an explicit clause on the applicable law, the practice of other international tribunals is relevant, whereby other international law, at the very least, fills the gaps in the DSU.[129] This also accords with the view that limited jurisdiction does not necessarily limit the applicable law of a tribunal. For Pauwelyn, this leaves two avenues in which to apply non-WTO law: as a fall-back where the panel is faced with questions not regulated by the WTO covered agreements, or in defence of a claim of a WTO violation.[130] As such, we have two competing views on the role of general principles in WTO law: to fill gaps or not?

Despite the lack of a clear answer in the WTO DSU on the scope of the applicable law in WTO disputes, it is clear that panels and the Appellate Body have turned to rules and principles of international law to complement or gap-fill WTO covered agreements.[131] For example, the Appellate Body referred to the

126 'Negotiations on Improvements and Clarifications of the Dispute Settlement Understanding, Further Contribution of the United States on Improving Flexibility and Member Control in WTO Dispute Settlement – Communication from the United States' (World Trade Organization, Dispute Settlement Body 2005) TN/DS/W/82.

127 PJ Kuijper, 'A Legal Drafting Group for the Doha Round: A Modest Proposal' (2003) 37 Journal of World Trade 1031, 1032.

128 As Hilf and Goettsche argue, 'therefore, apart from the limited jurisdiction of both Panels and the Appellate Body and apart from special conflict rules either in the WTO agreement, general international law or other non-WTO agreements, international law from all sources is potentially applicable as WTO law, unless the DSU or any other WTO rule has expressly contracted out of them': Hilf and Goettsche (n 120) 14–15. However, the silence is also used in favor of a narrow interpretation, in only referring to customary rules of interpretation, the drafters demonstrated 'an intent to exclude other international law by virtue of their decision not to mention it': Joel P Trachtman, 'The Jurisdiction of the WTO' (2004) 98 American Society of International Law Proceedings 139, 140; see also Trachtman (n 118) 342.

129 Van Damme (n 117) 317; Forteau (n 106) 433–434.

130 Pauwelyn (n 117); Joost Pauwelyn, 'The Role of Public International Law in the WTO: How Far Can We Go?' (2001) 95 The American Journal of International Law 535.

131 Trachtman (n 128) 139; Bartels, 'The Appellate Body and Public International Law' (n 125) 56.

inclusion of customary rules of interpretation for the requirement that WTO law is not to be read "in clinical isolation from public international law".[132] The panel in *Korea – Government Procurement* also referred to the fact that customary international law "applies generally to the economic relations between WTO Members", meaning that such law "applies to the extent that the WTO treaty agreements do not 'contract out' from it."[133] It has, therefore, become moot to ask whether panels and the Appellate Body have applied non-WTO law. Rather, it is clear such a practice is occurring.[134] However, the uncertainty in the legal sources on applicable law still leaves open the question whether the panels are in fact allowed to do so within the states' consent to WTO dispute settlement. If the extent of the panel's authority to apply other international law is indeterminate, the door to inconsistency is left open.

In this way, resolving this uncertainty in the applicable law of WTO disputes does involve taking a position on the relationship between the opening and closing tools of international law. Where there is no applicable law clause, should this be read as a lack of consent to wide applicable law? Or does a residual power to apply international law lie with any grant of jurisdiction to an international tribunal? As the above discussion illustrates, the answer is not neatly available on the formal sources of law.

3.2.2 ISDS

In comparison to the practice of applicable law under the WTO DSU, the applicable law in international investment disputes is much more directed by the parties to each individual dispute.[135] Applicable law is usually considered to be

---

132 *United States – Standards for Reformulated and Conventional Gasoline (Report of the Appellate Body)* (29 April 1996), WT/DS2/AB/R 17.

133 *Korea – Measures Affecting Government Procurement (Report of the Panel)* (1 May 2000) WT/DS163/R [7.96].

134 As Flett notes, '[a]gain, one has the impression that difficult doctrinal discussions about applicable law and the rules of interpretation might be overlooking the fact that, in the background, international law is steadily trickling into the WTO acquis , apparently without any of the WTO Members taking particular exception': James Flett, 'Importing Other International Regimes into World Trade Organization Litigation' in Margaret A Young (ed), *Regime Interaction in International Law: Facing Fragmentation* (Cambridge University Press 2012) 282; similarly, see Bartels, 'The Appellate Body and Public International Law' (n 125) 56; Van Damme (n 117) 320. This is also confirmed in the empirical results in Chapter 3.

135 The arbitral rules usually adopted in ISDS, including the ICSID Convention, UNCITRAL Rules and ICA Arbitration Rules, direct the tribunal to apply the law designated by the parties to the dispute first: ICSID Convention, article 42(1); UNCITRAL Arbitration Rules (with new article 1, paragraph 4, as adopted in 2013), article 35(1); International Court of Arbitration of the International Chamber of Commerce, Arbitration Rules (in force as from 1 March 2017), article 21(1); Permanent Court of Arbitration Optional Rules for

wider or more flexible than its counterpart in the WTO, leading to an assumption of a more open regime to other international law. However, determining the applicable law in investor-state disputes still matters considerably for two reasons. First, the law applicable to the dispute can have a very clear impact on the dispute, including the ultimate outcome. For example, the difference in compensation from expropriation (or other breaches) may differ significantly from domestic law to customary international law to the specific IIA.[136] The applicable law may also influence the availability of counterclaims in the dispute.[137] Secondly, the disregard of the applicable law may also amount to an excess of power and provide grounds for the setting-aside of the award or annulment of the award under the ICSID Convention.[138] Ultimately, the determination of the applicable law involves broad margins of discretion to the tribunals in their interpretation of applicable law clauses, allowing room for other international law to be included or excluded in the determination of the dispute, not simply in interpretation of the IIA.[139]

Applicable law is quite commonly regulated through applicable law clauses in IIAs, which set out the applicable sources of substantive law in investment

---

Arbitrating Disputes Between Two Parties of Which Only One Is a State (effective 6 July 1993), Article 33(1).

136 See, for example, *Mobil Corporation (now Venezuela Holdings BV) v Venezuela* (ICSID Case No ARB/07/27), Decision on Annulment, 9 March 2017 [157 ff]; Emmanuel Gaillard and Yas Banifatemi, 'The Meaning of "and" in Article 42 (1), Second Sentence, of the Washington Convention: The Role of International Law in the ICSID Choice of Law Process' (2003) 18 ICSID Review 375, 380; see also, Andrea K Bjorklund, 'Applicable Law in International Investment Disputes' in Chiara Giorgetti (ed), *Litigating International Investment Arbitration Disputes* (Brill Nijhoff 2014) 262, referring to the fact that there may not be a violation of domestic law but a violation of international law, applicable under the applicable law clause.

137 Bjorklund (n 136) 262; Gabriel Bottini and Elisa Méndez Bräutigam, 'Investment Claims against Latin American States: Environmental Protection and the Applicable Law' in Kate Miles (ed), *Research Handbook on Environment and Investment Law* (Edward Elgar Publishing 2019).

138 The failure to apply the applicable law may be grounds for annulment under Article 52(1)(b) of the ICSID Convention: *Azurix v Argentina (I)* (ICSID Case No ARB/01/12), Decision on the Application for Annulment of the Argentine Republic, 1 September 2009 [132 ff]; the non-application of the applicable law must be distinguished from the correctness of the application of the applicable law, which is not an annullable error: *Micula v Romania (I)* (ICSID Case No ARB/05/20), Decision on Annulment, 26 February 2016 [186]; Bjorklund (n 136) 262; Kurtz (n 43) 281; Reece, Massot and Bartoli (n 119) 212–3.

139 Crina Baltag, 'Applicable Law under Article 26(6) the Energy Charter Treaty and Environmental Protection: Promoting Sustainable Development in the Energy Field' (2019) 16 Transnational Dispute Management (TDM) 2; Surya P Subedi, *International Investment Law: Reconciling Policy and Principle* (3rd edn, Hart Publishing 2016) 131.

disputes.[140] In a large empirical study of 1017 investment treaties, Atanasova found that 38% of those treaties which provide consent to ISDS contain an applicable law clause, although applicable law clauses were significantly more common in recent treaties (65% of treaties signed between 2013 and 2016 contain an applicable law clause).[141] Within these applicable law clauses, the language also tends to be mandatory, with all but 3 treaties containing language similar to "the tribunal *shall* decide in accordance with …".[142] The clauses almost invariably refer to the investment treaty as a source of applicable law and then includes two other broad sources of law, without assigning any particular questions to any specific source. The two broad sources include domestic law and international law. Domestic law is only included in just over half of Atanasova's surveyed clauses.[143] Comparatively, international law (beyond the investment treaty itself) is included in over 80% of the applicable law clauses.[144] However, the references to international law are not consistent between clauses. The clauses most commonly refer to the "rules of international law" (44% of such clauses) or the "general principles of international law" (38% of such clauses), but only 10% of treaties expressly designate as applicable any other treaties in force between the parties.[145] This variation of language opens up the possibility for divergence between investment tribunals when determining the applicable international law, including what are "rules" or

140 Dafina Atanasova, 'Applicable Law Provisions in Investment Treaties: Forever Midnight Clauses?' (2019) 10 Journal of International Dispute Settlement 396, 4; Yas Banifatemi and Elsie Edson, 'Jurisdiction of the Center' in Julien Fouret, Rémy Gerbay and Gloria Alvarez (eds), *The ICSID Convention, Regulations and Rules: A Practical Commentary* (Edward Elgar Publishing 2019) 485; Christoph H Schreuer, *The ICSID Convention: A Commentary* (2nd edn, Cambridge University Press 2009) 550.

141 Atanasova (n 140) 12. While not the complete universe of investment treaties, the study included all investment treaties signed between 2013 and 2016, a near-exhaustion of the broad international economic treaties with substantive investment protection provisions, and the full investment treaty networks of nine states.

142 ibid 13.

143 ibid. The inclusion of domestic law in the clause may be relevant to other public international law where the international law has somehow been incorporated into the domestic legal system but is not otherwise a rule or principle of international law captured by the applicable law clause. However, this international law is then treated as part of the corpus of domestic law and is less relevant for the purposes of this research.

144 ibid.

145 Other variations include referring to both 'rules and principles of international law' or 'general rules of international law'. The most recent treaties tend to refer to the 'rules and principles' of international law: ibid 14–16.

"principles" of international law and whether a narrow or wide interpretation of the terms of the clause are used.[146]

In arbitral proceedings before ICSID, where parties have not made a choice as to the applicable law, whether through an applicable law clause or another method, Article 42(1) of the ICSID Convention provides a subsidiary rule. Article 42(1) states:

> The Tribunal shall decide a dispute in accordance with such rules of law as may be agreed by the parties. In the absence of such agreement, the Tribunal shall apply the law of the Contracting State party to the dispute (including its rules on the conflict of laws) and such rules of international law as may be applicable.

In the early days of ICSID arbitration, the reference to international law in Article 42(1) was seen to have a mere corrective function. This view of Article 42(1) was based on ICSID negotiating history, in which international law was referred to as coming into play "both in the case of a lacuna in domestic law as well as in the case of inconsistency between the two"[147] and was popularized in the *Klöckner* case.[148] However, many scholars consider that this view excessively limited the scope of the application of international law, which was neither supported by the drafting history of the ICSID Convention nor by

146 A narrow interpretation would limit the rules and principles to those that have a direct bearing on investment law while a wide interpretation would include broader international law, such as human rights and environment treaties: Christoph H Schreuer, 'Jurisdiction and Applicable Law in Investment Treaty Arbitration' (2014) 1 McGill Journal of Dispute Resolution 1, 16.

147 The full quote states that 'the final provision relating to international law (which would bring it into play both in the case of a lacuna in domestic law as well as in the case of inconsistency between the two) was adopted by a majority of 24 to 6': Summary Proceedings of the Legal Committee Meeting, 7 December 1964, Document No. 81 in International Center for Settlement of Investment Disputes, *The History of the ICSID Convention: Documents Concerning the Origin and the Formulation of the Convention on the Settlement of Investment Disputes between States and Nationals of Other States*, vol II (1970) 804; see also Ole Spiermann, 'Investment Arbitration: Applicable Law' in Marc Bungenberg and others (eds), *International Investment Law: A Handbook* (Hart Publishing 2015).

148 The Ad Hoc Committee noted the 'dual role' of international law under Article 42, that is "complementary (in the case of lacuna ...), or corrective, should the State's law not conform on all points to the principles of international law: *Klöckner Industrie-Anlagen GmbH and others v United Republic of Cameroon and Société Camerounaise des Engrais* (ICSID Case No ARB/81/2), Ad Hoc Committee Decision on Annulment, 3 May 1985 [69]; see also, *Amco Asia Corporation and others v Republic of Indonesia* (ICSID Case No ARB/81/1), Decision on the Application for Annulment, 16 May 1986 [148].

the fact that the international law referred to in Article 42 is to be understood within the meaning of Article 38 of the ICJ Statute.[149] The tension between the complementary/corrective function and the more expansive role of Article 42(1) was discussed by the Annulment Committee in *Wena Hotels,* determining that both legal orders have a role and that "international law can be applied by itself".[150] Following this clarification by the Annulment Committee, international law has commonly been applied as a separate source of law, as the empirical results in Chapter 3 also confirm.

Where there is no applicable law clause in the IIA and the parties have not brought the proceedings under the ICSID Convention, the tribunal will have to determine the applicable law.[151] International law will likely still be found to be applicable to the dispute, even in the absence of explicit textual direction.[152] This argument is based on the fact that IIAs themselves are creatures of international law, thereby requiring the application of customary international law, which applies to all states unless clear contracting out of such rules occurs.[153]

149 See Gaillard and Banifatemi (n 136) 397 ff. Gaillard and Banifatemi refer to the drafting history to support the view that international law is to be understood in the sense of Article 38 of the ICJ Statute; see also, the Memorandum from the General Counsel and Draft Report of the Executive Directors to accompany the Convention, 19 January 1965, Document No. 128, which stated that 'the term "international law" as used in this context should be understood in the sense given to it by Article 38(1) of the Statute of the International Court of Justice, allowance being made for the fact that Article 38 was designed to apply to inter-State disputes': International Center for Settlement of Investment Disputes (n 147) 962.

150 *Wena Hotels Limited v Arab Republic of Egypt* (ICSID Case No ARB/94/4), Decision on the Application by the Arab Republic of Egypt for Annulment, 5 February 2002 [39–41].

151 This is supported by the rules of other arbitral institutions: UNCITRAL Arbitration Rules, article 35(1) which states that the tribunal shall apply the law 'which it determines to be appropriate'.

152 For example, see decisions in which there was no applicable law clause in the constitutive treaty but the tribunal considered relevant international law to be applicable: *Cargill v Poland* (ICSID Case No ARB(AF)/04/2), Award, 29 February 2008 [228]; *Oztas Construction v Libya* (ICA Case No 21603/ZF/AYZ), Final Award, 14 June 2018 [23]; *South American Silver Limited (Bermuda) v The Plurinational State of Bolivia* (PCA Case No 2013–15), Award, 22 November 2018 [207]; see further Spiermann (n 147) 1385 ff; Kurtz (n 43) 283; Patrick Dumberry, *The Formation and Identification of Rules of Customary International Law in International Investment Law* (Cambridge University Press 2016) 351.

153 For example, the Annulment Committee in *Azurix v Argentina (I)* stated: "[b]earing in mind that an investment treaty, whether bilateral or multilateral, is itself a source of international law as between the States parties to that treaty, the law applicable in any claim for a breach of that treaty can thus be said to be the treaty itself specifically, and international law generally': *Azurix v Argentina (I)* (n 138) para 146; see further, Kurtz (n 43) 283. Kurtz also refers to the fact that there is a close historical connection between the development of the treaty-based investment protections and the evolution of customary rules as a reason for the application of customary international law; similarly, Banifatemi notes

However, it is certainly not clear how far beyond the application of customary international law tribunals are able to go. Even with this ambiguity, it is still much less controversial that international law is generally applicable in investor-state disputes when compared to its WTO counterpart.

In relation to the applicable law in the decisions analysed in this book, the empirical results indicate that most of the decisions are subject to a predefined choice of law, either through an applicable law clause in the IIA or through the fall-back provision of the ICSID Convention. Only a small number of decisions were left with no guidance on the applicability of international law in the dispute. Figure 2 illustrates these results.[154]

When we consider the applicable law clauses of IIAs in more detail, we identify a number of different variations in the language referring to the other

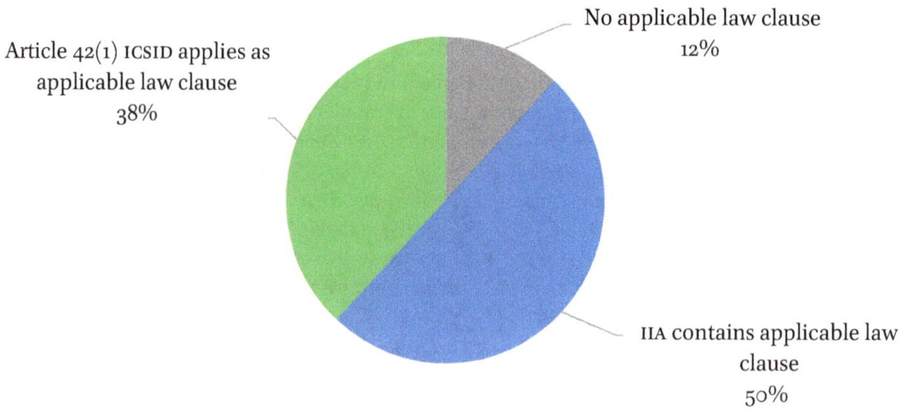

FIGURE 2 Applicable law clauses in ISDS decisions

that the role of international law in investment treaty arbitration is essential and, by the very nature of investment treaty arbitration, certain issues can be resolved only through the application of international law: Yas Banifatemi, 'The Law Applicable in Investment Treaty Arbitration' in Katia Yannaca-Small (ed), *Arbitration under International Investment Agreements: A Guide to the Key Issues* (Oxford University Press 2010) 204; see Forteau (n 106) 433–434 for general discussion of the principle in other dispute settlement mechanisms.

154 The results on the IIA containing applicable law clauses in this study is slightly higher than the empirical results of Atanasova, although they are certainly within the same range. Whether there is a reason based on the types of IIAs that are litigated could be a question for further research.

sources of law applicable in the dispute. For an overwhelming majority of the decisions with an applicable law clause, international law is included as one of the sources, whether through the IIA or the ICSID Convention. Only a small fraction of the decisions is covered by an applicable law clause that does not refer to any sources of international law. Importantly, these applicable law clauses do not *exclude* the application of other international law. For example, Article 8.3 of the Czech-UK BIT states: "the arbitrator or arbitral tribunal to which the dispute is referred under paragraph (2) shall, in particular, base its decision on the provisions of this Agreement."[155] In such circumstances, the tribunal would then be required to consider which other international law may apply.

The vast majority of decisions are subject to the ICSID Convention language of "such rules of international law as may be applicable", either as a result of the use of Article 42(1) as a fall-back provision or by the IIA adopting similar language in its applicable law clause. However, there remain several variations on the potential sources of applicable international law in the other applicable law clauses, as illustrated in Figure 3.

Although some variety in language is used, the commonality between the provisions is generally broad (or perhaps more accurately vague) language on the applicable international law, without excluding specific sources of international law. The question of interpretation then becomes whether terminological differences in the broad language used, such as between references to "rule" and "principle" or between "relevant principles" and "general principles", suggest differences in the applicable international law. The clauses referring to "general principles of international law" are most similar to the language of Article 38(1)(c) of the ICJ Statute, albeit recognizing the international character of the general principles, rather than of "civilized nations".[156]

---

155 Agreement between the Government of the United Kingdom of Great Britain and Northern Ireland and the Government of the Czech and Slovak Federal Republic for the Promotion and Protection of Investments (Prague, 10 July 1990). This BIT was raised in three intra-EU objection decisions.

156 On the distinction between general principles derived from domestic compared to international law, see Marcelo Vázquez-Bermúdez, 'Second Report on General Principles of Law' (International Law Commission 2020) A/CN.4/741; Marija Đorđeska, *General Principles of Law Recognized by Civilized Nations (1922–2018): The Evolution of the Third Source of International Law Through the Jurisprudence of the Permanent Court of International Justice and the International Court of Justice* (Brill Nijhoff 2020) ch 3; on how ISDS tribunals have ascertained general principle of law, see Valentina Vadi, *Analogies in International*

FIGURE 3 Common references to international law in applicable law clauses in ISDS[157]

In a limited number of cases, there are some more specific formulations of applicable international law that, on an ordinary meaning, could appear to be more restrictive formulations[157]. As set out in Table 3, these formulations fall into two categories. First, those formulations that refer to the requirement that the principles of international law be "accepted by both Contracting States". This first formulation suggests a greater limitation on the applicable international law, since the rules and principles must be accepted by the state parties to the IIA. Secondly, formulations which refer to "universally recognized" principles of international law. However, whether "universally recognized" leads to a different set of applicable principles than "general principles of law recognized by civilized nations" under Article 38(1)(c) of the ICJ Statute has not been the subject of debate in the tribunal decisions.

Investment Law and Arbitration (Cambridge University Press 2015) ch 6, who notes that no quantitative test for determining whether a particular legal principle is a general principle of law has ever been set up.

157 Some of the decisions are brought under more than one IIA, which may have different applicable law clauses. As such, the total numbers do not directly match the total number of relevant decisions. The numbers included in "general principles of international law" consist of slight variations in language including "generally recognized principles of international law", "generally accepted rules and principles of international law" and "generally recognized rules and principles of international law".

TABLE 3 Specific formulations of applicable law clauses in ISDS

	Language of clause	BIT	Decisions (#)
1	"generally recognized principles of international law accepted by both Contracting States"	China-Laos BIT China-Peru BIT	3
	"the principles of international law recognized by the two Contracting Parties"	Italy-Lithuania BIT Italy-Tanzania BIT	2
2	"the universally accepted principles of international law"	Egypt-Spain BIT Algeria-Spain BIT	2
	"universally acknowledged rules and principles of international law"	Hungary-Netherlands BIT	2
	"the universally recognized norms and principles of international law"	USSR-Spain BIT	1

Only a small number of tribunals dwell on the specific terminology of the applicable law clause and how this affects the scope of the applicable law. For example, in *Cube Infrastructure*, the tribunal defined "principles of international law" in the ECT's applicable law clause in excluding the application of EU law:

> The reference is to "principles" of international law, not to every rule of international law that might be binding upon an ECT Contracting Party. The natural and ordinary meaning of the phrase is that it refers to the principles of public international law in general, as it applies to relations between any set of States, and not to principles that are peculiar to a sub-system of international law, such as EU law, to which some but by no means all ECT Contracting Parties are subject. ... While the EU treaties are of course international agreements made within the framework of, and governed by, public international law, they do not thereby become "principles of international law.[158]

This has not been a view widely discussed by other tribunals. More frequently, tribunals have not restricted themselves to a narrow reading of "applicable

158 *Cube Infrastructure Fund SICAV v Kingdom of Spain* (ICSID Case No ARB/15/20), Decision on Jurisdiction, Liability and Partial Decision on Quantum, 19 February 2019 [158].

rules and principles of international law".[159] Perhaps reflective of a pragmatic approach to applicable law, one in which the inclusion of fairly broad applicable law clauses does not overly restrict the tribunal.

3.2.3 Conclusions on Applicable Law

Although it is not possible to detail all the potential iterations of applicable law provisions relevant to the investor-state dispute settlement mechanism, the short survey identifies not only the potential for variation between tribunals on their approach to other public international law based on the variety of treaty terms, but also their generally wider scope of applicable law in investor-state disputes than WTO disputes. The variable applicable law between ISDS and WTO is one of the factors explaining the assumption that WTO is more restrictive in its approach to other public international law. Investor-state tribunals have clearly affirmed the application of general international law, perhaps illustrating the broad tribunal authority to determine the law applicable.[160] Comparatively, the debate over the possible scope for WTO panels to apply any rules other than the customary rules of interpretation remains unresolved.

3.3 *Interpretation*

Interpretation, hermeneutically speaking, is the process of giving meaning to a particular text, in the case of international law, treaties.[161] The traditional voluntarist aim of interpretation was to give effect to the state parties' intention and, as such, was supposed to be an objective act in cognizing positive law.[162] However, many scholars identified a greater role of interpretation in international law by international courts and tribunals than merely a cognitive exercise in clarification of existing norms.[163] The process of interpretation has

---

159 On the intra-EU objection, see *Belenergia SA v Italian Republic* (ICSID Case No ARB/15/40), Award, 6 August 2019 [292] and cases referred to therein.

160 Bjorklund (n 136) 274.

161 Oliver Dörr, 'Article 31: General Rule of Interpretation' in Oliver Dörr and Kirsten Schmalenbach (eds), *Vienna Convention on the Law of Treaties: A Commentary* (2nd edn, Springer Berlin Heidelberg 2018) 560.

162 Arnold Duncan McNair, *The Law of Treaties* (Clarendon Press 1961) 365; Gleider I Hernández, 'Interpretation' in Jorg Kammerhofer and Jean D'Aspremont (eds), *International Legal Positivism in a Post-Modern World* (Cambridge University Press 2014) 330.

163 The ILC Report on Fragmentation referred to interpretation as 'legal reasoning', rather than merely cognition of the law: Koskenniemi, 'Fragmentation of International Law: Difficulties Arising from the Diversification and Expansion of International Law, Report of the Study Group of the International Law Commission' (n 6) para 35; McLachlan referred to the integrating process of legal interpretation: Campbell McLachlan, 'The Principle of Systemic Integration and Article 31(3)(c) of the Vienna Convention' (2005) 54 International & Comparative Law Quarterly 279, 286; see the discussion in Kammerhofer (n 82) 80 ff.

been argued to provide one of the largest avenues for arbitrators to exercise their discretionary judicial power:

> This creative power is exacerbated when a rule has to adapt to the evolving needs of the international society. Allowing such 'breathing' of the rules is perhaps the essential (and unspoken) function of interpretation and is particularly important in international law, where it fills the absence of a specialized and centralized legislator.[164]

The interpretative power is guided by the obligatory customary rules of interpretation, expressed in Articles 31 to 33 of the VCLT[165] as well as certain other canons of interpretation. These Articles apply in both WTO and investor-state disputes. In the first award under ICSID, the tribunal noted the "sound universally accepted rules of treaty interpretation as established in practice ... and as codified in Article 31".[166] Since then, ISDS adjudicators have frequently referred to the VCLT to guide their interpretative discretion, albeit not always in a methodologically consistent way.[167] For the WTO, Article 3.2 of the DSU refers to the application of the "customary rules of interpretation of public international law" in clarifying the provisions of the WTO agreements, thereby incorporating Articles 31 to 33.[168] The customary status of the rules of interpretation are

164 Alain Pellet, 'Canons of Interpretation under the Vienna Convention' in Joseph Klingler, Yuri Parkhomenko and Constantinos Salonidis (eds), *Between the Lines of the Vienna Convention? Canons and Other Principles of Interpretation in Public International Law* (Kluwer Law International 2019) 2.

165 Richard K Gardiner, *Treaty Interpretation* (2nd edn, Oxford University Press 2015) 12; The ICJ has referred to Article 31 and 32 as expressing customary international law, see for example *Legal Consequences of the Construction of a Wall in the Occupied Palestinian Territory, Advisory Opinion* [2004] ICJ Reports 38 [94].

166 *Asian Agricultural Products Ltd v Republic of Sri Lanka* (ICSID Case No ARB/87/3), Award, 27 June 1990 [38].

167 See, for further discussion, Nicola Strain, 'Methodological Consistency in the Interpretation of International Treaties in Investor-State Arbitration: An Empirical Study' in Guiditta Cordero-Moss and Diego P Fernández Arroyo (eds), *Applicable Law Issues in International Arbitration / Questions de droit applicable dans l'arbitrage international*, vol 25 (Brill Nijhoff 2022); Esme Shirlow and Kiran Nasir Gore, *The Vienna Convention on the Law of Treaties in Investor-State Disputes: History, Evolution and Future* (Wolters Kluwer 2022); J Romesh Weeramantry, *Treaty Interpretation in Investment Arbitration* (Oxford University Press 2012).

168 Early on, the Appellate Body recognized that Article 31 and 32 of the VCLT have attained the status of a rule of customary or general international law and are therefore applicable interpretation rules under Article 3.2 of the DSU: *Japan – Alcoholic Beverages* (*AB*) (n 37) 10; panels and the Appellate Body have then routinely referred to Articles 31 and 32 as customary international law applicable in the dispute. For recent examples, see *United States – Tariff Measures on Certain Goods from China* (*Report of the Panel*) (15 September 2020),

particularly important in disputes where one of the contracting states has not ratified the VCLT.[169]

The existence of such rules and guides may suggest some limitations on the exercise of the interpretative process.[170] However, the interpretation rules themselves are indeterminate. The rules of interpretation in the VCLT have been drafted in such a way that it is not possible to point to one "method" of treaty interpretation.[171] Further, adjudicators may not always be sanctioned for failure to comply with the VCLT if such interpretation is "acceptable".[172] This opens up space for adjudicators to decide cases in accordance with their own theoretical or normative preferences.[173]

WT/DS543/R [7.156]; and *European Union – Cost Adjustment Methodologies and Certain Anti-Dumping Measures on Imports from Russia* (*Second Complaint*) (*Report of the Panel*) (24 July 2020), WT/DS494/R [7.1] where the Panel uses the common language on the treaty interpretation process: 'Article 3.2 of the DSU provides that the WTO dispute settlement system serves to clarify the existing provisions of the covered agreements "in accordance with customary rules of interpretation of public international law". … The principles codified in Articles 31 and 32 of the [VCLT] are generally accepted as such customary rules'.

169 See, for example, *Chevron and TexPet v Ecuador* (*I*) (PCA Case No 2007–02/AA277), Interim Award, 1 December 2008 [118]; *US – Gasoline* (n 132) 17.

170 The treaty interpretation process could also endow the decision with a judicial seal of objectivity: Duncan French, 'Treaty Interpretation and the Incorporation Of Extraneous Legal Rules' (2006) 55 International & Comparative Law Quarterly 281, 285.

171 See, for example, Koskenniemi who discusses the indeterminacy of treaty interpretation and the tension between evaluative arguments and objectiveness: Koskenniemi, *From Apology to Utopia* (n 60) 338 ff; or, Pauwelyn and Elsig who discuss the varying degree of interpretation space within which tribunals can select between different interpretative techniques: Joost Pauwelyn and Manfred Elsig, 'The Politics of Treaty Interpretation: Variations and Explanations Across International Tribunals' in Jeffrey L Dunoff and Mark Pollack (eds), *Interdisciplinary Perspectives on International Law and International Relations: The State of the Art* (Cambridge University Press 2012); similarly, Hernández notes that even if the VCLT cannot be taken as gospel, it provides an analytical frame that has attempted to systematize and to structure the various possible methods for discerning the meaning of a legal text: Hernández, 'Interpretation' (n 162) 326.

172 Kammerhofer (n 82) 108. As with jurisdiction, it remains a question who may sanction an incorrect failure to comply with treaty interpretation methods.

173 See Sean Murphy, 'The Utility and Limits of Canons and Other Interpretative Principles in Public International Law' in Joseph Klingler, Yuri Parkhomenko and Constantinos Salonidis (eds), *Between the Lines of the Vienna Convention? Canons and Other Principles of Interpretation in Public International Law* (Kluwer Law International 2019) 23; Hernández, 'Interpretative Authority and the International Judiciary' (n 76) 168: 'even the process of identifying legal norms requires a choice as to which theory of sources one privileges, thus further demonstrating how the claim to objectivity in law-identification can be problematic'.

3.3.1 Role of Interpretation in International Law

How the tribunals approach interpretation and the method of legal interpretation and reasoning can affect whether they "build systemic relationships between rules and principles by envisaging them as parts of some human effort or purpose".[174] As such, treaty interpretation is seen as part of the solution to fragmentation: a unified and coherent method of interpretation confirms the coherence of international law as a system.[175] However, tribunals have a certain amount of "interpretation space",[176] which can then become part of the problem of fragmentation, providing potential for the interpretation of the same rules differently.[177]

An example of the role of interpretation in developing a coherent international legal system is the priority or conflict rules in international law. The ILC's Fragmentation Report placed significant emphasis on the role of interpretative maxims in resolving conflicts in international law:

> … legal reasoning will either have to seek to harmonize the apparently conflicting standards through interpretation or, if that seems implausible, to establish definite relationships of priority between them. Here interpretative maxims and conflict-solution techniques such as the lex specialis, lex posterior or lex superior become useful. They enable seeing a systemic relationship between two or more rules, and may thus justify a particular choice of the applicable standards, and a particular conclusion. They do not do this mechanically, however, but rather as "guidelines", suggesting a pertinent relationship between the relevant rules in view of the need for consistency of the conclusion with the perceived purposes or functions of the legal system as a whole.[178]

---

174 Koskenniemi, 'Fragmentation of International Law: Difficulties Arising from the Diversification and Expansion of International Law, Report of the Study Group of the International Law Commission' (n 6) para 35.

175 Eirik Bjorge, 'The Convergence of the Methods of Treaty Interpretation: Different Regimes, Different Methods of Interpretation?' in Mads Andenas and Eirik Bjorge (eds), *A Farewell to Fragmentation* (Cambridge University Press 2015) 533 ff.

176 See Pauwelyn and Elsig (n 171).

177 For example, Hernández refers to the vagueness of the general rule on the interpretation of positive acts in international law has created enormous discretion for judicial institutions: Hernández, 'Interpretative Authority and the International Judiciary' (n 76) 167.

178 Koskenniemi, 'Fragmentation of International Law: Difficulties Arising from the Diversification and Expansion of International Law, Report of the Study Group of the International Law Commission' (n 6) para 36.

In this way, *lex specialis* is described as a pragmatic mechanism for dealing with situations where two rules of international law that are both valid and applicable deal with the same subject-matter differently.[179] The *lex specialis* principle is set out in Article 55 of the ILC Articles of State Responsibility:

> These articles do not apply where and to the extent that the conditions for the existence of an internationally wrongful act or the content or implementation of the international responsibility of a State are governed by special rules of international law.[180]

There is no express hierarchy of the sources of international law. However, Article 38(1) of the ICJ Statute likely indicates the order in which the sources would ordinarily present themselves in the mind of an international judge, with treaties being the most important and specific source.[181] The application of *lex specialis* as a method of legal reasoning then suggests an informal hierarchy between general and specialized international law, which is often set out in international conventions. Consequently, the *lex specialis* principle is likely to be one of the most common interpretative maxims used by the WTO and investor-state tribunals in determining whether other international law should be excluded since it plays an influential role in resolving conflicts between general international law and specific regime law. In comparison to *lex specialis*, Article 31(3)(c) and the principle of systemic integration enables the inclusion of other international law and will be examined in Chapter 4.

3.3.2 Distinguishing Applicable Law and Interpretation

The distinction between direct applicability and interpretative guidance of external laws and norms is often overlooked, despite the fact that such distinction matters for normative approaches[182] and systemic challenges in international law.[183] Put simply, it is a question of what law tribunals are authorized

---

179 ibid 46; see also Dirk Pulkowski, 'Lex Specialis Derogat Legi Generali / Generalia Specialibus Non Derogant' in Joseph Klingler, Yuri Parkhomenko and Constantinos Salonidis (eds), *Between the Lines of the Vienna Convention? Canons and Other Principles of Interpretation in Public International Law* (Kluwer Law International 2018) 164.

180 Responsibility of States for Internationally Wrongful Acts (adopted by the International Law Commission at its fifty-third session, 2001).

181 James Crawford, *Brownlie's Principles of International Law* (9th edn, Oxford University Press 2019) 20; Bin Cheng, *General Principles of Law as Applied by International Courts and Tribunals* (reprint 2006, Steven & Sons 1953) 22.

182 See discussion in Gardiner (n 165) 27.

183 Kurtz (n 43) 280.

to interpret (the applicable law) and what law is capable of being used in that interpretation (interpretation of the applicable law): "interpretation, is [the process] of determining the meaning of a rule, while ... application, is ... that of determining the consequences which the rule attaches to ... a given fact".[184]

Applicable law clauses that stipulate international law as one of the sources could be read as imposing "a positive affirmative duty" to apply those other rules.[185] Comparatively, interpretation is supposedly a secondary process, only necessary when the meaning of the treaty to be applied is not clear: one cannot apply a law unless its precise meaning is known.[186] However, in practice, the two concepts often lapse into each other.[187] For the purposes of this book, the primary distinction between application and interpretation is limiting any use of external norms in gap-filling the investment treaty, a process more distinctly a question of applicability.

3.3.3 Conclusion on Interpretation

Interpretative techniques play a key role in legal reasoning. The interpretation process could be both a solution to fragmentation, providing "unity in fragmentation", or add to the problem of fragmentation with the possibility of conflicting interpretations of similar norms. This difficulty was summarized, albeit in relation to coherency of the WTO agreements themselves, in a concurring opinion of an Appellate Body member in relation to the interpretation of zeroing in the Anti-Dumping Agreement:

> The interpretation of the covered agreements requires scrupulous adherence to the disciplines of the customary rules of interpretation of public international law. Those disciplines are directed towards arriving at a coherent and harmonious interpretation to develop an answer to an interpretative problem and thereby provide certainty as to the rights and obligations of the parties. Variability, contradiction, and uncertainty stalk the interpretative enterprise, but they are the hallmarks of its failure, not its success. Just as the interpreter of a treaty strives for coherence, there is an inevitable recognition that a treaty bears the imprint of many hands. And what is left behind is a text, sometimes negotiated to a point where an agreement to regulate a matter could only be reached on the basis of

184 *Factory at Chorzów (Germany v Poland), Jurisdiction* [1927] PCIJ Rep Series A No 9 39 (Dissenting Opinion of Judge Ehrlich).
185 Kurtz (n 43) 280.
186 Weeramantry (n 167) 30; McNair (n 162) 365.
187 Weeramantry (n 167) 30; see also Gardiner (n 165) 27; Kammerhofer (n 82) 85.

> constructive ambiguity, carrying both the hopes and fears of the parties. Interpretation is an endeavour to discern order, notwithstanding these infirmities, without adding to or diminishing the rights and obligations of the parties.[188]

3.4 *Conclusions and Implications*

This section has analysed the jurisdiction, applicable law and interpretation provisions of the WTO and investor-state dispute settlement mechanisms. While relatively uncertain and subject to significant debate on the scope of these provisions, some preliminary conclusions on the jurisdiction and applicable law provisions of each of the mechanisms can be made. The first and uncontroversial conclusion is that the jurisdiction of these tribunals is limited by the consent of the states. The limited jurisdiction is a reflection of the power balance between states and international tribunals: the scope of the power granted by the states to the international tribunal to settle a set of limited and defined disputes. For the WTO and investor-state tribunals, this jurisdiction is limited to disputes under the WTO covered agreements and investment disputes under IIAs, respectively. There is no general jurisdiction to settle disputes not falling within one of these formal sources.

Secondly, the applicable law of investor-state disputes is generally more open and flexible than disputes under the WTO covered agreements. As applicable law is used to "incidental ends" in determining the dispute within the jurisdiction of the tribunal, applicable law may be less rigidly restricted to the source of the tribunal's jurisdiction. This is apparent in investor-state disputes in which the applicable law is generally quite wide and includes broad definitions of rules and principles of international law. For the WTO, the scope of the applicable law beyond the terms of the WTO covered agreements is unclear and has been interpreted by international scholars in different ways. This uncertain conclusion on the applicable law in WTO illustrates the questions left unanswered by the treaty provisions. In identifying the indeterminate features of these treaty provisions, the section shows where there is potential for the creative and discretionary interpretative function of the tribunals to come into play.

In analysing the jurisdiction, applicable law and interpretation provisions of the dispute settlement mechanisms, the section also elucidates some of the potential legal sources of authority for the tribunal to include or exclude other international law:

---

188 *United States – Continued Existence and Application of Zeroing Methodology* (*Report of the Appellate Body*) (4 February 2009), WT/DS350/AB/R [306].

a. From the discussion of jurisdiction, we can identify a potential basis for the rejection of the application of other international law: the tribunal refers to its limited jurisdictional mandate in rejecting the application of the other law.

b. The applicable law of the dispute settlement mechanisms may also provide a legal basis for the inclusion of the other international law or, alternatively, finding that the other international law does not fall within the legal sources in the applicable law clause of the dispute settlement mechanism.

c. The interpretative maxims and priority rules in international law may also ground a decision on the application of other international law. The tribunal may refer to *lex specialis* to reject the application of general international law or may invoke *lex superior* to apply other international law.

These legal sources of authority for the application (or rejection) of other international law will be employed, and expanded upon, in the following Chapter.

CHAPTER 3

Empirical Perspective

The following Chapters build on the preliminary findings in Chapter 2 on the indeterminacy of applying other international law in dispute settlement by turning to the comparative doctrinal study of the decisions of the WTO and investor-state dispute settlement mechanisms. Beginning with this Chapter, the Chapters illustrate that this indeterminacy has resulted in a substantial amount of other international law being incorporated into the WTO and investor-state disputes, but at a cost. Chapter 3 sets the empirical stage for the doctrinal analysis and consideration of how the opening and closing tools operate in Chapters 4 and 5.

1 Empirical Perspectives on the Force of International Law

This section begins our examination of how WTO and ISDS adjudicators may be influenced by the political and legal forces of (de)fragmentation through an empirical analysis of the approach of the tribunals. The section does this in two different ways. First, the section presents a bird's eye view of fragmentation, reviewing the number of relevant decisions, the proportion of international law taken into account and the timeline of cases. This illustrates a background of incorporation within the general framework of the international legal system. The section then delves deeper into the approach of the tribunals, considering the impact of sources of international law, the method of reasoning of the tribunals and the relationship to the broader responses to fragmentation. These empirical results develop the complicated story of the adjudicator's toolkit, resulting in inconsistency and uncertainty, to be continued in the second half of the Chapter.

1.1 *Responding to Fragmentation: Relevant Decisions*

First, we must ascertain: how many decisions raised relevant other international law? Such an investigation begins to uncover whether these dispute settlement mechanisms act as "self-contained regimes" and the possibility for jurisdictional collisions and substantive fragmentation. In addition, these results begin to unpick the assumption that the WTO dispute settlement mechanism is more restrictive in its application of other international law.

 | DOI:10.1163/9789004700932_004

To determine how many decisions raised relevant international law, it is first necessary to define what is "relevant other international law". The first limitation is: *who*. Whose arguments on other international law have been taken into account in the study? The review focused on adjudicator's legal reasoning, thereby excluding alternative or further supportive arguments of the parties from the analysis,[1] as well as other international law that may be raised as part of the factual matrix.[2] Since this research is centered on the legal reasoning of adjudicators, other law is only relevant where the tribunal engages with that law in some meaningful way. The research does not attempt to infer why the tribunal chose not to deal with one of the parties' arguments.

The second limitation is: *what*. What is the relevant "other" law? "Other international law" was defined broadly as any international law, rules or principles that is not within the text of the constitutive treaty of the dispute settlement mechanism. As the research is concerned with the relationship between the opening and closing tools, which includes issues of jurisdiction, applicable law and interpretation, all international law referred to in the reasoning of the adjudicators was considered. However, some important exclusions of "other international law", otherwise falling within this broad definition, were excluded from the empirical study based on the scope of the research questions. This included:

1. Customary rules of treaty interpretation and other interpretative maxims: as these are applicable interpretative methods in both regimes, their inclusion would suggest that almost all decisions of the mechanisms

---

1 In the analysis, where a tribunal does not deal with an argument is distinguished from instances of other law where the tribunal noted that it was not necessary to deal with a source of other international law raised by one of the parties. In doing so, the tribunal has acknowledged the alternative argument of the parties. Those instances of other law were included in the analysis. As such, the analysis only excludes other international law that was raised by parties but never referred to by the tribunal. Two reasons support the exclusion. First, to exclude the "spaghetti on the wall" arguments of the parties that may not in fact be relevant in the dispute. Secondly, since it is not possible to infer why tribunals have not referred to alternative arguments of parties, it is difficult to say whether those arguments were simply irrelevant, or the tribunal considered the other law inapplicable.

2 For example, the use of the Framework Convention on Tobacco Control Guidelines used as evidence in relation to measures being taken to protect public health, rather than used as an interpretative tool in defining public health or police powers in the plain packaging disputes: *Australia – Certain Measures Concerning Trademarks, Geographical Indications and Other Plain Packaging Requirements Applicable to Tobacco Products and Packaging* (*Reports of the Appellate Body*) (9 June 2020), WT/DS435/AB/R ; WT/DS441/AB/R [6.702]; *Philip Morris Brands SARL v Oriental Republic of Uruguay* (ICSID Case No ARB/10/7), Award, 8 July 2016 [391 ff].

incorporated "other" international law, which would be a redundant exercise.[3] However, these are treated as potential legal bases for the incorporation of international law in section 1.2 below.[4]

2. Soft law: non-legal principles and other soft law instruments,[5] while often interwoven in the fabric of international law,[6] raise a debate about the role of soft law in international law,[7] which is beyond the scope of this study. For the purposes of WTO and ISDS decisions, examples of soft law that have been excluded from "other international law" are international guidelines used in defining investment law concepts and procedure, such

---

3 See discussion in Chapter 2. Prior quantitative and qualitative studies of interpretation in investment law identify the prevalence of the rules of the VCLT as the starting point of the interpretative exercise by these tribunals. See, on ISDS, for example, Nicola Strain, 'Methodological Consistency in the Interpretation of International Treaties in Investor-State Arbitration: An Empirical Study' in Guiditta Cordero-Moss and Diego P Fernández Arroyo (eds), *Applicable Law Issues in International Arbitration / Questions de droit applicable dans l'arbitrage international*, vol 25 (Brill Nijhoff 2022); August Reinisch, 'The Interpretation of International Investment Agreements' in Marc Bungenberg and others (eds), *International Investment Law: A Handbook* (Hart Publishing 2015); on the use of the VCLT interpretation rules in WTO disputes, see Asif H Qureshi, *Interpreting WTO Agreements: Problems and Perspectives* (2nd edn, Cambridge University Press 2015) 3 ff; and, Isabelle Van Damme, *Treaty Interpretation by the WTO Appellate Body* (Oxford University Press 2009).

4 In particular, Articles 30 and 31(3)(c) of the VCLT, along with other priority rules such as lex specialis, deal with whether other substantive international law is to be applied or excluded and as such, are treated as a legal basis for the incorporation of other international law within this study. This approach is in line with the ILC's treatment of conflict rules in its Fragmentation Report as important tools in the harmonization of international law. The ILC's Fragmentation Report considers *lex specialis*, Article 30, Article 31(3)(c) as well as *jus cogens/erga omnes* obligations as potential conflict/priority rules in the harmonization of international law: Martti Koskenniemi, 'Fragmentation of International Law: Difficulties Arising from the Diversification and Expansion of International Law, Report of the Study Group of the International Law Commission' (International Law Commission 2006) A/CN.4/L.682; similarly, see Kerstin von der Decken, 'Article 30: Application of Successive Treaties Relating to the Same Subject Matter', *Vienna Convention on the Law of Treaties: A Commentary* (2nd edn, Springer Berlin Heidelberg 2018) 540.

5 In short, "soft law" are non-binding instruments and adjudicators have discretion whether or not to apply them. Some examples that are often referred to as "soft law" include international standards and guidelines of intergovernmental institutions, declarations of the ILC (to the extent that such work does not become an expression of customary international law) or treaty interpretation by non-judicial bodies: Melaku Geboye Desta, 'Soft Law in International Law: An Overview' in Andrea K Bjorklund and August Reinisch (eds), *International Investment Law and Soft Law* (Edward Elgar Publishing 2012) 42.

6 See Moshe Hirsch, 'Sources of International Investment Law' in Andrea K Bjorklund and August Reinisch (eds), *International Investment Law and Soft Law* (Edward Elgar Publishing 2012).

7 See the debate in Desta (n 5) 42 ff.

as the OECD or the International Bar Association guidelines,[8] or international standards relevant to the Agreement on Sanitary and Phytosanitary Measures (SPS) Agreement.[9]

3. International law incorporated in domestic law: instead, this is considered part of the application of domestic law, which is a different question than this research asks. For example, this includes disputes where the domestic constitution enshrines environmental rights commonly found in international law[10] or international instruments having "direct effect" through domestic legislation.[11]
4. Customary international law standards incorporated within the provisions of the constitutive treaties: for example, customary standards of expropriation or fair and equitable treatment in investment protection.[12] Such standards are no longer "other" international law since the customary international law falls within the text of the constitutive treaty.
5. References to other IIAs or jurisprudence of other investment tribunals: this exclusion recognizes that such references to other investor-state decisions is a relatively common practice of ISDS tribunals, without attempting to enter into a debate on the "multilateralization" of investment law.[13]

---

8 See the discussion in Andrea K Bjorklund, 'Assessing the Effectiveness of Soft Law Instruments in International Investment Law' in Andrea K Bjorklund and August Reinisch (eds), *International Investment Law and Soft Law* (Edward Elgar Publishing 2012) 74.

9 Article 3.1 of the SPS Agreement refers to Members basing 'their sanitary or phytosanitary measures on international standards, guidelines or recommendations': Agreement on the Application of Sanitary and Phytosanitary Measures, Marrakesh Agreement Establishing the World Trade Organization, Annex 1A (15 April 1994), 1867 UNTS 493.

10 For example, *Perenco Ecuador Ltd v Republic of Ecuador and Empresa Estatal Petróleos del Ecuador* (ICSID Case No ARB/08/6), Decision on Jurisdiction, 30 June 2011.

11 For example, international instruments and environmental principles on climate change being part of the 'laws and regulations' in Article XX(d) of the GATT were only applicable if they had direct effect through domestic legislation: *India – Certain Measures Relating to Solar Cells and Solar Modules* (*Report of the Appellate Body*) (24 February 2016), WT/DS456/AB/R [5.138 ff]; or any rules of procedure applicable through the seat of arbitration, such as waiver of jurisdictional objections applicable as a result of Swiss procedural law in *Europa Nova v The Czech Republic* (PCA Case No 2014–19), Award, 15 May 2019 [438 ff].

12 This is to be distinguished from a case in which customary international law is raised as a separate cause of action for expropriation, for example: *Emmis International v Hungary* (ICSID Case No ARB/12/2), Decision on Respondent's Objection under ICSID Arbitration Rule 41(5), 11 March 2013 [79].

13 Schill promotes a view of multilateralization of international investment law, arguing that the network of investment treaties form "a unitary treaty-overarching legal framework that is based on largely uniform principles of international investment law and arbitration": Stephan W Schill, 'The Multilateralization of International Investment Law:

The issue of whether EU law is to be categorized as international or domestic law requires special attention in this empirical study. For WTO disputes, EU law is akin to domestic law since the EU is both a party to, and EU legislation is the subject of, the WTO agreements and therefore would not form part of the relevant other international law in WTO disputes. Comparatively, investor-state tribunals have referred to the "multiple" or "dichotomous" nature[14] of the *sui generis* EU regime, with the EU treaties usually treated as international but EU regulations as domestic law. For this reason, only some issues of EU law have been categorized as relevant other international law. For example, circumstances where the tribunal has found EU law applicable as a result of the domestic legal order are excluded.[15] Comparatively, where EU law is argued to be international law pursuant to the international legal sources under the applicable law clause or as relevant international rules within Article 31(3)(c) of the VCLT, this has been categorized as a relevant decision (even if the tribunal rejects such application of EU law). For the most part, this concerns the intra-EU objection that relied on the international character of the EU

Emergence of a Multilateral System of Investment Protection on Bilateral Grounds' (2010) 2 Trade, Law and Development 59, 61; see further Stephan W Schill, *The Multilateralization of International Investment Law* (Cambridge University Press 2009); such a view is shared by some tribunals, for example, the Berschader v Russia tribunal considered that international investment case law was a persuasive source of law, even if the respondent was not a party to the ICSID Convention: *Berschader v Russia* (SCC Case No 080/2004), Award, 21 April 2006 [97]. The arguments for and against the multilateralization of investment law are not within the scope of this research; see also, Kammerhofer who argues that legal scholarship can systematically portray a process of concretization 'without claiming that arbitral awards are (an expression of) a unified, multilateralized or general norm and without thus drawing generalizing conclusions as to the content of (all) IIAs': Jörg Kammerhofer, *International Investment Law and Legal Theory: Expropriation and the Fragmentation of Sources* (Cambridge University Press 2021) 155; see, also, the similar approach of Di Benedetto who describes international investment law as 'quasi-unitary': Saverio Di Benedetto, *International Investment Law and the Environment* (Edward Elgar Publishing 2013) 9 ff.

14 *Electrabel SA v Hungary* (ICSID Case No ARB/07/19), Award, 25 November 2015 [4.117 ff]; *SunReserve Luxco Holdings SARL v The Italian Republic* (SCC Arbitration V 2016/32), Final Award, 25 March 2020 [374 ff].

15 For example, in *SunReserve*, the tribunal found that EU law was only applicable to jurisdiction as part of the Swedish legal order, operating to create the outer limits to the tribunal's jurisdiction as the lex arbitri: *SunReserve Luxco Holdings SARL v The Italian Republic* (n 14) para 395; similarly, EU secondary legislation on state aid rules have been treated on multiple occasions as domestic law: *Cube Infrastructure Fund SICAV v Kingdom of Spain* (ICSID Case No ARB/15/20), Decision on Jurisdiction, Liability and Partial Decision on Quantum, 19 February 2019 [159].

treaties.[16] However, as will be set out in the relevant sections of the study, the intra-EU objection decisions are often removed from the empirical results where the sheer number of (essentially) the same outcome on the application of other international law would detrimentally affect the comparative exercise.

In the ISDS data collection, 406 decisions were found to contain other international law in the tribunal's reasoning, including citations, mentions, application of, or other references to other international law by the tribunal,[17] out of 499 collected decisions.[18] For the WTO disputes, 128 decisions contained relevant references out of 402 decisions.

As set out in Figure 4, there is a significant difference in the percentage of decisions of the two dispute settlement mechanisms that refer to other international law. However, this is not an accurate depiction of the openness of the regimes to other international law. First, as discussed in the introduction, the

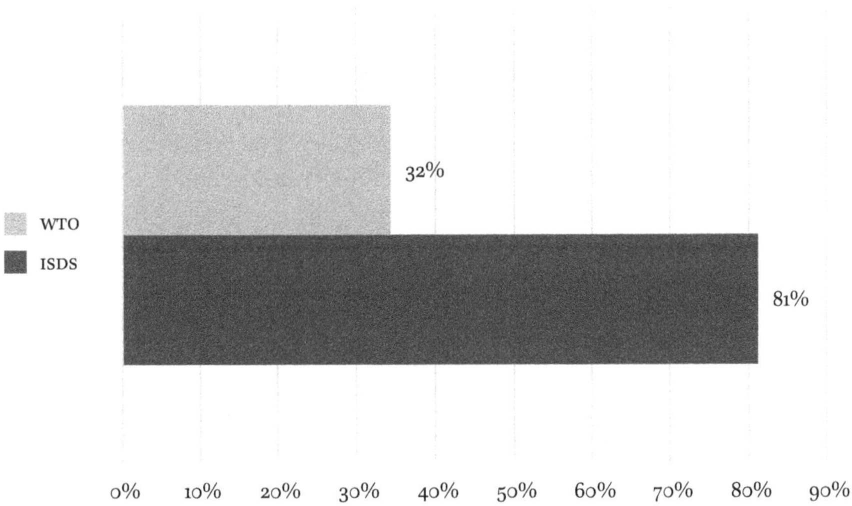

FIGURE 4 Percentage of total decisions referring to other international law in data collection

16 See, for example, *Vattenfall AB and others v Federal Republic of Germany (II)* (ICSID Case No ARB/12/12), Decision on the Achmea Issue, 31 August 2018; *Electrabel SA v Hungary* (ICSID Case No ARB/07/19), Decision on Jurisdiction, Applicable Law and Liability, 30 November 2012.

17 This also includes Annulment Committee decisions which found no annullable error in the tribunal's treatment of the other international law.

18 Five of the non-relevant cases were brought under multiple bases of jurisdiction, both under an IIA and an investment law or contract, but the tribunal found it did not have jurisdiction under the IIA, only the investment law or contract. There was no discussion of other law in the dismissal of jurisdiction under the IIA.

ISDS decisions analysed represent only a portion of total decisions, unlike the WTO data collection which covered *all* publicly available decisions. The first stage of the data collection of ISDS decisions was designed to find as many potentially relevant decisions as possible, thereby creating a larger proportion of relevant decisions in the total data collection compared to the WTO.

The second factor to consider in coming to a more accurate empirical conclusion relates to the dispute settlement design of the two mechanisms. There is probably a greater likelihood of the same issues being litigated multiple times in ISDS, compared to the WTO. The nature of ISDS proceedings is usually unsuitable for the consolidation of similar disputes, given the individual investor identity claims in ISDS compared to aggregated state-based claims in the WTO. While there may be some policy reasons for consolidation, for example disputes by shareholders of the same company, it is not a feature of ISDS to require consolidation, as explained by the *Eskosol* tribunal:

> The Tribunal is not called upon to decide whether, as a matter of either efficiency or fairness, it would be preferable for all shareholders of an entity affected by a challenged State measure to be heard in a single forum at a single time, together with the entity that they collectively own. The Tribunal previously observed that it is "not unsympathetic to Italy's circumstances, having to face claims now that are closely related to those it already successfully vanquished in a prior proceeding." But ultimately, these are system design questions that present policy issues, none of which are before the Tribunal. As the Tribunal also noted in its prior decision, "States have the power to create [such a system] if they so wish," but the fact remains that they have not done so in either instrument relevant to this case. Specifically, "neither the ICSID system as presently designed, nor the ECT itself, incorporate clear avenues (much less a requirement)" for such joinder or consolidation.[19]

Even if the dispute was heard with others and the reasoning is almost identical for each dispute, the tribunal may still issue separate decisions, for example, the Yukos disputes.[20] Comparatively, Article 9 of the WTO DSU encourages

19 *Eskosol S.pA in liquidazione v Italian Republic* (ICSID Case No ARB/15/50), Award, 4 September 2020 [262].

20 The tribunals in each of the three Yukos disputes stated that '[t]he three arbitrations were heard in parallel with the full participation of the Parties at all relevant stages of the proceedings. Mindful of the fact that each of the three Claimants maintains separate claims in separate arbitrations that require separate awards (the "Final Awards"), the Tribunal nevertheless shall discuss these arbitrations as a single set of proceedings, except where

the establishment of a single panel "whenever feasible" to deal with situations where multiple members request the establishment of a panel related to the same matter.[21] Further, third parties to the WTO disputes are also able to have their interests taken into account under Article 10 of the DSU, reducing the need for such parties to bring their own disputes. This essentially results in an "apples and oranges" comparison if we simply consider the total number of relevant decisions in each of the dispute settlement mechanisms. Therefore, a more accurate representation of the openness of the regimes to other international law is to look at the specific number of instances of other law in the decisions. In this way, such an empirical approach overcomes any problems in the data collection method and solely relies on the doctrinal analysis of the collected data.[22]

An "instance" of other international law identifies each time that a law, rule or principle is referred to by the tribunal. For example, as shown in the Appendix, the tribunal in *Cairn Energy PLC and Cairn UK Holdings Limited (CUHL) v*

circumstances distinct to particular Claimants necessitate separate treatment': *Hulley Enterprises v Russia* (PCA Case No 2005–03/AA226), Final Award, 18 July 2014 [2]; *Veteran Petroleum Limited v The Russian Federation* (PCA Case No 2005–05/AA28), Final Award, 18 July 2014; *Yukos Universal Limited (Isle of Man) v The Russian Federation* (PCA Case No 2005–04/AA27), Final Award, 18 July 2014. References to any one of these decisions in the analysis should also be read as including the other two proceedings.

21 The WTO Analytical Index indicates the prevalence with which the practice of single panels are used, with around 75 complaints being consolidated into 29 single panels: 'WTO Analytical Index: Guide to the WTO Law and Practice' (World Trade Organization 2020), DSU – Article 9 (Jurisprudence and Practice). The practice of separate reports for single panel proceedings has also been used sparingly, with only two examples of jurisprudential practice: the Panel in EC – *Bananas* issued four separate reports for each of the complainants upon the EC's request *European Communities – Regime for the Importation, Sale and Distribution of Bananas – Complaint by the United States (Report of the Panel)* (22 May 1997), WT/DS27/R/USA [7.55–7.57]; in the EC – Frozen Boneless Chicken Cuts dispute, the Panel agreed to issue two separate reports for the jointly held hearings: *European Communities – Customs Classification of Frozen Boneless Chicken Cuts – Complaint by Brazil (Report of the Panel)* (30 May 2005), WT/DS269/R [6.19–6.21]; *European Communities – Customs Classification of Frozen Boneless Chicken Cuts – Complaint by Thailand (Report of the Panel)* (30 May 2005), WT/DS286/R; although only one Appellate Body report was issued for both of these disputes: *European Communities – Customs Classification of Frozen Boneless Chicken Cuts (Report of the Appellate Body)* (12 September 2005), WT/DS269/AB/R ; WT/DS286/AB/R; *European Communities – Regime for the Importation, Sale and Distribution of Bananas (Report of the Appellate Body)* (9 September 1997) WT/DS27/AB/R.

22 ISDS decisions still encounter the problem of confidentiality and missingness. See discussion in Appendix 4 of Nicola Strain and others, 'Compliance Politics and International Investment Disputes: A New Dataset' (2024) 27 Journal of International Economic Law 70.

TABLE 4 Comparison of instances of international law before the regimes

	WTO	ISDS
Total instances	191	917
Total relevant decisions	128	406
Average instances of other law per decision	1.5	2.2

India[23] addressed nine separate instances of other law while *RWE Innogy GmbH and RWE Innogy Aersa S.A.U. v Spain*[24] raised only one instance. This analysis puts the WTO and ISDS regimes in a more similar footing when it comes to the relevance of other international law to the disputes, as shown in Table 4.

While ISDS tribunals consider the question of other international law more often, it is not quite as dramatically different from the instances of other international law before the WTO. A preliminary conclusion on the openness of the regimes shows very little difference between them once the factors that affect the ability to properly compare the two dispute settlement mechanisms are removed. Yet, this certainly does not conclude that the assumption of WTO restrictiveness is entirely unwarranted.

1.1.1 A Timeline of Fragmentation Responses?

The emergence of the concerns of fragmentation at the end of the 20th century and the development of coordinated responses of defragmentation suggest an inquiry into the timeline of other international law in the regimes. However, a simple comparison of the number of decisions referring to other international law in the decisions does not take us very far. The problem for making an inference from these empirical results is that very few cases exist for either regime before 2000. As the late 1990s and early 2000s mark the peak of the proliferation of courts and tribunals as part of institutional and substantive fragmentation, it would be difficult to draw any conclusions (beyond the general conclusion of increasing international dispute settlement) if the prevalence of other international law increases. This problem is neatly identified in the timeline of relevant decisions of the ISDS tribunals in Figure 5.

23 *Cairn Energy PLC and Cairn UK Holdings Limited (CUHL) v Republic of India* (PCA Case No 2016-07), Award, 21 December 2020.

24 *RWE Innogy GmbH and RWE Innogy Aersa SAU v Kingdom of Spain* (ICSID Case No ARB/14/34), Award, 18 December 2020.

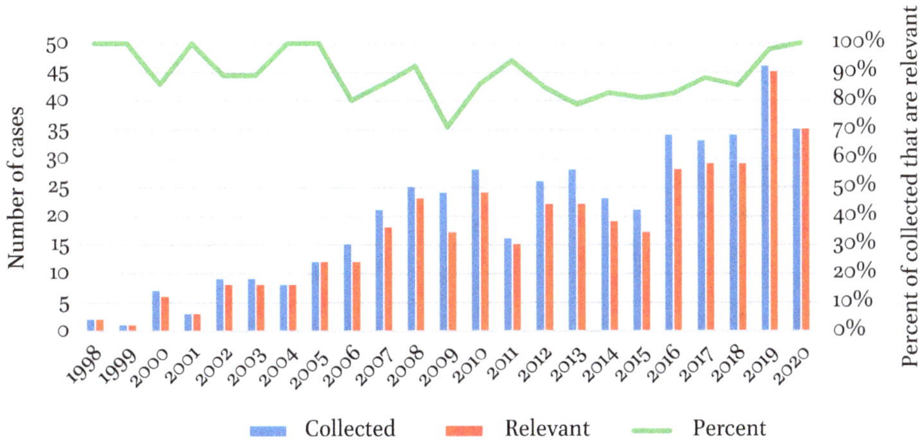

FIGURE 5 Year-spread of relevant ISDS cases[25]

For ISDS, we see a general increase in the number of decisions dealing with other international law, also reflecting the general increase in decisions throughout this period.[25] While we may dismiss the high percentage of relevant decisions due to the data collection process which favored the collection of potentially relevant decisions, the year-sampling stage of data collection enables some interesting results to be drawn. For the years 1998, 2008 and from 2018 to 2020, almost all decisions contain at least one instance of other international law. This certainly suggests a very open regime, one that relies on other international law to provide coherency to the network of IIAs. However, on a timeline analysis, only the total number of decisions seems to change between 1998 and 2020. This makes it difficult to find any timeline for defragmentation responses.

Comparatively, we have the *total* number of WTO decisions with which we can compare to the number of *relevant* WTO decisions. Figure 6 below maps the number of decisions each year. Given the analysis of the complete universe of WTO decisions, the timeline is much more random than in ISDS. There seems to be a peak in 2009 and then a downward trend over the past few years. This aligns with the completion of a number of complex disputes that dealt with a range of international law issues, including the *EC – Hormones* and *EC – Bananas* disputes. This could signify a tipping point in the development of the WTO dispute settlement mechanism's own jurisprudence on various

25 The results from 1990 to 1997 have been excluded from the figure since there were no decisions or only 1 decision in each of these years.

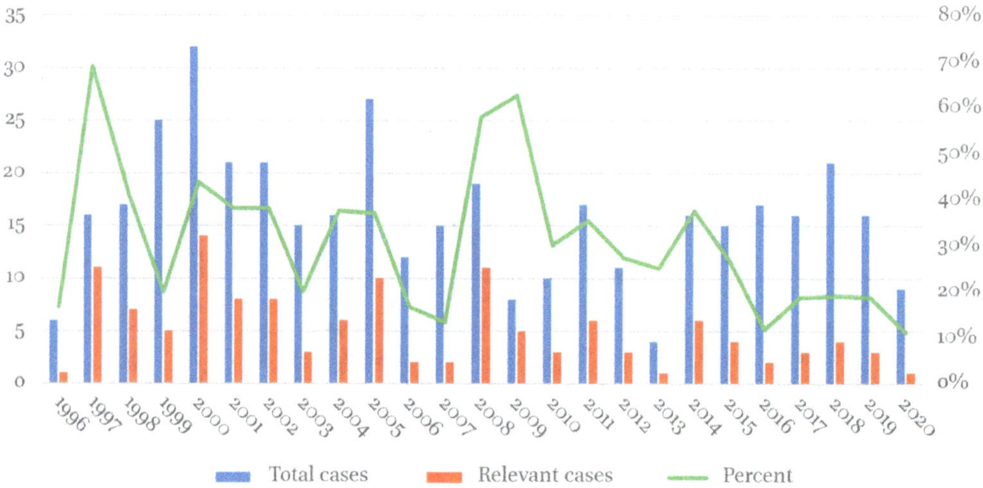

FIGURE 6 Year-spread of WTO cases

international law issues. However, it is difficult to identify a clear pattern from these numbers.

These limited empirical results do not allow us to identify a clear trend across the two systems. We may draw some correlations to events and influential cases during the time period, however, this would require further research. The only conclusion that we draw when we compare the percentage of relevant decisions from year-to-year is the overwhelming relevance of other international law across investor-state disputes, rather than the more ad-hoc relevance in WTO disputes. Combined with the results from the previous section, a preliminary conclusion can be drawn that the WTO is less likely to be faced with the question of other international law, pointing us toward an assumption of WTO-restrictiveness.

1.1.2 Acceptance of Other International Law

While the results in the preceding sections clearly indicate more investor-state disputes raise other international law than WTO disputes, the more interesting question is to consider what the tribunals actually do with that other international law. Could we still argue that ISDS is more receptive to other international law as those tribunals are more likely to apply such law?

Figure 7 and Figure 8 below indicate that the WTO panels and Appellate Body are not in fact less likely to take into account the other law in the relevant decisions. In fact, there is a slightly higher proportion of other law taken into account. Yet, at the same time, the WTO panels and Appellate Body are

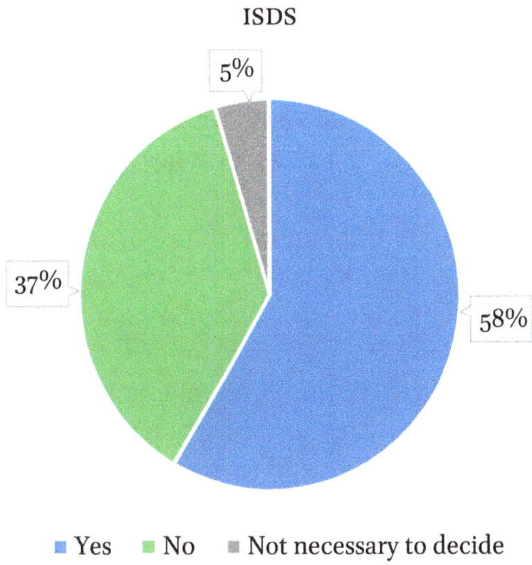

FIGURE 7
Instances of other international law taken into account: ISDS

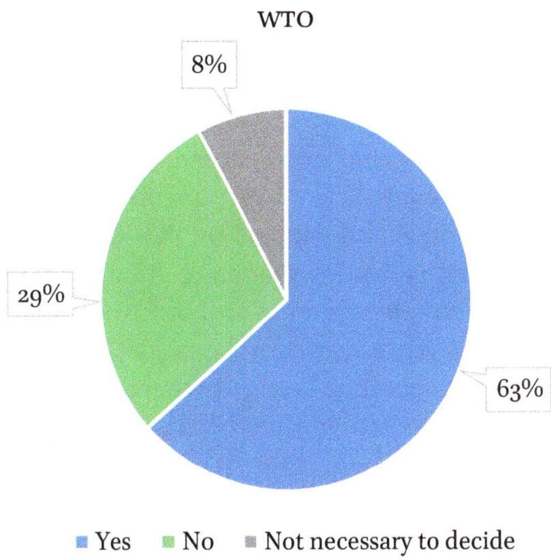

FIGURE 8
Instances of other international law taken into account: WTO

more likely to consider that they do not have to determine the applicability of the other law, rather relying on other arguments of the parties based on WTO agreements and jurisprudence (the "not necessary to decide" category).[26]

26 The "not necessary to decide" category is where the tribunal turns its mind to the other international law but finds it is not required to determine its applicability. This is to be

This could suggest the greater prevalence of alternative arguments based on other law within the WTO, combined with the exercise of judicial economy, compared to other law taking front stage in parties' arguments before ISDS tribunals and therefore requiring determination of applicability. If so, this result is unlikely to have greater systemic relevance than how disputes are argued before the tribunals.

We can make two preliminary conclusions from these results. First, the dispute settlement mechanisms are not isolated, "self-contained regimes". The regimes do, in fact, interact with general international law and other regimes, an unsurprising result, both from a systemic and positivist approach, given the various methods through which positive law enables other international law to be incorporated. Taking this conclusion one step further, scholars may take comfort that the results do not indicate substantive fragmentation since the tribunals are actively including other public international law: more than half of other international law raised is taken into account in the tribunal's decision. However, this further conclusion is overly optimistic based on such empirical data. Additional investigation of the type of international law applied and how the tribunal interprets such law is required.

Secondly, ISDS tribunals are not more likely to apply or take into account the other international law. Certainly, investor-state disputes are faced with relevant other international law more commonly than WTO disputes, which we can explain through some of the design choices, in particular the brevity of IIAs and the consequent need to fill lacunae in these agreements. However, the more similar rates of acceptance of other international law in tribunal reasoning may challenge our understanding of features that make dispute settlement mechanisms more or less open to other international law. This initial test of the assumption of WTO-restrictiveness certainly supports the scholarly discussion in Chapter 2 that the real question is not whether panels and the Appellate Body have applied non-WTO law but the extent to which they are authorized to bring in other international law. However, these results are merely a bird's-eye-view of the approach of the tribunals and further examination of the legal reasoning, the sources of law that are being applied and the method of incorporation of that law will put this assumption to the test in the proceeding discussion.

1.2 *Impact of Dispute Settlement Design*

The next section turns to relevant issues in assessing the role of dispute settlement design in fragmentation and its responses, including the source of

---

distinguished from other international law raised by parties that is never addressed by the tribunals and was not included as relevant other international law.

the other international law, and the basis for including or excluding the other international law. The results of these questions illustrate the extent to which some of the individual characteristics of the dispute settlement mechanisms may influence the outcome of the application of other international law as well as the use of the opening tools of international law by each of the dispute settlement mechanisms' adjudicators.

1.2.1 Sources of Law

Does the source of the other international law have any impact on whether the law is taken into account by the tribunal? This question is pertinent, in the first place, as it is the first step in determining whether the sources of law fit within the applicable law clause or not. This question also has significant relevance for concerns about fragmentation, both whether the WTO and investor-state dispute settlement systems act as "self-contained regimes" and whether the tribunals deal with law beyond the general and customary law brackets. A more open approach to sources of law, such as treaty and jurisprudence, goes beyond a limited "self-contained regime" methodology, which is more concerned with how the tribunal situates itself within general international law.[27]

The categorization of the sources in this empirical analysis is based on Article 38(1) of the ICJ Statute. Delimiting particular law within the sources of Article 38(1) is not an exact science, particularly when it comes to custom and general principles.[28] As a result, the analysis of the source of law primarily categorizes the sources according to how the tribunal themselves refer to the law. While this may not always be the correct categorization according to the rules and principles of international law, it is appropriate for an empirical study into the adjudicators' approach.

A particular note is to be made in relation to how judicial decisions and teachings in subparagraph (d) of Article 38(1) have been used in this analysis. This exercise is particularly concerned with where that jurisprudence is

---

27 For example, the general application of the secondary rules on state responsibility were considered by Simma and Pulkowski to help bury the self-contained regime myth: Bruno Simma and Dirk Pulkowski, 'Of Planets and the Universe: Self-Contained Regimes in International Law' (2006) 17 European Journal of International Law 483.

28 On the distinction between custom and general principles, see Marcelo Vázquez-Bermúdez, 'Second Report on General Principles of Law' (International Law Commission 2020) A/CN.4/741 51–2, noting that general principles that are widely recognized in treaties and other international instruments, may overlap with custom, 'given that the materials through which the requirement of recognition can be ascertained also serve as evidence to determine the existence of a rule of customary international law'; see also, 'Report of the International Law Commission on the Work of Its Seventy-Second Session' (International Law Commission 2021) A/76/10 paras 213–4 on the difficulty with the distinction.

somehow setting out a separate source of international law. As such, it is not a citation analysis, which has been undertaken very extensively in other empirical works[29] nor is it a cross-fertilization analysis.[30] Such cross-fertilization is relevant to the cooperation technique of defragmentation,[31] however, it has less relevance for questions of the opening and closing tools as the treaty law (for example) is the other law that is actually being applied, with jurisprudence as merely interpretive material of that other law.

Table 5 and Figure 9 set out the results on the source of law: Table 5 presents the aggregate number of decisions of each regime while Figure 9 provides the percentage of relevant decisions (from Figure 4) that raise a particular source of international law.

As illustrated in Figure 9 and Table 5, the most significant difference in the sources of other international law brought before the dispute settlement mechanisms is in the instances of judicial decisions. The empirical results suggest that investor-state tribunals treat the decisions of other international courts and tribunals as a separate source of other international law (compared to the use of judicial decisions in a citation analysis) much more frequently than their WTO counterparts. Part of the explanation for this incongruity is how certain decisions of international courts have been categorized in the analysis, particularly the *Factory at Chorzów* decision on reparation in international law. Such decisions could be considered general principles or customary

29 See, for example, Damien Charlotin, 'The Place of Investment Awards and WTO Decisions in International Law: A Citation Analysis' (2017) 20 Journal of International Economic Law 279; Niccolò Ridi, 'The Shape and Structure of the "Usable Past": An Empirical Analysis of the Use of Precedent in International Adjudication' (2019) 10 Journal of International Dispute Settlement 200.

30 An example of the cross-fertilization that is excluded from such analysis is the Appellate Body's reference to the ICJ's *Gabčíkovo-Nagymaros* judgment in determining whether the precautionary principle was part of customary international law. For this case, the other law is the precautionary principle and the assistance of the ICJ in interpreting that principle is not included in the analysis: *European Communities – Measures Concerning Meat and Meat Products (Hormones) (Report of the Appellate Body)* (16 January 1998), WT/DS26/AB/R; WT/DS48/AB/R [123]; *Gabčíkovo-Nagymaros Project (Hungary v Slovakia), Judgment* [1997] ICJ Rep 7.

31 Cross-fertilization has been defined as a 'method used by international courts to fill in gaps in their statutes and rules of procedure, as well as to strengthen their conclusions in line with other international courts and tribunals. In doing so, international courts routinely reference customary international law, general principles of law and rules developed in other international judicial and arbitral practice': Chiara Giorgetti, 'Cross-Fertilization of Procedural Law Among International Courts and Tribunals: Methods and Meanings' in Arman Sarvarian and others (eds), *Procedural Fairness in International Courts and Tribunals* (British Institute of International and Comparative Law 2015) 224.

TABLE 5 Sources of other law in the regimes

	Source under Art 38(1) ICJ	WTO	ISDS
a.	International conventions, whether general or particular[a]	37	143
b.	International custom	52	212
c.	General principles of law	65	299
d.	Judicial decisions and teachings	36	263

a Whether the treaty law is general or particular (*lex specialis / lex generalis*) is considered in more detail in section 2.1 below.

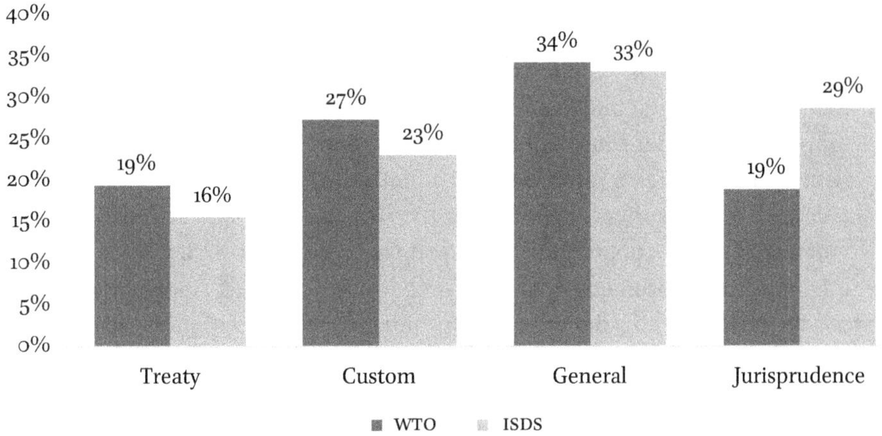

FIGURE 9 Proportion of sources of law in decisions

law rather than as judicial decisions.[32] Nonetheless, the choice in the study to refer to these as judicial decisions, rather than general principles or customary law, reflects the choice by the tribunals themselves to refer to that particular international court decision as the general principle. Since investor-state tribunals are required to gap-fill such state responsibility issues more frequently

32 For example, the *Factory at Chorzów* case itself refers to obligation to make reparation as a 'principle of international law': *Factory at Chorzów (Germany v Poland), Jurisdiction* [1927] PCIJ Rep Series A No 9; and was then referred to in the commentary to Article 31 of the ILC Articles: Responsibility of States for Internationally Wrongful Acts (adopted by the International Law Commission at its fifty-third session, 2001) 91.

than WTO panels, this largely accounts for the discrepancy between the two dispute settlement mechanisms.

When we consider treaties as a source of other international law, the WTO dispute settlement mechanism has a somewhat higher proportion of treaty-based and customary international law than its ISDS counterpart. Analysing the sources in more detail, the rationale for this higher proportion can be explained through the terms of the WTO covered agreements themselves and international trade law more broadly. The interpretation of the general exceptions in Article XX of the GATT often involve reference to other international legal regimes, particularly environmental law following the reasoning in *US – Shrimp*.[33] In addition, regional and bilateral free trade agreements are also often referred to within the scope of WTO disputes.[34]

It can be difficult to precisely separate custom from general principles. However, if we broadly group them together as "general international law," we can see a substantial discrepancy between conventional international law, being treaties, and general international law. General principles make up the largest proportion of other international that is brought before the two dispute settlement regimes. This result fits within both the cooperation and managerial approaches to international law and the link with the international judicial function. For the cooperation approach, procedural tools play an important role in the management of plurality, such procedural tools often falling within the scope of general principles rather than other sources of international law. In addition, as will be discussed in more detail in Chapter 4, general principles are also a primary aspect of the international judicial function in systematizing international law and resolving indeterminacy. The use of customary international law also plays in to debunking the "self-contained" regime myth.

1.2.2 Legal Basis and Method of Reasoning: Application of International Law

The next step in the empirical assessment is answering the question of the tribunal's legal basis for including (or excluding) the other law. This question illustrates which authority (if any) the adjudicators refer to when incorporating (or excluding) law, whether formal, legal sources of authority or others. This investigation is important for two reasons. First, it links to defragmentation techniques and the opening tools of international law, in particular the

---

33 *United States – Import Prohibition of Certain Shrimp and Shrimp Products* (*Report of the Appellate Body*) (12 October 1998), WT/DS58/AB/R. See discussion in 2.3 below.

34 *For example, Peru – Additional Duty on Imports of Certain Agricultural Products* (*Report of the Appellate Body*) (20 July 2015) WT/DS457/AB/R.

potential relevance of the interpretative techniques of defragmentation highlighted in the ILC Fragmentation Report. Secondly, it is also significant to the methodology of international adjudication. In assessing the methodology of adjudicators when undertaking their discretionary interpretative exercise, the first and foremost criterion is the adjudicator "consciously and transparently" applies their reasoned judgment.[35] The extent to which defragmentation is a political question, rather than a legal standard reconcilable with legal sources, could lead to suggestions of an embrace of politics and potential loss of judicial authority.[36] As such, this taps into Peters' call for the actors of international law to justify their interpretations "in general rather than parochial terms" and consider the extent to which outside perspectives have been internalized.[37]

The assessment of the legal basis and method of reasoning of adjudicators is where we expect more divergence between the WTO and investor-state tribunals. Investor-state tribunals should be more likely to refer to applicable law as the basis of taking into account the other law, whereas the limited applicable law of the WTO may restrict the reference to such legal basis, perhaps relying on the established practice of Appellate Body decisions on international law.

Based on the examination of the legal concepts of dispute settlement and the various legal methods by which those concepts enabled or restricted the

35 Here, Paulus' international legal positivist perspective on the role of international judges is particularly apt, in attempting to reconcile a positivist and postmodernist approach: Andreas Paulus, 'International Adjudication' in Samantha Besson and John Tasioulas (eds), *The Philosophy of International Law* (Oxford University Press 2010) 223. Although international legal positivism has its critics, there is agreement on this aspect of Paulus' methodology in that moral disagreements should be expressed in legal reasoning. See, for example, Nahuel Maisley, 'Better to See International Law This Other Way: The Case against International Normative Positivism' (2021) 12 Jurisprudence 151; for more detailed discussion on the role of international legal positivism in answering the questions of this research, see Nicola Strain, 'Jurisdiction and Applicable Law in Investor-State and WTO Dispute Settlement: Comparing Consent and Inconsistency in the Application of Other International Law' (University of Oslo, Faculty of Law 2022), from which this book is based.

36 Drawing on the words of Hernández, '[are] international judges, when interpreting and applying international law, making a claim to normative (or semantic) authority? Are they more modest "agents" in the international legal process? More ominously, are they cloaking themselves in the formalism of classical legal positivism so as to abdicate political responsibility for the constitutive role of their interpretations?': Gleider I Hernández, 'Interpretative Authority and the International Judiciary' in Andrea Bianchi and Matthew Windsor (eds), *Interpretation in International Law* (Oxford University Press 2015) 168.

37 Anne Peters, 'The Refinement of International Law: From Fragmentation to Regime Interaction and Politicization' (2017) 15 International Journal of Constitutional Law 671, 703.

application of other international law in Chapter 2, the decisions were categorized into the following legal bases for applying other international law:

a. Applicable law clause: tribunal refers to the other law as falling within the specific language of the applicable law clause;
b. General principle of law: tribunal refers to other law as "general principle of law" or "well-established" principle either within the scope of Article 38(1)(c) of the ICJ Statute or without referring to particular legal basis for applying general principles;
c. Customary international law: the tribunal refers to the other law as customary without referring to any other legal basis for applying such customary law, thereby indicating the regime has not "contracted out" of such law;
d. Article 31(3)(c) of the Vienna Convention: tribunal considers the application of the law through the prism of Article 31(3)(c) specifically; and
e. Priority of other law over treaty: for example, *lex superior* or *jus cogens*. In addition, other bases of reasoning were also identified in the relevant decisions and were thus included in the categorization. These "sources" of authority for inclusion of other international law are not properly defined as "legal bases" as there is no clear link to a formal consent-based authority to include the other international law:
f. Established practice: tribunal refers to prior WTO or investor-state tribunal decisions, respectively, applying that other law and considers that its approach is in line with that prior practice of regime tribunals, thereby almost suggesting a *jurisprudence constante* or precedent basis of authority;
g. Parties agree on the application of the law: tribunal refers to parties' agreement on the issue and makes no further independent investigation into the legal source or basis for applying that law; and
h. No clear legal authority stipulated.[38]

Presented empirically in Figure 10, the legal reasoning used by the WTO and investor-state tribunals appears relatively homogenous with some differences partly attributable to the working methods of the tribunals. The WTO panels and Appellate Body more frequently rely on the established practice reasoning

38 While one of the parties to the dispute may have provided a legal basis for the incorporation of the rule or principle, the analysis focuses on the tribunal's reasoning. As such, even if a party has provided a clear legal basis, if the tribunal has not made it apparent that it relied on that parties' reasoning, then the tribunal's approach has been categorized as "unclear". This category also includes any vague references to the other law being "international law" and therefore applicable without further substantiation of the applicability.

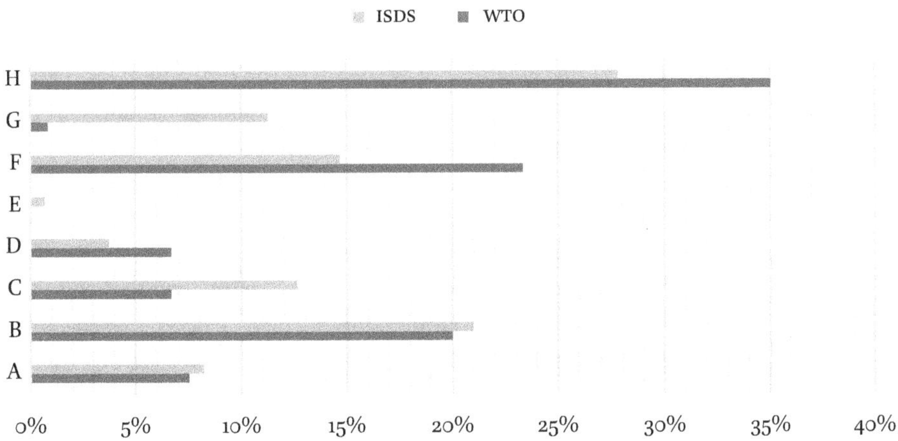

FIGURE 10 Legal basis and reasoning for application of other international law[39]

(category F), indicating the "cogent reasons"[39] approach is also used in the application of other international law. Comparatively, investor-state adjudicators refer to, and rely on, the fact that the parties to the dispute agree on the application of the other international law much more frequently (category G). We could hypothesize that the application of other international law is generally less controversial in the eyes of the parties to investor-state dispute or that there is less need for independent tribunal analysis of issues in investor-state arbitration than WTO panels, due to the bilateral vs multilateral nature of the adjudication. As this basis of legal reasoning only accounts for 11% of the instances of other international law incorporated within the ISDS decisions, it is not that interesting to investigate why investor-state tribunals do so.

Although the WTO tribunals more frequently fail to provide a legal basis for incorporation (category H), a notable homogeneity between the tribunals is that the largest percentage of other international law is brought in without the tribunals identifying any legal or other basis of authority for such inclusion. For the WTO, this may not be as problematic given almost half of those applications of other international law were only used to support the conclusion it had already arrived at solely on the basis of WTO law, rather than a gap-filling exercise. This purely supportive role accounts for 45% of instances of other law within category H, compared to only 18% of instances in ISDS. Nevertheless, this basis of legal reasoning (or more accurately, lack of legal reasoning)

39 Where the tribunal may refer to multiple reasons for the application of the other international law, each of the bases has been included in the empirical results.

illustrates the tension between systemic theoretical approaches and the consensual basis of international law. From a systemic point of view, this may not be concerning but rather a reflection of the state of the normative legal environment's preference for a coherent international legal order. For some of the instances of unclear reasoning, there may be little need to explain the legal basis as a result of the system of international law. One such example is the application of secondary rules, such as the ILC Articles on State Responsibility and the application of the rules on attribution and compensation in investor-state arbitration.[40] As many instances of other international law that would be considered uncontroversial in their application are also custom, it is certainly not clear why adjudicators may not have simply referred to the customary source of the law as a reason for its application. However, this does not explain many other applications of international law that are not so clear-cut from a systemic point of view.

From a more positivist and consensual standpoint, incorporation of other international law without clear stipulation of legal reasoning does not meet a conscious and transparent standard of reasoned judgment. This reflects that adjudicators should not disregard the legal sources from which they derive their authority,[41] which they may in fact do when they fail to engage with the legal basis for the incorporation of other international law. The potential disregard of the legal sources is particularly concerning where the adjudicators are applying rules from other international regimes, such as human rights[42] and environmental law,[43] which are the subject of inconsistent reasoning by the tribunals in other decisions. A further example is the incorporation of general principles that other tribunals have considered not appropriate to

40 See Simma and Pulkowski (n 27); Bruno Simma and Dirk Pulkowski, 'Two Worlds. but Not Apart: International Investment Law and General International Law' in Marc Bungenberg and others (eds), *International Investment Law: A Handbook* (Hart Publishing 2015).

41 This invokes Paulus' arguments on an 'enlightened positivism' or modern international legal positivism, which attempts to reconcile a positivist and postmodernist approach. One of the remaining stalwarts of the positivist approach is deriving authority from relevant legal sources. See: Paulus (n 35); Bruno Simma and Andreas Paulus, 'The Responsibility of Individuals for Human Rights Abuses in Internal Conflicts: A Positivist View' (1999) 93 American Journal of International Law 291.

42 For example, referring to the margin of appreciation in European human rights law: *Philip Morris v Uruguay* (n 2) para 399, an issue further discussed below.

43 See, for example, *China – Measures Related to the Exportation of Various Raw Materials (Reports of the Panel)* (5 July 2011), WT/DS394/R; WT/DS395/R; WT/DS398/R [7.372] where the Panel referred to definitions of conservation in environmental agreements. While the Panel went on to refer to Article 31(3)(c) in relation to the principle of sovereignty of natural resources, the Panel did not provide any ground for referring to the environmental agreements in an earlier paragraph of the decision.

transpose to the international arena.[44] The lack of clear legal reasoning not only creates concern from a consensual viewpoint but also contributes to inconsistency on the application of other international law, which is discussed in section 2 below.

A further similarity in the reasoning of the WTO and investor-state tribunals is also interesting: the treatment of the opening tools. For both dispute settlement mechanisms, there is limited use of the principle of systemic integration (category D) and a wide use of general principles of law (category B) in the two regimes (without necessarily explaining why such principles are applicable). As set out in the Introduction and to be further examined in Chapter 4, these legal bases for incorporation of other international law are part of an "international judicial function", enabling the opening (and possibly harmonization) of the regimes of international law within the broader system of international law. The implications of the use of opening tools in this way will be addressed in Chapter 5.

In relation to the first opening tool, broad applicable law clauses (category A), the results are relevant to the limited role of dispute settlement design in directing the method of reasoning of adjudicators. As expected, investor-state tribunals more commonly rely on the broad scope of the applicable law clause of the IIA in incorporating other international law, compared to WTO panels and the Appellate Body. But not as commonly as we might expect. The broad applicable law clauses could provide ample room for the tribunal to incorporate customary rules or general principles. For example, in *Inceysa v El Salvador*, the tribunal applied general international law on international public policy, prohibition against unlawful investment and good faith in relation to investor conduct where the IIA did not contain substantive rules that permit the determination whether the investment was made in accordance with the law of the host state.[45] The tribunal referred to the applicable law clause of the IIA, which referred to the "generally recognized rules and principles of international law" in justifying the incorporation of the general rules:

> the reference made in the Agreement to the generally recognized rules and principles of International Law obliges this Tribunal, first of all and before analyzing the legal provisions issued by the internal entities of the

44 For example, estoppel, which is also discussed in Chapter 4: *Karkey Karadeniz Elektrik Uretim AS v Islamic Republic of Pakistan* (ICSID Case No ARB/13/1), Award, 22 August 2017 [628].

45 *Inceysa Vallisoletana SL v Republic of El Salvador* (ICSID Case No ARB/03/26), Award, 2 August 2006 [223]; referring to Article XI.3 of the Agreement between the Kingdom of Spain and the Republic of El Salvador on the Reciprocal Promotion and Protection of Investments (San Salvador, 14 February 1995).

> government of El Salvador, to determine whether, according to said principles and rules, Inceysa's investment can be considered legally made.[46]

Yet, this accounts for a much smaller proportion of other international law in investor-state disputes than expected when we compare to the WTO panels and Appellate Body that also utilize "applicable law" as a legal basis, albeit in a minority of decisions. An inference we could draw, based on the results on the source of law investigation in Figure 9 above, which showed the predominance of custom and general principles, is that the investor-state tribunal may not deem it necessary to refer back to the broad applicable law clause when the source of the other international law is enough to suggest its application. In this respect, many tribunals start with an examination of the scope of the applicable law clause, noting its application to general international law. However, when dealing with the particular instance of other international law, the tribunals do not always refer back to their earlier interpretation of the scope of the applicable law clause.

This inference is supported by decisions which provide divergent reasoning for different instances and sources of international law: applicable law as the basis for specialized treaty law and no basis stipulated for general international law. For example, in *RREEF v Spain*, the tribunal considered that the margin of appreciation was applicable through the applicable law clause of the ECT:

> This does not mean, however, that the ECT regulates fully and integrally all matters which can be relevant in the present case. As recalled above, in conformity with Article 26(6) ECT and Article 42(1) of the ICSID Convention, in case the Treaty is mute, the Tribunal must decide the issues in dispute in accordance with other applicable rules and principles of international law as may be applicable. Hence, it is indeed not because the ECT does not expressly provide for the States' right to regulate, or because it does not formally recognize a margin of appreciation in their favour, that it must, nor can, be interpreted as excluding them.[47]

Comparatively, when considering the application of general international law on the principle of non-retroactivity and other ICJ decisions,[48] the tribunal

46 *Inceysa Vallisoletana S.L. v Republic of El Salvador* (n 45) para 224.

47 *RREEF v Spain* (ICSID Case No ARB/13/30), Decision on Responsibility and the Principles of Quantum, 30 November 2018 [241].

48 Including, *Elettronica Sicula S.pA (ELSI) (United States of America v Italy)*, Judgment [1989] ICJ Reports 15 [128] on arbitrariness; *Pulp Mills on the River Uruguay (Argentina v Uruguay)*, Judgment [2010] ICJ Reports 14 [168] on expert evidence.

appeared to only refer to the customary status of those rules or the established jurisprudential practice as the reason for their application.[49] The contested nature of the application of margin of appreciation in international investment law, discussed in section 2.2 below, may require the tribunal to more clearly explain the legal basis of its application than less controversial issues of general international law on restitution. However, it is difficult to draw inferences since there is such limited tribunal reasoning on applicable law clauses in investor-state decisions.

1.2.3 Legal Basis and Method of Reasoning: Rejection of International Law

The same empirical analysis is undertaken for the bases used in rejecting the application of other international law. Based on the legal sources in Chapter 2 and the results of the review, the categories used, both legal authority and non-legal reasoning, when dismissing the application of other international law included:

a. Dismissed on facts: tribunal considered that the facts of the dispute do not meet the elements of the other law but does not consider how that source of law may apply;[50]
b. Reliance on treaty terms: tribunal refers to the treaty as *lex specialis*, (or similar conflict rule)[51] or finds the ordinary meaning of the treaty does

---

49 *RREEF v Spain* (n 47), [326] on the principle of non-retroactivity and [461], [514] on the relevance of the ICJ decisions.

50 The dismissal on facts also covers decisions in which the tribunal "assumes" the principle applies in order to reject its application on the facts. It may be possible to argue that when a tribunal dismisses the application of the other law on the basis of the facts of the case that it is implicitly applying that other law However, this is not the correct approach, as will be further explained when discussing the results. As the tribunal only "assumes" the principle's relevance, it arguably does not apply that principle. See for example, *Guris Construction and Engineering Inc and others v Arab Republic of Syria* (ICA Case No 21845/ZF/AYZ), Final Award, 31 August 2020 [224] where the tribunal stated: '[t]he Tribunal cannot accept the Respondent's argument. No finding concerning the "clean hands" doctrine need or indeed can be made here. Assuming that a "clean hands" doctrine exists in general international law and applies in investor-State disputes, on any view the unclean hands must be those of the investor, not those of its home State. In addition, this Tribunal does not have jurisdiction under Article VII(2) of the Treaty – this being the sole source of the Tribunal's jurisdiction – to determine whether Turkey's conduct is internationally wrongful. And as Turkey is not a party to this arbitration, it is impermissible for the Tribunal to pass judgment on the lawfulness or otherwise of Turkey's conduct.'

51 On the relevant conflict rule, see Dirk Pulkowski, 'Lex Specialis Derogat Legi Generali / Generalia Specialibus Non Derogant' in Joseph Klingler, Yuri Parkhomenko and Constantinos Salonidis (eds), *Between the Lines of the Vienna Convention? Canons and Other Principles of Interpretation in Public International Law* (Kluwer Law International 2018).

not otherwise support application of other law or some other similar reason relying solely on the interpretation of the treaty terms;

c. Not applicable law: tribunal does not consider the other international law to be applicable law based on the applicable law clause, some other source of applicable law or does not meet the criteria under Article 31(3)(c) of the VCLT;[52]

d. No such rule or principle as argued by parties exists: tribunal finds that the particular way in which a party has referred to the other law is not in fact the way in which that other law should be understood or, alternatively, the tribunal finds that there is insufficient evidence that there is in fact a rule or principle of international law;

e. Not applicable in specific context of the regime: tribunal relies on the general nature or context of the regime. This is distinct from the *lex specialis* method of reasoning as there is no particular provision in the WTO agreements or IIA that is relied on by the tribunal. It is also distinguishable from the dismissal on the facts as the tribunal rather refers to something inherent in the regime or disputes generally, rather than the particular facts of the individual dispute;[53]

f. Limited jurisdiction: tribunal refers to its limited jurisdictional mandate in rejecting the application of the other law; and

g. Not relevant: the tribunal considers that the argument of the parties is ultimately not relevant to its reasoning.

We should note that this list of categories does not include an unclear or "not stipulated" basis, unlike the reasoning on the application of other international law in the preceding section. The review of the decisions found that tribunals did seek to provide a legal basis for the rejection of the other law.

---

52 This also covers reasoning where the tribunal notes that the law is not applicable law to determining its jurisdiction.

53 An example of such reasoning is the rejection of the diplomatic protection rules on derivative claims in investor-state disputes. See, for example, *Daimler Financial v Argentina* where the tribunal stated that "Argentina's arguments regarding the *Barcelona Traction* decision and what Argentina terms 'conventional international law' are equally unpersuasive. As noted both by the Claimant and by numerous other investor-State tribunals, the *Barcelona Traction* decision dealt with an attempt by one State to exercise diplomatic protection in favor of its nationals who had invested in a company incorporated in a second State with respect to disputed measures taken against the company by a third State. This is a significantly different factual scenario from the present one. Moreover, in reaching its decision to disallow the claim in *Barcelona Traction*, the ICJ itself noted that international treaties could provide shareholders with a direct right of action against foreign governments for certain claims. The present instance is precisely such a case": *Daimler Financial v Argentina* (ICSID Case No ARB/02/1), Award, 22 August 2012 [90].

Comparatively, in accepting other law, a large number of instances of other law were brought in without stipulation of the legal basis or otherwise clear method of reasoning. From this, we may seek to infer a systemic view of international law as the tribunals consider it necessary to substantiate the rejection of other international law, thereby suggesting other international law is applicable unless clearly excluded. However, making such an inference is likely an overly optimistic view of an "international legal order". Taking into account the adversarial nature of these dispute settlement mechanisms, it is more probable that the tribunals consider it necessary to respond to the party that has raised that other international law in a clear and unobjectionable manner. Due to the uncontroversial nature of many instances of law applied by the tribunal, as discussed above, the same need to substantiate the application may not arise or be subject to appeal by the affected parties.

As with the acceptance of other law, there are some similarities between the legal reasoning of investor-state and WTO tribunals shown in Figure 11. Two notable similarities of the legal reasoning are the use of *lex specialis* (or related type of reliance on specific treaty terms, category B) and limited jurisdiction (category F) arguments. First, the large reliance on the terms of the treaty by both dispute settlement mechanisms demonstrates the specialization of these regimes. For investor-state tribunals, this is a more surprising result given the brevity of the provisions of many IIAs and need to supplement such provisions with other international law. Second, in relation to the limited jurisdiction method of reasoning, both tribunals use this argument sparingly. This should not be read as suggesting a less important role for the consent-based and limited jurisdiction of the tribunals. The narrow use is more likely a result of the

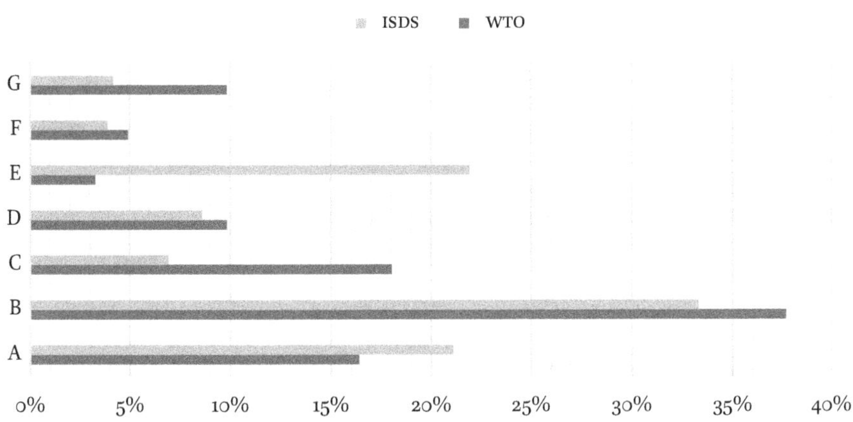

FIGURE 11 Legal basis for the rejection of other law

wariness with which parties themselves would seek to openly enlarge the jurisdictional scope of the tribunal. Nevertheless, the similarity in reasoning is particularly meaningful for the tension between consensual jurisdiction and the system of international law and how this affects the adjudicator's balancing of the opening and closing tools.

A further convergence is dismissing the application of the other law on the facts (category A), rather than by considering whether that other law is in fact applicable. This prompts the question whether dismissing a principle on the facts of the dispute amounts to the incorporation of the international legal principle. For example, Dumberry argues that the fact that the tribunals did not "hesitate to concretely apply" general principles like *lis pendens* is evidence of the tribunals' belief that the principle is to be applied in investment arbitration.[54] However, the present author does not consider that such belief should be implied. The divergent views on whether a principle, such as *lis pendens*, is in fact a general principle within the meaning of Article 38(1)(c) of the ICJ Statute[55] and the fact that tribunals have undertaken the task of determining the status of other principles[56] argues against any inferred application of rules and principles. Indeed, the existence of general principles should not be lightly presumed.[57] The dismissal of the principle on the facts is likely a more

54 Patrick Dumberry, *A Guide to General Principles of Law in International Investment Arbitration* (Oxford University Press 2020) 192; drawing from the conclusion in Philipp Janig and August Reinisch, 'General Principles and the Coherence of International Investment Law: Of Res Judicata, Lis Pendens and the Value of Precedents' in Mads Andenas and others (eds), *General Principles and the Coherence of International Law* (Brill Nijhoff 2019) 257 that 'while investor-state tribunals have so far not explicitly confirmed its status as a general principle of law, they have done so at least implicitly, as its rejection has consistently been based on the lack of fulfillment of its requirements'.

55 After reviewing the case law of international courts and tribunals, Shany concludes that there is insufficient case law to establish the existence of *lis pendens* as a general rule or principle in international law, although there may be a 'plausible case': Yuval Shany, *The Competing Jurisdictions of International Courts and Tribunals* (Oxford University Press 2004) 244; Pasquet summarizes the normative status and implications of the principle of *lis pendens* as 'controversial': Luca Pasquet, 'De-Fragmentation Techniques', *Max Planck Encyclopedia of International Procedural Law* (Oxford University Press 2018) para 6.

56 See, for example, *Hulley Enterprises v Russia* (n 20) para 1347 ff in which the tribunal found that clean hands was not a general rule or principle under Article 38(1)(c) of the ICJ Statute.

57 As the tribunal stated in *Renco Group Inc v Republic of Peru (II)* (PCA Case No 2019–46), Decision on Expedited Preliminary Objections, 30 June 2020 [214]: 'the existence of such principles is not lightly presumed. In order for a principle to rise to the level of a "general principle of law" under Article 38(1)(c) of the ICJ Statute, it must be "generally accepted" across national legal systems. The exact degree of acceptance required remains a subject of debate'. Similarly, the ILC's draft conclusions set a relatively high standard for

convenient method of rejecting the argument without having to deal with the more complex question of the status of the principle.[58] As such, the similarity in dismissing on the facts demonstrates the pragmatism in adjudicator reasoning. It may simply be easier to consider the facts do not meet "the law" rather than determine whether it is in fact "law". Particularly when the customary or general principle status of that law is not accepted by the parties to the dispute, this may be the route of least resistance.

The most significant divergences in the legal reasoning of the adjudicators occurs in the "not relevant" (category G), "not applicable in the context of the regime" (category E) and "not applicable law" (category C) bases of rejection. The differentiation in the legal reasoning in relation to category E, namely that the ISDS tribunals appear to use this reasoning much more frequently, could be an indication that there may be greater attempts at regime interactions by parties to ISDS disputes. This line of argument is further developed in the subsection below. Comparatively, the greater reliance in the rejection of the other law on the basis that it was "not applicable law" certainly reflects the assumption that what falls within "WTO law" is more restrictively interpreted.

Ultimately, the deeper empirical analysis of the legal reasoning of the two tribunals exhibits some interesting similar trends. Turning back to the assumption of WTO-restrictiveness, the investigation of the legal authority for including (or excluding) the other law was expected to provide more divergence between the WTO and investor-state tribunals, based on the disparities between the mechanisms and their constitutive treaties. However, the analysis provides more noteworthy similarities in tribunal reasoning than differentiation, including the combined failure to provide a conscious and transparent legal basis for application of other law and the limited utilization of applicable law and systemic integration bases of authority to incorporate other international law.

1.2.4 Regime Interactions: Courts and Tribunals

This section considers the regime interactions with other international courts and tribunals as part of the jurisprudence source of international law

---

identifying general principles, whether formed within the international legal system or national systems: Vázquez-Bermúdez (n 28) 58–9.

58 In determining the application of other general principles, tribunals have made it clear that they are dismissing the principle on the facts without ruling on the applicability of the principle to investor-state dispute settlement. See, for example, *Mason Capital LP and Mason Management LLC v Republic of Korea* (PCA Case No 2018–55), Decision on Preliminary Objections, 22 December 2019 [189]; *Thomas Gosling and others v Republic of Mauritius* (ICSID Case No ARB/16/32), Award, 18 February 2020 [127].

(subparagraph (d) of Article 38(1) of the ICJ Statute), providing an indication of regime interaction and potential for defragmentation, as discussed in Chapter 2. By considering the interaction of investor-state tribunals and the WTO panels and Appellate Body with other international courts, we can elucidate whether forms of judicial cooperation are occurring. Table 5 and Figure 9 above set out the number of instances of other international law based on the source of law in the judicial decisions of other international courts. Table 6 below provides a breakdown of this source of law according to the international court or tribunal referred to.

For both the WTO and investor-state disputes, the ICJ is the most commonly referred to in terms of its judicial decisions as a source of law. A focus on the ICJ is relevant to the hierarchical structure arguments of defragmentation and the systematization of international court jurisprudence, whereby the ICJ remains the "prodigious force" on general international law.[59] While the ICJ is not the "supreme court of international law", the maintenance of the ICJ's "special prestige and highly qualified judges" plays a leading role in the coherence

TABLE 6 Breakdown of the sources of jurisprudence by court

	ICJ[a]	Regional human rights courts	Other economic tribunals[b]	Various[c]
ISDS	77%	9%	6%	8%
WTO	61%	3%	11%	26%

a Also includes references to jurisprudence of the PCIJ.
b Other international economic tribunals includes WTO and ISDS, as well as other tribunals (ad hoc or otherwise) dealing with disputes under FTAS or other regional economic regimes, such as MERCOSUR. The investor-state decisions which refer to the Court of Justice of the European Union *Achmea* decision in relation to the intra-EU objection have been removed from the data-set for this analysis, as explained at the beginning of section 1.1 on the relevance of other international law.
c This captures instances where the tribunals refer to multiple courts, usually for issues of procedure and general interpretation issues, such as provisional measures and evidential rules.

59 Jonathan Charney, 'Is International Law Threatened by Multiple International Tribunals?' (1998) 271 Collected Courses of the Hague Academy of International Law 101, 355 ff; see also, Vadi, who refers to the perceived authority and persuasiveness of the ICJ and PCIJ in ISDS awards: Valentina Vadi, *Analogies in International Investment Law and Arbitration* (Cambridge University Press 2015) ch 3.

of international law.[60] This is exemplified in the ICJ's own consideration of the control tests in the *Nicaragua* and *Tadić* decisions:

> the Court attaches the utmost importance to the factual and legal findings made by the ICTY in ruling on the criminal liability of the accused before it … The situation is not the same for positions adopted by the ICTY on issues of general international law which do not lie within the specific purview of its jurisdiction.[61]

In addition, reference to the ICJ and its constituting Statute also plays into the narrative of a system of international law, for example, through the defragmentation role of Article 38(1) of the ICJ Statute.

For the WTO, most references to ICJ jurisprudence are taken into account in some way, albeit primarily in clarifying the meaning of WTO provisions or supporting the conclusion of the panel or Appellate Body on procedural and evidential issues.[62] A notable exception is *EC – Bananas*, in which the Appellate Body considered that the PCIJ and ICJ jurisprudence raised did not establish a general rule that a complaining party must have a "legal interest". As such, the Appellate Body rejected the relevance of the jurisprudence to the dispute.[63] In ISDS, the most common references to ICJ jurisprudence is to those cases that could also be labeled as general principles, such as *Monetary Gold*,[64]

60 Charney (n 59) 361; Lang similarly refers to the ICJ taking a 'reflexivity enhancing role', which conceives of the ICJ as the apex of an institutional hierarchy, tasked with resolving normative conflicts and clarifying divergent jurisprudence: Andrew Lang, 'The Role of the International Court of Justice in a Context of Fragmentation' (2013) 62 International and Comparative Law Quarterly 777, 779.

61 *Application of the Convention on the Prevention and Punishment of the Crime of Genocide (Bosnia and Herzegovina v Serbia and Montenegro)*, Judgment [2007] ICJ Reports 43 [403].

62 For example, panels have applied ICJ jurisprudence on consultations and negotiations between states: *European Union – Measures Affecting Tariff Concessions on Certain Poultry Meat Products (Report of the Panel)* (28 March 2017), WT/DS492/R [7.486]; and ICJ jurisprudence on the weight to be given to domestic court decisions: *United States – Certain Methodologies and their Application to Anti-Dumping Proceedings Involving China (Report of the Panel)* (19 October 2016), WT/DS471/R [7.326].

63 *EC – Bananas III* (n 21) para 133.

64 *Monetary Gold Removed from Rome in 1943 (Italy v France, UK and USA)*, Preliminary Question, Judgment [1954] ICJ Reports 19, 33, also known as the indispensable third-party principle.

Barcelona Traction[65] and *Factory at Chorzów*.[66] While the tribunals distinguish the context of investment law from the ICJ's decision on shareholder claims in *Barcelona Traction*,[67] drawing from the other principles established by the ICJ supports the defragmentation role of the ICJ and the application of general principles in the international judicial function.[68] The reference to the ICJ jurisprudence on the balance of examining merits at the jurisdictional stage[69] also confirms such a conclusion.

1.3 *Conclusions on Responses to Fragmentation in ISDS and WTO*

The empirical approach to other international law presented in this Chapter provides mixed results. At a very basic level, these empirical results indicate that these regimes do not merely pay lip service to not being read "in clinical isolation from international law": they are not self-contained regimes operating outside the general international law framework and thereby creating opportunity for substantive fragmentation in that way. Building on the initial results that indicate the WTO dispute settlement mechanism is almost as open as investor-state tribunals to the application of other international law, the investigation of the role of dispute settlement design in addressing the application of other international law shows significant similarities. In particular, similarities in the sources of the other law and the relevance of other international courts and tribunals. The examination of the legal reasoning of the tribunals in the application of other international law provided particularly interesting similarities that indicate limitations of the opening tools in explaining the application of other international law.

---

65 *The Barcelona Traction, Light and Power Company Limited (New Application: 1962) (Belgium v Spain)*, Second Phase, Judgment [1970] ICJ Reports 3 on derivative claims.

66 *Factory at Chorzów (Germany v Poland), Jurisdiction* (n 33) 21 on reparations and compensation in international law.

67 See, for example, *Anglo American v Venezuela* (ICSID Case No ARB(AF)/14/1), Award, 18 January 2019 [203]; *Daimler Financial v Argentina* (n 53) para 90; *Azurix v Argentina (I)* (ICSID Case No ARB/01/12), Decision on the Application for Annulment of the Argentine Republic, 1 September 2009 [86 ff]; in *Berschader v Russia*, the tribunal considered that it could not be excluded that the Barcelona Traction dictum had some influence on the drafting of the treaty, even if it no longer reflects the current state of international law: *Berschader v Russia* (n 13) para 141.

68 Vadi similarly argues that the *Factory at Chorzów* case serves as a sort of legitimizing function in ISDS, since parties would expect arbitral tribunals to mention this leading case: Vadi (n 59) ch 3.

69 The tribunals commonly refer to Judge Higgins' separate opinion as a clear formulation of the test: *Oil Platforms (Islamic Republic of Iran v United States of America), Judgment* [2003] ICJ Reports 161, 856. See, for example, *Impregilo v Pakistan (II)* (ICSID Case No ARB/03/3), Decision on Jurisdiction, 22 April 2005 [237 ff]; *Casinos Austria v Argentina* (ICSID Case No ARB/14/32), Decision on Jurisdiction, 29 June 2018 [201 ff].

2 Beyond the Numbers: Consistently Inconsistent?

While the preceding empirical assessment sheds some light on the approach of the adjudicators to other public international law, it fails to capture the complexities of analysing this aspect of their work. With the empirical background established, we turn to detailed analysis of the language used by the tribunals and specific case studies. This analysis reveals a similarity between the systems: inconsistency in approach to other international law within the systems, a "consistency in inconsistency". We expect some inconsistency within ISDS as a result of the heterogeneity of the system, with some inconsistency necessary based on this heterogeneity. On the other hand, following the cogent reasons approach of the WTO Appellate Body, we would expect less inconsistency within the WTO dispute settlement mechanism; at least once the Appellate Body has provided guidance to panels on how other international law may be relevant. While we see more inconsistency across ISDS, the WTO dispute settlement system also suffers from internal inconsistency.

This inconsistency has implications for defragmentation. Inconsistency could be evidence of substantive fragmentation within the regimes as well as potentially detrimental to the coherence of international law more generally. To illustrate this point, this section considers some specific examples of inconsistency: interactions with other treaty-based regimes of international law (environmental law in WTO and human rights in investor-state disputes) and customary international law on state responsibility.

2.1 *Treaty Interactions: Overview*

Section 1.2 above illustrated that other regime law, namely treaty law, is less commonly invoked in WTO and investor-state decisions compared to general international law, being custom and general principles. Nevertheless, there is still a wide variety of treaty law brought before the tribunals, both specific and more general treaty law. Broadly speaking, specific treaty law captures such issues as human rights and environmental instruments, EU law and international economic regimes (such as regional agreements) that are the subject of specific regimes of international law. Comparatively, "general treaty law" covers international procedural rules, such as the New York Convention,[70] or broad treaties covering relations between states, such as the UN Charter and the Vienna Conventions on Diplomatic and Consular Relations,[71] that are not

70 Convention on the Recognition and Enforcement of Foreign Arbitral Awards (New York, 10 June 1958), 330 UNTS 3.

71 Vienna Convention on Diplomatic Relations (Vienna, 18 April 1961), 500 UNTS 95; Vienna Convention on Consular Relations (Vienna, 24 April 1963), 596 UNTS 261. All these

limited to a specific regime of international law. The following section expands this analysis in considering the extent to which that treaty law is particular regime law. In doing so, the section provides some indication of the level of treaty interaction and potential for defragmentation within the WTO and investor-state tribunals. The section focuses on human rights and environmental legal regimes given the increasing attention on whether international economic law balances these other important public interests.

Table 7 provides the results of the types of treaties sought to be applied within investor-state and WTO disputes.

Perhaps unsurprisingly, one of the most common types of treaty law referred to in each dispute settlement mechanism is other economic regimes, indicating the overlap between areas of international economic law. The results also indicate the potential lack of integration of these regimes of international law with human rights and environmental concerns. In relation to environmental concerns in ISDS, this may be a result of most international environmental

TABLE 7 Proportion of types of treaty law in the regimes

	Human rights[a]	Environment/ sustainable development	Other economic regimes[b]	Other[c]
ISDS	39%	5%	30%	26%
WTO	0%	17%	51%	31%

a For regional human rights instruments, this includes only the treaty itself and jurisprudence of the regional human rights courts are counted as a source of jurisprudence. For example, the margin of appreciation used by the ECtHR is categorized as jurisprudence, rather than treaty law.

b This includes regional economic agreements, other FTAs, the reference to GATT in ISDS as well as treaties relating to the regulation of economic activities, including the UN Convention against Corruption, IMF treaties and taxation treaties. The intra-EU objections based on the EU treaties have been excluded from this analysis.

c "Other" includes general treaty law as well as any other specific treaty law not falling within one of the other regimes.

---

examples of specific and general treaty law have been considered by the tribunals in the comparative study. References to the VCLT (that are not simply to interpretation under that treaty and therefore not the subject of relevant other law) have been categorized as customary law since not all Members of the WTO are parties to the VCLT. This broadly accords with the approach of the WTO panels and Appellate Body when considering the VCLT.

concerns being captured within domestic law environmental obligations.[72] The next sections develop the inconsistent practice of each of the dispute settlement mechanisms in relation to human rights in investor-state disputes and environmental agreements in WTO disputes, given the greater prevalence of those areas of treaty law in the regimes. The inconsistency in relation to both the environmental and human rights regimes also indicates a more fundamental problem: the coherence of international law. This leaves us to question what other underlying objectives or views may be in play for the adjudicators, a question of balancing the coherence of international law with the settlement of individual disputes.

2.2 *Human Rights in ISDS*

Table 7 illustrates that the proportion of human rights instruments raised in ISDS (as a percentage of the total instances of treaties as a source of other international law) is much higher than its WTO counterpart. The extent of the balancing of human rights and economic interests has been argued as part of a normative hierarchy or constitutionalism of international law.[73] A normative hierarchy under the constitutional vision of international law also relies on *jus cogens* and Article 103 of the UN Charter. The *Methanex v USA* tribunal recognized that:

> as a matter of international constitutional law a tribunal has an independent duty to apply imperative principles of law or jus cogens and not to give effect to parties' choices of law that are inconsistent with such principles.[74]

72 For example, some domestic constitutions have enshrined environmental rights commonly found in international law, thereby those obligations become domestic law within the investment regime, rather than international law. See *Perenco v Ecuador* (n 10).

73 See, for example, Ernst-Ulrich Petersmann, 'Constitutional Theories of International Economic Adjudication and Investor-State Arbitration' in Pierre-Marie Dupuy, Ernst-Ulrich Petersmann and Francesco Francioni (eds), *Human Rights in International Investment Law and Arbitration* (Oxford University Press 2009) 180 ff. Petersmann states: '[a]s the universal recognition of inalienable human rights has constitutionally limited the power-oriented premises of the Westphalian "international law among states", international economic courts should examine – like European courts – the potential impact of human rights and other "principles of justice" (for example, of non-discrimination, necessity, and proportionality) on the interpretation of economic rules and on judicial justifications of judgments' (p 183).

74 *Methanex Corporation v United States of America* (ad hoc, UNCITRAL), Final Award, 3 August 2005, Part IV, Chapter C [24].

However, there was no violation of a *jus cogens* rule in that case. This captures the general approach of tribunals to such concepts: recognition of their fundamentality but ultimately no application based on the facts of the dispute. There is very little in the ISDS or WTO jurisprudence to indicate a normative hierarchy of human rights concerns. The explanation for the relatively high percentage of human rights instruments referred to in investor-state tribunals lays more in the nature of investor rights and state obligations and does not seem to depart from the economic interests. The relevance of *jus* cogens is further expanded on in Chapter 7 in assessing justice as a standard of legitimacy.

There is ample evidence of investor-state tribunals taking human rights obligations into account and the substantive judgments of human rights courts,[75] potentially reducing fragmentation between investment and human rights law. In the collected data, 55 decisions consider the application of international human rights law or the jurisprudence of human rights courts, in particular the European Court of Human Rights (ECtHR). Some examples of how human rights law has been taken into account by investor-state disputes illustrate the potential for harmonization. As international investment law concerns property rights, the use of economic rights in human rights instruments, such as the ICCPR,[76] the European Convention on Human Rights (ECHR)[77] and the Universal Declaration of Human Rights (UDHR),[78] have been used to interpret investor rights. This has included the interpretation of fair trial rights,[79] the

75 See, for example, Freya Baetens, 'Invoking Human Rights: A Useful Line of Attack or a Defence Tool for States in Investor-State Dispute Settlement?' in Martin Scheinin (ed), *Human Rights Norms in 'Other' International Courts* (Cambridge University Press 2019); Pierre-Marie Dupuy, Ernst-Ulrich Petersmann and Francesco Francioni (eds), *Human Rights in International Investment Law and Arbitration* (Oxford University Press 2009); Vivian Kube and Ernst-Ulrich Petersmann, 'Human Rights Law in International Investment Arbitration' in Andrea Gattini, Attila Tanzi and Filippo Fontanelli (eds), *General Principles of Law and International Investment Arbitration* (Brill Nijhoff 2018); Bruno Simma and Theodore Kill, 'Harmonizing Investment Protection and International Human Rights: First Steps toward a Methodology' in Christina Binder and others (eds), *International Investment Law for the 21st Century* (Oxford University Press 2009).

76 International Covenant on Civil and Political Rights (19 December 1966), 999 UNTS 171.

77 European Convention for the Protection of Human Rights and Fundamental Freedoms (4 November 1950, as amended by Protocols No. 11 and 14), ETS 5.

78 Universal Declaration of Human Rights (adopted 10 December 1948), UNGA Res 217 A(III).

79 See, for example, *Tulip Real Estate v Turkey* (ICSID Case No ARB/11/28), Decision on Annulment, 30 December 2015 [86–92], on the use of human rights treaties in the interpretation of a fundamental rule of procedure under the annulment procedures of the ICSID Convention; similarly, *Churchill Mining PLC and Planet Mining Pty Ltd v Republic of Indonesia* (ICSID Case No ARB/12/14 and 12/40), Decision on Annulment, 18 March 2019;

standards of denial of justice[80] and the prohibition on expropriation,[81] in light of human rights instruments and jurisprudence.

Nevertheless, the study reveals two concerns with the application of human rights in international investment law. First, the creation of obligations for the investor through the application of human rights may raise concern with the limited jurisdiction of the tribunal, addressed in Chapter 6. Secondly, the threat of substantive fragmentation is still prevalent, exemplified where inconsistent application of human rights concepts has occurred.

Taking just one example of jurisprudence from the human rights regime, we can consider the inconsistency in relation to the margin of appreciation. In the context of ISDS, the margin of appreciation draws primarily from the ECtHR's jurisprudence. Albeit within different IIA contexts, two cases indicate the diverse approach to the margin of appreciation in ISDS. In *RREEF v Spain*, the tribunal applied the margin of appreciation on the basis that the IIA in question (the ECT) did not expressly exclude the doctrine. The tribunal considered "there can be no doubt that States enjoy a margin of appreciation in public international law".[82] In a remarkably different direction, the tribunal in *von Pezold v Zimbabwe* considered there must be "due caution in importing concepts from other legal regimes". The tribunal did not recognize that the margin of appreciation had achieved customary status and, as such, refused to apply the doctrine in the dispute.[83] Only the home states of the investors were a party to the ECHR in *von Pezold* (Germany/Switzerland),[84] compared to

---

On the use of the ICCPR on interpreting the fair and equitable treatment standard, see *Hesham Talaat M Al-Warraq v The Republic of Indonesia* (ad hoc, UNCITRAL), Final Award, 15 December 2014 [621]; and *Chevron and TexPet v Ecuador (II)* (PCA Case No 2009–23), Second Partial Award on Track II, 30 August 2018 [8.57 ff], referring to the ICCPR and the UDHR; and *The Rompetrol Group NV v Romania* (ICSID Case No ARB/06/3), Award, 6 May 2013 [169], referring to the ECHR on fair trial standards.

80 *Toto v Lebanon* (ICSID Case No ARB/07/12), Decision on Jurisdiction, 11 September 2009 [154 ff].

81 *Víctor Pey Casado and President Allende Foundation v Republic of Chile (I)* (ICSID Case No ARB/98/2), Award, 8 May 2008 [604 ff]; *Saipem S.pA v The People's Republic of Bangladesh* (ICSID Case No ARB/05/07), Decision on Jurisdiction and Provisional Measures, 21 March 2007 [132].

82 *RREEF v Spain* (n 47) paras 241–2.

83 *Bernhard von Pezold v Republic of Zimbabwe* (ICSID Case No ARB/10/15), Award, 28 July 2015 [465–7]; See also, *Quasar de Valors v Russia* (SCC Case No 24/2007), Award, 20 July 2012 [158] in which the tribunal noted that the reliability of investment protection treaties should not be diluted by the same notions of margin of appreciation that apply to human rights conventions; and the concurring and dissenting opinion of Gary Born in *Philip Morris v Uruguay* (n 2) para 87.

84 The decision concerned conjoined proceedings brought under different IIAs.

both home and host state in *RREEF v Spain* (Spain and UK). It may be arguable that this justifies a different approach to the margin of appreciation in the two disputes.

However, the applicable law clauses of the IIAs were relatively similar referring to the "rules of international law".[85] This begs the question whether jurisprudence of a regional court, developed in the scope of a particular human rights treaty, is an applicable rule of international law. As Born et al argue, this doctrine has been applied without meaningful explanation of the doctrine's relevance to international investment law, nor the limitations of the doctrine.[86]

2.3 *Environment in WTO*

In the opposite direction, environmental instruments, including sustainable development, are more commonly invoked in WTO proceedings. However, as with human rights in ISDS, it has not proved a simple process.[87] International environmental law has been used in interpreting WTO covered agreements following the decision of the Appellate Body in *US – Shrimp*. In *US – Shrimp*, the Appellate Body expressly turned to international environmental agreements, including the Convention on Biological Diversity,[88] to interpret parts of the Article XX(g) GATT exception.[89] Following the example set by the Appellate

85 Article 10.3 of the Agreement between the Swiss Confederation and the Republic of Zimbabwe on the Protection of Investments (Harare, 15 August 1996) refers to the 'rules of international law as may be applicable'; Article 11(2) Agreement between the Republic of Zimbabwe and the Federal Republic of Germany concerning the Encouragement and Reciprocal Protection of Investments (Harare, 29 September 1995) is perhaps even broader, referring to 'any treaties in force between the Contracting Parties, such rules of general international law as may be applicable'; Article 26(6) of the ECT refers to 'applicable rules and principles of international law': The Energy Charter Treaty (Lisbon, 17 December 1994), 2080 UNTS 95.

86 Gary Born, Danielle Morris and Stephanie Forrest, 'A Margin of Appreciation: Appreciating Its Irrelevance in International Law' (2020) 61 Harvard International Law Journal 65. See further, Raymond Yang Gao, 'What Are We Talking About When We Talk About Deference in Investment Treaty Arbitration?' (2022) 13 Journal of International Dispute Settlement 472; Joshua Paine, 'Standard of Review: Investment Arbitration', *Max Planck Encylopedia of International Procedural Law* (Oxford University Press 2018).

87 See, for example, Daniel Bodansky and Jessica C Lawrence, 'Trade and Environment' in Daniel Bethlehem and others (eds), *The Oxford Handbook of International Trade Law* (Oxford University Press 2009); Francesco Francioni (ed), *Environment, Human Rights and International Trade* (Hart 2001); Joel P Trachtman, 'WTO Trade and Environment Jurisprudence: Avoiding Environmental Catastrophe' (2017) 58 Harvard International Law Journal 273.

88 Convention on Biological Diversity (Rio de Janeiro, 5 June 1992), 1760 UNTS 79.

89 Article XX is the general exceptions provision of the GATT and paragraph (g) refers to measures "relating to the conservation of exhaustible natural resources if such

Body, the decisions illustrate the use of environmental principles for interpretation of the scope of general exceptions, but caution must be exercised in changing any standards or obligations of WTO covered agreements.

This is exemplified in the application of the precautionary principle in WTO disputes. Different approaches to whether the principle is reflected in the provisions of the WTO agreements or is incompatible with (or otherwise override) the provisions of the WTO agreements can be seen in the *Biotech* and *Hormones* disputes. In EC – *Hormones*, the Appellate Body declined to reach a conclusion on whether the precautionary principle had crystallized into a general principle of customary environmental law.[90] Despite some reflection in Article 5.7 of the SPS Agreement, in the view of the Appellate Body, the precautionary principle could not override the provisions of Article 5.1 and 5.2 of the SPS Agreement.[91] A similar approach was taken by the Panel in EC – *Biotech*. The Panel considered that the precautionary principle would be a relevant rule under Article 31(3)(c) of the VCLT if it was in fact a general principle.[92] The Panel noted that the legal debate over the status of the precautionary principle was still ongoing and, as it was not necessary to settle the complex issue, the Panel chose not to take a position on the status of the principles.[93]

EC – *Biotech* also demonstrates another inconsistency with the approach to environmental agreements in WTO dispute settlement. In an example that will be dealt with in more detail in Chapter 4, *US – Shrimp* and EC – *Biotech* are inconsistent in determining whether environmental agreements are relevant in interpretation. Faced with the same Convention on Biological Diversity as the Appellate Body in *US – Shrimp*, the Panel in EC – *Biotech* rejected the application of this Convention under the Article 31(3)(c) interpretative method

measures are made effective in conjunction with restrictions on domestic production or consumption".

90 The Appellate Body stated: 'The precautionary principle is regarded by some as having crystallized into a general principle of customary international environmental law. Whether it has been widely accepted by Members as a principle of general or customary international law appears less than clear. We consider, however, that it is unnecessary, and probably imprudent, for the Appellate Body in this appeal to take a position on this important, but abstract, question. We note that the panel itself did not make any definitive finding with regard to the status of the precautionary principle in international law and that the precautionary principle, at least outside the field of international environmental law, still awaits authoritative formulation': EC – *Hormones* (n 30) para 123.

91 ibid [124–5].

92 *European Communities – Measures Affecting the Approval and Marketing of Biotech Products (Report of the Panel)* (29 September 2006), WT/DS291/R; WT/DS292/R; WT/DS293/R [7.67].

93 ibid [7.88–9].

since the US was not a party to the Convention.[94] These decisions and their inconsistency is examined in more detail in Chapter 4 given its relevance to the approach to systemic integration by WTO adjudicators.

2.4 *Customary International Law*

Turning to secondary rules of customary international law, a positive sign for defragmentation and burying the self-contained regime myth is the general application of the secondary rules on state responsibility.[95] However, the general law nature of these secondary rules, codified in the ILC Articles on State Responsibility,[96] does not avoid the inconsistency found in the preceding discussion of regime collisions. Article 4 and 5 of the ILC Articles on State Responsibility[97] are generally accepted in ISDS and the WTO. For the WTO, even though certain issues of attribution are covered by *lex specialis* WTO provisions,[98] the ILC Articles maintain a relevancy in interpretation. Since the Appellate Body in *US – Definitive Anti-Dumping* (*China*) determined

---

94 *European Communities – Regime for the Importation, Sale and Distribution of Bananas – Recourse to Article 21.5 of the DSU by the United States* (*Report of the Panel*) (19 May 2008), WT/DS27/RW/USA [7.74].

95 See Simma and Pulkowski (n 27); Simma and Pulkowski (n 40).

96 Crawford notes that the fact that the ILC Articles have been so widely used does not mean that they necessarily constitute general international law: James Crawford, 'Investment Arbitration and the ILC Articles on State Responsibility' (2010) 25 ICSID Review 127, 128; however, the ILC Articles are generally accepted as an accurate codification of the customary international law of state responsibility: James Crawford, *State Responsibility: The General Part* (Cambridge University Press 2013) 43; this status has been confirmed by the ICJ, amongst countless other courts and tribunals: *Application of the Convention on the Prevention and Punishment of the Crime of Genocide* (*Bosnia and Herzegovina v Serbia and Montenegro*), *Judgment* (n 61) 209.

97 Article 4 and 5 attributes conduct of state organs and persons or entities exercising elements of governmental authority to that state under international law: ILC Articles on State Responsibility.

98 Attribution is covered by a number of provisions of the WTO agreements but there is no major *lex specialis* on conduct of state organs: Santiago M Villalpando, 'Attribution of Conduct to the State: How the Rules of State Responsibility May Be Applied Within the WTO Dispute Settlement System' (2002) 5 Journal of International Economic Law 393. Comparatively, the necessity defence is covered in Article XXI of the GATT on security exceptions and countermeasures are covered by the WTO rules on suspension of concessions in the DSU, thereby *lex specialis* rules. For discussion of countermeasures, see Martins Paparinskis, 'Equivalent Primary Rules and Differential Secondary Rules: Countermeasures in WTO and Investment Protection Law' in Tomer Broude and Yuval Shany (eds), *Multi-Sourced Equivalent Norms in International Law* (Bloomsbury Publishing 2011).

that Articles 4 and 5 on attribution were relevant interpretative elements under Article 31(3)(c) of the VCLT, later decisions have considered that the ILC Articles support their reasoning on interpretation of the WTO covered agreements.[99] The ILC Articles on countermeasures have also been utilized as material to support the proportionality requirement in safeguard measures under the Agreement on Textiles and Clothing[100] and the Agreement on Safeguard Measures.[101] However, attempts to transpose the customary regime of countermeasures to WTO law is not appropriate given the *lex specialis* nature of the WTO regime.[102]

In ISDS, such rules have been used "like a drowning man might grab a stick at sea in the hope of having certainty".[103] While there has been some "slightly awkward handling" of the customary rules on attribution, tribunals have generally been careful and conscientious in their application of the ILC Articles.[104] Yet, inconsistency is easily identifiable in investor-state tribunals' consideration of the necessity defence, encapsulated in Article 25 of the ILC Articles.

The discussion of the relationship between the customary international law defence and the IIA defence rose to particular prominence following the

99 *United States – Definitive Anti-Dumping and Countervailing Duties on Certain Products from China* (*Report of the Appellate Body*) (11 March 2011), WT/DS379/AB/R [308–316]; see, further *Saudi Arabia – Measures concerning the Protection of Intellectual Property Rights* (*Report of the Panel*) (16 June 2020), WT/DS/567/R; *United States – Anti-Dumping and Countervailing Measures on Certain Coated Paper from Indonesia* (*Report of the Panel*) (6 December 2017), WT/DS491/R.

100 *United States – Transitional Safeguard Measure on Combed Cotton Yarn from Pakistan* (*Report of the Appellate Body*) (8 October 2001) WT/DS192/AB/R [120]; Agreement on Textiles and Clothing, Marrakesh Agreement Establishing the World Trade Organization, Annex 1A (15 April 1994, terminated 1 January 2005), 1868 UNTS 14.

101 *United States – Definitive Safeguard Measures on Imports of Circular Welded Carbon Quality Line Pipe from Korea* (*Report of the Appellate Body*) (15 February 2002), WT/DS202/AB/R [257–9]; Agreement on Safeguards, Marrakesh Agreement Establishing the World Trade Organization, Annex 1A (15 April 1994), 1869 UNTS 154; although countermeasures are not relevant to the Article XX(d) general exception since the exception related to compliance with domestic law: *Mexico – Tax Measures on Soft Drinks and Other Beverages* (*Report of the Panel*) (7 October 2005) WT/DS308/R [8.180–1]; *Mexico – Tax Measures on Soft Drinks and Other Beverages* (*Report of the Appellate Body*) (6 March 2006) WT/DS308/AB/R [72].

102 *United States – Import Measures on Certain Products from the European Communities* (*Report of the Panel*) (17 July 2000), WT/DS165/R [6.133].

103 Crawford (n 96) 128.

104 See, Crawford's assessment of the handling of the field of attribution: Crawford (n 96).

Argentine financial crisis. The crisis led to a number of disputes under the United States – Argentina IIA, which included a state of emergency clause that the treaty:

> shall not preclude the application by either Party of measures necessary for the maintenance of public order, the fulfillment of its obligations with respect to the maintenance or restoration of international peace or security, or the Protection of its own essential security interests.[105]

Writing following the handing down of the first five of the awards, Kurtz provides a useful typology of interpretative methods through which the tribunal treated the relationship between the treaty exception and the customary defence of necessity: confluence, *lex specialis* and primary-secondary application methods. The confluence approach is the most restrictive approach as it "conflates" the treaty defence with the customary defence.[106] At the time of writing, Kurtz considered that the confluence approach was most dominant in the awards having been utilized in three out of the five of the arbitral awards.[107] However, the confluence approach has been strongly criticized, evidenced both in Kurtz's work and the subsequent findings of annullable error

105 Treaty between United States of America and The Argentine Republic concerning the Reciprocal Encouragement and Protection of Investment (Washington, 14 November 1991), Article XI; comparatively, Article 25 of the ILC Articles is much more determinative and states that '1. Necessity may not be invoked by a State as a ground for precluding the wrongfulness of an act not in conformity with an international obligation of that State unless the act: (a) is the only way for the State to safeguard an essential interest against a grave and imminent peril; and (b) does not seriously impair an essential interest of the State or States toward which the obligation exists, or of the international community as a whole. 2. In any case, necessity may not be invoked by a State as a ground for precluding wrongfulness if: (a) the international obligation in question excludes the possibility of invoking necessity; or (b) the State has contributed to the situation of necessity': ILC Articles on State Responsibility.

106 Jürgen Kurtz, 'Adjudging the Exceptional at International Investment Law: Security, Public Order and Financial Crisis' (2010) 59 International & Comparative Law Quarterly 325, 341.

107 ibid 341; Kurtz refers to the awards in; *CMS Gas Transmission v Argentina* (ICSID Case No ARB/01/8), Award, 12 May 2005; *Sempra v Argentine Republic* (ICSID Case No ARB/02/16), Award, 28 September 2007; *Enron Creditors Recovery Corp and Ponderosa Assets, LP v Argentine Republic* (ICSID Case No ARB/01/3), Award, 22 May 2007. Kurtz's analysis does not take into account the reasoning of the Annulment Committees in *Sempra* and *Enron*, which had not been decided at the time of Kurtz's publication.

in the *CMS*[108] and *Sempra*[109] cases.[110] The second method prioritizes the treaty exception through the *lex specialis* rule, "constituting a specific elaboration or updating of the general customary norm."[111] The LG&E award[112] falls within this approach as the treaty provision is "not set in isolation" and is applied as an expression of *lex specialis*, however, a rather unprincipled approach is taken by the tribunal, in Kurtz's view.[113] Kurtz also finds some "intriguing hints" in the direction of this approach in the *Continental* award.[114] Finally, the primary-secondary application method is Kurtz's preferred method,[115] which would characterize:

> all of the treaty provisions at issue, both forms of obligation and exception, as primary legal standards that determine whether a State has committed a wrongful act at international law. It is only if breach is determined by the composite application of these rules that an adjudicator would examine the secondary possibility of the customary defence.[116]

While not directly adopted by the tribunals, Kurtz finds support for the approach in the *Continental* award[117] and then is ultimately endorsed by the Annulment Committee in the *CMS* case.[118]

---

108 *CMS Gas Transmission v Argentina* (ICSID Case No ARB/01/8), Decision of the ad hoc Committee on Argentina's Application for Annulment, 25 September 2007 [128–134].
109 *Sempra v Argentine Republic* (ICSID Case No ARB/02/16), Decision on the Argentine Republic's Application for Annulment of the Award, 29 June 2010 [197–209].
110 See also August Reinisch, 'Necessity in International Investment Arbitration – An Unnecessary Split of Opinions in Recent ICSID Cases – Comments on CMS v. Argentina and LG&E v. Argentina' (2007) 8 Journal of World Investment & Trade 191, 205; Jürgen Kurtz, 'The Paradoxical Treatment of the ILC Articles on State Responsibility in Investor-State Arbitration' (2010) 25 ICSID Review 200, 210–214; Campbell McLachlan, 'Investment Treaties and General International Law' (2008) 57 International & Comparative Law Quarterly 361, 390.
111 Kurtz (n 106) 352.
112 *LG&E v Argentine Republic* (ICSID Case No ARB/02/1), Decision on Liability, 3 October 2006 [229, 245, 258].
113 Kurtz (n 106) 355–356.
114 Kurtz (n 106), referring to; *Continental Casualty v Argentina* (ICSID Case No ARB/03/9), Award, 5 September 2008 [168].
115 Kurtz (n 106) 360.
116 ibid 356–7.
117 *Continental Casualty v Argentina (Award)* (n 114) paras 166–167, 192; the Annulment Committee found no annullable error in the tribunal's decision on the necessity defence: *Continental Casualty v Argentina* (ICSID Case No ARB/03/9), Decision on the Application for Partial Annulment, 16 September 2011 [124].
118 Kurtz (n 106) 357; referring to *CMS v Argentina (Annulment)* (n 108) paras 124–134.

Other than these five awards discussed, there has been little movement on the necessity defence in international investment disputes. The additional cases dealing with the relationship between the treaty and customary defence still appear to follow Kurtz's three interpretative methodologies. However, with the annulment committee decisions in some cases and cases under other IIAs, the dominance of the confluence approach has been replaced by the *lex specialis* approach. The only remaining case that appears to support the confluence approach is *Enron*. Unlike *CMS* and *Sempra*, the Annulment Committee in *Enron* found that it was a matter for the tribunal to determine the substantive operation, content and interplay of the treaty and custom defence. As the tribunal's reasoning was tainted by annullable error for different reasons, the Annulment Committee found it had no occasion to go further and to express any view on the correctness of the tribunal's decision.[119] Comparatively, the Annulment Committee in *Sempra* found an annullable error in the tribunal's confluence approach, stating that it may be appropriate to look to customary international law as a guide but parties may contract otherwise.[120] Later cases under the US-Argentina IIA also appear to favor the *lex specialis* approach, with the *El Paso* tribunal explicitly endorsing the treaty exception as *lex specialis*[121] and the *Mobil Exploration* tribunal only referring to the customary defence for "gap-filling" purposes.[122] Although under different IIAs, the awards of *Deutsche Telekom v India*[123] and *Devas CC v India*[124] also seem to support the *lex specialis* approach.

---

119 *Enron Creditors Recovery Corp and Ponderosa Assets, LP v Argentine Republic* (ICSID Case No ARB/01/3), Decision on the Application for the Annulment of the Argentine Republic, 30 July 2010 [405]. The Committee determined that the finding that Argentina was precluded from relying on the necessity defence under the IIA and customary international law were both tainted by an annullable error, namely, the reliance on economic expert opinion rather than legal opinion.

120 *Sempra v Argentina* (Annulment) (n 109) para 197.

121 *El Paso Energy International Company v The Argentine Republic* (ICSID Case No ARB/03/15), Award, 31 October 2011 [552].

122 *Mobil Exploration and Development v Argentine Republic* (ICSID Case No ARB/04/16), Decision on Annulment, 8 May 2019 [93–97]. The tribunal also applied the treaty exception before the customary defence. However, it did so in a manner which applied the customary defence as interpretative guidance in circumstances where there was no uncertainty or ambiguity in the treaty text: *Mobil Exploration and Development v Argentine Republic* (ICSID Case No ARB/04/16), Decision on Jurisdiction and Liability, 10 April 2013 [1015, 1064–5], see also Separate Opinion of Professor Brotons.

123 *Deutsche Telekom v India* (PCA Case No 2014–10), Interim Award, 23 December 2017 [228–229]. The tribunal refers to the *CMS* Annulment Committee in determining that the IIA provision was to be 'distinguished' from the customary international law defence.

124 *Devas v India* (PCA Case No 2013–09), Award on Jurisdiction and Merits, 25 July 2016 [255–256]. The tribunal noted that the IIA provision would guide the tribunal in

2.5 *Conclusions on Inconsistency*

This short examination of inconsistency within the regimes overlooks many other examples. However, this snapshot identifies some of the different reasoning of the tribunals that can lead to these inconsistent results. In addition, this discussion highlights the substantive fragmentation within the international legal regimes, highlighting that defragmentation techniques may create new versions of fragmentation where tribunals have indeterminate discretion to pick and choose how to deal with the other public international law. These examples of inconsistency may evidence the tension between coherence of international law and settling disputes. How this inconsistency links with the adjudicator's toolkit is examined in the following chapters.

---

determining whether or not the respondent was in breach and considered this approach to be consistent with the *Continental Casualty* award and CMS annulment.

CHAPTER 4

Opening Tools

The Introduction set the stage for the ability of applicable law, general principles and systemic integration to open the regimes to the wider system of international law. This Chapter digs deeper into the use of these opening tools. How are adjudicators using these opening tools to address the indeterminacy of international law? Do these opening tools function as we expect them to in these international economic regimes? Chapter 3's empirical results exhibited relatively insignificant utilization of applicable law and systemic integration to ground the application of international law. Further, while general principles were the most applied source of law, it was not as high as expected. This Chapter expands on these findings and considers the extent to which the opening tools in the adjudicator's toolkit are being utilized in a consistent and coherent way and how they contribute to the methodology of international adjudication and the system of international law.

1 Applicable Law

As introduced in Chapter 2, applicable law concerns what legal norms an international tribunal may use when determining the dispute. The concept of applicable law can be used as an opening tool of international law. As explained in the ILC's Fragmentation Report:

> It is sometimes suggested that international tribunals or law-applying (treaty) bodies are not entitled to apply the law that goes "beyond" the four corners of the constituting instrument … But, if … all international law exists in systemic relationship with other law, no such application can take place without situating the relevant jurisdiction-endowing instrument in its normative environment. This means that although a tribunal may only have jurisdiction in regard to a particular instrument, it must always interpret and apply that instrument in its relationship to its normative environment – that is to say "other" international law.[1]

1 Martti Koskenniemi, 'Fragmentation of International Law: Difficulties Arising from the Diversification and Expansion of International Law, Report of the Study Group of

 | DOI:10.1163/9789004700932_005

An applicable law clause may provide the source of authority for a tribunal to apply customary international law, general principles of law and other treaties beyond the constitutive instrument. However, not all dispute settlement mechanisms have broadly drafted applicable law clauses. So, to what extent does applicable law, as a legal concept, function as an opening tool? This section digs deeper into the concept of applicable law and the legal reasoning of the WTO and ISDS adjudicators to see how perceptions of applicable law may explain the opening or closing of the regimes to international law. As discussed in Chapter 2, the applicable law of the WTO dispute settlement mechanism illustrates the different sides of the debate on whether international law is applicable while the applicable law of investor-state disputes provides broader support for the applicability of international law.

The following section examines the role of applicable law clauses in two different ways. First, the relevance of different applicable law language in ISDS decisions. Secondly, the relevance of there being no applicable law clause in the IIA. This second type of decision is a closer analogy to WTO decisions, where there is no applicable law clause, let alone one with open language and broad sources. Here, we can ask two questions: does the lack of applicable law clause impact on the likelihood that ISDS tribunals apply other international law, and are the legal basis and authority given for the incorporation or rejection of other international law similar to WTO disputes?

1.1 *Applicable Law in ISDS Practice: the Relevance of Different Applicable Law Language*

What is the relevance of different applicable law clause language? Chapter 2 identified the different applicable law clauses that applied to the disputes in the empirical study. These differences ranged from the same wording as Article 38(1)(c) of the ICJ Statute ("general principles of international law") to more specific formulation of principles ("accepted by both Contracting States") (see Figure 3 and Table 3 above). It is not necessary to consider in detail the precise meaning of these phrases. It is more important to question whether the different language has any impact on adjudicator reasoning. Given the small number of decisions that are brought within the more specific formulation of applicable law clauses, it is difficult to compare the approach of tribunals in much detail. We have just two examples that we can compare of other international law in which their applicability was raised under different applicable law clause wording: the margin of appreciation and illegality.

---

the International Law Commission' (International Law Commission 2006) A/CN.4/L.682 para 423.

First, as discussed in Chapter 3 (section 2.2), the application of the margin of appreciation has been inconsistently applied, and often without meaningful explanation of the doctrine's relevance to international investment law. The decisions discussed there contained broad applicable law provisions: the ECT's language in *RREEF v Spain* referring to "applicable rules and principles of international law" and the BIT language of "such rules of international law as may be applicable" in *von Pezold v Zimbabwe*. An example of stricter terminology for relevant international law sources in an applicable law clause is the *Quasar de Valors v Russia* decision. The relevant IIA referred to the more restrictive formulation of "universally recognized norms and principles of international law".[2] Although the adjudicators considered they were bound by the terms of the applicable IIA, rather than the ECtHR's wide margin of appreciation, the adjudicators did not turn their attention to the particular applicable law language.[3] Nothing in the reasoning of the adjudicators provides any further clarity on the scope of applicable law and the application of the margin of appreciation than the inconsistent application in *RREEF v Spain* and *von Pezold v Zimbabwe*.

Secondly, the different applicable law clauses in particular cases of illegality in the conduct of the investor. In section 2.2 below, the general principle of good faith is analysed in more detail. Under the China-Laos IIA, which contains the stricter applicable law wording of "generally recognized principles of international law accepted by both Contracting States",[4] the tribunal in *Sanum Investments v Laos (I)* recognized illegality as part of the general principles of international law of good faith.[5] The Respondent also relied on the doctrine of clean hands, which the tribunal noted that, if incorporated, could risk opening investment disputes to open-ended and vague principles. However, the tribunal decided to put aside the label of clean hands and incorporate more broadly corruption being incompatible with good faith obligations.[6] Similarly in *Unión Fenosa Gas v Egypt*, whose IIA required "the rules and the universally accepted

---

2 Article 10 of the Convention for the Promotion and Reciprocal Protection of Investments between Spain and the Russian Federation (Madrid, 26 October 1990). Official languages of the treaty are Spanish and Russian and the translation of the applicable law clause is from the decision.

3 *Quasar de Valors v Russia* (SCC Case No 24/2007), Award, 20 July 2012 [126–7].

4 Article 8.7 of the Agreement between the Government of the People's Republic of China and the Government of the Lao People's Democratic Republic concerning the Encouragement and Reciprocal Protection of Investments (Vientiane, 31 January 1993).

5 *Sanum Investments v Laos (I)* (PCA Case No 2013–13), Award, 6 August 2019 [103].

6 ibid 104.

principles of international law",[7] the tribunal accepted the application of the doctrine of international public policy.[8] Comparatively, under the ECT applicable law clause which refers to "applicable rules and principles of international law", the tribunal in *Hulley Enterprises v Russia* was not convinced that there existed a "general principle of law recognized by civilized nations" of unclean hands. Arguably, based on the ordinary meaning of the different applicable law clauses, the tribunal in *Sanum Investments v Laos (I)* should have considered whether the principle was in fact "accepted by both Contracting States". The tribunal's catch-all incorporation of the doctrine of clean hands is problematic if we do not take a flexible approach to applicable law. These examples also demonstrate the pragmatic approach to applicable law and general principles, which is further discussed below.

1.2 *Applicable Law in ISDS Practice: the Relevance of the Absence of an Applicable Law Clause*

Secondly, what if there is no applicable law clause? Does this affect the reasoning of ISDS adjudicators? Within the study, there are 49 decisions[9] which were brought under an IIA that had no applicable law clause or otherwise did not refer to international law within such a clause. This amounts to 13% of the analysed decisions (see Figure 2 above).[10]

---

7 Article 11 of the Agreement for the Reciprocal Promotion and Protection of Investments between the Kingdom of Spain and the Republic of Egypt (Madrid, 3 November 1992).

8 *Unión Fenosa Gas v Egypt* (ICSID Case No ARB/14/4), Award, 31 August 2018 [7.48].

9 There were also five decisions which were brought under multiple IIAs where one of the IIAs did not include an applicable law clause. However, those five decisions are excluded in the analysis of this section to ensure proper comparability between decisions with and without an applicable law clause of the entire dispute.

10 In addition, there are also five relevant decisions which are brought under more than one IIA, being the ECT and a BIT (which did not include an applicable law provision). In four of the decisions, the tribunals declined jurisdiction over the BIT, without referring to any other international law in the process: *Europa Nova v The Czech Republic* (PCA Case No 2014–19), Award, 15 May 2019; *ICW v Czech Republic* (PCA Case No 2014–22), Award, 15 May 2019; *Photovoltaik Knopf Betriebs v The Czech Republic* (PCA Case No 2014–21), Award, 15 May 2019; *Voltaic Network v Czech Republic* (PCA Case No 2014–20), Award, 15 May 2019 (all these decisions involved the same tribunal members and reasoning but the disputes were not formally consolidated). The final decision also found no jurisdiction over the BIT claim. However, in doing so, the tribunal considered the applicable law to the BIT to be the same approach as it had applied to the ECT, without developing its reasoning for that position. In determining jurisdiction under the BIT, the tribunal relied largely on its prior reasoning under ECT jurisdiction, with the exception that *ratione materiae* jurisdiction was not found under the BIT: *Energoalians v Mongolia* (ad hoc), Award, 23 October 2013

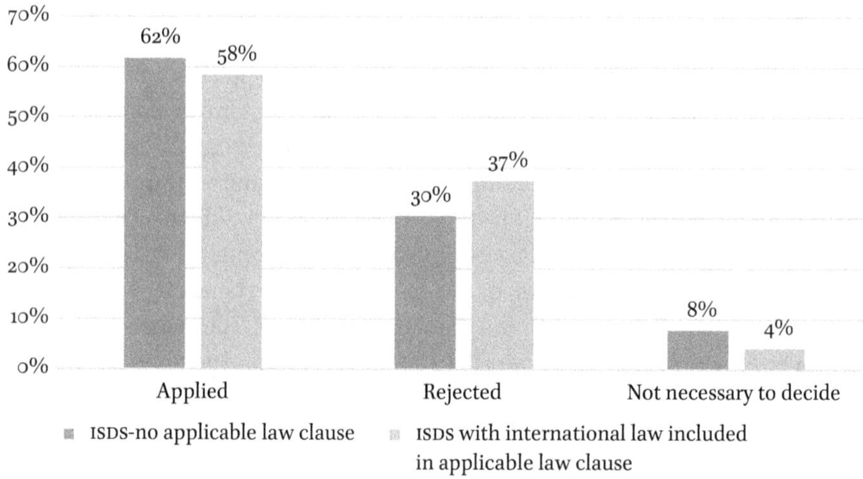

FIGURE 12 Comparison of acceptance of other international law in ISDS decisions with and without applicable law clauses

Beginning with the question of the impact of applicable law clauses on acceptance of other international law, an empirical assessment suggests the existence of applicable law clauses do not play a very large role in the application of other international law in ISDS. The empirical results of decisions dealing with IIAs with no applicable law clause look almost identical to the results of decisions where the IIA included international law as part of an applicable law clause. Figure 12 identifies only a small difference in the rejection of other international law in the no-applicable law clause disputes but a more similar acceptance rate in these disputes.

In relation to the method of reasoning of the adjudicators, decisions with no-applicable law clause refer to the applicable law of the dispute as a legal basis for the inclusion just as commonly (or more accurately as rarely) as the aggregated investor-state results. For 6 instances of other international law, the tribunal referred to the applicable law as the legal basis for the inclusion of the other international law, accounting for 7.6% of instances of applied other international law in no-applicable law clause disputes, compared to the aggregate of 8% for all disputes (see Figure 10 above).

From these comparative results, some implications can be drawn. The results confirm the discussion of the applicable law in Chapter 2 that international law generally applies to investor-state disputes. The existence of an

[277 ff]. These decisions have not been included in the comparison in this section to the WTO given the jurisdiction under the BITS was declined.

applicable law clause, or lack thereof, does not greatly affect the application of other international law.[11] Further, the application of international law where no applicable law clause exists does not appear to be controversial nor necessitate a greater inquiry into whether the other international law is in fact applicable. This is demonstrated in the limited discussion of the law applicable in disputes in which the IIA does not contain an applicable law clause. As set out in Chapter 2, in the absence of party agreement, the tribunal has to determine the applicable law,[12] which would suggest the necessity of the tribunal undertaking such a determination. Nevertheless, examples of such determinations in the context of specific applications of other international law are rare. In *AMF v Czech Republic*, when dealing with the intra-EU objection, the tribunal narrowed the applicable law to the provisions of the IIA and general principles of international law, primarily based on its view that there was no contradiction between the positions of the parties as to the law applicable.[13] The exception was the application of EU law, which the tribunal reasoned must be excluded:

> Therefore, when a bilateral investment treaty, such as the Germany-Czech Republic BIT, remains silent as to the applicable law to disputes arising under it, it cannot be considered that the Contracting States, one of which was not even a Member State of the EU at the time of the

11 As noted in Chapter 2, five decisions were brought pursuant to an IIA that included an applicable law clause that did not refer to international law (but nor did the clause exclude international law). For three of these decisions, only the intra-EU objection was raised: *A11Y LTD v Czech Republic* (ICSID Case No UNCT/15/1), Decision on Jurisdiction, 9 February 2017; *WNC Factoring Limited v The Czech Republic* (PCA Case No 2014–34), Award, 22 February 2017; *Anglia Auto Accessories Ltd v Czech Republic* (SCC Case No 2014/181), Final Award, 10 March 2017. A fourth decision also related to the intra-EU objection but also dismissed the application of *lis pendens* on the facts of the dispute: *Ivan Peter Busta and James Peter Busta v Czech Republic* (SCC Case No V2015/014), Final Award, 10 March 2017; The final decision found it not necessary to decide whether the ILC Articles or the *Barcelona Traction* dictum on reflective loss were applicable as the tribunal dismissed the jurisdictional objection on other grounds: *Louis Dreyfus Armateurs SAS v Republic of India* (PCA Case No 2014–26), Award, 11 September 2018. As such, these decisions do not affect the aforementioned results.

12 Supported by the arbitration rules commonly used in ISDS, including UNCITRAL Arbitration Rules (with new article 1, paragraph 4, as adopted in 2013), Art 35(1) which refers to the tribunal applying the law 'which it determines to be appropriate'; see also International Court of Arbitration of the International Chamber of Commerce, Arbitration Rules (in force as from 1 March 2017), Art 21(1).

13 *AMF Aircraftleasing Meier & Fischer GmbH & Co v The Czech Republic* (PCA Case No 2017–15), Final Award, 11 May 2020 [503–4].

> conclusion of the BIT, intended for EU law, a regional sub-system of international law, to apply to the disputes under the BIT.[14]

The reasoning of the tribunal illustrates why broad statements on applicable law are not made in such disputes as the application of general international law is rarely controversial.[15] When dealing with the application of international law disputed between the parties, such as treaty law, the tribunals appear to deal with the specific question and the sources of authority raised by the parties rather than abstract questions of applicable law.

In relation to the language of tribunals, there also appears to be little differentiation based on the existence or lack thereof of an applicable law clause. Some tribunals that are faced with no applicable law clause undertake extensive analysis of the sources of international law to be applied and their authority to do so. For example, in *Chevron and TexPet v Ecuador (II)*, where the tribunal extensively discussed judicial estoppel and its relationship to good faith, with good faith applicable as a general principle of international law under Article 38(1)(c) of the ICJ Statute.[16] However, this does not align with the common legal reasoning used throughout such ISDS decisions. Just like the majority of ISDS decisions with applicable law clauses, tribunals still rely heavily on vague authority and sweeping statements of the applicability of general international law.

1.3 *Comparing ISDS and WTO Practice*

From here, we can consider the second part to the question of the relevance of not having an applicable law clause: whether the similarities between ISDS decisions and the WTO decisions increase when we focus on IIAs lacking an applicable law clause. Given the similarities identified in the previous section between ISDS decisions with applicable law clauses and decisions without

---

14 ibid 374. While this quotation is taken from the tribunal's determination of its jurisdiction, with such law applicable to jurisdiction potentially being different law applicable to the merits, the tribunal reaffirms its conclusion on applicable law in relation to the alleged breaches of the IIA (see [504]).

15 For example, the tribunal in *RosInvest v Russia* noted that the parties agreed that the law applicable to the jurisdictional question was public international law: *RosInvestCo UK Ltd v The Russian Federation* (SCC Case No V079/2005), Award on Jurisdiction, October 2007 [33]; the tribunal made a similar finding in the Final Award: *RosInvestCo UK Ltd v The Russian Federation* (SCC Case No 079/2005), Final Award, 12 September 2010 [249].

16 *Chevron and TexPet v Ecuador (II)* (PCA Case No 2009–23), Second Partial Award on Track II, 30 August 2018 [7.83–87, 7.106–8].

applicable law clauses, together with the tribunals' limited consideration of applicable law where no such clause exists, there seems to be limited utility in comparing this small subset of ISDS decisions to WTO decisions. Rather, we can conclude that there is nothing remarkable between ISDS decisions with or without applicable law clauses that would somehow affect the comparison to WTO decisions. No particular implication from the existence (or lack thereof) of an applicable law clause, nor the language of the applicable law clause, seems to affect this comparative exercise.

Based on these conclusions, applicable law clauses do not play as large a role as the institutional assumption of ISDS may suggest. Applicable law clauses themselves are not enough to explain the openness of dispute settlement mechanisms to other international law. Additional features or something inherent in the nature of the regime may fill the role of broad applicable law clauses in opening the regime to harmonization with general international law, especially when we compare the position of ISDS and WTO decisions where no applicable law clause exists.

Perhaps it is better to understand narrow applicable law clauses as closing tools, rather than wide applicable law clauses (or no clause at all) as opening tools. Nonetheless, the question still remains about how such clauses interact with the closing tool of limited jurisdiction, to be discussed in Chapter 6.

1.4 *Applicable Law and General Principles: the Avoidance of* Non Liquet

From this conclusion, we can turn to the question of narrow applicable law and its impact on the applicability of international law. Prescribing the limits of the law applicable to a dispute reflects the balance between the political and legal actors and institutions: what may States have excluded the tribunal from applying? This balance is reflected in the principle of *non liquet*: the tribunal has jurisdiction but cannot make a substantive legal conclusion on the basis that there is no applicable law, or the applicable law is unclear.[17] It is important to understand this balance when considering the application of other opening tools, particularly general principles which may (or may not) be an applicable source of law under the constitutive treaty. If the applicable law does not include general principles, how is the tribunal to deal with gaps or indeterminacy in the applicable law? This touches the divide between consensual and

17 Joost Pauwelyn, *Conflict of Norms in Public International Law: How WTO Law Relates to Other Rules of International Law* (Cambridge University Press 2003) 454, citing; *Monetary Gold Removed from Rome in 1943 (Italy v France, UK and USA)*, Preliminary Question, Judgment [1954] ICJ Reports 19, 32.

systemic approaches: is the tribunal to fill the gaps through general principles under a systemic approach or must the tribunal adhere to the limited scope of its applicable law?

The inclusion of general principles in the Statute of the PCIJ,[18] the precursor to Article 38 of the ICJ Statute, was designed to avoid the possibility of *non liquet*.[19] Declarations of *non liquet* are rare, yet the ICJ may have implied a *non liquet* in relation to the question of the threat or use of nuclear weapons as an act of self-defence. The ICJ found the law applicable to the question was the use of force enshrined in the UN Charter and the law applicable in armed conflict, together with any specific treaties on nuclear weapons.[20] According to the ICJ, neither international customary law nor any general principle contained any specific prescription authorizing the threat or use of nuclear weapons.[21] By the President's casting vote, the ICJ then held that, while the threat of nuclear weapons would generally be contrary to international law:

> in view of the current state of international law, and of the elements of fact at its disposal, the Court cannot conclude definitively whether the threat or use of nuclear weapons would be lawful or unlawful in an extreme circumstance of self-defence, in which the very survival of a State would be at stake.[22]

---

18 Article 36 of the Statute of the Permanent Court of International Justice (16 December 1920, as amended by Protocol of 14 September 1929). Article 36 is in almost identical terms to Article 38 of the ICJ Statute.

19 See the discussion of the drafting history of the Statute of the PCIJ by Judge Schwebel: *Legality of the Threat or Use of Nuclear Weapons, Advisory Opinion* [1996] ICJ Reports 226, 323; see, further, Pellet who notes that the first purpose of Article 38(1)(c) was to avoid a non liquet: Alain Pellet and Daniel Müller, 'Article 38' in Andreas Zimmermann and others (eds), *The Statute of the International Court of Justice: a commentary* (3rd edn, Oxford University Press 2019) para 251 ff; Mads Andenas and Ludovica Chiussi, 'Cohesion, Convergence and Coherence of International Law' in Mads Andenas and others (eds), *General Principles and the Coherence of International Law* (Brill Nijhoff 2019) 14; Marija Đorđeska, *General Principles of Law Recognized by Civilized Nations (1922–2018): The Evolution of the Third Source of International Law Through the Jurisprudence of the Permanent Court of International Justice and the International Court of Justice* (Brill Nijhoff 2020) 31 ff; Patrick Dumberry, *A Guide to General Principles of Law in International Investment Arbitration* (Oxford University Press 2020) 50 ff.

20 *Legality of the Threat or Use of Nuclear Weapons, Advisory Opinion* (n 19) para 34; referring to Article 2 and 51 of the Charter of the United Nations (San Francisco, 24 October 1945), 1 UNTS XVI.

21 *Legality of the Threat or Use of Nuclear Weapons, Advisory Opinion* (n 19) para [52].

22 ibid 266, operative paragraph 2E and [97].

The ICJ did not expressly proclaim a *non liquet* in its reasoning, but some dissenting judges considered that this was the effect of the ICJ's position.[23] While declaration of *non liquet* may be more acceptable in advisory opinions,[24] there are still limited examples of *non liquet*. This reflects a general aversion to acknowledging any incompleteness to international law, whether based on an international judicial function approach or a state sovereignty approach. However, the approaches differ on why international law is "complete". On the one hand, international law has mechanisms in which to fill the indeterminacy of international law, namely the development of law as inherent in the judicial function through recourse to general principles of law. On the other hand, what is not explicitly prohibited by international law is permitted, thereby there is no lacuna in the law. This approach is based on the *Lotus* reasoning[25] and is generally thought to flow from the sovereignty of states.[26] This tension is played out in the separate and dissenting opinions in *Nuclear Weapons*. For example, Judge Higgins considered it was "precisely the role" of the ICJ and "exactly the judicial function to take principles of general application, to elaborate their meaning and to apply them to specific situations".[27] Comparatively, Judge Shahabuddeen considered there was no *non liquet*: whether the Court's position was one of prohibition or one of authorization, there is no room unoccupied by international law.[28] In this way, the principle of *non liquet* touches on the role of international adjudicators: is it appropriate for judges to decide issues according to their conception of the legal order or should courts play a more narrow technical role?[29]

Proclaiming a *non liquet* is to be distinguished from declining jurisdiction. Rather, the tribunal has jurisdiction but cannot make a substantive legal conclusion on the basis that there is no applicable law or it is impossible to

23 See, for example, Judge Higgins and Judge Shahabuddeen: ibid 389, 583.

24 See discussion in Prosper Weil, '"The Court Cannot Conclude Definitively" … Non Liquet Revisited' (1998) 36 Columbia Journal of Transnational Law 109, 114.

25 *SS Lotus (France v Turkey)*, Judgment [1927] PCIJ Series A No 10.

26 Fitzmaurice refers to these approaches as the 'extreme positivist' view and the 'natural law school' as considering gaps to be filled by general principles: Gerald Fitzmaurice, *The General Principles of International Law: Considered from the Standpoint of the Rule of Law* (Sitjhoff 1957) 55. See the discussion on the two approaches in Daniel Bodansky, 'Non Liquet and the Incompleteness of International Law' in Laurence Boisson de Chazournes and Philippe Sands (eds), *International Law, the International Court of Justice and Nuclear Weapons* (Cambridge University Press 1999) 161; and Weil (n 24) 110 ff.

27 *Legality of the Threat or Use of Nuclear Weapons, Advisory Opinion* (n 19) 591; see also, the opinion of Judge Schwebel, p 323.

28 ibid 390.

29 Bodansky (n 26) 166–7.

determine which two contradictory norms may be applied.[30] As Judge Higgins considered, reasons of propriety or important defects in procedure have been given in declining to answer questions, but the *non liquet* in prior ICJ cases had not been due to deficiencies in the law.[31] While declining jurisdiction may be common, particularly in investor-state tribunals, neither of the dispute settlement mechanisms have expressly proclaimed a *non liquet*.[32]

For the WTO, the DSU is not clear whether a tribunal can proclaim a *non liquet*. During negotiations, suggestions to the text of Article 3.2 of the DSU that would have enabled any indeterminacy to be referred to the General Council were not adopted.[33] According to the DSU, panels and the Appellate Body are only obliged to make decisions when this will assist the DSB in exercising its responsibilities. This explains the reasoning behind the exercise of judicial economy by panels and the Appellate Body:

> [A] panel has to address those claims on which a finding is necessary in order to enable the DSB to make sufficiently precise recommendations and rulings so as to allow for prompt compliance by a Member with those recommendations and rulings 'in order to ensure effective resolution of disputes to the benefit of all Members'.[34]

30 Pauwelyn (n 17) 151, 454; Bodansky (n 26) 155.

31 *Legality of the Threat or Use of Nuclear Weapons, Advisory Opinion* (n 19) 591, referring to *Monetary Gold Removed from Rome in 1943* (*Italy v France, UK and USA*), Preliminary Question, Judgment (n 17); and *Northern Cameroons* (*Cameroon v United Kingdom*), Preliminary Objections [1963] ICJ Reports 14.

32 Although there may be examples where the tribunal has identified a lacuna in the law but found it unnecessary to address how the lacuna is to be overcome. See, for example, *United States – Anti-Dumping Measures on Certain Hot-Rolled Steel Products from Japan* (*Report of the Appellate Body*) (24 July 2001), WT/DS184/AB/R [126], where the Appellate Body identified a lacuna in Article 9.4 of the Anti-Dumping Agreement but found it unnecessary to overcome since the issue was not raised in the appeal. As such, falling into the category of 'reasons of propriety' identified in Judge Higgins as reason to decline to answer a legal question.

33 Kenya suggested the addition of the following paragraph to Article 3.2: '[w]hen, in the course of proceedings before a panel or the Appellate Body, a question arises on whether or not there is a conflict between provisions of any covered Agreement or between any covered Agreements, the panel or Appellate Body shall refer the matter to the General Council for a determination. In reaching the determination, the General Council may exercise the authority conferred under paragraph 2 of Art IX of the WTO Agreement', cited in Lorand Bartels, 'The Separation of Powers in the WTO: How to Avoid Judicial Activism' (2004) 53 International and Comparative Law Quarterly 861, 873.

34 *Australia – Measures Affecting the Importation of Salmon* (*Report of the Appellate Body*) (6 November 1998), WT/DS18/AB/R [233].

Based on this reasoning, Bartels concludes that it is reasonable to suggest that where the law is indeterminate, it would be more appropriate in discharging their duty to address the relevant provisions of the covered agreements for panels and the Appellate Body to make a statement to this effect, rather than a finding based on indeterminate law.[35] Pauwelyn, on the other hand, considers that a panel can only proclaim a *non liquet* in extreme circumstances of non-resolvable conflicts, more likely between provisions within the WTO agreements rather than between WTO provisions and other norms.[36] No panel or the Appellate Body has expressly referred to the principle of *non liquet*, with only some limited references in submissions of the EC in two disputes.[37] Instead, panels and the Appellate Body seek to resolve the silence and obscurity of the law through the application of non-WTO law, as confirmed by the empirical results in this study.

The greater flexibility assumed in the applicable law in ISDS is reflected in the prohibition on *non liquet* in investor-state disputes, both in practice and under the ICSID Convention. Tribunals have expressly recognized that they should not declare *non liquet*. For example in *Windstream Energy v Canada*, the tribunal recognized that it cannot simply declare *non liquet* in circumstances where parties had not adduced evidence of the content of a rule of customary international law.[38] In *Tenaris v Venezuela (II)*, the Annulment Committee noted that the burden of proof allows tribunals to avoid declaring *non liquet*.[39] This jurisprudence is supported by Article 42(2) of the ICSID Convention that prohibits the declaration of *non liquet* on the ground of silence or obscurity of the law.

In summary, while WTO panels and the Appellate Body have not expressly declared *non liquet*, scholarly debate exists on whether panels should declare *non liquet* in the absence of WTO law on the issue. Comparatively, investor-state tribunals have expressed the prohibition against *non liquet*. With the existence of indeterminacy in the applicable treaties and in the absence of declarations of *non liquet*, it is clear from Chapter 3 that other international law is being

35 Bartels (n 33) 877.

36 Pauwelyn (n 17) 419–22, 454.

37 *United States – Measures Affecting Trade in Large Civil Aircraft (Second Complaint) – Recourse to Article 21.5 of the* DSU *by the European Union (Report of the Panel)* (9 June 2017), WT/DS353/RW; *European Communities – Customs Classification of Frozen Boneless Chicken Cuts (Report of the Appellate Body)* (12 September 2005), WT/DS269/AB/R ; WT/DS286/AB/R [129].

38 *Windstream Energy v Canada* (PCA Case No 2013–22), Award, 27 September 2016 [351].

39 *Tenaris SA & Talta v Venezuela (II)* (ICSID Case No ARB/12/23), Decision on Annulment, 28 December 2018 [94].

applied by the dispute settlement mechanisms. The following section considers the gap-filling process and systemic integration used by the tribunals to "complete the law". When we start to drill further down into the application of different sources of law and the legal basis for that application, will we see further practical differences between the WTO and ISDS? An approach inspired by the international judicial function would suggest not as general principles and coherency of international law should be applicable in both regimes. On the other hand, a consensual approach may suggest a smaller role for general principles in WTO law, on the basis of the brevity of investment law treaties compared to the applicable WTO law as well as the limited jurisdiction and applicable law of the WTO dispute settlement mechanisms in relation to violations under specific treaty provisions.

2 General Principles

General principles fulfil an essential function of gap-filling international law.[40] Stemming from this function, they play a broader function in promoting the coherence of international law, contributing to the systemization of international law:

> The question of coherence in international law is an existential one. The lack of a centralized legislator at the international level has often triggered fears about the possible effect of contradictions between international legal norms. It has also raised questions about possible lacunae in international law, and its corollary, the potential declaration by the Court of a *non liquet*. General principles have proved effective in helping the Court to address both structural problems of law-making in international society and to promote coherence.[41]

40 Marcelo Vázquez-Bermúdez, 'Third Report on General Principles of Law by Marcelo Vázquez-Bermúdez, Special Rapporteur' (International Law Commission 2022) A/CN.4/753 15. Recently, there has been substantial academic work on general principles, which this section builds on. See, for example, Dumberry (n 19); Andrea Gattini, Attila Tanzi and Filippo Fontanelli (eds), *General Principles of Law and International Investment Arbitration* (Brill Nijhoff 2018); Mariana Clara de Andrade, 'General Principles of Procedural Law in the Practice of the WTO Appellate Body' (2021) 24 International Community Law Review 444; Đorđeska (n 19).

41 'Statement of H.E. Mr. Abdulqawi Ahmed Yusuf, President of the International Court of Justice before the Sixth Committee of the General Assembly, New York' para 37; cited by Vázquez-Bermúdez (n 40) 50; see also Campbell McLachlan, 'Investment Treaties and

This section compares the approach to general principles in investment arbitration and the WTO to reveal to what extent general principles are being utilized not only for their essential function of filling lacunae, but also their broader role in the coherency of international law.

Some investor-state tribunals have explained the basis for the gap-filling role of general principles, relying on the similarity in applicable law language to Article 38(1)(c) of the ICJ Statute[42] to ground the application of general principles. As the tribunal in *National Grid v Argentina* summarized:

> The Treaty, however, is not a self-contained, stand-alone legal framework, but rather an international bilateral treaty which must be "integrated" with underlying principles of international law in order to fill its gaps. Thus the remission in [the BIT's applicable law clause] to "the applicable principles of international law."[43]

WTO panels and the Appellate Body have not expressed the function of general principles quite as clearly. The *Korea – Government Procurement* panel referred to the role of customary international law as applicable where the WTO agreements do not "contract out" from it. In its reasoning, the Panel does not refer to the incompleteness of WTO law and the requirement to "fill its gaps" as investor-state tribunals have done, but rather the application of customary law where "there is no conflict or inconsistency, or an expression in a covered WTO agreement that implies differently."[44] Such language is in line with the DSU on

---

General International Law' (2008) 57 International & Comparative Law Quarterly 361, 361, who describes, '[i]nternational law ... may not contain, and generally does not contain, express rules decisive of particular cases; but the function of jurisprudence is to resolve the conflict of opposing rights and interests by applying, in default of any specific provisions of law, the corollaries of general principles, and so to find ... the solution of the problem'.

42 Article 38(1) of the ICJ Statute has been referred to by 19 investor-state tribunals within the study in relation to interpreting the applicable law clause of the IIA, the role of judicial decisions in international law or Article 31(3)(c) of the VCLT. See, for example, *Cairn Energy PLC and Cairn UK Holdings Limited (CUHL) v Republic of India* (PCA Case No 2016–07), Award, 21 December 2020 [1738]; *Renco Group Inc v Republic of Peru (II)* (PCA Case No 2019–46), Decision on Expedited Preliminary Objections, 30 June 2020 [214]; *Eskosol S.pA in liquidazione v Italian Republic* (ICSID Case No ARB/15/50), Decision on Termination Request and Intra-EU Objection, 7 May 2019 [115–6].

43 *National Grid PLC v The Argentine Republic* (ad hoc, UNCITRAL), Award, 3 November 2008 [87]. Although the tribunal referred to principles of international law, it went on to apply the customary defence of necessity.

44 *Korea – Measures Affecting Government Procurement (Report of the Panel)* (1 May 2000) WT/DS163/R [7.96].

the role in "clarifying" the existing provisions of the WTO covered agreements, the lack of an express prohibition on *non liquet* and no applicable law clause in the same vein as Article 38 of the ICJ Statute.[45]

Exemplifying the inconsistency of approaches, other investor-state tribunals have adopted more similar language to WTO panels, pointing away from the gap-filling role of general principles:

> The principles of international law, which have an unquestionable importance in treaty interpretation, do not allow an arbitral tribunal to write new, additional requirements – which the drafters did not include – into a treaty, no matter how auspicious or appropriate they may appear.[46]

As already elucidated, the applicable law clauses of IIAs are substantially similar. This is also the case for the two quotations above, for which both IIAs refer to "principles of international law",[47] which does not explain the different perspectives on the role of general principles. When we turn to analysing some general principles in action in these regimes, will we find greater similarity or even more divergence in the treatment of general principles. Can we distil a

45 As a result, the Appellate Body has only referred to Article 38(1) of the ICJ Statute in order to interpret the meaning of Article 31(3)(c) of the VCLT: *United States – Definitive Anti-Dumping and Countervailing Duties on Certain Products from China* (*Report of the Appellate Body*) (11 March 2011), WT/DS379/AB/R [308]; or, in the role of 'teachings' in international law: *United States – Section 110(5) of the US Copyright Act* (*Report of the Panel*) (15 June 2000), WT/DS160/R [6.111]. Although parties have raised arguments on Article 38(1) which were not dealt with by the panel or Appellate Body. For example, Canada's argument that the precautionary principle was an 'emerging principle' which may then crystallize into a general principle under Article 38(1)(c). *European Communities – Measures Concerning Meat and Meat Products (Hormones)* (*Report of the Appellate Body*) (16 January 1998), WT/DS26/AB/R ; WT/DS48/AB/R [122].

46 *Hulley Enterprises v Russia* (PCA Case No 2005–03/AA26), Interim Award on Jurisdiction and Admissibility, 30 November 2009 [415]; see, also, the decisions in the parallel proceedings: *Veteran Petroleum Limited v The Russian Federation* (PCA Case No 2005–05/AA28), Interim Award on Jurisdiction and Admissibility, 30 November 2009 [415]; and *Yukos Universal Limited (Isle of Man) v The Russian Federation* (PCA Case No 2005–04/AA27), Interim Award on Jurisdiction and Admissibility, 30 November 2009 [415].

47 The applicable law clause in *National Grid* refers to 'the applicable principles of international law': Agreement between the Government of the United Kingdom and Northern Ireland and the Government of the Republic of Argentina for the Promotion and Protection of Investments (London, 11 December 1990), Article 8.4; while the applicable law in *Hulley v Russia* is covered by Article 26(6) of The Energy Charter Treaty (Lisbon, 17 December 1994), 2080 UNTS 95, referring to the 'applicable rules and principles of international law'.

broader function of systemizing international law as present within the adjudicator's mind?

2.1 *General Principles in Numbers*

The empirical analysis of the decisions of these two dispute settlement mechanisms in Chapter 3 provided an indication of the abundance of general principles in disputes. As illustrated in Table 5 and Figure 9, general principles were the most considered source of law before the tribunals, accounting for roughly 33% of instances of other international law before both the WTO and investor-state tribunals. Expanding from this, we can also ask whether the source of the other international law influences tribunal reasoning. Are tribunals more likely to take into account or apply general principles of law? For this purpose, Figure 13 compares the percentage of instances in which treaties and general principles were taken into account. Treaties and general principles are two dissimilar sources of law, with different functions and different influences on the view of the system of international law: one based more clearly on state sovereignty and consent, and the other important in gap-filling and resolving indeterminacy from the state-created rules.

Comparing the raw percentages of instances of treaty and general international law taken into account by the tribunals is quite surprising. Figure 13 displays an almost even incorporation of treaties and general principles

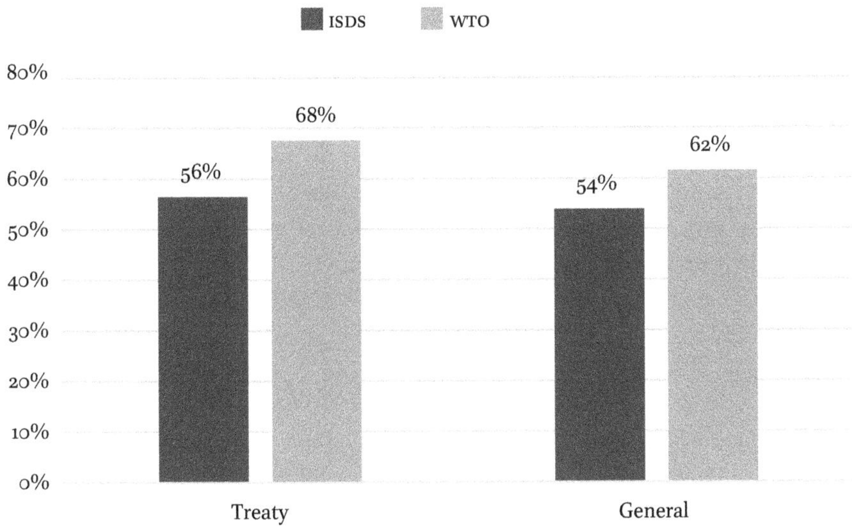

FIGURE 13 Percentage of instances of treaty and general principles taken into account

within each dispute settlement mechanism, with only a 2 to 6% difference.[48] Yet, a larger percentage of both treaties and general principles are taken into account in WTO disputes. The smaller percentage of general principles applied in investor-state tribunals is partly explainable by the choice in the study to classify dismissal on the facts as not taking that other international law into account, with the reasons for that choice set out in Chapter 3 (section 1.2.2) above. Many general principles, such as *res judicata, lis pendens* and estoppel, were treated by investor-state tribunals as not applicable on the facts of the dispute. If such reasoning was treated as an implicit acceptance of the general principle, then this likely creates a much more favorable treatment of general principles in ISDS, creating a parallel with the treatment of general principles by WTO panels and the Appellate Body. This would also tip the scales in favor of adoption of general principles in ISDS, compared to treaty-law.

The analogous acceptance of treaty and general principles of international law is not neatly explained based on an assumption of the openness of the regimes. Further digging would be required to consider whether the incorporation of other treaty law is a result of the general nature of a large number of treaties brought before the dispute settlement mechanism (as shown in Table 7). Nonetheless, the results illustrate the irrelevance of the source of law in explaining what other law is being taken into account by tribunals as well as the positive signs of a system of international law and consideration of other specialized areas of international law.

A further investigation is to consider for what purpose or function are general principles applied by the adjudicators. As set out in the Introduction (section 3), a number of questions were asked when reviewing the jurisprudence, the third of which is relevant here: how was that other international law used by the tribunal? The following categories were applied in the empirical analysis:

a. Gap-filling or supplementing treaty: tribunal does not refer to interpreting a particular provision but rather appears to apply other law where there is no relevant WTO or IIA provision;
b. Clarify meaning: tribunal refers to international law in interpreting a particular provision of the WTO agreements or IIA;

48 For this comparison, the references to the EU treaties have been taken out of the investor-state data. Due to the large number of decisions dealing with the intra-EU objection, the potential conflict between investor-state dispute settlement and the EU treaties and the overwhelming rejection of such conflict (and thus, rejection of the application of the EU treaties), the inclusion of the intra-EU objection decisions would not accurately reflect how investor-state tribunals deal with treaties on a more general basis.

c. Support conclusion: tribunal finds particular application or interpretation of the WTO agreements or IIA, based only on those agreements, and then refers to the other law as merely supporting that prior conclusion.

It is not always possible to clearly distinguish between these categories, particularly where the tribunal is gap-filling a treaty or clarifying the meaning of an existing provision.[49] To answer in simple terms, the distinction is whether a relevant treaty provision exists. If no such provision exists, then the tribunal is likely to be exercising a gap-filling function. A clear example is the application of the customary principles of reparation in investor-state claims relating to FET, where the IIA only provides for compensation for expropriation.[50] The more difficult case is where there is an existing treaty provision and the tribunal "reads in" a condition into an existing clause, for example, the condition of non-contribution in the customary rules on necessity, which is discussed in section 3.3 below. For the purposes of the classification on the use of other international law, the focus is on the tribunal's reasoning, rather than the "correctness" of the application of each instance of other international law by the tribunals. As such, while it may be difficult to clearly distinguish between the categories, the classification is guided by how the adjudicators themselves explain how they have used the other international law.

Figure 14 provides one of the greatest differences between WTO and investor-state tribunals in the empirical analysis, yet also one of the few empirical results that appears to prove the assumption of the restrictiveness of WTO dispute resolution. As suggested by its very name, gap-filling requires "gaps" in the substantive law of these regimes. We may not be surprised that there are less lacunae within the extensive WTO agreements compared to the handful of

49 While there may be some overlap between the clarification of the meaning of a provision and the tribunal referring to other international law to support its conclusion, the research is most interested in the gap-filling process so the important focus in the categorization is between gap-filling and the other two categories.

50 See, for example, *Siemens AG v Argentine Republic* (ICSID Case No ARB/02/8), Award, 6 February 2007 [349]: '[t]he law applicable to the determination of compensation for a breach of such Treaty obligations is customary international law. The Treaty itself only provides for compensation for expropriation in accordance with the terms of the Treaty'; see also, *Greentech Energy Systems A/S, NovEnergia II Energy & Environment (SCA) SICAR, and NovEnergia II Italian Portfolio SA v The Italian Republic* (SCC Case No V 2015/095), Award, 23 December 2018 [548]: '[t]he Tribunal agrees with Claimants that, absent an applicable treaty provision on damages, the Chorzów Factory "full compensation" standard is the appropriate starting point for quantum assessment. The Tribunal finds that this general standard applies to FET, umbrella clause, and other treaty violations, and is therefore not limited to cases of expropriation'.

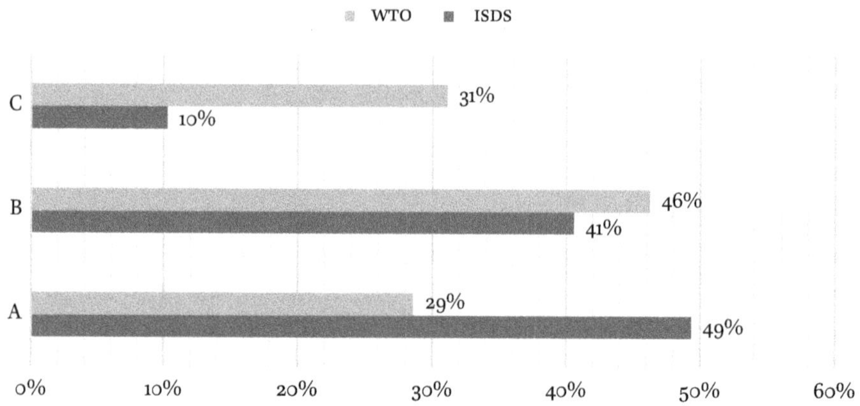

FIGURE 14 How other law is applied in the decisions

provisions in most litigated IIAs.[51] Particularly when we take into account the need to rely on the secondary rules of customary international law in investor-state disputes, which accounts for 44% of the gap-filling exercise. However, the greater proportion of other law being used simply to support the conclusion of the WTO panels and Appellate Body is noteworthy. Although other law is not playing a leading role in decisions of the WTO dispute settlement mechanism, the fact that WTO panels and the Appellate Body continue to refer to such law to support their conclusion, which is based otherwise on internal WTO law, lends support to a systemic view of international law and the possibilities for the international legal order to bring legitimacy to its regimes.

Limiting this analysis to how general principles were applied, the results become a lot more similar. The predominant use of general principles in the decisions of these tribunals is in gap-filling, supporting the international judicial function's direction to fill lacunae in law and create coherence between regimes. For investor-state tribunals, the use of general principles is proportionally higher in gap-filling than compared to all other international law (49% of all other international law compared to 61% of instances

51 Whether more recently negotiated IIAs may fill some of these gaps is a question for further research. Although, Alschner has concluded that the impact of arbitration on investment rulemaking is surprisingly small: Wolfgang Alschner, 'The Impact of Investment Arbitration on Investment Treaty Design: Myths versus Reality' (2017) 42 Yale Journal of International Law 1. In this respect, the average year of signature for IIAs in the relevant decisions is 1993, with the newest IIA in 2014.

of general principles). For the WTO panels and Appellate Body, it is an even more striking increase in gap-filling, with only 29% of all other law being used in gap-filling compared to 50% of general principles. Certainly, these results indicate a direction toward the international judicial function and the necessity of general principles to fill lacunae in both of the systems. When we compare the results of WTO and investor-state tribunals to each other, unsurprisingly, general principles are more frequently used in gap-filling in ISDS disputes, although perhaps not as significantly as the assumptions based on the treaty-texts would suggest. Interestingly, the WTO method of application of general principles much more closely matches the treatment given by investor-state adjudicators than the aggregated results on all other international law. As such, Figure 15 below appears much more homogenous than Figure 14.

2.2 *General Principles in Practice*

However, as with our empirical results in Chapter 3, quantitative approaches only show part of the story and more in-depth analysis of the legal reasoning on gap-filling is required. In this respect, general principles that relate to rights to bring action, such as those grounded in good faith and equity, are a good example of showing the gap-filling process at work in the jurisdictional phase. These principles are often raised as jurisdictional defences by the respondents or in order to coordinate jurisdictional collisions and are not expressly included in many of the treaties conferring jurisdiction on the tribunals.

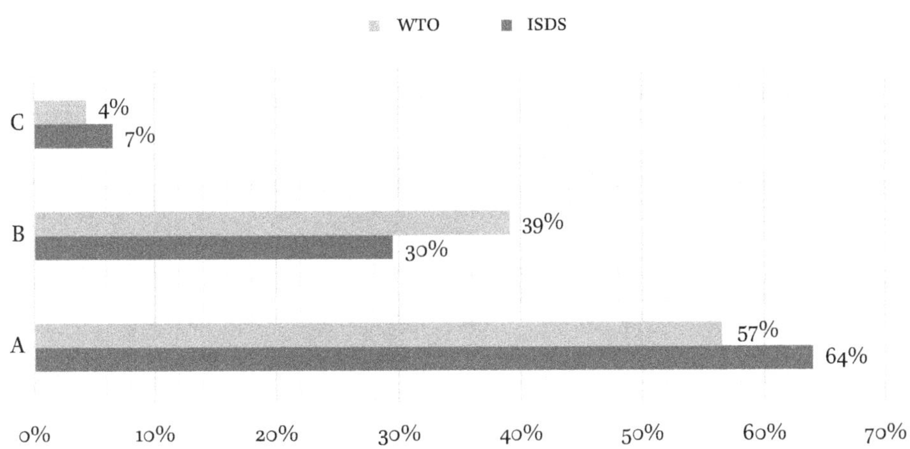

FIGURE 15 How general principles are applied

2.2.1 Good Faith

First, good faith as a limit on the exercise of treaty-based powers (rather than good faith as a limit on interpretative discretion).[52] This is a rather broad catch-all for a number of variations on "good faith"[53] relating to the performance of treaty obligations, ranging from Article 18 and 26 of the VCLT,[54] to clean hands[55] and abuse of rights.[56] As the ICJ explained in *Nuclear Tests*:

> One of the basic principles governing the creation and performance of legal obligations, whatever their source, is the principle of good faith. Trust and confidence are inherent in international co-operation, in particular in an age when this co-operation in many fields is becoming increasingly essential.[57]

The WTO DSU does refer to "good faith" in the narrow concept of engaging in dispute settlement procedures in good faith in an effort to resolve the dispute.[58] A broader notion of good faith in relation to substantive obligations is

---

52 On both aspects of good faith, including the distinction between the two, see Ulf Linderfalk, 'General Principles as Principles of International Legal Pragmatics: The Relevance of Good Faith for the Application of Treaty Law' in Mads Andenas and others (eds), *General Principles and the Coherence of International Law* (Brill Nijhoff 2019).

53 Good faith is a rather elusive concept, as Cheng explained: '[w]hat exactly this principle implies is perhaps difficult to define. As an English judge once said, such rudimentary terms applicable to human conduct as "Good Faith", "Honesty", or "Malice" elude a priori definition. 'They can be illustrated but not defined"': Bin Cheng, *General Principles of Law as Applied by International Courts and Tribunals* (reprint 2006, Steven & Sons 1953) 105.

54 Article 18 concerns the obligation not to defeat the object and purpose of a treaty prior to its entry into force while Article 26 codifies the *pacta sunt servanda* rule: Vienna Convention on the Law of Treaties (Vienna, 23 May 1969), 1155 UNTS 331.

55 'Clean hands' refers to the principle that 'he who comes to equity for relief must come with clean hands'. As Fitzmaurice transposed to the international sphere: 'thus a State which is guilty of illegal conduct may be deprived of the necessary *locus standi judicio* for complaining of corresponding illegalities on the part of other states, especially if these were consequential on or were embarked upon in order to counter its own illegality': Fitzmaurice (n 26) 119.

56 Abuse of rights 'is merely an application of this principle [of good faith] to the exercise of rights': Cheng (n 53) 121.

57 *Nuclear Tests* (*Australia v France*), Merits, Judgment [1974] ICJ Reports 253 [46].

58 Understanding on Rules and Procedures Governing the Settlement of Disputes, Marrakesh Agreement Establishing the World Trade Organization, Annex 2 (15 April 1994), 1869 UNTS 401, Article 3.10. The full text of that provision states: 'It is understood that requests for conciliation and the use of the dispute settlement procedures should not

not directly in the treaty-text, as such, a lacuna could be seen to exist. The WTO panels and Appellate Body have been generally reluctant to apply the general principle of good faith unless specific language in support of such inclusion can be found in WTO law, suggesting more of a role for general principles as supportive interpretive material rather than a separate obligation.[59] In *Peru – Agricultural Products*, the Appellate Body considered that good faith, in terms of Article 18 of the VCLT, only formally enters WTO law to the extent that it is incorporated through the texts of the covered agreements.[60] When it came to illegal acts,[61] the Appellate Body in *Mexico – Soft Drinks* refused to decide whether the doctrine was part of WTO law. Even if it had been applicable, the Appellate Body noted that it would require a determination of obligations under a treaty outside its jurisdiction.[62] In a similar fashion, the Appellate Body considered that the alleged breach of the international law principle of good faith in the performance of treaty obligations was not within the terms of reference of the panel in *US – Hot-Rolled Carbon Steel Flat Products from India*.[63] While breach of the general international obligation of good faith may be difficult to apply in WTO law, the presumption of good faith does find a

be intended or considered as contentious acts and that, if a dispute arises, all Members will engage in these procedures in good faith in an effort to resolve the dispute. It is also understood that complaints and counter-complaints in regard to distinct matters should not be linked'.

59 See, similar conclusion of Mitchell: 'WTO Tribunals have shown some reluctance to find that a Member has failed to act in good faith. At the same time, WTO Tribunals have sometimes been keen to leave open the possibility that they could make such a finding in an appropriate case. If a WTO Tribunal were ever to find a Member had failed to act in good faith independent of any WTO provision, it would need a solid legal basis for doing so within its mandate as a judicial body and taking into account the relevant provisions of the DSU. I see none': Andrew Mitchell, *Legal Principles in WTO Disputes* (Cambridge University Press 2008) 144.

60 *Peru – Additional Duty on Imports of Certain Agricultural Products* (*Report of the Appellate Body*) (20 July 2015) WT/DS457/AB/R [5.28].

61 This general principle, with substantive and procedural implications, refers to the fact that one party cannot avail themselves of the fact that the other has not fulfilled some obligations if the former party has, by some illegal act, prevented the fulfilment of that obligation: *Factory at Chorzów* (*Germany v Poland*), *Jurisdiction* [1927] PCIJ Rep Series A No 9 31; *Gabčíkovo-Nagymaros Project* (*Hungary v Slovakia*), *Judgment* [1997] ICJ Rep 7 [110]; Đorđeska (n 19) 112, 399.

62 *Mexico – Tax Measures on Soft Drinks and Other Beverages* (*Report of the Appellate Body*) (6 March 2006) WT/DS308/AB/R [55–56].

63 *United States – Countervailing Measures on Certain Hot-Rolled Carbon Steel Flat Products from India* (*Report of the Appellate Body*) (8 December 2014), WT/DS/436/AB/R [4.333–4].

foothold. In *US – Continued Suspension of Obligations in the* EC*-Hormones Dispute*, the Appellate Body considered that the principle of good faith was well recognized in international law and applies in WTO dispute settlement; therefore, Members may be presumed to have acted in good faith when implementing the DSB's recommendations.[64]

Unlike the WTO panels and Appellate Body, allegations of lack of good faith have been raised a significant number of times in investor-state disputes, in particular, good faith in relation to the conduct of the investor. Whether that is described in the form of the doctrine of clean hands, illegality or international public policy, its roots lie in good faith. Good faith may condition the eligibility for legal protection of the investment, as a jurisdictional or admissibility criterion, as well as assessing the host state's responsibility.[65] In considering the approach to good faith on the part of the investor, separate types of conduct must be distinguished: conduct at the time of making the investment and conduct during the investment. The condition for eligibility for legal protection, particularly in relation to the conduct at establishment of the investment, can be a jurisdictional issue as legality clauses requiring compliance with domestic laws are often found in an IIA's definition of investment.[66] Tribunals may then rely on that legality requirement as *lex specialis*.[67] Where such clauses are not included, tribunals have referred to the "well-established principle of international law that a tribunal constituted on the basis of an investment treaty has no jurisdiction over a claimant's investment which was made illegally in

64 *United States/Canada – Continued Suspension of Obligations in the* EC*-Hormones Dispute* (*Report of the Appellate Body*) (16 October 2008), WT/DS320/AB/R ; WT/DS321/AB/R [314–5].

65 Attila Tanzi, 'The Relevance of the Foreign Investor's Good Faith' in Andrea Gattini, Attila Tanzi and Filippo Fontanelli (eds), *General Principles of Law and International Investment Arbitration* (Brill Nijhoff 2018) 195.

66 ibid 197; whether the good faith objection is a bar to jurisdiction or a defence on the merits depends on the wording of the IIA: *Metal-Tech Ltd v Republic of Uzbekistan* (ICSID Case No ARB/10/3), Award, 4 October 2013 [127].

67 For example, in *Kim v Republic of Uzbekistan* (ICSID Case No ARB/13/6), Decision on Jurisdiction, 8 March 2017 [370], the tribunal noted that 'the presence of an explicit legality requirement … defines the jurisdictional impact of a legality requirement, thereby displacing any implicit legality requirement as regards jurisdictional questions'.

violation" of domestic laws.[68] If not a jurisdictional issue, a lack of good faith on the part of the investor may also result in the inadmissibility of the claims.[69]

Most successful jurisdictional objections based on good faith primarily concerned the establishment of the investment, rather than the conduct of the investment. Tribunals have used various terminology for issues falling within the good faith of investors and varied reasoning as to how that principle applies in decisions in which the IIA does not include such legality requirements. It is not necessary to consider whether there is a distinction in principle based on the different terminology used by the tribunals. Tribunals themselves seem to dwell little on the difference between these principles. The underlying feature, regardless of the terminology used, is the good faith on the part of the investor and its application to the time of entry of the investment, even in the absence of a legality clause in the IIA. For example:

a. In *Fraport v The Philippines (II)*, the IIA in question included an explicit legality requirement of "acceptance in accordance with host state laws". Nonetheless, the tribunal recognized illegality "as to essence of the investment" as an "increasingly well-established international principle which makes international legal remedies unavailable", even if there had been no explicit legality requirements in the IIA.[70] Since the IIA included an

68 *Ampal-American Israel Corporation v Arab Republic of Egypt* (ICSID Case No ARB/12/11), Award, 1 February 2016 [301]; see, also *Plama Consortium Limited v Republic of Bulgaria* (ICSID Case No ARB/03/24), Award, 27 August 2008 [138–9] which determined that, despite the lack of a domestic legality clause in the ECT, '[t]his does not mean, however, that the protections provided for by the ECT cover all kinds of investments, including those contrary to domestic or international law. [...] The Arbitral Tribunal concludes that the substantive protections of the ECT cannot apply to investments that are made contrary to law'; *Phoenix Action v Czech Republic* (ICSID Case No ARB/06/5), Award, 15 April 2009 [78]; *Mamidoil Jetoil Greek Petroleum Products Societe SA v Republic of Albania* (ICSID Case No ARB/11/24), Award, 30 March 2015 [294]; *Fraport AG Frankfurt Airport Services Worldwide v Republic of the Philippines (II)* (ICSID Case No ARB/11/12), Award, 12 December 2014 [332]; cf. *Stati v Kazakhstan* (SCC Case No 116/2010), Award, 19 December 2013 [812], where the tribunal considered that the drafters of the ECT could have written such a requirement into the text and so the tribunal could not see where such a requirement could come from.

69 Tanzi (n 65) 199, who notes that even if inadmissibility is not expressly mentioned, it can be read into the language of those decisions that do not mention a lack of jurisdiction but consider treaty protection does not apply to the investment. This reflects the blurred lines between jurisdiction and admissibility objections in international dispute settlement.

70 *Fraport v the Philippines* (II) (n 68) para 332.

explicit legality requirement, it was not strictly necessary for the tribunal to consider the applicability of good faith as a general principle.[71]

b. In *Blusun v Italy,* the tribunal recognized that even though the ECT does not lay down an explicit requirement of legality, the principle of international public order meant that the ECT did not cover investments which are unlawful at the time of establishment.[72] However, the tribunal found it was not necessary to decide whether there exists a generic "clean hands" defence or ground of inadmissibility in international investment law.[73]

c. In *Metal-Tech v Uzbekistan,* the tribunal found that a breach of the general prohibition of abuse of rights, which is a manifestation of the principle of good faith, may give rise to an objection to jurisdiction or to a defence on the merits.[74] Further, the investor could not rely on an MFN clause to overcome the legality requirement of the IIA.[75] After reviewing the text of the IIA, the tribunal concluded that the investment must be legal when it is initially established.[76]

As to the legality of the performance of an investment, the situation is opaquer. The tribunal in *Churchill Mining v Indonesia* had recourse to principles of international law to determine the consequences of such conduct given the IIA only contained admission requirements.[77] The tribunal referred to abuse of rights (as an emanation of the principle of good faith), international public policy and the "common law doctrine of unclean hands [that] has also found expression at the international level".[78] On the basis of "the legal principles just set forth", but particularly international public policy, the tribunal considered that forgery made the claim inadmissible.[79] However, we can also find examples in which tribunals have considered that one of these principles were not

71 ibid [333].

72 *Blusun SA, Jean-Pierre Lecorcier and Michael Stein v Italian Republic* (ICSID Case No ARB/14/3), Award, 27 December 2016 [264].

73 ibid [273].

74 *Metal-Tech Ltd. v Republic of Uzbekistan* (n 66) para 127. Although the tribunal considered this was based on the IIA and was not part of the objective definition of the term 'investment' in Article 25 of the ICSID Convention.

75 ibid [163].

76 ibid [193]. The tribunal ultimately found that there was corruption under domestic host state law. As such, the tribunal did not have to take the further step in finding conduct contrary to international public policy: [374].

77 *Churchill Mining PLC and Planet Mining Pty Ltd v Republic of Indonesia* (ICSID Case No ARB/12/14 and 12/40), Award, 6 December 2016 [488].

78 ibid [492–3].

79 ibid [507–8].

in fact a general principle applicable to the dispute. For example, in *Hulley v Russia*, the tribunal was not persuaded that the principle of unclean hands was a separate applicable source of law, within the meaning of "general principle of law" in Article 38(1)(c) of the ICJ Statute. As such, there was no legality requirement as to the conduct of the investment.[80] The tribunal did, however, find that a legality requirement at the establishment of the investment could be read into the ECT.[81]

2.2.2 Estoppel

Turning to the second general principle, estoppel, which is said to relate to principles of good faith and equity.[82] Broadly, estoppel involves a statement or representation by one party which is relied on by the other party to the second party's detriment.[83] The first party is then estopped from withdrawing that statement. Estoppel may relate to the jurisdiction of the tribunals by estopping one of the parties from relying on a particular jurisdictional avenue or objection[84] or, in very particular circumstances, for a state to be bound by a treaty to which it had not formally acceded.[85] In the WTO, estoppel has been

80 *Hulley Enterprises v Russia* (PCA Case No 2005–03/AA226), Final Award, 18 July 2014 [1357–8]; see, also, the parallel proceedings: *Veteran Petroleum Limited v The Russian Federation* (PCA Case No 2005–05/AA28), Final Award, 18 July 2014; *Yukos Universal Limited (Isle of Man) v The Russian Federation* (PCA Case No 2005–04/AA27), Final Award, 18 July 2014.

81 *Hulley Enterprises v Russia* (n 80) para 1347 ff; see also, the parallel proceedings: *Veteran Petroleum Limited v The Russian Federation* (n 80); *Yukos Universal Limited (Isle of Man) v The Russian Federation* (n 80).

82 For example, the ICJ observed that the concepts of acquiescence and estoppel, 'irrespective of the status accorded to them by international law, both follow from the fundamental principles of good faith and equity': *Delimitation of the Maritime Boundary in the Gulf of Maine Area (Canada v United States of America), Judgment* [1984] ICJ Reports 246 [130]; similarly, the ICJ has stated that '[t]he Court cannot regard Nicaragua's reliance on the optional clause as in any way contrary to good faith or equity; nor can Nicaragua be taken to come within the criterion of the North Sea Continental Shelf case, and the invocation of estoppel by the United States of America cannot be said to apply to it': *Military and Paramilitary Activities in and Against Nicaragua (Nicaragua v United States of America), Jurisdiction and Admissibility* [1984] ICJ Reports 392 [51].

83 As recently summarized in *Obligation to Negotiate Access to the Pacific Ocean (Bolivia v Chile)*, Judgment [2018] ICJ Reports 507 [158].

84 For example, the US argued that Nicaragua was estopped from invoking compulsory jurisdiction under Article 36 of the ICJ Statute: *Military and Paramilitary Activities in and Against Nicaragua (Nicaragua v United States of America), Jurisdiction and Admissibility* (n 82) para 48. Tanzi also notes that when states resort to the clean hands doctrine, claimants may counteract by invoking the principle of estoppel: Tanzi (n 65) 209.

85 For example, in *North Sea Continental Shelf (Federal Republic of Germany v Denmark), Judgment* [1969] ICJ Reports 3, 25, the ICJ considered that 'only the existence of a situation

raised in 9 decisions and was dismissed on the facts in 6 of the decisions. All decisions occurred in 2008 and before. Most relevantly, the Appellate Body in EC – *Sugar* chose not to decide whether estoppel was a general principle applicable in WTO law and, rather, dismissed the argument on the facts of the individual dispute. However, in doing so, the Appellate Body stated:

> We see little in the DSU that explicitly limits the rights of WTO Members to bring an action; WTO Members must exercise their "judgement as to whether action under these procedures would be fruitful", by virtue of Article 3.7 of the DSU, and they must engage in dispute settlement procedures in good faith, by virtue of Article 3.10 of the DSU. This latter obligation covers, in our view, the entire spectrum of dispute settlement, from the point of initiation of a case through implementation. Thus, even assuming arguendo that the principle of estoppel could apply in the WTO, its application would fall within these narrow parameters set out in the DSU.[86]

Prior to the Appellate Body's decision in *EC – Sugar*, panels had more decisively stated that there was no basis in WTO or international law for such an estoppel argument.[87]

---

of estoppel could suffice to lend substance to [the contention that the Federal Republic of Germany was bound by the Geneva Convention on the Continental Shelf] ... that is to say if the Federal Republic were now precluded from denying the applicability of the conventional regime, by reason of past conduct, declarations, etc., which not only clearly and consistently evinced acceptance of that regime, but also had caused Denmark or the Netherlands, in reliance on such conduct, detrimentally to change position or suffer some prejudice'.

86 *European Communities – Export Subsidies on Sugar* (*Report of the Appellate Body*) (28 April 2005), WT/DS265/AB/R ; WT/DS266/AB/R ; WT/DS283/AB/R [3.12]; this was then cited as the applicable standard in *European Communities – Regime for the Importation, Sale and Distribution of Bananas – Second Recourse to Article 21.5* (*Report of the Appellate Body*) (26 November 2008), WT/DS27/AB/RW/USA ; WT/DS27/AB/RW2/ECU [227]. A potential criticism of this decision is that it was not clear how the 'shared understanding' was supposed to fit into the elements of estoppel. As Mitchell argued, 'had the Appellate Body better shown more confidence in addressing this claim, it might have more carefully evaluated its meaning in international law, thereby providing clearer and better reasoning for its conclusion': Mitchell (n 59) 133.

87 *Guatemala – Definitive Anti-Dumping Measures on Grey Portland Cement from Mexico* (*Report of the Panel*) (24 October 2000), WT/DS156/R [8.24]; *European Communities – Anti-Dumping Duties on Imports of Cotton-Type Bed Linen from India – Recourse to Article 21.5 of the DSU by India* (*Report of the Panel*) (29 November 2002), WT/DS141/RW [6.91]. Mitchell refers to some of these decisions exhibiting 'unnecessary hostility to this important expression of the principle of good faith': Mitchell (n 59) 127.

Comparatively, estoppel has been raised in 54 decisions of investor-state tribunals. The tribunals have considered estoppel to be a general principle or "well established in international law".[88] Nevertheless, tribunals usually dismiss the application of estoppel on the basis of the facts of the dispute,[89] like their WTO counterparts, or find it unnecessary to decide after dealing with potentially "easier" jurisdictional arguments.[90] More detailed discussion of the application of estoppel is rare. In *Besserglik v Mozambique*, the tribunal emphatically rejected the estoppel argument whereby the claimant argued a state that had implicitly consented to jurisdiction through words, conduct or silence should be estopped from objecting to jurisdiction. The tribunal stated that the requirement of reciprocal notifications under the IIA could not be presumed to be in existence by the doctrine of estoppel, nor more generally can the jurisdiction of the tribunal be created by invoking estoppel.[91] This is a rather rare example of invoking the doctrine of estoppel, namely in implying consent. More commonly, estoppel is raised in relation to estopping the respondent from rescinding or withdrawing its consent to jurisdiction. As such, *Besserglik* does not represent a strong disavowal of the doctrine of estoppel in ISDS. When the tribunals do consider estoppel as a general principle, they fail to go any further in setting out their authority or reasoning for applying the general principles, thereby failing to apply a conscious and transparent standard of reasoning.

2.2.3 Coordinating Jurisdictions

The gap-filling role of general principles may also overcome the concerns of fragmentation through the application of general principles relevant to

88 *Canfor v USA* (ad hoc), Order of the Consolidation Tribunal, 7 September 2005 [168]; *Pan American Energy v Argentina; BP v Argentina* (ICSID Case No ARB/03/13 and 04/8), Decision on Preliminary Objection, 27 July 2006 [159]; *Mamidoil Jetoil v Albania* (n 68) paras 469–70; see, also, Dumberry (n 19) 166 ff.

89 Each of the decisions in the preceding footnote found the factual elements of estoppel were not fulfilled. See also, recent examples of *EuroGas Inc and Belmont Resources Inc v Slovak Republic* (ICSID Case No ARB/14/14), Award, 18 August 2017 [433]; *Tethyan Copper Company Pty Limited v Islamic Republic of Pakistan* (ICSID Case No ARB/12/1), Decision on Jurisdiction and Liability, 10 November 2017 [667], concerning issue/collateral estoppel; *UAB E energija (Lithuania) v Republic of Latvia* (ICSID Case No ARB/12/33), Award, 22 December 2017 [533].

90 See, for example, *Salini Impregilo S.pA v Argentine Republic* (ICSID Case No ARB/15/39), Decision on Jurisdiction and Admissibility, 23 February 2018 [150]; and *Kim v Republic of Uzbekistan* (n 67) para 539.

91 *Besserglik v Mozambique* (ICSID Case No ARB(AF)/14/2), Award, 28 October 2019 [418–423], although the tribunal did go on to confirm that even if estoppel were, in principle, capable of giving rise to jurisdiction, the factual circumstances for estoppel did not exist.

coordinating jurisdictions. In particular, procedural rules such as *res judicata* and *lis pendens* help to manage proceedings before a diverse set of fora. However, analysis of the decisions suggests that there is a long way to go in such a cooperation approach. As Boisson de Chazournes notes, adapting the traditional methods of dealing with conflicting jurisdiction through procedural rules to the international level is a new trend,[92] the kinks of which are still being worked out by WTO and ISDS adjudicators.

In the WTO, procedural and equitable tools, particularly *lis pendens* but also *res judicata*, are very rarely referred to, let alone applied. No WTO panel or Appellate Body has referred to the doctrine of *lis pendens*. In the first case to consider *res judicata*, the Panel in *India – Measures Affecting the Automotive Sector* avoided the question of the applicability of *res judicata*, in relation to India's argument that the US was re-litigating a matter decided in *India – Quantitative Restrictions*,[93] as the requirements of the doctrine had not been fulfilled on the facts.[94] Panels have received some assistance from the doctrine of *res judicata* in clarifying meaning of certain WTO provisions and doctrines, including the meaning of "judicial decisions" and the "preclusion doctrine", being the limitation on the scope of Article 21.5 compliance proceedings.[95] However, little more is said in relation to the application (or lack thereof) of the doctrine in WTO proceedings. While *res judicata* has been raised in

92 Laurence Boisson de Chazournes, 'Plurality in the Fabric of International Courts and Tribunals: The Threads of a Managerial Approach' (2017) 28 European Journal of International Law 13, 46.

93 *India – Quantitative Restrictions on Imports of Agricultural, Textile and Industrial Products* (*Report of the Appellate Body*) (23 August 1999), WT/DS90/AB/R.

94 The Panel noted that the 'general question as to the applicability of the doctrine of *res judicata* to WTO dispute settlement is of systemic importance… In the absence of any clear guidance, many interpretative issues would thus need to be considered in determining whether the doctrine of *res judicata* applies in WTO dispute settlement in circumstances where the facts would support such an assertion. However, the potential relevance of the notion of *res judicata* to this case would only arise if it is commonly understood conditions of application were met on the facts': *India – Measures Affecting the Automotive Sector* (*Report of the Panel*) (21 December 2001), WT/DS146/R ; WT/DS175/R [7.55–7.59, 7.103].

95 *Thailand – Customs and Fiscal Measures on Cigarettes from the Philippines – Recourse to article 21.5 of the DSU by the Philippines* (*Report of the Panel*) (12 November 2018), WT/DS371/RW, fn 1033.

6 decisions,[96] it has only been raised in the context of prior WTO decisions, rather than as a coordination tool between international tribunals.[97]

Comparatively, investor-state respondents seem more willing to argue for the application of such rules, at least *res judicata*. Yet, the international investment sphere has still proved a fairly inappropriate arena for the application of such principles given the difficulty with meeting the preconditions of these principles within the investor-state context. In particular, the triple identity test and the requirement of hierarchically similar courts is problematic where parallel proceedings are brought under different international investment agreements or before separate international courts.[98] Investment treaties and arbitration rules rarely include guidance on issues of concurrent proceedings.[99] In the analysed ISDS decisions *lis pendens* has been raised in 12 decisions but was ultimately not applied in any of those decisions.[100] Only one decision determined that the doctrine is not applicable law on the basis of the terms of the IIA, as reference to international arbitration was available

96 This denotes the number of decisions in which the panel or Appellate Body itself has referred to *res judicata*. The principle has been raised by parties to the dispute in 21 decisions but, ultimately not considered by the panel or Appellate Body in the majority of those decisions.

97 An exception to this would have been Paraguay's argument, as a third party, invoking *res judicata* in relation to the MERCOSUR rulings. However, Argentina did not raise the argument and the Panel considered that Paraguay did not have the right to determine the scope of any preliminary issues. As such, the Panel did not consider *res judicata* as a preliminary issue: *Argentina – Definitive Anti-Dumping Duties on Poultry from Brazil* (*Report of the Panel*) (22 April 2003), WT/DS241/R, fn 53.

98 See a summary of the preconditions for application of *res judicata* and *lis pendens* in Philipp Janig and August Reinisch, 'General Principles and the Coherence of International Investment Law: Of Res Judicata, Lis Pendens and the Value of Precedents' in Mads Andenas and others (eds), *General Principles and the Coherence of International Law* (Brill Nijhoff 2019) 258 ff.

99 'Possible Future Work in the Field of Dispute Settlement: Concurrent Proceedings in International Arbitration' (United Nations Commission on International Trade Law 2017) A/CN.9/915 para 10.

100 Boisson de Chazournes refers to *lis pendens* being applied in *SPP v Egypt*, in which the ICSID tribunal did suspend proceedings while parallel proceedings in the Cour de Cassation were ongoing: Boisson de Chazournes (n 92) 47–48. However, the tribunal's jurisdiction in this dispute was based on the Egyptian investment law, rather than an IIA. As such, it does not fall within the case selection of this research: *Southern Pacific Properties (Middle East) Ltd v Arab Republic of Egypt* (ICSID Case No ARB/84/3, Preliminary Objections to Jurisdiction, 14 April 1988.

"irrespective" of any domestic actions.[101] The remaining 11 decisions dismissed the application of the doctrine based on the facts of the case without considering the nature of the doctrine and its applicability in the context of international investment law.[102]

The applicability of *res judicata*, compared to *lis pendens*, appears to be more accepted in ISDS. *Res judicata* has been raised in 49 ISDS decisions but was only found applicable in 23 decisions. From this much smaller number of applications of the *res judicata* principle it should not be inferred that *res judicata* is not a general principle of international law, as may be the case for *lis pendens*. Rather, it reflects the difficulty with lumping all *res judicata* references together. Much like *lis pendens*, the different jurisdictional and applicable law clauses at play in the multiple proceedings may prohibit the application of *res judicata* in certain circumstances.[103] This is exemplified by the *Perenco v Ecuador* tribunal which was faced with two *rei judicatae*: *res judicata* of another investor-state tribunal and the *res judicata* effect of the tribunal's earlier decision in the *Perenco* proceedings. The earlier decision of the same tribunal was *res judicata* and, on general principle, binding on the parties, while the decision rendered in a parallel investor-state proceeding (reflected in a settlement in the *Burlington v Ecuador* proceedings)[104] was not.[105] In its reasoning, the tribunal referred to the de-centralized international legal regime in which tribunals only have jurisdiction over certain investment treaties and only over the particular parties to the dispute.[106] In this way, *res judicata* applied by investor-state tribunals has been a tool in avoiding multiple proceedings within ISDS, thereby ensuring

101 *Sedelmayer v Russia* (ad hoc), Arbitration Award, 7 July 1998 74.

102 *Thomas Gosling and others v Republic of Mauritius* (ICSID Case No ARB/16/32), Award, 18 February 2020; *Hydro S.r.l and others v Republic of Albania* (ICSID Case No ARB/15/28), Award, 24 April 2019; *Unión Fenosa Gas v Egypt* (n 8); *Busta v Czech Republic* (n 11); *Sanum Investments v Laos (I)* (PCA Case No 2013–13), Award on Jurisdiction, 13 December 2013; *EDF International v Argentina* (ICSID Case No ARB/03/23), Award, 11 June 2012; *EDF (Services) v Romania* (ICSID Case No ARB/05/13), Award, 8 October 2009; *AMTO v Ukraine* (SCC Case No 080/2005), Final Award, 26 March 2008; *SGS Société Générale de Surveillance SA v Islamic Republic of Pakistan* (ICSID Case No ARB/01/13), Decision on Jurisdiction, 6 August 2003; *CME Czech Republic BV v Czech Republic* (ad hoc), Final Award, 14 March 2003; *Lauder v Czech Republic* (ad hoc), Final Award, 5 September 2001.

103 For discussion, see Christoph H Schreuer, 'Multiple Proceedings' in Andrea Gattini, Attila Tanzi and Filippo Fontanelli (eds), *General Principles of Law and International Investment Arbitration* (Brill Nijhoff 2018).

104 *Burlington Resources Inc v Republic of Ecuador* (ICSID Case No ARB/08/5), Decision on Ecuador's Counterclaims, 7 February 2017.

105 *Perenco Ecuador Ltd v Republic of Ecuador and Empresa Estatal Petróleos del Ecuador* (ICSID Case No ARB/08/6), Award, 27 September 2019 [491–2].

106 ibid [496].

legal certainty within the regime of international law.[107] However, it has little application beyond the individual proceedings[108] and even its application to earlier decisions in the same proceedings has not been universal.[109]

These tools of coordinating jurisdiction could be effective in managing parallel litigations and addressing that key concern of fragmentation. While we can consider whether such principles should be applied on the basis of a systemic view or consensual view of international law, in filling gaps in the regime law, the results suggest that such an examination is not yet necessary. The use of such principles in the WTO and investor-state tribunal decisions appears to have little relevance to coordinating jurisdictions within the international legal order. Rather, such principles have primarily been used in ensuring consistency within the individual regimes or between the regime and domestic orders, rather than the international legal order more broadly.

2.2.4 Conclusion on General Principles in Practice

The preceding analysis of these general principles[110] indicates that the WTO panels and Appellate Body have generally been slower and more cautious in recognizing a role for general principles of international law.[111] For the Appellate Body, there has been more general reliance on refusing to decide either way, thereby avoiding the tough jurisdictional question. This supports our

107 In accepting *res judicata* of a denial of jurisdiction in the *Iberdrola (I)* proceedings, the tribunal in *Iberdrola Energía, SA v Republic of Guatemala (II)* (PCA Case No 2017–41), Final Award, 24 August 2020 [309] stated: 'the fact is that *res judicata* pursues an important policy objective, namely, avoiding that the same issues be litigated over and over again and thereby ensuring legal certainty. As noted by the ICJ, "the principle of *res judicata* [...] protects, at the same time, the judicial function of a court or tribunal and the parties to a case which has led to a judgment that is final and without appeal".'

108 *Res judicata* has also been raised in relation to domestic proceedings. While *res judicata* was found to be applicable to investor-state disputes as a matter of principle in some of these decisions, the application of the principle to domestic proceedings was dismissed in all decisions.

109 The tribunal in RWE *v Spain* considered its decision on jurisdiction was 'binding' but was not res judicata as such: *RWE Innogy GmbH and RWE Innogy Aersa SAU v Kingdom of Spain* (ICSID Case No ARB/14/34), Award, 18 December 2020 [89].

110 This is only a small snapshot of the application (or not) of general principles. There may be other explanations for the failure to apply general principles, such as the exceptional circumstances under which estoppel can be found or the legal insecurity that may surround good faith. See, for example, Tanzi who notes that tribunals might be wary of basing their decisions on good faith alone as its legal insecurity may lead to risks of arbitrariness: Tanzi (n 65) 194; similarly, Mitchell refers to the 'nebulous nature of good faith' as intensifying the difficulties with relying on the principle within the WTO: Mitchell (n 59) 143–4. As such, a complete conclusion is difficult to draw from this sample of cases.

111 See, also Andrew Lang, 'Twenty Years of the WTO Appellate Body's "Fragmentation Jurisprudence"' (2015) 14 Journal of International Trade Law and Policy 116, 118.

assumption of the openness of the WTO compared to ISDS in relation to other public international law, exemplified on the debate as to whether *non liquet* can be declared in WTO disputes.[112] While not a self-contained regime, as exemplified in the empirical results in Chapter 3, the WTO panels and Appellate Body do not lean into their international judicial function as much as their ISDS counterparts do (or perhaps are required to). In this way, the role of dispute settlement design becomes more apparent as we dig deeper into the quantitative and qualitative analysis of the decisions of these dispute settlement mechanisms.

2.3 *Coherence and Systemization: the Broader Function of General Principles*

As the ILC identified and confirmed in the previous subsections, the primary task of general principles is gap-filling the constitutive treaty of a tribunal. However, in filling lacunae, general principles may also contribute to the completeness of a legal system. When considered in light of the international legal system, this gap-filling function "reinforces and protects the systemic fabric" of international law.[113] In this way, general principles could:

> help [smooth] certain tensions inherent in legal pluralism, by ensuring a minimum openness and conversation between legal orders, regimes and sub-regimes, precluding them from living in clinical isolation from each other.[114]

From the examination of the general principles discussed in the previous subsection, the inconsistent approach to general principles in ISDS and the generally reluctant approach of WTO panels and the Appellate Body only just enables the conclusion of the gap-filling function of the general principles, let alone the positive use in the coherence of the international legal system. We find some examples of the tribunals applying general principles in this way, as illustrated in the empirical results and the analytical discussion the previous section. However, general principles could play a much larger role in situating the regimes within the general international legal order. This is exemplified in

112 Lang also refers to the structural position of the Appellate Body – asked to address sensitive questions without the clear legitimacy needed to do so: ibid 123.

113 Andenas and Chiussi (n 19) 14.

114 Jan Wouters and others, 'General Principles and the Coherence of International Law: Setting the Scene' in Mads Andenas and others (eds), *General Principles and the Coherence of International Law* (Brill Nijhoff 2019) 5.

the differential treatment of the principle of good faith. Special Rapporteur Vázquez-Bermúdez referred to good faith as an example of general principles that are aimed at performing the function of coherence and systemization in a more direct way.[115] While good faith is broadly accepted by the adjudicators, the particular principles falling within good faith, such as illegality and clean hands, remain blurry.

General principles, through their systemic function, could potentially shield the dispute settlement mechanisms from backlash against the legitimacy of the systems.[116] Such an approach would be in line with the international judicial function's lawmaking for coherency of international law, but may be problematic for these specialist and limited jurisdiction tribunals. As Kleinlein notes for specialized tribunals, there may be a tension between efficiently developing the specialized law of their regime, potentially contributing to fragmentation, and exercising lawmaking authority more generally in international law by mediating between different issue areas.[117] The significant amount of discretion placed in the hands of the arbitrator when it comes to general principles plays into the hands of uncertainty:

> Systematic use of discretion by third-party adjudicators, of course, would not contribute to strengthen the legitimacy of investment arbitration. General principles operate ad hoc, their application depending on specific instances of normative ambiguity or unusual factual patterns. They are more than gap-fillers, but they cannot attain the front stage; in a sense, systematic recourse to general principles would call into question the viability of the treaty régime that fuels and sustains investment arbitration.[118]

---

115 Vázquez-Bermúdez (n 40) 52; referring to Cheng (n 53) 118, who referred to good faith as 'necessary for the functioning of the legal system'.

116 This is also the conclusion of Dumberry: Dumberry (n 19).

117 Kleinlein notes that the general lawmaking authority beyond the individual regime requires opening up the perspective and broadening the applicable law: Thomas Kleinlein, 'Judicial Lawmaking by Judicial Restraint? The Potential of Balancing in International Economic Law' in Armin von Bogdandy and Ingo Venzke (eds), *International Judicial Lawmaking: On Public Authority and Democratic Legitimation in Global Governance* (Springer 2012) 258.

118 Andrea Gattini, Attila Tanzi and Filippo Fontanelli, 'Under the Hood of Investment Arbitration: General Principles of Law' in Andrea Gattini, Attila Tanzi and Filippo Fontanelli (eds), *General Principles of Law and International Investment Arbitration* (Brill Nijhoff 2018) 20; see also, Giorgio Gaja, 'General Principles of Law', *Max Planck Encyclopedia of Public International Law* (Oxford University Press 2020) para 31.

This ends with specialized courts locating themselves within the "embrace of general international law" but finding their own different (or perhaps limited) way to do so, according to their regime's particular culture.[119]

3 Systemic Integration

Article 31(3)(c) of the VCLT is described as the "clearest formal expression of the systemic nature of international law".[120] Although the principle of systemic integration, to which Article 31(3)(c) is said to give expression, was included in the treaty interpretation process in Article 31 of the VCLT, the principle was largely left undiscovered until the recent defragmentation efforts. In the ILC's Fragmentation Report, the principle of systemic integration was essential "to keep alive, any sense of the common good of humankind, not reducible to the good of any particular institution or 'regime'."[121] By utilizing the principle of systemic integration, the judge is offered the option of taking into account the system of international law, and thereby acts as a bridge between a single rule and the system of international law.[122] According to the ILC's Fragmentation Report:

> ... all international law exists in systemic relationship with other law, no such application can take place without situating the relevant jurisdiction-endowing instrument in its normative environment. This means that although a tribunal may only have jurisdiction in regard to a particular instrument, it must always interpret and apply that instrument in its relationship to its normative environment – that is to say "other" international law.[123]

119 Rosalyn Higgins, 'The ICJ, the ECJ, and the Integrity of International Law' (2003) 52 International and Comparative Law Quarterly 1, 9–10.

120 Koskenniemi (n 1) para 420; see also, Panos Merkouris, *Article 31(3)(c) VCLT and the Principle of Systemic Integration: Normative Shadows in Plato's Cave* (Brill Nijhoff 2015) 5.

121 Koskenniemi (n 1) para 480.

122 Merkouris (n 120) 6 and 303 in which Merkouris noted that '[b]y allowing judges to take into account rules of international law, within the limits prescribed by Article 31(3)(c), what is being achieved is what Klabbers very succinctly described as "unity in fragmentation"'; citing Jan Klabbers, 'Reluctant Grundnormen: Articles 31(3)(c) and 42 of the Vienna Convention on the Law of Treaties and the Fragmentation of International Law' in Matthew Craven, Malgosia Fitzmaurice and Maria Vogiatzi (eds), *Time, History and International Law* (Brill Nijhoff 2007) 159.

123 Koskenniemi (n 1) para 423.

Argued in this way, the function of the principle is more than merely restating the applicability of general international law, but rather "to take into account the normative environment more widely".[124] For McLachlan, this principle reflects the fact that treaties are themselves creatures of international law and so must be applied against the background of the general principles of international law.[125] The fundamental nature of this principle leads McLachlan to not simply describe Article 31(3)(c) as customary international law, but rather as a constitutional norm of the international legal system, a technique of interpretation that permits reference to other rules of international law, enabling the harmonization of rules and thereby avoiding conflict of norms.[126] As such, the principle of systemic integration attempts to partially restore the idea of determinacy within international law.[127] Article 31(3)(c) and the principle of systemic integration may also elucidate questions surrounding the relationship between different sources of international law and the consensual nature of international jurisdiction.[128] McLachlan credits the "interplay between the jurisdictional constraints upon the scope of the tribunal's competence and the interpretation of the law to be applied" as a possible explanation for the rising resurgence of Article 31(3)(c) in defragmentation attempts.[129]

3.1 *Systemic Integration and Its Indeterminacy*

The principle of systemic integration requires the tribunal to draw a distinction between using rules of international law as part of the interpretative process and applying the rules of international law directly to the facts, as discussed in Chapter 2 (section 3.3.2) above. However, a fine line must be trodden to ensure treaty interpretation using Article 31(3)(c) is not used "to displace the applicable law".[130] Systemic integration is not an exact science as the ILC's Fragmentation Report highlights. The level of generality with which Article 31(3)(c) has been drafted leaves us with significant uncertainty in how to apply

124 ibid [414–415].

125 Campbell McLachlan, 'The Principle of Systemic Integration and Article 31(3)(c) of the Vienna Convention' (2005) 54 International & Comparative Law Quarterly 279, 280.

126 ibid 280.

127 Gleider I Hernández, 'Interpretation' in Jorg Kammerhofer and Jean D'Aspremont (eds), *International Legal Positivism in a Post-Modern World* (Cambridge University Press 2014) 318.

128 Duncan French, 'Treaty Interpretation and the Incorporation Of Extraneous Legal Rules' (2006) 55 International & Comparative Law Quarterly 281, 283.

129 McLachlan (n 125) 288.

130 *Oil Platforms (Islamic Republic of Iran v United States of America)*, Judgment [2003] ICJ Reports 161, 238 (separate opinion of Judge Higgins).

the provision. The ILC's Fragmentation Report noted the following criticisms that have been levelled against the "substantive and temporal scope as well as the normative force" of the provision:

a. How widely should "other law" be taken into account?
b. What about prior or later law?
c. And what does "taking into account" really mean?[131]

These questions remain despite the application of Article 31(3)(c) by a number of international courts and tribunals. In *Oil Platforms,* where the ICJ acknowledged the pivotal role of Article 31(3)(c) for the first time, the Court gave no further guidance as to when and how it should be applied. This is particularly lamentable when we consider the criticisms of the reasoning in the separate opinions and the extensive application of customary international law using Article 31(3)(c).[132]

The ICJ invoked Article 31(3)(c) to apply general international law, including the UN Charter, on the use of force to assess a bilateral treaty of amity.[133] The Court found that it had jurisdiction under the compromissory clause to decide any question of interpretation or application as to whether the actions were "an unlawful use of force, by reference to international law applicable to this question".[134] Judge Higgins' criticism of the majority approach has gathered much attention, criticizing the majority's invocation of treaty interpretation

131 Koskenniemi (n 1) para 423.

132 McLachlan (n 125) 309.

133 Treaty of Amity, Economic Relations and Consular Rights between the United States and Iran (Tehran, signed 15 August 1955). The jurisdiction of the ICJ was based on Article XXI(2) of the Treaty, which stated that 'any dispute between the High Contracting Parties as to the interpretation or application of the present Treaty, not satisfactorily adjusted by diplomacy, shall be submitted to the [ICJ]'. The particular provision of the Treaty the subject of the interpretation states that the treaty shall not preclude the application of measures 'necessary to fulfill the obligations of a High Contracting Party for the maintenance or restoration of international peace and security, or necessary to protect its essential security interests'.

134 In determining the interpretative authority under article 31(3)(c), the ICJ stated: "under the general rules of treaty interpretation, as reflected in the 1969 Vienna Convention on the Law of Treaties, interpretation must take into account 'any relevant rules of international law applicable in the relations between the parties' (Art. 31, para. 3[c]). The Court cannot accept that Article XX, paragraph 1(d), of the 1955 Treaty was intended to operate wholly independently of the relevant rules of international law on the use of force, so as to be capable of being successfully invoked, even in the limited context of a claim for breach of the Treaty, in relation to an unlawful use of force. The application of the relevant rules of international law relating to this question thus forms an integral part of the task of interpretation entrusted to the Court by Article XXI, paragraph 2, of the 1955 Treaty": *Oil Platforms* (n 130) 182–183.

to displace the applicable law.[135] However, Judge Buergenthal's concerns with the Court's approach most emphatically draws out the tension between consensual jurisdiction and reference to "other" international law rules. For Judge Buergenthal, the evasion of the question of jurisdiction by the majority was particularly troubling:

> Whether one likes it or not, that is the consequence of the fact that the Court's jurisdiction, in resolving disputes between the parties before it, is limited to those rules of customary international law and to those treaties with regard to which the parties have accepted the Court's jurisdiction. If it were otherwise, a State that has submitted itself to the Court's jurisdiction for the interpretation of one treaty would suddenly find that it has opened itself up to judicial scrutiny with regard to other more or less relevant treaties between the parties to the dispute that are not covered by the dispute resolution clause of the treaty which conferred jurisdiction on the Court in the first place. This would be the natural consequence of the Court's reliance in this case on Article 31, paragraph 3(c), in order to interpret Article XX, paragraph 1(d). Such a result would conflict with the consensual basis of the Court's jurisdiction and would jeopardize the willingness of States to accept the Court's jurisdiction for the adjudication of disputes relating to the interpretation or application of specific rules of international law.[136]

Judge Buergenthal seemed concerned with the use of the interpretative technique to establish a framework of reasoning that enabled the ICJ to make a preliminary determination as to the legality of US action under general international law.[137] For Judges Buergenthal and Higgins, the crucial distinction between interpretation and application was blurred by the ICJ. In light of the other separate opinions supporting this aspect of the judgment,[138] we cannot

135 Judge Higgins considered that the ICJ did 'not [interpret] Article XX, paragraph 1(d), by reference to the rules of treaty interpretation. It has rather invoked the concept of treaty interpretation to displace the applicable law. It has replaced the terms of Article XX, paragraph 1(d), with those of international law on the use of force and all sight of the text ... is lost': ibid 238.

136 ibid 279.

137 French (n 128) 289.

138 See, for example, the separate opinion of Judge Simma in which he stated: "[t]he Court, in paragraph 41 of the Judgment, thus accepts, and rightly so, the principle according to which the provisions of any treaty have to be interpreted and applied in the light of the treaty law applicable between the parties as well as of the rules of general international

generalize on the appropriateness of the ICJ's approach based on Judge Buergenthal's criticism. However, the concern expressed in this separate opinion reveals the potential for this interpretative provision to be handled improperly, undermining the consensual nature of international dispute settlement and confidence in international justice more generally.[139] The way in which a tribunal approaches the question of the relationship between the opening and closing tools may affect the application of systemic integration to the dispute. The conflation of these two ideas in *Oil Platforms* demonstrates the fine line separating legitimate interpretative practices from others.

3.2 *Systemic Integration in Numbers*

A simple empirical assessment of the use of Article 31(3)(c) by the WTO and ISDS tribunals identifies an important commonality in the use of this interpretation method. Article 31(3)(c) (or references to the principle of "systemic integration") is rarely successfully invoked before these international economic tribunals, as shown in Figure 10. Limiting this empirical assessment to cases where a party or the tribunal has specifically turned their mind to the Article 31(3)(c) argument,[140] we find only 29 WTO panel or Appellate Body reports (representing 32 instances of "other" international law) and 42 ISDS awards (representing 46 instances of "other" international law).[141]

When we breakdown whether the systemic integration argument has been accepted by the tribunals in Table 8, we see a drastic difference between the two mechanisms: investor-state tribunals are more than twice as likely to accept the other international law on the basis of Article 31(3)(c). In comparison, WTO panel and Appellate Body reports are more likely to reject or not deal with the Article 31(3)(c) argument. The prevalence of times that WTO panels and the Appellate Body have determined that it was not necessary to decide or otherwise not deal with the Article 31(3)(c) argument may be partly explainable by the greater reliance on judicial economy in WTO reports and the larger proportion of other law not dealt with by the WTO panels and Appellate Body

law 'surrounding' the treaty. If these general rules of international law are of a peremptory nature, as they undeniably are in our case, then the principle of interpretation just mentioned turns into a legally insurmountable limit to permissible treaty interpretation." *Oil Platforms* (n 130) 330.

139 Richard K Gardiner, *Treaty Interpretation* (2nd edn, Oxford University Press 2015) 283.

140 This removes decisions containing only mere references to Article 31(3)(c) as part of general references to the Vienna Convention in the interpretation process.

141 For the purposes of this analysis, the decisions in which Article 31(3)(c) is only referred to in relation to the intra-EU objection have been excluded. This excludes 27 intra-EU objection decisions.

TABLE 8 References to systemic integration

	WTO		ISDS	
	Instances	Percent	Instances	Percent
Accepted	8	25%	25	54%
Rejected	11	34.3%	12	26%
Not necessary to decide (or not dealt with)[a]	13	40.6%	9	19.5%

a In contrast to earlier sections, the analysis includes references to systemic integration made by the parties to the dispute, even if the tribunals itself did not turn its mind to the argument.

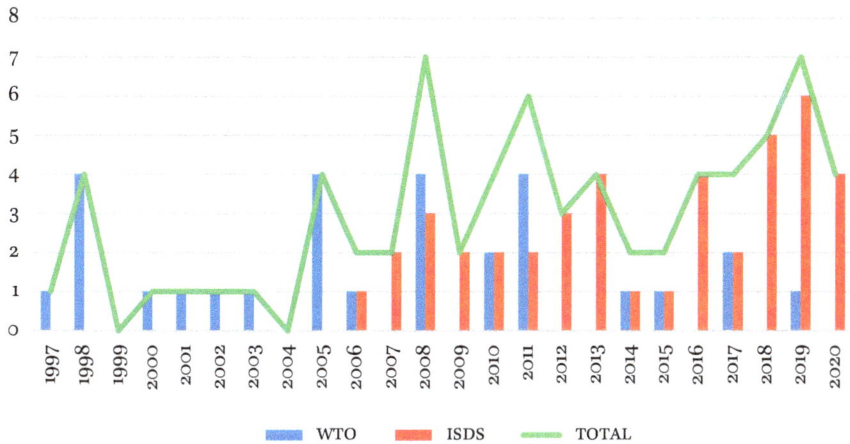

FIGURE 16 Timeline of systemic integration references

more generally, as shown in Figure 8. Continuing with the theme of this Chapter, this indicates a greater use of the adjudicator's toolkit in favor of an open international judicial function by investor-state adjudicators to overcome the otherwise isolated and vague bilateral investment agreements.

We can also see a difference in the temporal spread of decisions dealing with Article 31(3)(c) in Figure 16. In the WTO, there is a more even spread of decisions, whereas most ISDS cases are concentrated in the post-2010 period.[142] In

142 8 cases prior to 2010, compared to 34 cases post-2010.

fact, no ISDS decision considers the relevance of Article 31(3)(c) prior to 2006. As the number of decisions of investor-state tribunals referring to other international law increased in line with the total number of decisions (see Figure 5), it fails to fully explain why the principle was so under-utilized until the most recent decade. Perhaps it is simply a response to the renewed interest in Article 31(3)(c) after the *Oil Platforms* decision and the ILC Fragmentation Report.

When we compare to the total number of instances of other international law utilized by these tribunals, we can see the very small relevance of direct invocation by the parties and reliance by the adjudicators on Article 31(3)(c), illustrated in Table 9. From the standpoint of the formal sources on incorporation of other international law, this is not necessarily problematic as there are other ways in which other international law could be (and indeed has been) taken into account by the tribunals. However, it is problematic if other legal bases relied on by the tribunals are not in fact appropriate or no legal basis is actually supplied by the tribunal. Such concerns cut across jurisdictional authority, applicable law issues and judicial reasoning. As this study focuses on the legal reasoning of the tribunals and their "subjective view of legal correctness", comments on whether such problems in relation to the appropriateness of the legal bases relied on by the tribunals falls outside its scope. Nonetheless, the inconsistency in tribunal reasoning unravels some of the confidence in the objective legal correctness of tribunal reasoning. In addition, Chapter 3 also highlighted the large number of decisions in which the tribunals failed to provide any legal basis for the incorporation of other international law (see Figure 10). As to whether some of the ambiguity in the legal reasoning of the tribunals could be cured through a clear application of the principle of systemic integration is a question for further research.

TABLE 9 Comparison of total instances of PIL compared to systemic integration instances

	WTO		ISDS	
	Instances of systemic integration	**Total instances of other PIL**	**Instances of systemic integration**	**Total instances of other PIL**
Taken into account	8	121	25	536
Not taken into account or not decided	24	70	21	381
Total instances of PIL	32	191	46	917

The small number of direct invocations of Article 31(3)(c) also makes it difficult to conclude on how its use as part of the adjudicator's toolkit contributes to the systemization and coherence of international law. This small number of direct invocations of Article 31(3)(c) does not clearly indicate a system mindset of the adjudicators. However, nor does it indicate a rejection of such systemic ideas. Perhaps the small number of direct invocations is an attempt to avoid the difficult uncertainties still surrounding the formulation and limitations of the language of Article 31(3)(c).

Yet, the relatively low number of *direct* invocations of Article 31(3)(c) does not contribute to consistent approaches to defragmentation. *Indirect* applications of the principle, without referring to the principle as such, contribute to the uncertainty surrounding the system of international law. Arguably, the result of direct and indirect applications is the same, namely other international law is applied in interpreting the treaty in its normative environment. As the Appellate Body confirmed in in *US – Definitive Anti-Dumping*:

> If, as the Panel states, certain ILC Articles have been "cited as containing similar provisions to those in certain areas of the WTO Agreement" or "cited by way of contrast with the provisions of the WTO Agreement", this evinces that these ILC Articles have been "taken into account" in the sense of Article 31(3)(c) by panels and the Appellate Body in these cases.[143]

Inherent or implicit systemic integration may still enhance the coherence of substantive international law by acknowledging the normative environment of the regime.[144] However, it cannot enhance the coherence of the methodology of international law. Any indirect application of the principle of systemic integration without referring to it as such may suggest the tribunals have an insufficient legal basis or authority for the systemic integration of international law. Avoiding the direct reference could be an attempt at avoiding allegations of misapplication of the principle. But it also fails to meet a conscious and transparent standard of legal reasoning, important to the methodology of international adjudication. Indirect applications may obscure the source of judicial authority or normative goals of the adjudicator and thereby do not meet this standard of legal reasoning.

143 *US – Definitive Anti-Dumping (China)* (Appellate Body) (n 45) para 313.

144 See, further, Chapter 3 (section 1.2) on unclear legal bases in the tribunal's reasoning on the application of other international law.

3.3 *Systemic Integration in Practice*

The small number of direct invocations of Article 31(3)(c) begs the question whether it is indicative of a wider problem with the principle of systemic integration. In the regimes of this study, we can identify at least two occasions where the application of the principle of systemic integration has contributed to the consistent inconsistency: the relevance of environmental agreements in the WTO and the customary defence of necessity in investment arbitration.

3.3.1 Environmental Agreements in the WTO

The early decisions in *US – Shrimp* and EC *– Biotech* take competing approaches to the application of environmental agreements through the prism of Article 31(3)(c). While this section is limited to inconsistency in the approach of the WTO dispute settlement mechanism in these decisions, the differing approaches to Article 31(3)(c) also raises systemic questions of coherence of interpretation across international law, not simply the WTO.[145]

In *US – Shrimp*, the Appellate Body expressly turned to international environmental agreements to interpret parts of Article XX(g) of the GATT exception. However, the Appellate Body did not refer to Article 31(3)(c) in undertaking its now famous evolutionary interpretation.[146] Rather, the express reference to Article 31(3)(c) applied to the principle of good faith in interpreting the chapeau of Article XX. In a commonly cited passage, the Appellate Body noted that it was their task "to interpret the language of the chapeau, seeking additional interpretive guidance, as appropriate from the general principles of international law".[147] The Appellate Body then made a footnote reference to Article 31(3)(c).[148] Later, in reasoning the evolutionary interpretation of "exhaustible natural resources" in Article XX(g), the Appellate Body referred

---

145 See Freya Baetens, 'Muddling the Waters of Treaty Interpretation? Relevant Rules of International Law in the MOX Plant OSPAR Arbitration and EC – Biotech Case' (2008) 77 Nordic Journal of International Law 197.

146 *United States – Import Prohibition of Certain Shrimp and Shrimp Products (Report of the Appellate Body)* (12 October 1998), WT/DS58/AB/R [129–130]; on evolutionary interpretation in WTO disputes, see Isabelle Van Damme, 'Understanding the Choice for Evolutionary Interpretation' in Georges Abi-Saab, Gabrielle Marceau and Clément Marquet (eds), *Evolutionary Interpretation and International Law* (Hart 2019); Graham Cook, 'The Illusion of "Evolutionary Interpretation" in WTO Dispute Settlement' in Georges Abi-Saab, Gabrielle Marceau and Clément Marquet (eds), *Evolutionary Interpretation and International Law* (Hart 2019); Gabrielle Marceau, 'Evolutive Interpretation by the WTO Adjudicator' (2018) 21 Journal of International Economic Law 791.

147 *US – Shrimp* (n 146) para 158.

148 ibid fn 157.

to such instruments as UNCLOS,[149] the Rio Declaration,[150] the Convention on Biological Diversity[151] and the Convention on the Conservation of Migratory Species of Wild Animals.[152] These instruments which the Appellate Body considered were "recent acknowledgment by the international community of the importance of concerted bilateral or multilateral action to protect living natural resources" supported its determination that "it is too late in the day to suppose that Article XX(g) … may be read as referring only to the conservation of exhaustible mineral or other non-living natural resources."[153]

As the Appellate Body did not directly refer to Article 31(3)(c) in its interpretative exercise, it is not surprising that the Appellate Body did not undertake an examination of the elements of Article 31(3)(c), even in light of its acknowledgement that parties to the dispute had not ratified all of the international instruments. The Appellate Body in a footnote investigation noted that UNCLOS had not been ratified by Thailand (one of the complainants) or even signed by the US but the US had accepted that "for the most part" the fisheries law in UNCLOS reflects international customary law.[154] The extent that the customary law nature of general sovereign rights over fisheries covers the specific language of conserving and managing "natural resources, whether living or non-living" in UNCLOS is not entirely clear and likely requires a more rigorous consideration under Article 31(3)(c). This may explain the Appellate Body's lack of explicit reliance on Article 31(3)(c) for this section of its reasoning, perhaps reflecting a pragmatic approach to avoiding this question of treaty interpretation.

The Panel in the subsequent Article 21.5 compliance proceedings attempted to overcome this question of the Appellate Body's implicit application of Article 31(3)(c). First, the Panel explicitly referred to Article 31(3)(c) when addressing the Appellate Body's reference to the multilateral environmental

---

149 The Appellate Body referred to Article 56 on defining the jurisdictional rights of coastal states, and Articles 61–2 on the conservation of living resources: United Nations Convention on the Law of the Sea (Montego Bay, 10 December 1982), 1833 UNTS 397.

150 The Appellate Body referred to Agenda 21 as speaking broadly of 'natural resources': Agenda 21, adopted by the United Nations Conference on Environment and Development, 14 June 1992, UN Doc. A/CONF.151/26/Rev.1.

151 The Appellate Body referred to the concept of 'biological resources' in this Convention: Convention on Biological Diversity (Rio de Janeiro, 5 June 1992), 1760 UNTS 79.

152 The Appellate Body referred to the Resolution on Assistance to Developing Countries reciting 'living natural resources': Final Act of the Conference to Conclude a Convention on the Conservation of Migratory Species of Wild Animals (Bonn, 23 June 1979), 19 ILM 11 15.

153 *US – Shrimp* (n 146) para 131.

154 *US – Shrimp* (n 146), fn 110.

agreements,[155] something which the Appellate Body did not do itself. Then, the Panel appears to rectify the Appellate Body's potential error in its interpretation by noting that all parties to the dispute have accepted, or committed to comply with, the international instruments, except for the Convention on the Conservation of Migratory Species of Wild Animals.[156] The Panel did not indicate whether this exception did (or should) have any impact on the interpretative reasoning. In this reference to Article 31(3)(c), the Panel was dealing with a different section of the Article XX analysis, the line of equilibrium, in which the Appellate Body also referred to multilateral environmental agreements, rather than the interpretation of "exhaustible natural resources". However, the Article 31(3)(c) reference by the Panel is still highly pertinent since the same multilateral agreements were the subject of both parts of the Appellate Body's legal reasoning. In particular, it suggests a more flexible interpretation of Article 31(3)(c) that does not require all parties to the dispute to be parties to the treaty being relied on for interpretation. This analysis of Article 31(3)(c) stands in direct contrast with the approach of a later panel in *EC – Biotech*.

The later Panel in *EC – Biotech* appeared to substantially refine these approaches to Article 31(3)(c). Unlike earlier attempts to apply Article 31(3)(c) as an interpretative method, the Panel set out in detail the elements of this provision and considered the textual meaning of "rules of international law". The Panel's interpretation of the elements of Article 31(3)(c) led it to the conclusion that the "rules of international law applicable in the relations between the parties" requires the treaty interpreter to consider rules which are applicable in the relations between all parties to the treaty which is being interpreted. In the Panel's view, this enhances the consistency of the applicable rules and contributes to the avoidance of conflict between the relevant rules.[157] The Convention on Biological Diversity was again an interpretative tool before the Panel and, based on its earlier interpretation, the Panel rejected the application of this Convention under the Article 31(3)(c) interpretative method since the US was not a party to the Convention.[158] As the rules of international law

155 *United States – Import Prohibition of Certain Shrimp and Shrimp Products – Recourse to Article 21.5 by Malaysia (Report of the Panel)* (15 June 2001), WT/DS58/RW [5.57].

156 ibid, referring to para 168 of the Appellate Body report. Together with the preamble of the WTO Agreement and the Marrakesh Decision establishing the Committee on Trade and Environment, the international instruments influenced the positioning of the line of equilibrium toward multilateral solutions: see para 5.51–5.58.

157 *European Communities – Regime for the Importation, Sale and Distribution of Bananas – Recourse to Article 21.5 of the DSU by the United States (Report of the Panel)* (19 May 2008), WT/DS27/RW/USA [7.70].

158 ibid [7.74].

in this case were not argued by all parties to the dispute to be relevant to interpretation of the WTO agreements, the Panel did not need to take a position on whether this would change its analysis.[159]

After finding that it was not required to take into account the Convention (or the precautionary principle as a general principle or customary law), the Panel examined whether other rules of international law could be used in interpretation "even if these rules are not applicable in relations between the WTO Members and thus do not fall within the category of rules which is at issue in Article 31(3)(c)."[160] Prompted by comments from the EC, the Panel also distanced its conclusion from the Appellate Body in *US – Shrimp*. The Panel responded to the fact that the Appellate Body had referred to conventions that were not applicable to all disputing parties by noting that this mere fact "does not necessarily mean that a convention cannot shed light on the meaning and scope of a treaty to be interpreted."[161] To distance itself from *US – Shrimp*, the Panel referred more generally to the Appellate Body's use of the international instruments as informative aids and noted that the Appellate Body did not suggest it was doing so under Article 31(3)(c) requirements.[162] The Panel then found it not "necessary or appropriate" to rely on the provisions of the Convention in interpreting the WTO agreements.[163] However, this distancing is not reflected in scholarly commentary on the *US – Shrimp* case, in which the Appellate Body's interpretation of "exhaustible natural resources" is often cited as an example of the application of systemic integration.[164]

3.3.2 Necessity in ISDS

ISDS tribunals have also been plagued by inconsistent approaches to Article 31(3)(c). One clear example is the divergent approach to the relevance of the customary defence of necessity to interpret the IIA defence. The Argentine financial crisis cases, such as *CMS*[165] and *Enron*,[166] were the subject of extensive

159 ibid [7.72].

160 *European Communities – Measures Affecting the Approval and Marketing of Biotech Products (Report of the Panel)* (29 September 2006), WT/DS291/R; WT/DS292/R; WT/DS293/R [7.90].

161 *EC – Bananas (Art 21.5)* (n 157) para 7.94.

162 ibid 7.94, fn 271. The Panel noted that the Appellate Body had not even mentioned Article 31(3)(c).

163 *EC – Biotech* (n 160) para 7.95.

164 See, for example, McLachlan (n 125) 302; Merkouris (n 120) 47.

165 *CMS Gas Transmission v Argentina* (ICSID Case No ARB/01/8), Award, 12 May 2005.

166 *Enron Creditors Recovery Corp and Ponderosa Assets, LP v Argentine Republic* (ICSID Case No ARB/01/3), Award, 22 May 2007.

criticism for the inconsistent approach to the state of necessity defence in the US – Argentina IIA. The development of the jurisprudence in this series of disputes as they progressed through multiple annulment proceedings settled into a *lex specialis* view of the relationship between the customary and treaty defence, as discussed in Chapter 3 (section 2.4) above. Yet, the cases still illustrate an inconsistent approach to the extent to which the customary plea can be used to fill gaps in the IIA language. This question has been clearly played out in the inconsistent approach to the application of Article 31(3)(c) in the *Mobil Exploration* and *El Paso* decisions. In determining whether a condition of non-contribution was included in the IIA provision,[167] vastly different approaches to Article 31(3)(c) and the customary standard were reached.

In *El Paso*, the tribunal referred to the Iran-US Claims Tribunal's reasoning in the *Amoco* case for the fact that, even though a treaty is *lex specialis,* it does not mean that customary international law is not relevant.[168] Relying on this, the tribunal found that Article 25(2) of the ILC Articles was a rule of general international law, applicable between the parties, which, as such, could be used to interpret the IIA provision pursuant to Article 31(3)(c).[169] For the tribunal, this meant that the IIA provision could be interpreted as limiting the invocation of necessity where the party has not created or substantially contributed to it.[170] This was also the approach of the tribunal in *Mobil Exploration*, which was subject to strong dissent by Arbitrator Brotons, who considered the majority had misunderstood the *raison d'être* of Article 31(3)(c):

167 The non-contribution requirement is reflected in Article 25(2) of the ILC Articles which states that 'necessity may not be overlooked by a State as a ground for precluding wrongfulness if: … (b) the State has contributed to the situation of necessity': Responsibility of States for Internationally Wrongful Acts (adopted by the International Law Commission at its fifty-third session, 2001).

168 *El Paso Energy International Company v The Argentine Republic* (ICSID Case No ARB/03/15), Award, 31 October 2011 [616]; referring to *Amoco International Finance Corporation v The Government of the Islamic Republic of Iran and others* (1987) 15 Iran-US CTR 189 [112] where the tribunal stated: '[a]s a *lex specialis* in the relations between the two countries, the Treaty supersedes the *lex generalis*, namely customary international law. This does not mean, however, that the latter is irrelevant in the instant Case. On the contrary, the rules of customary international law may be useful in order to fill in possible lacunae of the Treaty, to ascertain the meaning of undefined terms in its text or, more generally, to aid interpretation and implementation of its provisions'.

169 *El Paso v Argentina* (Award) (n 168) para 621.

170 ibid 624. Argentina appealed this aspect of the tribunal's decision for failure to state reasons. The Annulment Committee dismissed Argentina's application in its entirety and did not comment on the appropriateness of the tribunal's approach to Article 31(3)(c): *El Paso Energy International Company v The Argentine Republic* (ICSID Case No ARB/03/15), Decision of the Ad Hoc Committee on the Application for Annulment of the Argentine Republic, 22 September 2014 [248, 254].

> Relying on Article 31.3(c) of the Vienna Convention to justify the incorporation into Article XI of the rigorous rule of 'state of necessity' is ignoring the raison d'être of a legal provision that, when requiring that interpretation takes into account, together with the context, 'any relevant rules of international law applicable in the relations between the parties,' attempts to save the unity of international law, ensure the observance of its imperative rules and consistency amongst different international obligations, without interfering with the interpretation of particular rules in accordance with the interpretative canon already established. The 'state of necessity' rule is certainly not pertinent to the interpretation of a rule such as Article XI of the Treaty, which is very different conceptually.[171]

The Annulment Committee in *Mobil Exploration* sided with the arguments of Arbitrator Brotons and noted that Article 31(3)(c) only has a role to play where the treaty is unclear or ambiguous and, therefore, merits interpretation.[172] While the Annulment Committee agreed with the initial tribunal and the *El Paso* tribunal that customary law can be used to fill the gaps in a treaty, the Annulment Committee found that the tribunal actually applied the customary defence "under the guise" of an interpretation of a specific phrase of the IIA.[173]

3.4 *Implications: Systemic Integration as Providing the Solution or the Problem of Fragmentation?*

The examination illustrates the complexity of systemic integration as an interpretative principle contributing to the harmonization of international law. Despite its purpose to bring determinacy to the interpretation of international norms, the principle itself is indeterminate. This indeterminacy has perhaps contributed to the underutilization of the principle by WTO and ISDS adjudicators. What is clear, however, is that this indeterminacy has led to inconsistent treatment of the principle by adjudicators. This necessitates a greater understanding of the principle and how different values or justifications for the application of the principle affect the outcome of the interpretative process.

The inconsistent approaches of WTO and ISDS adjudicators reveal two different justifications for the principle. Each justification defines different limits on the use of the principle. These justifications have been aptly described by

171 *Mobil Exploration and Development v Argentine Republic* (ICSID Case No ARB/04/16), Decision on Jurisdiction and Liability, 10 April 2013, separate opinion of Arbitrator Brotons para 26.

172 *Mobil Exploration and Development v Argentine Republic* (ICSID Case No ARB/04/16), Decision on Annulment, 8 May 2019 [93].

173 ibid 96–97.

Kammerhofer, drawing from Koskenniemi's duality of apology and utopia.[174] On the one hand, "apology": systemic integration is justified through recourse to party intentions. Systemic integration is limited to uncovering party intentions since that is the goal of all interpretation. This can be seen in the *EC – Biotech* panel requiring all WTO members to be parties to the treaty used in the interpretative exercise. According to the recourse to party intentions, a WTO member could not have intended an interpretation based on a treaty it has not consented to be bound by. On the other hand, "utopia": systemic integration is justified because it contributes to international law as a coherent system. Even if there is not a direct reference to the incorporation of another norm, the substantive coherence between norms exists, thereby requiring the application of systemic integration. While critical of how the principle was applied in *El Paso*, Arbitrator Brotons refers to this "utopia" vision of systemic integration as saving "the unity of international law" and ensuring the "observance of its imperative rules and consistency amongst different international obligations".

The principle could play an important role in defragmentation and connecting legal regimes and norms. However, systemic integration as a solution for fragmentation has its limits. Regardless of whether the principle is indirectly or directly referred to, the principle may also represent as much of a problem for fragmentation. An isolationist methodology, in which a tribunal rejects the application of Article 31(3)(c) could be detrimental to the coherent development of international law,[175] particularly if that reasoning on Article 31(3)(c) perpetuates throughout the regime. Article 31(3)(c) may also add to the contradictions as there may not be a "clear and unequivocal" solution to conflicts in relation to the development of international law between various sub-regimes.[176] International tribunals should be cautious about how far systemic integration is desirable, as illustrated in the *Oil Platforms* decision and to be continued in the next Chapters.

174 See Jörg Kammerhofer, *International Investment Law and Legal Theory: Expropriation and the Fragmentation of Sources* (Cambridge University Press 2021) ch 4; referring to Martti Koskenniemi, *From Apology to Utopia: The Structure of International Legal Argument* (Cambridge University Press 2005). Kammerhofer adopts an international legal positivist approach to evaluating the approach of ISDS tribunals to the expropriation obligation. He refers to Koskenniemi's postmodernist critique.

175 See, for example, Baetens' conclusion on the application of Article 31(3)(c) in two different legal regimes: Baetens (n 145).

176 Andreas Paulus, 'International Adjudication' in Samantha Besson and John Tasioulas (eds), *The Philosophy of International Law* (Oxford University Press 2010) 222.

CHAPTER 5

Closing Tool

The previous Chapter analysed the opening tools used by adjudicators, in furtherance of an international judicial function, as a method to explain the exercise of discretion in relation to the application of other international law, such discretion being important for defragmentation of international law. This Chapter considers the counter-argument to the opening tools: jurisdiction as the limiting factor of the adjudicator's discretion. Under this argument, the limited jurisdiction of an international tribunal has flow-on effects for applicable law and interpretation that affects the potential for substantive fragmentation between regimes.

1 Jurisdiction and Its Indeterminacy

Chapter 2 referred to consent to jurisdiction as the foundational source of legitimacy for international courts and tribunals, and the key ingredient in the consensual basis of international adjudication. The act of granting jurisdiction to a tribunal contains the limits of the adjudicator's power. However, jurisdiction is an elusive concept. This section asks what powers and functions are embedded in the general concept of jurisdiction and how the indeterminate concept acts as a limiting tool. The section starts by exploring general discussions of the concept, before examining the understanding of the concept by trade and investment adjudicators.

When considering the jurisdiction and applicable law of the WTO and investor-state dispute settlement systems "[t]erminological clarity has always been, and always will be, the first step in any analysis of legal terms and concepts."[1] As lawyers, we have an intuitive understanding of the concept of jurisdiction.[2] However, the terminological clarity of such a fundamental term

1 Daniel Costelloe, 'Conceptions of State Jurisdiction in the Jurisprudence of the International Court of Justice and the Permanent Court of International Justice' in Stephen Allen and others (eds), *The Oxford Handbook of Jurisdiction in International Law* (Oxford University Press 2019) 458.

2 Stephen Allen and others, 'Introduction: Defining State Jurisdiction and Jurisdiction in International Law' in Stephen Allen and others (eds), *The Oxford Handbook of Jurisdiction in International Law* (Oxford University Press 2019) 4.

 | DOI:10.1163/9789004700932_006

as "jurisdiction"[3] is far from achieved.[4] Despite our intuitive sense, we struggle to provide a comprehensive definition of the meaning of jurisdiction and the outer boundaries of what should be considered a "jurisdictional" power.

The complicating factors for defining jurisdiction are many and appear to cross boundaries between dispute resolution bodies, regardless of the language in the constitutive treaties. The first and most important complicating factor arises from the usage of "jurisdiction" in a variety of ways, leaving its specific meaning to be determined by context. "Jurisdiction" is used in both a legislative[5] and adjudicative context, as well as in reference to jurisdiction of states[6] and jurisdiction of an international court or tribunal. While the adjudicative context is our sole focus here, which refers to the jurisdiction of courts, rather than the reach of state laws,[7] this diversity of contexts in which the same word is used complicates our understanding of what should be a clear and fundamental concept. The second factor that contributes to the blurred definition of jurisdiction is that the question of jurisdiction also has significant political importance.[8] As such, the concept of jurisdiction can be caught up within political issues, some of which may be better left to state parties. This could potentially incentivize an uncertain concept of jurisdiction, allowing states and courts' discretion to return a judicial dispute back to the political realm. These complicating factors leave us with an elusive definition, which

3 In French, the term 'compétence' is used in a similar way to the English term of 'jurisdiction'. While the book considers the English use of the term 'jurisdiction', it is noteworthy that the French term 'compétence' is used in similar contexts and suffers the same difficulty in being used in a variety of contexts: HWA Thirlway, 'The Law and Procedure of the International Court of Justice 1960–1989: Part Nine' (1999) 69 British Yearbook of International Law 1, 4.

4 Noll argues that general international law offered a terminology of jurisdiction, yet lacked a coherent conception underpinning it: Gregor Noll, 'Theorizing Jurisdiction' in Anne Orford and Florian Hoffmann (eds), *The Oxford Handbook of the Theory of International Law*, vol 1 (Oxford University Press 2016) 616.

5 'Legislative' or 'prescriptive jurisdiction' refers to jurisdiction to make law applicable to the activities, relations or status of persons, whether by legislation, by executive act or order. Prescriptive jurisdiction relates to the geographical reach of state laws: Cedric Ryngaert, *Jurisdiction in International Law* (2nd edn, Oxford University Press 2015) 9; see, also, FA Mann, 'The Doctrine of Jurisdiction in International Law' (1964) 111 Collected Courses of the Hague Academy of International Law 1, 9.

6 In a generic sense, 'state jurisdiction' can encompass notions such as 'domestic jurisdiction' and the 'reserved domain' (matters that fall within domestic jurisdiction by default) as well as the extent of a state's regulatory authority, governed by international law: Costelloe (n 1) 458.

7 Ryngaert (n 5) 9.

8 Shabtai Rosenne, The Law and Practice of the International Court, 1920–2005 (4th edn, Brill Nijhoff 2006) 803.

has significant implications for our understanding of state consent to jurisdiction. As with other areas of indeterminacy revealed in this study, the uncertainty can then be leveraged based on an adjudicator's normative goals and view of their function.

A second issue also arises when we attempt to define the function of "jurisdiction": to what extent do terminological differences between treaties affect a tribunal's definition of "jurisdiction"? This question relates to whether "jurisdiction" is a term, which is capable of being interpreted in the same way across different regimes, even in circumstances where treaties may adopt different language. This is particularly relevant for the WTO DSU, which does not refer to "jurisdiction" at all. Rather, the WTO DSU uses terminology more aligned with non-judicial bodies, although with some judicial language dotted throughout the text.

1.1 *Jurisdiction in General International Law*

While the concept of jurisdiction is not clearly defined at the international level, the usage of terms such as "jurisdiction" and "competence" are generally considered to be "evidence of the judicial nature" of a tribunal.[9] The term "jurisdiction" is frequently employed by international lawyers yet the definition is hardly self-evident.[10] Generally, jurisdiction relates to sovereignty and power,[11] but beyond that, we struggle to provide a more detailed definition. The following section reviews attempts at defining jurisdiction at the international level, highlighting the lack of any definitions in the treaty texts and the generality with which jurisdiction is defined by international courts and tribunals. The section also explores related concepts and potential analogies for assistance in defining jurisdiction. The analysis highlights that jurisdiction is ultimately about power: balancing the grant of power from states to international

9 *Effect of Awards of Compensation made by the United Nations Administrative Tribunal, Advisory Opinion* [1954] ICJ Reports 47, 51–52: the ICJ referred to terms such as 'tribunal', 'judgment', competence to 'pass judgment upon applications' used in the Statute of the United Nations Administrative Tribunal as generally used with respect to judicial bodies.

10 Ryngaert (n 5) 5; see also, *United Phosphorus, Ltd v Angus Chemical Co.*, 322 F 3d 942, 948 (7th Cir. 2003), which states 'jurisdiction is a word of many, to many, meanings', cited in Allen and others (n 2) 4.

11 Ryngaert (n 5) 5; see also, Shabtai Rosenne, *The International Court of Justice: An Essay in Political and Legal Theory* (AW Sijthoff 1957) 247; Malcolm N Shaw, *Rosenne's Law and Practice of the International Court: 1920–2015, vol II* (5th edn, Brill Nijhoff 2016) para 148 in volume 2, Chapter 9; Thirlway (n 3) 4; and Xue Hanqin, *Jurisdiction of the International Court of Justice* (Brill Nijhoff 2017) 34; Relja Radović, *Beyond Consent: Revisiting Jurisdiction in Investment Treaty Arbitration* (Brill Nijhoff 2021) 19 ff.

tribunals and the appropriate limits on that judicial power. However, we do not have a clearer definition of jurisdiction in general international law.

1.1.1 Understandings in Treaty

Article 36 of the ICJ Statute, which sets out the jurisdiction of the ICJ, states that "the jurisdiction of the Court comprises all cases which the parties refer to it and all matters specially provided for in the Charter of the United Nations (UN) or in treaties and conventions in force."[12] The Statute refers to both "competence" and "jurisdiction", which may seem to confuse whether there is a separate definition of these terms. However, for the purposes of the Statute, the separate usage of these terms appears to have little practical relevance.[13] Similarly, the Seabed Disputes Chamber of the International Tribunal for the Law of the Sea (ITLOS) "shall have jurisdiction … relating to disputes" falling within a closed list of categories in Article 187 of the United Nations Convention on the Law of the Sea (UNCLOS).[14] The jurisdiction of the PCA uses the terminology of "competence" in that the PCA "is competent for all arbitration cases" under Article 41 of the 1907 Hague Convention.[15] However, Article 45 of the 1907 Hague Convention also refers to "jurisdiction": "Arbitrators called upon to form the Tribunal with jurisdiction to decide this difference must be chosen from the general list". Article 47 goes on to enable the extension of "the jurisdiction of the Permanent Court … to disputes between non-Contracting Powers".

Further obscuring the potential to identify a treaty definition of jurisdiction across constitutive instruments is the fact that some political and other non-judicial bodies also use terminology like jurisdiction and competence. One such example is the Human Rights Committee under the International Covenant on Civil and Political Rights (ICCPR). The ICCPR refers to the Committee and its activities with both judicial and non-judicial terminology. The Committee is referred to with non-judicial language, such as submitting reports and comments to state parties.[16] However, in more judicial terms, state parties may

12 Statute of the International Court of Justice (San Francisco, concluded 26 June 1945), 3 Bevans 1179.

13 Shaw (n 11) para 149 in volume 2, Chapter 9; Hanqin (n 11) 33.

14 United Nations Convention on the Law of the Sea (Montego Bay, 10 December 1982), 1833 UNTS 397.

15 1907 Convention for the Pacific Settlement of International Disputes (The Hague, concluded 18 October 1907), 1 Bevans 577.

16 International Covenant on Civil and Political Rights (19 December 1966), 999 UNTS 171, Article 40.

recognize "the competence" of the Committee to consider communications that a state party is not fulfilling its obligations.[17]

This brief review of jurisdictional clauses of some international dispute resolution bodies indicates the common use of the term "jurisdiction" without elaboration of the concept within the treaty texts. From here, we can consider how jurisprudence has sought to bring clarity to this concept (if at all). [18]

1.1.2 Understandings in Jurisprudence

International court judgments often describe jurisdiction quite broadly, referring to "the power of the Court to 'do justice' between the litigating States, to decide the case before it with final and binding force on those States"[19] or "the power of a tribunal to determine a case in accordance with the law creating the tribunal or a law prescribing its jurisdiction".[20] In early advisory opinions on the international administrative tribunals, the ICJ used the phrase "do justice" several times and set out its understanding of what to "do justice" required. In the *Effect of Awards of Compensation* advisory opinion, the ICJ described the process as including "considering the arguments of the parties, appraising the evidence produced by them, establishing the facts and declaring the law applicable to them."[21] Similarly, in the *Judgments of the ILO Administrative Tribunal* advisory opinion, the ICJ referred to the jurisdiction of the administrative tribunal as whether the tribunal was "legally qualified to examine the complaints submitted to it and to adjudicate on the merits of the claims set out therein".[22]

Despite these attempts at defining the concept, the term "jurisdiction" does not appear to be a term of art and it has been applied to many areas of a court's activity, which may appear to be unconnected. Jurisdiction is said to be a technical word with a precise meaning[23] but, as identified by the Iran-US Claims

17 ibid, Article 41.

18 As Boisson de Chazournes notes, the meaning of consent and jurisdiction and their limits remain susceptible to being given meaning and interpretation by courts and tribunals, even in the face of clear treaty language: Laurence Boisson de Chazournes, 'Variations around the Notion of Consent in Investment Arbitration' in Samantha Besson (ed), *Consenting to International Law* (1st edn, Cambridge University Press 2023) 247.

19 Shaw (n 11) para 149 in volume 2, Chapter 9.

20 *Genie Lantman Elton (USA) v United Mexican States* (Mexico-United States, General Claims Commission, 13 May 1929) (1929) IV UNRIAA 529, p 533.

21 *Effect of Awards of Compensation made by the United Nations Administrative Tribunal*, Advisory Opinion (n 9) 56.

22 *Judgments of the Administrative Tribunal of the ILO upon complaints made against the UNESCO*, Advisory Opinion [1956] ICJ Reports 77, 87.

23 *Cases of Dual Nationality – Decision No 22* (Anglo-Italian Conciliation Commission) (1954) 14 UNRIAA 27, 35.

Tribunal, there is a "large variety of situations in which matters of jurisdiction may arise".[24] The diverse application of the term "jurisdiction" to various areas of a court's activity range from the question whether a tribunal has the authority to commence and continue the examination of a dispute,[25] to the question whether the court may interpret a judgment once given.[26] Judge ad hoc Daxner summarized the diversity of connotation of the term "jurisdiction" in noting that "jurisdiction" has two fundamental meanings in international law. First, it means to recognize the Court as an organ instituted for the purpose *jus dicere* and in order to acquire the ability to appear before it. The second meaning is to determine the competence of the Court, i.e., to invest the court with the right to solve concrete cases.[27]

The elusiveness of the concept is compounded by the reluctance of courts and tribunals to define the meaning of the word "jurisdiction" in general. For example, in the *Nottebohm* case, the ICJ noted that:

> The Court is not concerned with defining the meaning of the word 'jurisdiction' in general. In the present case, it must determine the scope and meaning of the Declaration made by Guatemala on the basis of Article 36, paragraph 2, a Declaration which, together with that provision and the corresponding Declaration by Liechtenstein, contains the law governing the question under consideration.[28]

Whilst understandable, based on the elusiveness of the concept, this reluctance by the ICJ (and other courts and tribunals) has made it difficult to systematically define the boundaries and ramifications of the concept of jurisdiction. This provides the required wriggle-room for the international judicial function to develop around the edges of consent to jurisdiction.

---

24 *Islamic Republic of Iran v United States* (IUSCT Case No A/1), Decision (DEC8-A1-FT), 17 May 1982, (1982) 1 Iran-US CTR 144 152; see, further, CF Amerasinghe, *Jurisdiction of International Tribunals* (Kluwer Law International 2003) 51, 58–64.

25 *Judgments of the Administrative Tribunal of the ILO* (n 22) 87.

26 *Request for Interpretation of the Judgment of 15 June 1962 in the Case Concerning the Temple of Preah Vihear (Cambodia v Thailand)*, Judgment [2013] ICJ Reports 281, 295.

27 *Corfu Channel Case (United Kingdom v Albania)*, Preliminary Objection [1948] ICJ Reports 15, 39.

28 *Nottebohm (Liechtenstein v Guatemala)*, Preliminary Objections [1953] ICJ Reports 111, p 122.

1.1.3 Distinguishing Jurisdiction and Admissibility

The consideration of the admissibility of disputes may shed further light on the concept of "jurisdiction" and what falls within a "jurisdictional" decision. At times, the distinction between jurisdiction and admissibility has neither been entirely transparent nor formally observed.[29] However, we can identify a general understanding that a plea of inadmissibility usually relates to whether the claim is "inadmissible on some ground other than its ultimate merits" whereas a jurisdictional objection argues that the tribunal itself is incompetent to give any ruling on the merits, or even on the admissibility of the claim.[30] In *Application of the Genocide Convention* (*Croatia v Serbia*), the ICJ distinguished between jurisdiction and admissibility in the following way:

> If the objection is a jurisdictional objection, then since the jurisdiction of the Court derives from the consent of the parties, this will most usually be because it has been shown that no such consent has been given by the objecting State to the settlement by the Court of the particular dispute. A preliminary objection to admissibility covers a more disparate range of possibilities. ... Essentially such an objection consists in the contention that there exists a legal reason, even when there is jurisdiction, why the Court should decline to hear the case, or more usually, a specific claim therein.[31]

29 For example, the ICJ has been faced with objections to jurisdiction presented by the parties as arguments of inadmissibility. In the *Nicaragua Case*, the United States argued that the application was inadmissible on five separate grounds. The ICJ noted that some of these grounds 'have in fact been presented in terms suggesting that they are matters of competence or jurisdiction rather than admissibility.' However, the Court noted that 'it does not appear to be of critical importance how they are classified in this respect': *Military and Paramilitary Activities in and Against Nicaragua* (*Nicaragua v United States of America*), *Jurisdiction and Admissibility* [1984] ICJ Reports 392, 492; similarly in *Northern Cameroons*, the ICJ noted that it did 'not find it necessary ... to determine whether all of them are objections to jurisdiction or to admissibility or based on other grounds. During the course of the oral hearing little distinction if any was made by the Parties themselves between "jurisdiction" and "admissibility"': *Northern Cameroons* (*Cameroon v United Kingdom*), *Preliminary Objections* [1963] ICJ Reports 14, 27.

30 Gerald Fitzmaurice, *The Law and Procedure of the International Court of Justice*, vol 2 (Cambridge University Press 1993) 438.

31 *Application of the Convention on the Prevention and Punishment of the Crime of Genocide* (*Croatia v Serbia*), Preliminary Objection, Judgment [2008] ICJ Reports 412 [120]; also citing: *Oil Platforms* (*Islamic Republic of Iran v United States of America*), Judgment [2003] ICJ Reports 161 [29].

This division between jurisdiction and admissibility, as set out in this general definition by the ICJ,[32] could be analytically described as one of power: jurisdiction is a question of power, the legal power to adjudicate, whereas admissibility denotes that this judicial power is a right, not a duty, a court may decline to exercise the power to adjudicate.[33] This further reinforces the concept of jurisdiction as a fundamental judicial power but does not further elaborate on a precise definition.

1.2 *Jurisdiction in the WTO*

In a design choice reflecting the balance between political and judicial actors in the WTO, the DSU makes both "political" and "legal" methods of dispute settlement available, with the panel and Appellate Body procedures representing the legal side.[34] Article 2.1 of the DSU established the DSB to administer the rules and procedures of the WTO dispute settlement mechanism. By the power granted in that Article, the DSB is responsible for establishing panels, adopting reports, maintaining surveillance of implementation of rulings and recommendations and authorizing suspension of concessions and other obligations under the covered agreements. The DSB is made up of all Member governments, being the General Council convening as the DSB to deal with dispute settlement issues.[35] The vesting of the ultimate authority to adopt reports is a legacy of the GATT system, which was often criticized as being "more diplomatic and political than judicial in nature."[36] However, the reverse consensus rule introduced in the DSU, by which panel and Appellate Body reports will be adopted by the DSB unless the DSB decides by consensus not to adopt,[37] brings the dispute settlement mechanism "closer to a system resembling binding

32 For further examples, see *Nottebohm* (n 28) 122; *Ambatielos Case (Greece v United Kingdom), Judgment* [1953] ICJ Reports 10, 22–23.

33 Yuval Shany, 'Jurisdiction and Admissibility' in Cesare Romano, Karen Alter and Yuval Shany (eds), *The Oxford Handbook of International Adjudication* (Oxford University Press 2013) 787.

34 Ernst-Ulrich Petersmann, *The GATT/WTO Dispute Settlement System: International Law, International Organizations and Dispute Settlement* (Kluwer Law International 1997) 182–3.

35 Article IV:3 of the Marrakesh Agreement Establishing the World Trade Organization (15 April 1994), 1867 UNTS 154.

36 Peter Van den Bossche and Werner Zdouc, *The Law and Policy of the World Trade Organization: Text, Cases and Materials* (Cambridge University Press 2017) 212.

37 See Article 16.4 for panel reports and Article 17.14 for Appellate Body reports: Understanding on Rules and Procedures Governing the Settlement of Disputes, Marrakesh Agreement Establishing the World Trade Organization, Annex 2 (15 April 1994), 1869 UNTS 401.

arbitration or litigation among Member States."[38] Combined with the independence of the panel and Appellate Body members, the reverse consensus implies a significant "legalization" and "quasi-judicialization" of dispute settlement in the WTO.[39]

A review of these articles of the DSU shows a significant departure from other treaties conferring jurisdiction on an international tribunal, including the ICJ Statute or UNCLOS discussed in the previous section. We can find similarities with non-judicial bodies, such as the Human Rights Committee, with language referring to "reports" of the Human Rights Committee to be submitted to the state parties, similar to reports of panels to be sent to the DSB for approval. Language such as "terms of reference" is used alongside concepts such as "legal complaint". We could infer two different, but perhaps linked, design choices of the drafters of the DSU in including quasi-judicial and political language within the DSU. First, that the drafters of the DSU did not turn their mind to general concepts of dispute resolution or, perhaps more drastically, that they did not consider such judicial concepts to be applicable to the newly created WTO dispute settlement mechanism. As the drafting history of the DSU is not conclusive on this issue, the more likely inference is that drafters did not turn their mind to general concepts of dispute resolution, instead preferring to remain within the previous GATT framework of dispute settlement. The legal ramifications for the introduction of a more legal dispute resolution body in the Appellate Body may not have been perceived by negotiators of the DSU.

Despite the lack of reference to "jurisdiction" in the DSU, panels and the Appellate Body frequently use this term themselves. A total of 320 reports (out of 402), 98 from the Appellate Body and 222 from panels, contain a reference to the term "jurisdiction".[40] While "jurisdiction" is used in different contexts elsewhere in the WTO agreements,[41] the majority of these 320 reports

38 Gregory Spak and Gisele Kapterian, 'The World Trade Organization' in Chiara Giorgetti (ed), *The Rules, Practice and Jurisprudence of International Courts and Tribunals* (Martinus Nijhoff Publishers 2012) 140.

39 Petersmann (n 34) 186.

40 These numbers are the result of a search conducted on "WTO Documents Online" for panel or Appellate Body Reports using the term "jurisdiction" on 1 October 2021 (https://docs.wto.org/dol2fe/Pages/FE_Search/FE_S_S005.aspx).

41 For example, Article 2.1 of the Agreement on Subsidies and Countervailing Measures refers to the "jurisdiction of the granting authority", being a reference to jurisdiction in the sense of domestic or national jurisdiction: Agreement on Subsidies and Countervailing Measures, Marrakesh Agreement Establishing the World Trade Organization, Annex 1B (15 April 1994), 1869 UNTS 14.

use "jurisdiction" in the adjudicative context. The references to "jurisdiction" include both references by the panel and Appellate Body as well as by parties in their submissions. In several cases, the term "jurisdiction" has also been included in a panel's Working Party Procedures.[42]

In an early report of the Appellate Body, the Appellate Body made the link between a panel's terms of reference and jurisdiction:

> A panel's terms of reference are important for two reasons. First, terms of reference fulfil an important due process objective – they give the parties and third parties sufficient information concerning the claims at issue in the dispute in order to allow them an opportunity to respond to the complainant's case. Second, they establish the jurisdiction of the panel by defining the precise claims at issue in the dispute.[43]

We find similar references to jurisdiction repeated throughout the reports of the panels and Appellate Body in relation to the panel's terms of reference, ranging from "the jurisdiction of a panel is established by that panel's terms of reference"[44] to "a panel request governs a panel's terms of reference and thereby 'delimits the scope of [its] jurisdiction'".[45] Additionally, the power and

42 See, for example, *Philippines – Taxes on Distilled Spirits* (*Report of the Panel*) (15 August 2011), WT/DS396/R ; WT/DS403/R, which in paragraph 17 of the Working Procedures stated: 'Any request for a preliminary ruling (including rulings on jurisdictional issues) to be made by the Panel shall be submitted no later than in a party's first written submission.'; see, also, the working procedures in *Australia – Measures Affecting the Importation of Apples from New Zealand* (*Report of the Panel*) (9 August 2010), WT/DS367/R.

43 *Brazil – Measures Affecting Desiccated Coconut* (*Report of the Appellate Body*) (21 February 1997), WT/DS22/AB/R p 22.

44 *India – Patent Protection for Pharmaceutical and Agricultural Chemical Products* (*Report of the Appellate Body*) (19 December 1997), WT/DS50/AB/R [92].

45 *Ukraine – Anti-Dumping Measures on Ammonium Nitrate* (*Report of the Appellate Body*) (12 September 2019), WT/DS493/AB/R [6.20], citing: *China – Measures Imposing Anti-Dumping Duties on High-Performance Stainless Steel Seamless Tubes* (HP-SSST) *from Japan / China – Measures Imposing Anti-Dumping Duties on High-Performance Stainless Steel Seamless Tubes* (HP-SSST) *from the European Union* (*Report of the Appellate Body*) (14 October 2015), WT/DS454/AB/R; WT/DS460/AB/R [5.12]; See also: *United States – Definitive Anti-Dumping and Countervailing Duties on Certain Products from China* (*Report of the Appellate Body*) (11 March 2011), WT/DS379/AB/R [4.6]; *United States – Countervailing Duties on Certain Corrosion-Resistant Carbon Steel Flat Products from Germany* (*Report of the Appellate Body*) (28 November 2002), WT/DS213/AB/R [124].

functions of the panels in relation to Article 21.5 compliance proceedings has also been described in jurisdictional terms.[46]

To some degree, the panels and Appellate Body discuss their understanding of the powers and functions that fall within their jurisdiction. For example, the Appellate Body has recognized implied jurisdictional powers:

> … panels cannot simply ignore issues which go to the root of their jurisdiction [but must] deal with such issues – if necessary, on their own motion – in order to satisfy themselves that they have authority to proceed.[47]

These implied jurisdictional powers are based on a "widely accepted rule" that "international adjudicative tribunals, including WTO dispute settlement panels, possess inherent jurisdiction which derives from the exercise of their adjudicative function."[48] In adopting the general language of jurisdiction, the panels and Appellate Body have incorporated some of the functions of "jurisdiction" from general international law. The discussion of panel and Appellate Body references to "jurisdiction" illuminates that, regardless of the lack of such a term in the DSU, the general international law concept of jurisdiction, and its elusive definition, have been adopted by the WTO dispute settlement mechanism. The extent to which this is in fact in line with the intentions of the drafters of the DSU is not entirely clear. However, at the very least, the design choice to judicialize the WTO DSU, departing from the GATT model, enabled the closer alignment with international courts and tribunals.

---

46 See, for example: *US – Measures Affecting Trade in Large Civil Aircraft (Second Complaint) – Recourse to Article 21.5 of the DSU by the European Union (Report of the Panel)* (9 June 2017), WT/DS353/RW [7.358]; *Thailand – Customs and Fiscal Measures on Cigarettes from the Philippines – Second recourse to Article 21.5 of the DSU by the Philippines (Report of the Panel)* (12 July 2019), WT/DS/371/RW2 [7.29].

47 *Mexico – Anti-Dumping Investigation of High Fructose Corn Syrup (HFCS) from the United States – Recourse to Article 21.5 of the DSU by the United States (Report of the Appellate Body)* (22 October 2001) WT/DS132/AB/RW [36].

48 *Russia – Measures Concerning Traffic in Transit (Report of the Panel)* (5 April 2019), WT/DS512/R [7.53] and reference in footnote 49, including: *United States – Anti-Dumping Act of 1916 (Report of the Appellate Body)* (28 August 2000) WT/DS136/AB/R ; WT/DS/162/AB/R [54]; *Mexico – Corn Syrup (Article 21.5) (n 47) para 36; United States – Measures Affecting Trade in Large Civil Aircraft (Second Complaint) – Recourse to Article 21.5 of the DSU by the European Union (Report of the Panel)* (n 46) para 7.358.

1.3 *Jurisdiction in ISDS*

In comparison to the WTO dispute settlement mechanism, the term "jurisdiction" is more readily found within investor-state dispute settlement, both in the documents conferring jurisdiction on tribunals[49] and in tribunal decisions.[50]

As a consequence of the historical divergence on multilateral/bilateral relations, there is no single document setting out the design choices of ISDS to compare to the WTO DSU. However, the ICSID Convention provides a good reference point, both for comparison to the WTO and as representing a large proportion of investor-state disputes. While the ICSID Convention does not apply to all investor-state disputes, arbitration before ICSID accounts for the largest number of investor-state disputes.[51] The ICSID Convention is also referred to as a forum for dispute settlement in the vast majority of IIAs.[52] Further, the ICSID Convention is the only arbitral institution designed for investor-state disputes. Other arbitral institutions were designed either for inter-state disputes (the PCA) or commercial arbitration (such as the LCIA, ICA, SCC) and their rules and institutions have been adapted to deal with investor-state disputes. Finally, the treaty character of the ICSID Convention enables us to review the drafting history to consider how treaty negotiators may have used the term "jurisdiction", in the same way as the drafting of the WTO DSU has been examined, which is often not available for negotiation of IIAs. The ICSID Convention was the result of the inability of investment protection negotiations to provide a multilateral treaty such as the GATT. Faced with difficult negotiations on a substantive agreement, World Bank General Counsel Aron

49 For example, Chapter II of the ICSID Convention is titled 'Jurisdiction of the Center'. NAFTA also refers to the jurisdiction of tribunals numerous times, including in relation to consolidation of disputes (Article 1126) and interim measures of protection (Article 1134): North American Free Trade Agreement (17 December 1992), 32 ILM 289.

50 A simple example is the issuance of "Decisions on Jurisdiction" by investor-state tribunals.

51 As at 31 December 2020, ICSID had registered 721 cases under the ICSID Convention, with a further 69 cases under its Additional Facility Rules: 'The ICSID Caseload – Statistics' (International Center for Settlement of Investment Disputes 2020) Issue 2021–1 9; based on results from PITAD as at 1 January 2020, there were 1,126 total cases based on substantive bilateral investment and free trade agreements, complemented by a further 157 cases based on contracts and domestic foreign investment laws: Daniel Behn, Malcolm Langford and Laura Létourneau-Tremblay, 'Empirical Perspectives on Investment Arbitration: What Do We Know? Does It Matter?' (2020) 21 The Journal of World Investment & Trade 188, 191.

52 A search on the International Investment Agreements Navigator managed by UNCTAD identifies 2185 out of 2575 mapped treaties using ICSID as an ISDS forum option (search on 29 March 2021): United Nations Conference on Trade and Development, 'International Investment Agreements Navigator' (*UNCTAD Investment Policy Hub*) <https://investmentpolicy.unctad.org/international-investment-agreements> accessed 27 April 2021.

Broches advanced the formula of "procedure before substance".[53] In this way, the development of ICSID is within the same negotiation framework as the GATT/WTO of creating a specific treaty for protection of international economic activity, albeit a more limited focus on dispute settlement. Analysing the development of the ICSID Convention's dispute settlement provisions provides us with an indication of states' historical preferences on the nature of investor-state arbitration.

The distinct nature of the ICSID Convention must be noted when comparing jurisdictional powers to the WTO dispute settlement mechanisms. Consent to jurisdiction of the investment dispute will be found outside the ICSID Convention, namely (for the disputes analysed in this study) in the IIA setting out the substantive obligations of the parties. Nevertheless, the jurisdiction clause of the ICSID Convention still has a role to play. The jurisdiction clause of the ICSID Convention provides an objective requirement on the nature of the dispute and the parties, the outer limits of which cannot be overridden by party consent:[54]

> While consent of the parties is an essential prerequisite for the jurisdiction of the Centre, consent alone will not suffice to bring a dispute within its jurisdiction. In keeping with the purpose of the Convention, the jurisdiction of the Centre is further limited by reference to the nature of the dispute and the parties thereto.[55]

This creates a "dual" or "double barrel" test whereby the objective criteria of the ICSID Convention must be met, along with meeting the definition of consent to arbitration in the IIA,[56] an additional jurisdictional step that is not required in WTO proceedings.

Although the ICSID Convention does not provide any substantive international investment obligations, invoking ICSID jurisdiction has important

---

53 Rudolf Dolzer and Christoph Schreuer, *Principles of International Investment Law* (2nd edn, Oxford University Press 2012) 9; Armin von Bogdandy and Ingo Venzke, 'In Whose Name? An Investigation of International Courts' Public Authority and Its Democratic Justification' (2012) 23 European Journal of International Law 7, 9.

54 Christoph H Schreuer, *The ICSID Convention: A Commentary* (2nd edn, Cambridge University Press 2009) 83.

55 'Report of the Executive Directors on the Convention on the Settlement of Investment Disputes between States and Nationals of Other States' (International Bank for Reconstruction and Development 1965) para 25.

56 See, for example, *Ceskoslovenska Obchodni Banka, AS v The Slovak Republic* (ICSID Case No ARB/97/4), Decision on Objections to Jurisdiction, 24 May 1999 [68].

consequences. By invoking ICSID jurisdiction, parties are thereby incorporating the procedural and enforcement rules of the ICSID Convention. This is to be distinguished from invoking the Additional Facility Rules, whereby access to ICSID may be granted to non-Contracting States, but the Convention itself is not applicable to the proceedings,[57] more akin to bringing proceedings to the other arbitral institutions. Consequently, the language of jurisdiction in the WTO DSU and the ICSID Convention is not directly comparable if we take into account the different nature of the dispute treaties. However, the ICSID Convention does provide an objective test of jurisdiction similar to the WTO DSU that we can compare for the purposes of understanding the limiting scope of jurisdiction as a closing tool of international law.

In a departure from the approach of the WTO DSU, the ICSID Convention specifically refers to "jurisdiction". Article 25(1) of the ICSID Convention sets out the jurisdiction of ICSID:

> The jurisdiction of the Centre shall extend to any legal dispute arising directly out of an investment, between a Contracting State (or any constituent subdivision or agency of a Contracting State designated to the Centre by that State) and a national of another Contracting State, which the parties to the dispute consent in writing to submit to the Centre. When the parties have given their consent, no party may withdraw its consent unilaterally.

The reference to jurisdiction is quite similar to other treaties creating international tribunals or conferring jurisdiction on international tribunals as "jurisdiction" is used like a term of art, without definition of its meaning. However, it must be noted that the reference to the jurisdiction of the Center stands in stark contrast to the lack of similar language in the WTO DSU. We can perhaps mark the divergence between the use of the term "jurisdiction" in the ICSID Convention, compared to the WTO DSU, as partially influenced by the style of the negotiations of the ICSID Convention. While the WTO DSU negotiation process was undertaken through diplomatic channels and negotiating groups comprising solely of states represented by their ambassadors to the GATT,[58]

---

57 ICSID Additional Facility Rules (effective as of 27 September 1978), art 2 and 3; Schreuer (n 54) 84–5.

58 The Dispute Settlement Negotiating Group (NG13) was responsible for negotiations on the dispute settlement mechanism and the Ambassadors of Uruguay and the United States were appointed as the first chairmen of the group. Terence P Stewart, *The GATT Uruguay Round: A Negotiating History (1986–1992)*, vol 2 (Kluwer Law and Taxation Publishers 1993) 2726.

the drafting of the ICSID Convention took a much less political approach. Based on an extensive review of the drafting history of the ICSID Convention, St John concluded that the ICSID Convention "emerged nearly fully formed out of the World Bank's Legal Department".[59]

Although the ICSID Convention refers to the jurisdiction of the Center, no particular definition of jurisdiction is given. The absence of such a definition was considered to allow a broad interpretation of the term, as set out in the Report of the Executive Directors:

> The term "jurisdiction of the Centre" is used in the Convention as a convenient expression to mean the limits within which the provisions of the Convention will apply and the facilities of the Centre will be available for conciliation and arbitration proceedings.[60]

It becomes clear from the negotiating history of the ICSID Convention that the drafters were influenced by previous international conventions in using the term "jurisdiction". The World Bank officials leading the meetings of state representatives noted that the Hague Conventions of 1899 and 1907 had been used as precedents for the jurisdiction of ICSID:

> The term "jurisdiction" is used in Section 1 and in the title of Article II in its broadest sense to denote the scope of the facilities made available by the Center. The terminology used follows the precedent of the Hague Convention of 1907 which speaks of the "jurisdiction of the Permanent Court" (see for example Article 47 of the Convention) even though that Court, like the proposed Center does not itself exercise judicial or quasi-judicial functions.[61]

59 Taylor St John, *The Rise of Investor-State Arbitration: Politics, Law, and Unintended Consequences* (Oxford University Press 2018) 14.

60 'Report of the Executive Directors on the Convention on the Settlement of Investment Disputes between States and Nationals of Other States' (n 55) para 22..

61 Working Paper for Consultative Meetings of Legal Experts Designated by Governments, 15 October 1963 (COM/AF/WH/EU/AS/1): International Center for Settlement of Investment Disputes, *The History of the ICSID Convention: Documents Concerning the Origin and the Formulation of the Convention on the Settlement of Investment Disputes between States and Nationals of Other States*, vol II (1970) 203; see also, Consultative Meeting of Legal Experts in Addis Ababa, December 16–20, 1963 (Summary Record of Proceedings), on p 255 in which the Chairman of the meeting also noted the term 'jurisdiction' may be questioned.

Some experts pointed out during meetings that "jurisdiction" could be read "as implying an element of compulsion which was quite inconsistent with the character of the Convention".[62] The Chairman submitted that "scope of activity" could be used instead of "jurisdiction".[63] However, the term "jurisdiction" remained in all versions of the draft convention and no specific definition of "jurisdiction" was ultimately included.[64] We can also identify in the negotiations that other general ideas related to jurisdiction of courts and tribunals informed the understanding of the jurisdiction of ICSID. For example, in relation to the voluntary nature of arbitration, the General Counsel Broches noted that "the question of 'jurisdiction' must be decided by some authority" and that it was "a well-established rule of international law that, unless the parties otherwise provide, the arbitral tribunal is the judge of its own jurisdiction."[65]

However, even with this greater frequency of usage of the term "jurisdiction" in treaty documents, investor-state arbitral decisions still suffer the same problem as general international law: no clear definition of "jurisdiction" emerges. In terms of jurisprudence, there is very limited discussion of the concept and meaning of "jurisdiction" in general terms. In the Decision on Jurisdiction in *Urbaser v Argentina*,[66] a tribunal under the ICSID Convention explored the meaning of "jurisdiction" in its attempt to distinguish between jurisdiction and admissibility. The tribunal's general definition is in similarly broad terms to that found in judgments of other international courts: "[j]urisdiction in the judicial or adjudicative context means the authority to render legal decisions.

62 Consultative Meeting of Legal Experts, Bangkok, 27 April 1964 (Summary Record of Proceedings): ibid 491.

63 ibid.

64 See, also: A Broches, 'Convention on the Settlement of Investment Disputes: Some Observations on Jurisdiction' (1966) 5 Columbia Journal of Transnational Law 263, 265–266.

65 Note by the General Counsel transmitted to the Executive Directors, 19 January 1962 (SecM 62–17): International Center for Settlement of Investment Disputes (n 61) 16.

66 The claim was brought pursuant to Argentina's offer to arbitrate contained in Article X of the BIT: Agreement for the Promotion and Reciprocal Protection of Investments between the Kingdom of Spain and the Republic of Argentina (Buenos Aires, 3 October 1991), 1699 UNTS 203. Article X states:

"3. The dispute may be submitted to an international arbitral tribunal in any of the following circumstances:

a. At the request of either party to the dispute, when no decision has been reached on the substance 18 months after the judicial proceeding provided for in paragraph 2 of this article began or

b. When such a decision has been reached, but the dispute between the parties persists;

c. When both parties to the dispute have so agreed."

It includes consideration of the sphere of such authority, i.e., the scope of the judicial competence."[67]

In *Abaclat v Argentina*, another tribunal constituted under the ICSID Convention, the dissenting opinion of Arbitrator Abi-Saab provides useful comments on the definition of jurisdiction in seeking to distinguish from admissibility.[68] Abi-Saab disagreed with the majority award, on both substantive points, and "the understanding of some basic principles, rules and concepts of international law, such as jurisdiction and admissibility."[69] In the course of his dissenting opinion, Abi-Saab commented on the general definition of jurisdiction:

> Jurisdiction as a concept in international law, partakes of its generic meaning in the general theory of law; but is further specified and particularized in function of the fundamental principle of the consensual basis of international adjudication.
>
> The term "jurisdiction" (from the latin "jurisdictio", literally to "pronounce" or "enunciate the law", dire le droit), when used in the judicial or adjudicative context, denotes "the legal power of an organ to decide cases (in general) or a case (in particular) by application of law". In other words, it is the empowerment to exercise the judicial function. Thus, jurisdiction refers first and foremost to a legal power to exercise a certain type of activity, the judicial function.[70]

However, similar to decisions in other international courts and tribunals, Abi-Saab also does not elaborate on what falls within this "jurisdictional power". Precisely what activities of the tribunal should be said to be jurisdictional, compared to admissibility or applicable law questions, are not set out. Rather,

---

67 *Urbaser SA v Argentine Republic* (ICSID Case No ARB/07/26), Decision on Jurisdiction, 19 December 2012 [125].

68 Article 8(3), the relevant jurisdictional provision, of the Agreement between the Argentine Republic and the Italian Republic on Investment Promotion and Protection (Buenos Aires, 22 May 1990) states: "If, after 18 months from the notification of commencement of an action before the national courts indicated in the above paragraph 2, the dispute between the Contracting Party and the investors still continues to exist, it may be subject to international arbitration. With this purpose and under this Agreement, each Contracting Party grants its anticipated and irrevocable consent that any dispute may be subject to arbitration." (Unofficial translation provided by Claimants in the dispute, authorized versions in Spanish and Italian).

69 *Abaclat and Others vs Argentina* (ICSID Case No ARB/07/5), Decision on Jurisdiction and Admissibility, 4 August 2011 [4].

70 ibid [9–10].

we are left with the same elusive definition that is only somewhat clarified when it is compared against what falls within the admissibility criterion.

While the tribunal decisions just discussed were brought under the ICSID Convention, the elusive definition arguably also applies to jurisdiction of tribunals before other arbitral institutions. A short survey of IIAs suggest that, like the WTO DSU, the term "jurisdiction" is rarely used in dispute settlement provisions.[71] However, as with the WTO DSU, such tribunals still refer to concepts of jurisdiction under general international law, thereby invoking the elusive definition.[72] For example, in *García Armas v Venezuela*, a dispute facilitated by the PCA under the UNCITRAL rules, the tribunal's starting point was "jurisdiction" in general international law[73] and referred to Abi-Saab in *Abaclat* on the limited jurisdiction of tribunals.[74] In determining the burden of proof in relation to its jurisdiction, the tribunal then determined that the content of international law must be determined by the tribunal, according to the *jura novit curia* principle.[75] Application of such principle can be seen as inherent to the proper administration of the tribunal's judicial function, even if not ultimately an inherent jurisdictional power.[76]

1.4 *Implications of the Indeterminacy: Unclear Power and Authority*

International actors and adjudicators have attempted to define the term "jurisdiction" and to what extent it limits the powers and functions pursuant to a consensual approach to international law. However, the concept remains elusive before international court and tribunals.[77] Perhaps all we can gain from

---

71 For example, see the list of typical dispute settlement provisions contained in BITS: Campbell McLachlan, Laurence Shore and Matthew Weiniger, *International Investment Arbitration: Substantive Principles* (2nd edn, Oxford University Press 2017) para 3.02 ff.

72 For example, tribunals invoke the inherent jurisdictional powers: *Austrian Airlines v The Slovak Republic* (ad hoc, UNCITRAL), Final Award, 9 October 2009 [117]; or, refer to concepts such as compulsory and general jurisdiction in determining that the tribunal only has 'compétence d'attribution': *ST-AD v Bulgaria* (PCA Case No 2001–06), Award on Jurisdiction, 18 July 2013 [361].

73 *García Armas and others v Venezuela* (PCA Case No 2016–08), Award on Jurisdiction, 13 December 2019 [628].

74 ibid [629].

75 ibid [638].

76 See discussion of the principle in Luigi Fumagalli, 'Jura Novit Curia', *Max Planck Encyclopedia of International Procedural Law* (Oxford University Press 2018).

77 Judge Higgins summarized the position of the PCIJ and ICJ as follows: '[i]t is clear from the jurisprudence of the [PCIJ] and of the [ICJ] that there is no rule that requires a restrictive interpretation of compromissory clauses. But equally, there is no evidence that the various exercises of jurisdiction by the two Courts really indicate a jurisdictional presumption in favor of the plaintiff [...] The Court has no judicial policy of being either

international jurisprudence is to set out the basic function of jurisdiction: the expression of power to exercise the judicial function. In this way, jurisdiction reflects the grant of power by states to international courts and tribunals. If we are unable to identify precisely what "power" is within its jurisdiction, how can we determine the extent of a state's consent to jurisdiction? Exactly what this expression of power specifically authorizes may not be possible to identify at the abstract level. Yet, the concept of jurisdiction is still maintained as fundamental to the proper functioning of international dispute resolution and the usage of jurisdictional terminology denotes judicial functions and powers. Whether this "judicial function" is limited to law-applying in the settlement of the dispute or extends to lawmaking in the sense of the international judicial function is not clear and complicates our understanding of how limited jurisdiction interacts with the adjudicator's opening tools.

2 Jurisdiction as a Closing Tool in Practice

If jurisdiction reflects the powers of an adjudicator, which is limited by the terms of a state's consent to the judicial resolution of the dispute, we expect that the limited jurisdiction of a tribunal is used as a basis of reasoning by adjudicators in rejecting the application of public international law in the dispute. However, Figure 9 in Chapter 4 demonstrated the rather sporadic use of limited jurisdiction as a reason for denying a party's attempts to include other areas of public international law. Only 5% of WTO disputes and 4% of relevant ISDS disputes rely on limited jurisdiction as a basis for rejecting other international law.

From the viewpoint of comparative design choices, the similarity of the results between the WTO and ISDS adjudicators is interesting. The political and legal balance in the WTO dispute settlement mechanism, the terms of reference and exhaustive nature of the covered agreements should provide clearer guidance on the limitations of the WTO adjudicator's jurisdiction. Yet, ISDS shares a similar result with the more restrictive compulsory jurisdiction of the WTO.

From the viewpoint of consent, what does this mean for jurisdiction as a limiting tool? Does this suggest a less important role for the consent-based and

---

liberal or strict in deciding the scope of compromissory clauses: they are judicial decisions like any other': *Oil Platforms (Islamic Republic of Iran v United States of America), Preliminary Objection, Judgment* [1996] ICJ Reports 803, 857, para 36; see also, *Austrian Airlines v The Slovak Republic* (n 72) para 119 ff.

limited jurisdiction of the tribunals in the normative goals of the adjudicators? Perhaps more likely is the wariness with which parties themselves would seek to openly enlarge the jurisdictional scope of the tribunal. When we consider the small number of disputes in which this basis is used, we find support for the latter. The other international law raised (and rejected on the basis of limited jurisdiction) primarily relates to a claim outside the dispute submitted to the tribunals.[78] For example, in *US – Certain Hot-Rolled Carbon*, India sought to argue that the US had also breached the international law principle of good faith in performing treaty obligations. The Appellate Body upheld the Panel's finding that such a claim was not within the terms of reference.[79] Or, in the ISDS context, Uzbekistan sought to rely on abuse of rights as a ground for its counterclaim in *Oxus Gold v Uzbekistan*.[80]

The use, or more accurately lack thereof, of the "limited jurisdiction" basis as rejecting other international law does not invalidate the importance of jurisdiction as the limiting factor. Rather, it illustrates how jurisdiction may already act as the closed door: parties are unlikely to bring clear cases of applying international law beyond the tribunal's jurisdiction. When arguments pass this initial test, the questions become more difficult and borderline decisions appear.

2.1 *Jurisdictional Objections*

Tribunals are cautious to cede their jurisdiction on the basis of other international law, in line with the role of jurisdiction as a closing tool. However, general principles and customary international law can still be used to legitimize a consensual approach to jurisdiction, thereby protecting the carrying out of judicial functions. Chapter 4 (section 2.3) already examined how general principles stemming from good faith have been used to ground objections. Although not always clear on whether issues of jurisdiction or admissibility, the result of finding such an objection is the same, namely the dismissal of the claim.[81]

78 Many of the disputes in which limited jurisdiction has been raised are further discussed in the following Chapter.

79 *United States – Countervailing Measures on Certain Hot-Rolled Carbon Steel Flat Products from India* (*Report of the Appellate Body*) (8 December 2014), WT/DS/436/AB/R [4.334].

80 *Oxus Gold v Uzbekistan* (ad hoc), Final Award, 17 December 2015 [935].

81 As Abi-Saab noted: '[a]ccording to the general rules of law and rules of general international law, non-compliance begets the inevitable legal sanction of dismissing the case, as falling outside the jurisdiction of the tribunal or as inadmissible': *Abaclat and Others vs Argentina* (n 69) para 28 (dissenting opinion of Abi-Saab); see also, on how the distinction has been inconsistently applied in relation to the corruption defence and waiting periods: August Reinisch, 'Jurisdiction and Admissibility in International Investment

Estoppel is more commonly (and more appropriately) raised in relation to the respondent withdrawing or rescinding its consent to jurisdiction. The claimant's attempt in *Besserglik v Mozambique* to use estoppel to imply consent to jurisdiction, which stands out from the other decisions on estoppel in ISDS, clearly highlights the necessary difference between using general principles to imply, presume or otherwise create consent compared to interpreting jurisdictional conditions. In rejecting the argument of the respondent, the tribunal asserts the fundamental nature of consent to jurisdiction, which cannot be presumed to be in existence through general principles.[82] Although the claimant's attempt in *Besserglik v Mozambique* is an extreme example of the line between the appropriate and non-appropriate use of general principles in jurisdiction, such extreme examples are often needed to elucidate the nuanced arguments on jurisdiction.

Similarly, the application of the futility exception has also been applied in interpreting jurisdictional conditions of IIAs. As the tribunal in *Daimler v Argentina* considered:

> the requirement for waiving treaty-based jurisdictional pre-requisites in international law is not nonsensicality but futility. Sovereign States are free to agree to any treaty provisions they so choose – whether concerning substantive commitments or dispute resolution provisions or otherwise – provided these provisions are not futile and are not otherwise contrary to peremptory norms of international law.[83]

However, it is important to consider the text of the specific IIA and the circumstances of the dispute as to whether the jurisdictional condition is in fact futile, compared to waiving jurisdictional pre-requisites where the IIA is silent on the

Law' in Andrea Gattini, Attila Tanzi and Filippo Fontanelli (eds), *General Principles of Law and International Investment Arbitration* (Brill Nijhoff 2018).

82 *Besserglik v Mozambique* (ICSID Case No ARB(AF)/14/2), Award, 28 October 2019 [421–422].

83 *Daimler Financial v Argentina* (ICSID Case No ARB/02/1), Award, 22 August 2012 [198]. The tribunal also described the restrictions on interpreting dispute settlement provisions: '[i]n interpreting dispute resolution provisions in BITS – just as with any other treaty provision – the ultimate goal is to determine what the contracting parties actually consented to. Thus, the fact that dispute resolution clauses should be construed neither liberally nor restrictively does not authorize international tribunals to interpret such clauses in a manner which exceeds the consent of the contracting parties as expressed in the text. To go beyond those bounds would be to act ultra vires' (at [172]); see also, *ST-AD v Bulgaria* (n 72) paras 364–5, although neither tribunal found futility existed within the circumstances of the dispute.

effects of non-compliance in each particular IIA. This appears to be the source of the concern of Abi-Saab in *Abaclat* on the majority's finding of jurisdiction despite the claimant's failure to comply with the local courts requirement.[84]

On this point of jurisdictional objections, the intra-EU objection is illustrative of how other international law may shield the jurisdiction of a tribunal. The intra-EU objection failed to gain traction before ISDS tribunals, commonly finding that the jurisdiction of the tribunals did not conflict with EU law.[85] Importantly, in undertaking this exercise and finding that the jurisdictional objection based on the other international law did not deprive the tribunal of jurisdiction, general international law played the central role in resolving the jurisdictional questions. The intra-EU objection cases are an example of the system (defragmentation) vs positivist tension (consent to jurisdiction) co-inhabiting. General international law concepts are applied to determine the jurisdictional objection of the conflict between EU law and international investment law, even if such conflict rules are not present in the treaties. Yet, the consent to the jurisdiction of the ISDS tribunal remains despite any other treaty regime pushing against it. The tribunals are also careful to ensure that EU law is noted as potentially relevant applicable law to the merits of the dispute, further distancing the fundamental jurisdiction requirements from more flexible approaches to international law at the merits.

The *Tatneft v Ukraine* decision makes a similar point in relying on general international procedural tools on concurrent jurisdiction. In that decision, the tribunal had to decide which two sets of treaties governed the dispute as far as jurisdiction was concerned: the respondent relied on the 1994 Fuel and Energy Cooperation Treaty and the Ukrtatnafta Treaty, while the claimant relied on the Investment Cooperation Agreement and the Russia-Ukraine BIT.[86] Determining which treaty governed the dispute was particularly crucial

---

84 *Abaclat and Others vs Argentina* (n 69) para 28 (dissenting opinion of Abi-Saab), although the majority decided on the basis of 'weighing of the specific interests at stake' rather than from the general principle of futility (at [584]); Abi-Saab's reasoning was cited with approval in the dissenting opinion in *Ambiente Ufficio S.pA and others v Argentine Republic* (ICSID Case No ARB/08/9), Decision on Jurisdiction and Admissibility, 8 February 2013 [340–341] (dissenting opinion of Bernárdez).

85 See, for example, *Electrabel SA v Hungary* (ICSID Case No ARB/07/19), Decision on Jurisdiction, Applicable Law and Liability, 30 November 2012; *Vattenfall AB and others v Federal Republic of Germany (II)* (ICSID Case No ARB/12/12), Decision on the Achmea Issue, 31 August 2018; For the alternative view, see Kohen's dissenting opinion in *Adamakopoulos v Cyprus* (ICSID Case No ARB/15/49), Decision on Jurisdiction, 7 February 2020.

86 *Tatneft v Ukraine* (PCA Case No 2008–8), Partial Award on Jurisdiction, 28 September 2010 [87].

to the tribunal's jurisdiction since only the treaties relied on by the claimant provided for investor-state arbitration.[87] The tribunal relied on the principle of *lex specialis* to determine that the dispute fell "most accurately" within the ambit of the dispute resolution arrangements in the Russia-Ukraine BIT.[88] The tribunal also addressed the various decisions of other international courts and tribunals invoked by the parties, noting that "in all the pertinent cases", the international court decided in favor of its jurisdiction in spite of concurrent jurisdiction arguments.[89]

From such examples, we can draw two conclusions. First, the tribunals are cautious to give up their jurisdiction on the basis of other law or other regimes.[90] Secondly, in doing so, general international law is used to "legitimize" the exercise of the tribunal's jurisdiction. General international law may be used to interpret jurisdictional requirements or provide conflict rules in absence of such treaty rules. However, the line is drawn when other international law may expand jurisdiction or otherwise cede jurisdiction of a properly constituted tribunal, thereby imposing jurisdiction as a closing tool.

2.2 *Inherent and Procedural Powers*

While the grant of jurisdiction can be a limiting tool, by delimiting what issues a tribunal may determine, it also grants the tribunal "a sweeping hold" over the scope of that consent.[91] By granting a tribunal jurisdiction to settle particular disputes, this comes with a grant of certain powers that are governed by essential general principles to "ensure the fulfilment of the fundamental purpose of all judicial proceedings, the final settlement of a dispute by an impartial

---

87 Comparatively, the treaties relied on by the respondent only envisaged negotiation and consultation for disputes concerning the application or interpretation of the treaties at issue and domestic proceedings for dispute related to agreements entered into by 'entities' of the parties. Indeed, there had been domestic litigation before Russian and Ukrainian courts but no competing jurisdiction between different international tribunals: ibid [88–9].

88 ibid [90–100].

89 ibid [96]; referring to the PCIJ decisions *of The Mavrommatis Palestine Concessions* (*Greece v United Kingdom*), Objection to Jurisdiction [1924] PCIJ Rep Series A No 2; *Factory at Chorzów* (*Germany v Poland*), Jurisdiction [1927] PCIJ Rep Series A No 9; and *Rights of Minorities in Upper Silesia* (*Minority Schools*) (*Germany v Poland*), Judgment [1928] PCIJ Rep Series A No 15.

90 The exception to this conclusion is fundamental rules of international law, such as *jus cogens*. However, such rules have not arisen in disputes before the WTO and investor-state dispute settlement mechanisms.

91 Christian J Tams, 'Controlling Consent: Insights from Binding Dispute Settlement' in Samantha Besson (ed), *Consenting to International Law* (1st edn, Cambridge University Press 2023) 82.

authority in a manner just and equitable to the parties on the basis of respect for law".[92]

As the starting point, inherent jurisdictional powers, such as *la compétence de la competence*,[93] indicate the potential for conflict between consent and judicial powers.[94] As Fitzmaurice noted, the soundness of this generally accepted principle could be questioned on the basis that the power of the tribunal to determine questions of jurisdiction "is scarcely consistent with the fundamental principle that the jurisdiction of an international tribunal is derived from and depends on the will of the parties".[95] Arguably, if the tribunal determines a jurisdictional issue *propio motu*, it will do so contrary to the expressed views of one or both of the parties. As Fitzmaurice noted, this argument may have theoretical force but it would render international arbitration and adjudication impossible.[96] However, this somewhat practically flawed argument demonstrates the tension in inherent jurisdiction: balancing the intent of the parties against the necessity of the tribunal to exercise an inherent power, which arises from the very existence of a tribunal and the need to perform its functions.[97]

Similarly, Thirlway challenged the notion of inherent jurisdiction as contradicting the fundamental principle of consent. In relation to inherent jurisdiction over provisional measures, Thirlway cautioned that:

92 Bin Cheng, *General Principles of Law as Applied by International Courts and Tribunals* (reprint 2006, Steven & Sons 1953) 389–90; see further, Charles Kotuby and Luke Sobota, *General Principles of Law and International Due Process: Principles and Norms Applicable in Transnational Disputes* (Oxford University Press 2017) ch 3 on the principle of due process.

93 Powers in relation to interim protection, preliminary objections and intervention are also often considered to be exercised in the inherent jurisdiction of a tribunal, in the absence of express statutory provisions: Elihu Lauterpacht, '"Partial" Judgments and the Inherent Jurisdiction of the International Court of Justice' in Vaughan Lowe and Malgosia Fitzmaurice (eds), *Fifty Years of the International Court of Justice* (Cambridge University Press 1996) 477; Chester Brown, 'The Inherent Powers of International Courts and Tribunals' (2006) 76 British Yearbook of International Law 195, 216.

94 Inherent jurisdictional powers were not included in the empirical analysis of "other international law" but clearly remain relevant to the doctrinal analysis of this research.

95 Fitzmaurice (n 30) 453.

96 Fitzmaurice considers that 'in the absence of a hierarchical system, or of special agreement, there is no other method by which any judicial determination of jurisdictional issues – which are after all legal issues – can be obtained, if not from the tribunal itself': ibid 454.

97 Friedl Weiss, 'Inherent Powers of National and International Courts' in Federico Ortino and Ernst-Ulrich Petersmann (eds), *The WTO Dispute Settlement System 1995 – 2003* (Kluwer 2003) 178.

> It needs to be recalled once more that the essence of jurisdiction is consent: if the Statute expresses the consent of States to a limited power to indicate provisional measures, it is self-contradictory to argue that, by creating a court, they implicitly consented to a wider power.[98]

However, Thirlway also noted that the justification of inherent jurisdiction is that it "is a necessary condition of ... any court of law ... being able to function at all".[99] In sourcing the justification for inherent jurisdiction in the functions of international tribunals, it is arguable that this jurisdiction derives ultimately from the consent of the state: "for it is the state parties who, in framing the constitutive instruments of international courts, have conferred those functions upon them."[100] Even without these jurisdictional powers expressed in constituting instruments, "as a general rule, any body possessing jurisdictional powers has the right in the first place to determine the extent of its jurisdiction."[101] Consequently, general principles[102] play an important part in interpreting limited consent to jurisdiction.[103]

For some tribunals, some of these inherent powers are set out in their constituting instruments,[104] thereby no longer being inherent but rather express

98 Thirlway (n 3) 21.

99 ibid 41.

100 Brown (n 93) 229; Thirlway (n 3) 43–44; see also, *Abaclat and Others vs Argentina* (n 69) para 13 (dissenting opinion of Abi-Saab): 'the consent of the parties cannot go beyond the objective limits of the general jurisdiction of the organ, but can restrict its jurisdiction further within these objective limits, by the parties subjecting their consent to additional limits, conditions or reservations. These can relate to any of the four dimensions of the ambit. But they can also relate to the powers of the organ as such (the primary meaning of jurisdiction), as long as this does not touch the hard core requirements of the judicial function, for example by excluding from its powers the indication of provisional measures'.

101 *Interpretation of the Greco-Turkish Agreement of December 1st, 1926*, Advisory Opinion [1928] PCIJ Rep B No 16 20; see also, *Northern Cameroons* (*Cameroon v United Kingdom*), Preliminary Objections (n 29) 103 (Separate Opinion of Judge Fitzmaurice).

102 The source of inherent jurisdictional powers is not necessarily clear. Brown identifies four possible sources of inherent jurisdiction: general principles of law, implied powers, derived from the identity of courts as judicial bodies or as necessary to ensure the fulfilment of the functions of international courts. Brown considers that the most likely source of inherent jurisdiction is found in the necessity of international courts to fulfil their functions: Brown (n 93) 221–228.

103 See also, Sarah Thin, 'Guardians of Legality? The International Judicial Function in an Era of Community Interest' (2023) 92 Nordic Journal of International Law 499, 503, who notes that implied powers are still part of a state-centric adjudicative function, but such powers are limited only to those necessary for an agreed purpose.

104 For example, Article 36(6) of the ICJ Statute states: "In the event of a dispute as to whether the Court has jurisdiction, the matter shall be settled by the decision of the Court." In

jurisdictional powers. However, these rules in the constituting instruments merely reflect the general principle and the necessity for "the very essence of the arbitral function and one of the inherent requirements for the exercise of this function".[105] Importantly, the ICJ has noted that the inherent jurisdiction of *la compétence de la competence* is *reflected* in Article 36(6) of the ICJ Statute, rather than the Statute *conferring* such a power, further illustrating the inherent nature of such powers.[106] This is also the case for ISDS tribunals under the ICSID Convention, which authorizes the exercise of certain inherent powers. Specifically, Article 41(1)[107] of the ICSID Convention reiterates "the well-established principle that international tribunals are to be the judges of their own competence".[108] Similarly, Article 23(1) of the UNCITRAL Rules provides that "the arbitral tribunal shall have the power to rule on its own jurisdiction".[109]

In comparison, for the WTO dispute settlement mechanism, the application of the "well-established" inherent jurisdictional powers is somewhat more

addition, the ICJ Statute also includes powers in relation to preliminary objections (article 36[6]), intervention (articles 62 and 63) and interim protection (article 41) that may also be considered to be matters in the exercise of 'inherent jurisdiction'. The ICJ has affirmed that Article 36(6) reflects the general principle that international tribunals possess inherent power to determine their own jurisdictions: *Nottebohm* (n 28) 119.

105 The Rapporteur of the Hague Convention of 1899, cited in ibid.

106 *Legality of the Use of Force* (*Serbia and Montenegro v Belgium*), Preliminary Objections [2004] ICJ Reports 279, 294; Brown (n 93) 214.

107 Article 41, in full, states:

1. The Tribunal shall be the judge of its own competence.
2. Any objection by a party to the dispute that that dispute is not within the jurisdiction of the Center, or for other reasons is not within the competence of the Tribunal, shall be considered by the Tribunal which shall determine whether to deal with it as a preliminary question or to join it to the merits of the dispute.

108 'Report of the Executive Directors on the Convention on the Settlement of Investment Disputes between States and Nationals of Other States' (n 55) para 38; see also, *Standard Chartered Bank (Hong Kong) Limited v Tanzania Electric Supply Company Limited* (ICSID Case No ARB/10/20), Decision on Annulment, 22 August 2018) [158, 321]; *Pac Rim Cayman LLC v Republic of El Salvador* (ICSID Case No ARB/09/12), Award, 14 October 2016) [5.33]; *HOCHTIEF Aktiengesellschaft v Argentine Republic* (ICSID Case No ARB/07/31, Decision on Jurisdiction, 24 October 2011) [11].

109 Article 23(1), in full, states: 'The arbitral tribunal shall have the power to rule on its own jurisdiction, including any objections with respect to the existence or validity of the arbitration agreement. For that purpose, an arbitration clause that forms part of a contract shall be treated as an agreement independent of the other terms of the contract. A decision by the arbitral tribunal that the contract is null shall not entail automatically the invalidity of the arbitration clause': UNCITRAL Arbitration Rules (with new article 1, paragraph 4, as adopted in 2013).

debateable.[110] There is no recognition within the DSU that either the WTO panels or the Appellate Body possess any inherent jurisdictional powers. Nevertheless, the Appellate Body has confirmed the existence of the "widely accepted rule that an international tribunal is entitled to consider the issue of its own jurisdiction on its own initiative, and to satisfy itself that it has jurisdiction in any case that comes before it."[111] This "widely accepted rule" has since been applied in several WTO disputes. In *Mexico – Corn Syrup* (*Article 21.5*) decision, the Appellate Body referred to the "proper exercise of the judicial function" and the requirement to address and dispose of "certain issues of a fundamental nature" as requiring panels to deal with "issues which go to the root of their jurisdiction ... if necessary, on their own motion – in order to satisfy themselves that they have authority to proceed."[112] In the subsequent *Mexico – Corn Syrup* decision, the Appellate Body agreed with Mexico that WTO panels "have certain implied jurisdictional powers that derive from their nature as adjudicative bodies", stating:

> WTO panels have certain powers that are inherent in their adjudicative function. Notably, panels have the right to determine whether they have jurisdiction in a given case, as well as to determine the scope of their jurisdiction.[113]

The Appellate Body went on to limit the implied jurisdictional powers of panels by determining that a WTO panel is not in a position to freely choose whether

110 For example, Weiss refers to the WTO dispute settlement mechanism as an atypical judicial body. As such, the Appellate Body does not possess inherent powers to review awards or issue interim orders. The fact that the Appellate Body examines issues propio motu is merely in the interests of efficiency. Weiss (n 97) 185–189 Weiss considers that the inherent powers are exercised in the interests of justice and so the completion of the legal analysis in the interests of efficiency of dispute resolution is not an inherent power. The fact that panels and the Appellate Body formally only act as servants of the DSB may suggest that it is not necessary for panels and the Appellate Body to have all the powers required to exercise the judicial function: see discussion in Lorand Bartels, 'The Separation of Powers in the WTO: How to Avoid Judicial Activism' (2004) 53 International and Comparative Law Quarterly 861, 885.

111 *United States – Anti-Dumping Act of 1916* (*Report of the Appellate Body*) (n 48) para 56 fn 30.

112 *Mexico – Corn Syrup* (*Article 21.5*) (n 47) para 36. The Appellate Body also cited *United States – Anti-Dumping Act of 1916* (*Report of the Appellate Body*) (n 48) para 54 fn 32, that 'the vesting of jurisdiction in a panel is a fundamental prerequisite for lawful panel proceedings.'

113 *Mexico – Tax Measures on Soft Drinks and Other Beverages* (*Report of the Appellate Body*) (6 March 2006) WT/DS308/AB/R [45].

or not to exercise its validly established jurisdiction. In the Appellate Body's opinion, this would "seem to 'diminish' the right of a complaining Member to 'seek the redress of a violation of obligations'" as it "would not be consistent with a panel's obligations under Articles 3.2 and 19.2 of the DSU."[114] However, the Appellate Body "express[ed] no view" on whether other legal impediments could exist which would preclude a panel from ruling on the merits of the claim.[115] Also relevantly for the consent-judicial lawmaking tension, the "law-making" of the Appellate Body in the *Mexico – Soft Drinks* decision is limited to the jurisdictional powers, with the Appellate Body ultimately rejecting the relevance of international law in the other aspects of the dispute.[116]

A less straightforward example than inherent powers is the concept of good faith. Good faith is at the intersection of procedure and substance[117] and, as such, it illustrates how procedural questions interact differently with the opening and closing tools. This is captured in the WTO decision of *US – Hot-Rolled Carbon Steel Flat Products from India* in which good faith as a substantive obligation was not available based on the limited jurisdiction of the tribunal.[118] There, the Appellate Body noted that India drew a distinction between the principle of good faith in relation to treaty interpretation and the exercise of good faith in the performance of treaty obligations. The latter claim of breach of the international law principle of good faith did not fall within the Panel's terms of reference.[119]

However, when good faith falls towards procedural rules and rules of evidence, such as abuse of process issues, tribunals are willing to read in good faith obligations. Procedure, when defined broadly, rather than narrowly,

114 ibid [53].

115 ibid [54].

116 The Appellate Body rejected the illegality arguments of Mexico: *Mexico – Soft Drinks (Appellate Body)* (n 113); comparatively, the Appellate Body in *US – Anti-Dumping Act of 1916* only raised the issue of inherent jurisdictional powers, while the Panel reports in the dispute only raised issues of evidence in relation to municipal laws: *United States – Anti-Dumping Act of 1916 – Complaint by the European Communities (Report of the Panel)* (31 March 2000), WT/DS136/R; *United States – Anti-Dumping Act of 1916 – Complaint by Japan (Report of the Panel)* (29 May 2000), WT/DS162/R.

117 As Tanzi notes, good faith affects legal obligations at each stage and bears on a formidably wide range of aspects, procedural and substantive alike: Attila Tanzi, 'The Relevance of the Foreign Investor's Good Faith' in Andrea Gattini, Attila Tanzi and Filippo Fontanelli (eds), *General Principles of Law and International Investment Arbitration* (Brill Nijhoff 2018) 194.

118 *United States – Countervailing Measures on Certain Hot-Rolled Carbon Steel Flat Products from India (Report of the Appellate Body)* (n 79) para 4.333–4.

119 ibid [4.334].

incorporates rules devoted to the enforcement of the rules of substantive law and rules determining organization and functioning of judicial proceedings.[120] These powers concern the ability of dispute settlement tribunals to manage their own proceedings.[121] Rules of evidence also fall within procedure and the principles of international due process, explaining the common relevance of international legal rules of burden of proof and evidence finding its way into WTO[122] and ISDS decisions.[123] In regards to good faith and evidential rules, the Panel in *Thailand – Cigarettes from the Philippines (Art 21.5)* identified issues of due process and "the good faith conduct of WTO Members as fundamental to the substantive obligations of the Members as well as the dispute settlement system as a whole" in dealing with a question of lawyer-client privilege.[124] The Panel was required to decide whether there was a violation of due process rights in circumstances where the complainant had submitted privileged documents in breach of lawyer-client privilege. While the DSU sets out good faith and due process requirements, the Panel considered there were no WTO rules

---

120 Robert Kolb, 'General Principles of Procedural Law' in Andreas Zimmermann and others (eds), *The Statute of the International Court of Justice: A Commentary* (3rd edn, Oxford University Press 2019) 965.

121 This also aligns with the US's suggested parameters for use of public international law in WTO dispute settlement, whereby the US recognized that 'each WTO adjudicative body is tasked with managing its own proceedings, including developing its own working procedures. It is natural that in managing its proceedings, a body may wish to consider how other adjudicative bodies have approached similar procedural issues, including other international adjudicative bodies as well as those in an individual Member. Ultimately, however, such consideration is a question of the body exercising its discretion as to how to manage its proceedings; such consideration is not a question of interpreting a covered agreement in accordance with public international law': 'Negotiations on Improvements and Clarifications of the Dispute Settlement Understanding, Further Contribution of the United States on Improving Flexibility and Member Control in WTO Dispute Settlement – Communication from the United States' (World Trade Organization, Dispute Settlement Body 2005) TN/DS/W/82 7.

122 The Appellate Body first referred to the applicable rules on burden of proof in *United States – Wool Shirts and Blouses* (*Report of the Appellate Body*) (25 April 1997), WT/DS33/AB/R 13 ff.

123 Like its WTO counterpart, the first decision under ICSID also relied on the general international law rules on burden of proof and evidence: *Asian Agricultural Products Ltd v Republic of Sri Lanka* (ICSID Case No ARB/87/3), Award, 27 June 1990 [56]; for a more recent acceptance of the general principles on burden of proof see *Churchill Mining PLC and Planet Mining Pty Ltd v Republic of Indonesia* (ICSID Case No ARB/12/14 and 12/40), Decision on Annulment, 18 March 2019 [215].

124 *Thailand – Customs and Fiscal Measures on Cigarettes from the Philippines – Recourse to article 21.5 of the DSU by the Philippines* (*Report of the Panel*) (12 November 2018), WT/DS371/RW [7.29].

governing lawyer-client privilege.[125] As such, the Panel looked to the practice of other international courts and tribunals to identify general principles of lawyer-client privilege "that may be equally appropriate to dealing with issues of lawyer-client privilege in the WTO dispute settlement context".[126] Although to some extent the Panel is supplementing (not necessarily gap-filling or merely interpreting) WTO principles of due process and good faith with general principles arising from jurisprudence, the Panel does so without establishing any hierarchy between the sets of principles.[127]

Such distinctions of substance and procedure are not always clear and can be criticised as abstract, vague or artificially applied.[128] This criticism comes across in Arbitrator Abi-Saab's dissenting opinion in *Abaclat* to the tribunal's treatment of the mass claims. Although the mass claims part of the majority decision does not relate to the application of other international law, Abi-Saab's discussion of the limits of "procedural improvisation" highlights the possibility for artificial distinction between jurisdictional and procedural concerns. The majority considered that there was a "gap" in the ICSID framework, "which was unintended and which the Tribunal has the power to fill" through the exercise of its procedural powers[129] under Article 44 of the ICSID Convention[130] and Rule 19 of the ICSID Arbitration Rules.[131] For Abi-Saab, the issue of collective proceedings was more than a mere "technical gap" but related to the limits of the tribunal's powers in exercising its judicial or arbitral function,

125 ibid [7.30].

126 ibid [7.34].

127 'We do not consider that either applies to the exclusion of the other, or that it would be correct to establish any hierarchy between these sets of principles': ibid [7.32].

128 See, for example, Shany's discussion of the difficulty in classifying claims as procedural or substantive in nature: Yuval Shany, *Questions of Jurisdiction and Admissibility before International Courts* (Cambridge University Press 2015) 98 ff.

129 In doing so, the majority distinguished between a 'qualified silence', meaning an intended silence indicating that it does not allow for something that is not provided, compared with a 'gap' which was unintended and which the Tribunal has the power to fill: *Abaclat and Others vs Argentina* (n 69) para 517.

130 Article 44 states that '[a]ny arbitration proceeding shall be conducted in accordance with the provisions of this Section and, except as the parties otherwise agree, in accordance with the Arbitration Rules in effect on the date on which the parties consented to arbitration. If any question of procedure arises which is not covered by this Section or the Arbitration Rules or any rules agreed by the parties, the Tribunal shall decide the question': Convention on the Settlement of Investment Disputes Between States and Nationals of Other States (Washington, 18 March 1965), 575 UNTS 159.

131 Rule 19 states that '[t]he tribunal shall make the orders required for the conduct of the proceeding': ICSID Arbitration Rules (effective as of 10 April 2006).

thereby it was an issue of jurisdiction.[132] In this way, the issue of mass claims relates to the consent of the respondent state, rather than mere procedural powers of a tribunal and therefore is to be assessed as a strict requirement of consent to jurisdiction.

2.3 *Implications*

This Chapter examined the consensualist approach to the force of international law: the concept of jurisdiction and the restrictive nature of state consent as a closing tool. Consent to jurisdiction is a fundamental concept in international dispute resolution and international tribunals continue to refer to the importance of consent to jurisdiction. However, as this Chapter has illustrated, consent to jurisdiction is more difficult to understand in practice. Most notably, there is no clear understanding of the definitional limits of the concept of "jurisdiction".

By identifying these difficulties, we are left with the question of how to interpret consent to jurisdiction. We continue to wonder what states mean when they use the term "jurisdiction" in treaties establishing such international tribunals. Perhaps all we can clearly ascertain is that the function of this term as used by states is to set out the power and authority of the adjudicatory mechanism. However, this does not get us far. We are still faced with the question of how a tribunal can interpret a state's consent to jurisdiction when it does not understand the definition and boundaries of this concept and its relationship to other concepts.

The blurriness of the opening and closing tools highlighted in this and the previous Chapters leaves room for discretion and normative judgements by adjudicators on the importance of each of the tools. The next Chapter unpacks how the indeterminacy of the toolkit leads to inconsistency from one adjudicator to the next.

---

132 *Abaclat and Others vs Argentina* (n 69) para 196 (dissenting opinion of Abi-Saab).

CHAPTER 6

Unpacking Inconsistency

Following the revelation of the inconsistency created through the application of the adjudicator's toolkit in the book, this Chapter elucidates how the different normative goals of adjudicators influences the indeterminacy of the adjudicator's toolkit. These disparate goals, often hidden within the opaque reasoning of adjudicators, is argued in this Chapter to be the source of the "consistent inconsistency". Defragmentation and the international judicial function challenge a restrictive interpretation of jurisdiction, with the systemic approaches to international law conflicting with a traditional and more consensual view of jurisdiction. However, the balance between the international judicial function and jurisdiction is not clear, resulting in inconsistency when it comes to the relationship between jurisdiction and the opening tools.

1 Source of Inconsistency: Relationship between Jurisdiction and Applicable Law

This section examines the source of inconsistency in the tribunals' approach to other public international law as uncertainty surrounding the foundational legal concepts of jurisdiction and the opening tools. This uncertainty is most evident in understanding the relationship between jurisdiction and applicable law and how limitations within jurisdiction affect applicable law and interpretation.

As the previous section highlighted, the concept of jurisdiction is not clearly defined at the international level, nor is there any particular rule on how jurisdictional clauses are to be interpreted. This has made it difficult to systematically define the boundaries and ramifications of the concept of jurisdiction. One of the questions arising from the lack of a clear delimitation of the boundaries of the concept of jurisdiction is how this concept relates to other expressions of the tribunal's authority, in particular, the tribunal's authority to apply particular law. Defining the relationship between jurisdiction and applicable law must be the first step to understanding the authority of international trade and investment tribunals to decide questions related to other norms and rules of public international law.

This section begins with an examination of the relationship between jurisdiction and applicable law, both under general international law and within

 | DOI:10.1163/9789004700932_007

the WTO and ISDS regimes. The implications of the relationship between jurisdiction and applicable law for the application of other international law is then analysed in two ways. First, the consequences of tribunals taking different approaches to the relationship between jurisdiction and applicable law, with the countermeasures defence in ISDS as a clear example of such problems. Secondly, the relationship between jurisdiction and interpretation, noting the particular complexity of systemic integration.

Some may consider the relationship between jurisdiction and applicable law to be a moot or uncontroversial issue, particularly when we consider how parties approach jurisdiction and applicable law. When presenting their argument to the international court or tribunal, jurisdiction and applicable law will usually be treated as separate issues and dealt with in different sections of memorials and submissions. Further, jurisdictional issues may already have been dealt with in preliminary objections. As such, when it is time to consider applicable law, jurisdiction may no longer be in doubt. Such an approach to jurisdiction and applicable law may assist in structuring legal arguments and ensuring all issues are addressed before the court or tribunal in a succinct way.[1] However, this distinction between jurisdiction and applicable law may be illusory. Analysis of tribunal approaches to the issue identifies that tribunals do not necessarily consider this distinction to be real. This can lead to confusion on the nature and scope of a tribunal's jurisdictional power and the applicable law, leading to fragmentation between regimes and the "consistency in inconsistency" that has been identified within the WTO and investor-state tribunal reasoning.

The relationship between jurisdiction and applicable law can be viewed through two different lenses: first, whether applicable law plays a role in defining the jurisdiction of the tribunal, and secondly, whether jurisdiction somehow defines or limits the applicable law of the dispute. Confusion arises in both aspects of the relationship, illustrating the potential for diverging views of adjudicators and misunderstanding of the relationship between these concepts. This confusion provides an opportunity for incongruence between adjudicator approaches to law outside the four corners of the treaty conferring jurisdiction on the tribunal.

The relationship between jurisdiction and applicable law becomes particularly relevant for cases arising in the context of a broader political disagreement. As the ICJ explained in *Ukraine v Russia*:

---

1 On the intertwined nature of jurisdiction and substantive questions in the structure of legal arguments before international tribunals, see Yuval Shany, *Questions of Jurisdiction and Admissibility before International Courts* (Cambridge University Press 2015) 84–6.

> applications that are submitted to [the ICJ] often present a particular dispute that arises in the context of a broader disagreement between the parties ... The fact that a dispute before the Court forms part of a complex situation that includes various matters, however important, over which the States concerned hold opposite views, cannot lead the Court to decline to resolve that dispute, provided that the parties have recognized its jurisdiction to do so and the conditions for the exercise of its jurisdiction are otherwise met.[2]

Such cases that arise within a broader political dispute clearly illustrate the problem of a tribunal's jurisdiction to consider any other aspects of the dispute. Whether the tribunal recognizes a distinction between jurisdiction and applicable law will affect the understanding of its scope to consider other international law issues. On the one hand, a tribunal could recognize the distinction. As considered in the ILC's Fragmentation Report, quoted above in Chapter 4 (section 1), a limited jurisdiction may not equal limited applicable law.[3] This distinction approach is linked to the view of applicable law as an opening tool of international law. By separating it from the limited jurisdiction, applicable law can act as the gateway for other normative considerations beyond the individual legal regime and thereby avoid the pessimistic view of the risks of fragmentation.

On the other hand, the primary importance of state consent to international dispute resolution may suggest another view. In line with the demands of state sovereignty, no State may be compelled to submit to any form of dispute settlement without its consent.[4] If we consider that applicable law is intimately connected to the concept of jurisdiction, which, in turn, is limited by State consent, this will affect the extent beyond the treaty limits that the tribunal may go in applying other law: courts have limited jurisdiction and, as such, are not permitted to exceed their mandates and infer jurisdiction to apply other

2 *Application of the International Convention for the Suppression of the Financing of Terrorism and of the International Convention on the Elimination of all Forms of Racial Discrimination* (*Ukraine v Russian Federation*), Preliminary Objection [2019] ICJ Reports 558 [28] (citations omitted).

3 Martti Koskenniemi, 'Fragmentation of International Law: Difficulties Arising from the Diversification and Expansion of International Law, Report of the Study Group of the International Law Commission' (International Law Commission 2006) A/CN.4/L.682 para 423.

4 See, for example, *Status of Eastern Carelia*, Advisory Opinion [1923] PCIJ Report Series B No 5 27; *Ambatielos Case* (*Greece v United Kingdom*), Judgment [1953] ICJ Reports 10, 19.

law.[5] As such, whether jurisdiction and applicable law are distinct concepts will affect the authority of the international tribunal to consider any law beyond the particular treaty conferring jurisdiction on the tribunal.[6] Both approaches have normative force, depending on the concept and source of legitimacy of international law: the former "crucial distinction" approach by recognizing the systemic relationship within different branches of international law and the latter by recognizing the primacy of state consent to jurisdiction.

Confusing the picture further is the middle ground between these two dichotomous approaches, which recognizes a complex relationship between jurisdiction and applicable law. One example of such an approach is the "gate-keeper approach". While this approach sees jurisdiction and applicable law as conceptually distinct, compromissory clauses often act as the gatekeepers of the law to be used by the court: the dispute "passes through the gate of the jurisdictional clause, which in turn influences the tribunal's determination of the applicable law".[7] Under this approach, the applicable law clause may also influence how a tribunal conceives of its jurisdictional mandate.[8]

---

5 Joel P Trachtman, 'Jurisdiction in WTO Dispute Settlement' in Bruce Wilson and Rufus Yerxa (eds), *Key Issues in WTO Dispute Settlement: The First Ten Years* (Cambridge University Press 2005) 135.

6 An example of how the effect of these two approaches on the law used by the tribunal can be seen in the debate between Pauwelyn and Trachtman on the extent to which the WTO panels and Appellate Body may take into account other norms of public international law: Joost Pauwelyn, *Conflict of Norms in Public International Law: How WTO Law Relates to Other Rules of International Law* (Cambridge University Press 2003) 460–465; Joel P Trachtman, 'Review of Conflict of Norms in Public International Law: How WTO Law Relates to Other Rules of International Law' (2004) 98 The American Journal of International Law 855, 858; Trachtman (n 5) 135.

7 Michael Waibel, 'Investment Arbitration: Jurisdiction and Admissibility' in Marc Bungenberg and others (eds), *International Investment Law* (Beck Nomos Hart 2015) 1221.

8 A number of other investment law scholars also refer to a link between jurisdiction and applicable law that may fall within the gatekeeper approach. For example, Schreuer considers that jurisdiction and applicable law are intimately linked but are not necessarily always coextensive: Christoph H Schreuer, 'Jurisdiction and Applicable Law in Investment Treaty Arbitration' (2014) 1 McGill Journal of Dispute Resolution 1, 2; see also, Eric De Brabandere, *Investment Treaty Arbitration as Public International Law: Procedural Aspects and Implications* (Cambridge University Press 2014) 135; Bjorklund also finds that the scope of the tribunal's authority dictates the law applicable to the dispute and that "substantive law that the treaty directs the tribunal to apply will govern the breadth of the tribunal's jurisdiction to grant relief by giving it the authority to enforce only a limited set of rules: Andrea K Bjorklund, 'Applicable Law in International Investment Disputes' in Chiara Giorgetti (ed), *Litigating International Investment Arbitration Disputes* (Brill Nijhoff 2014) 263, 265.

1.1 *The Murky Waters of International Jurisprudence*

In an attempt to understand the concept of "jurisdiction" in the international field, Amerasinghe reviewed the jurisprudence of international courts and tribunals and proposed that "jurisdiction" covers many aspects of judicial activity. Relevantly for the relationship between jurisdiction and applicable law, Amerasinghe considered one aspect of jurisdictional activity to involve "the initial power of a tribunal to determine whether it may determine (or has the authority to determine) that it has the appropriate authority to begin and continue judicial examination of a case."[9] This area of judicial activity may require a tribunal to decide:

a. the authority to proceed to exercise the power to apply rules of procedure and substance to decide the dispute referred to the tribunal;
b. the power to grant what in the broadest terms may be called remedial measures once a decision has been taken on the merits; and
c. sometimes to select particular rules of substance or procedure in deciding the merits, i.e., what it may do in settling the dispute once it has been established that it has the authority to do so.

In Amerasinghe's view, the third category refers to what law should or should not be applied in relation to substance or procedure,[10] as such, identifying a close link between the boundaries of jurisdiction and the limits of the applicable law.

Beyond the scholarly debate, there is limited assistance provided in the jurisprudence of international courts and tribunals. In *Jurisdiction of the Courts of Danzig*, the PCIJ considered that "jurisdiction implies the right to decide what substantive law is applicable in a given case to which the jurisdiction extends"[11] but goes little farther in explaining this. More recent jurisprudence of international courts and tribunals fails to provide any clearer understanding of this relationship. The distinction often ends up blurred in practice:

> Because there is no real system of compulsory jurisdiction in international law, jurisdictional disputes occupy a quite disproportionate part of the Courts' time. (…) [This] also gives rise to real difficulties in great

9 CF Amerasinghe, *Jurisdiction of International Tribunals* (Kluwer Law International 2003) pp 58–62.

10 CF Amerasinghe, *Jurisdiction of Specific International Tribunals* (Martinus Nijhoff 2008) p 6.

11 *Judgments of the Courts of Danzig*, Advisory Opinion [1928] PCIJ Report Series B No 15 p 26.

> many cases in trying to squeeze a case that is really about one subject into a jurisdictional clause that was designed to deal with something else.[12]

We can find some discussion of the relationship between jurisdiction and applicable law when international courts and tribunals have been faced with disputes under compromissory clauses. While limited in number and breadth of analysis in such cases, the following discussion suggests that the relationship is not simple and applicable law is not to be read as entirely separate from jurisdictional limitations, contrary to the liberal reading by the ILC Fragmentation Report.

In his dissenting opinion in *Military and Paramilitary Activities*, Judge Jennings quite emphatically discussed his concerns with expansion of jurisdiction. Judge Jennings considered that the compromissory clause of the bilateral treaty between the US and Nicaragua of 1956[13] did not include matters that could be inconsistent with the object and purpose of the treaty but not referred to as specific articles of the treaty:

> The jurisdiction clause of such a treaty could not be regarded as conferring a jurisdiction to pass upon matters external to the actual provisions of the treaty, even though such matters may affect the operation of the treaty … If it were otherwise, there would be no apparent limit to the kinds of dispute which might in certain circumstances be claimed to come under such a jurisdiction clause.[14]

The ICJ's decision was slightly less emphatic, noting the fact that it had jurisdiction under Art 36(2) of the ICJ Statute as well as the bilateral treaty, meant that it could examine Nicaragua's claim, but such a claim was not provided for under the bilateral treaty.[15] Perhaps in a slightly less explicit manner, the ICJ was also recognizing the inherent and primary role of jurisdictional clauses.

12 Sir Christopher Greenwood's Friday Lunchtime Lecture, Lauterpacht Center for International Law, 7 October 2011, cited in Waibel (n 7) 1221.

13 Article XXIV:2 of the treaty states, 'any dispute between the Parties as to the interpretation or application of the present Treaty, not satisfactorily adjusted by diplomacy, shall be submitted to the International Court of Justice, unless the Parties agree to settlement by some other pacific means': Treaty of Friendship, Commerce and Navigation between the United States of America and the Republic of Nicaragua (Managua, 21 January 1956), 3567 UNTS 3.

14 *Military and Paramilitary Activities in and Against Nicaragua* (*Nicaragua v United States of America*), Judgment [1986] ICJ Reports 14, 539 (Dissenting Opinion of Judge Jennings).

15 ibid 276. Judge Jennings agreed with this point: see 539.

The issue of the relationship between different international laws at the jurisdictional and applicable law stage was also the subject of the *Genocide Convention* cases.[16] In the first case in *Bosnia and Herzegovina v Serbia and Montenegro*, the ICJ made it very clear that it had no jurisdiction outside of the Genocide Convention.[17] The ICJ stated that it:

> has no power to rule on alleged breaches of other obligations under international law, not amounting to genocide, particularly those protecting human rights in armed conflict. That is so even if the alleged breaches are of obligations under peremptory norms, or of obligations which protect essential humanitarian values, and which may be owed *erga omnes*.[18]

The ICJ went on to note that, in determining a breach of the Convention, it would only have recourse to the Convention itself, and the rules of general international law on treaty interpretation and State responsibility.[19]

The later decision in *Croatia v Serbia* seems to take its jurisdiction one step further. The ICJ referred to the above-cited paragraph from the *Bosnia and Herzegovina* case, but went on to state that:

> [it] does not prevent the Court from considering, in its reasoning, whether a violation of international humanitarian law or international human rights law has occurred to the extent that this is relevant for the

16 *Application of the Convention on the Prevention and Punishment of the Crime of Genocide (Bosnia and Herzegovina v Serbia and Montenegro)*, Judgment [2007] ICJ Reports 43; *Application of the Convention on the Prevention and Punishment of the Crime of Genocide (Croatia v Serbia)*, Judgment [2015] ICJ Reports 3.

17 Article 9 of the Genocide Convention is the compromissory clause and states: 'Disputes between the Contracting Parties relating to the interpretation, application or fulfilment of the present Convention, including those relating to the responsibility of a State for genocide or for any of the other acts enumerated in article III, shall be submitted to the International Court of Justice at the request of any of the parties to the dispute': Convention on the Prevention and Punishment of the Crime of Genocide (9 December 1948), 78 UNTS 277.

18 *Application of the Convention on the Prevention and Punishment of the Crime of Genocide (Bosnia and Herzegovina v Serbia and Montenegro)*, Judgment (n 16) para 147.

19 ibid [149]; see also, *Application of the Convention on the Prevention and Punishment of the Crime of Genocide (Croatia v Serbia), Judgment* (n 16) para 125. Relevantly, the Genocide Convention does not include an applicable law clause in the event that disputes are brought before the ICJ.

> Court's determination of whether or not there has been a breach of an obligation under the Genocide Convention.[20]

This passage suggests a role for laws outside the Genocide Convention beyond mere interpretation assistance. The Court accepted the possibility of finding a violation of international humanitarian law so long as that is somehow "relevant" to the ultimate determination that falls within its jurisdiction. In this respect, the two passages require us to distinguish between the "power to rule" against "considering violations", a potentially very narrow differentiation based on the legal consequences for the violation. When the Court turned to the applicable law, it determined that the Convention and international humanitarian law are "two distinct bodies of rules" but, where both of these bodies of rules are applicable to an armed conflict, "the rules of international humanitarian law might be relevant in order to decide" whether the acts alleged by the parties constitute genocide under the Convention.[21] However, as a result of the limitation of its jurisdiction to violations of the Convention, it does not have to rule "in general or in abstract terms" on the relationship between the Convention and international humanitarian law.[22] The Court did not indicate how international humanitarian law might be relevant to the dispute and, in the context of Serbia's counterclaim, went so far as to note that an act may be lawful under international humanitarian law but at the same time constitute a violation of the Convention.[23]

The application of other international treaties was also the subject of discussion in relation to the jurisdiction of the ICJ in the *Pulp Mills* case. Argentina brought a dispute against Uruguay on the basis of a bilateral treaty, which provided for jurisdiction of the ICJ for disputes "concerning the interpretation or application" of the 1975 Statute of the River Uruguay.[24] Argentina attempted to argue that certain clauses of the 1975 Statute were "referral clauses", having the effect of incorporating into the Statute the obligations of the parties under general international law and a number of multilateral conventions, and thereby allowing the ICJ to determine whether Uruguay had complied with

20 *Application of the Convention on the Prevention and Punishment of the Crime of Genocide (Croatia v Serbia)*, Judgment (n 16) para 85 (emphasis added).

21 ibid [153].

22 ibid, see also [474] where a similar statement is made in relation to Serbia's counterclaim.

23 ibid [474].

24 Article 60 states that 'any dispute concerning the interpretation or application of the Treaty and the Statute which cannot be settled by direct negotiations may be submitted by either Party to the International Court of Justice': Statute of the River Uruguay, a treaty signed by Argentina and Uruguay (26 February 1975), 1295 UNTS 340.

its obligations under certain other conventions.[25] The ICJ rejected the "referral clause" argument based on its interpretation of the 1975 Statute and found it had no jurisdiction to rule whether Uruguay had complied with its obligations under other multilateral conventions.[26] On an alternative argument of Argentina relating to interpretation using Article 31(3)(c) of the VCLT, the ICJ relevantly noted that:

> In the interpretation of the 1975 Statute, taking account of relevant rules of international law applicable in the relations between the Parties, whether these are rules of general international law or contained in multilateral conventions to which the two States are parties, nevertheless has no bearing on the scope of the jurisdiction conferred on the Court under Article 60 of the 1975 Statute, which remains confined to disputes concerning the interpretation or application of the Statute.[27]

The relationship between jurisdiction and applicable law became murkier when Argentina argued that Uruguay had breached its "other obligations deriving from general, conventional and customary international law which are necessary for the application of the 1975 Statute".[28] This flows from a requirement under Article 41 to ensure rules and measures adopted at the domestic level are "in accordance with applicable international agreements" and take account of internationally agreed technical standards.[29] However, the Court did not ultimately consider breach of other international agreements, but rather through their incorporated version in domestic regulations and rules adopted by the treaty body.[30]

While it may be tempting to rely on this rather broad view of its jurisdiction and power to determine the applicable law that has been taken by the ICJ, this approach is not appropriate for specialized tribunals. Although the ICJ is not

25 *Pulp Mills on the River Uruguay (Argentina v Uruguay), Judgment* [2010] ICJ Reports 14 [53]. Argentina referred to Article 1 (purposes and definitions) and 41 (undertaking to protect and preserve aquatic environment in accordance with applicable international agreements) of the Statute.

26 ibid [63].

27 ibid [66].

28 ibid [169].

29 ibid [196–197].

30 ibid [202] (the treaty body refers to the Administrative Commission of the River Uruguay, established under the 1975 Statute). General international law is still relevant to interpreting Article 41, namely using the requirement of environmental impact assessment under general international law to interpret Article 41: [204].

a court of general jurisdiction, as Crawford and Nevill have argued, the ICJ has taken a broad view of the notion of dispute arising under a treaty, on the basis of Article 38(1) of the ICJ Statute.[31] For the ICJ, a broad approach to jurisdiction and applicable law may not be particularly problematic: "the Court, having been let into the arena of putative general jurisdiction via a particular treaty, could then range across the international law terrain, something the judges like to do, if only in an impressionistic mode."[32] This presumption of general jurisdiction may not be applicable to more specialist tribunals,[33] dealing with a single regime of international law.

As an example of specialist tribunals, decisions within the UNCLOS framework present an inconsistent and confusing picture. Even on the first stage of the relationship (concerning whether applicable law plays a role in defining jurisdiction), there is inconsistent jurisprudence on whether the applicable law provision could expand the jurisdiction of UNCLOS tribunals.[34] In the *Guyana v Suriname* decision, the tribunal (administered by the PCA) explicitly considered that Article 293(1) of UNCLOS[35] gave it "competence" and rejected Suriname's contention that it had no "jurisdiction" over the claim relating to violations of the UN Charter and general international law.[36] The tribunal went on to find a violation of the prohibition on the use of force and, as such, clearly exercised jurisdiction in relation to this claim.[37]

In *The MOX Plant* case, the tribunal (also administered by the PCA) famously referred to a "cardinal distinction" between the scope of the tribunal's

---

31 James Crawford and Penelope Nevill, 'Relations between International Courts and Tribunals: The "Regime Problem"' in Margaret A Young (ed), *Regime Interaction in International Law: Facing Fragmentation* (Cambridge University Press 2012) 249.

32 ibid 250.

33 ibid 241.

34 Tzeng identifies three cases as showing the applicable law provision being effectively invoked to expand the tribunals' jurisdiction and four cases in which the 'well-established' principle is applied and the tribunal rejects any expansion of jurisdiction under the applicable law clause: Peter Tzeng, 'Jurisdiction and Applicable Law Under UNCLOS' (2016) 126 The Yale Law Journal 242, 243.

35 Article 293(1) is the applicable law clause of UNCLOS, stating that "a court or tribunal having jurisdiction under this section shall apply this Convention and other rules of international law not incompatible with this Convention": United Nations Convention on the Law of the Sea (Montego Bay, 10 December 1982), 1833 UNTS 397. Arguably, a rather wide applicable law clause.

36 *Guyana v Suriname* (PCA Case No 2004–04), Award of the Arbitral Tribunal, 17 September 2007, (2007) 47 ILM 166 [405–6]. The arbitration was commenced under UNCLOS and administered by the PCA.

37 ibid [488].

jurisdiction and the law to be applied.[38] The tribunal provided little analysis nor set out the implications of this "cardinal distinction", which it referred to as arising from the UK's submissions. In its submissions, the UK strongly criticized Ireland's contention on the applicable law. The UK noted that Ireland brought the dispute under UNCLOS, thereby prescribing the jurisdiction of the tribunal.[39] However, the UK disagreed with Ireland's contention that UNCLOS incorporates and requires the application of other international law not inconsistent with UNCLOS. The UK argued this "dramatically enlarged" the jurisdiction of the tribunal "through the prism of applicable law".[40] After reviewing various other international legal decisions, the UK concluded that compromissory clauses, such as the one in UNCLOS, extend "only to matters that come within the scope of that clause and does not include the interpretation or application of other international agreements or of customary international law."[41] The tribunal noted its agreement with the "cardinal distinction" referred to by the UK but perhaps confused the issue by going on to refer to inadmissibility of claims under other legal instruments, rather than jurisdiction.[42] Ultimately, the procedural decision turned on problems arising from some aspects of European Community law[43] and we are not provided with a more detailed consideration of the aspect of the relationship between jurisdiction and applicable law in *The MOX Plant* case.

Although not in the UNCLOS context, it is helpful to consider the related *Ireland v United Kingdom* proceedings under the Convention for the Protection of the Marine Environment of the North-East Atlantic (referred to as the

38 *The MOX Plant Case (Ireland v United Kingdom)* (PCA 2002–01), Suspension of Proceedings on Jurisdiction and Merits, Order of 24 June 2003 [19]; on how some scholars have interpreted the meaning of 'cardinal distinction', see Joost Pauwelyn, 'How to Win a World Trade Organization Dispute Based on Non-World Trade Organization Law' (2003) 37 Journal of World Trade 997, 1000; Lorand Bartels, 'Jurisdiction and Applicable Law Clauses: Where Does a Tribunal Find the Principal Norms Applicable to the Case before It?' in Tomer Broude and Yuval Shany (eds), *Multi-Sourced Equivalent Norms in International Law* (Hart Publishing 2011) 124; Campbell McLachlan, 'The Principle of Systemic Integration and Article 31(3)(c) of the Vienna Convention' (2005) 54 International & Comparative Law Quarterly 279, 301.

39 Article 288(1) of UNCLOS, on which Ireland relied in bringing the dispute to the tribunal, states: "A court or tribunal referred to in Article 287 shall have jurisdiction over any dispute concerning the interpretation or application of this Convention which is submitted to it in accordance with this Part."

40 *The MOX Plant Case (Ireland v United Kingdom)* (PCA 2002–01), Counter-Memorial of the United Kingdom, 9 January 2003 [4.6].

41 ibid [4.30].

42 *The MOX Plant Case (Ireland v United Kingdom)* (n 38) para 19.

43 ibid [20–28].

"OSPAR Convention") as well. The OSPAR Convention includes a similar applicable law clause to UNCLOS, which includes the applicability of the "rules of international law".[44] The tribunal noted that it was able to apply customary international law and general principles unless there was *lex specialis* in the OSPAR Convention.[45] However, it was a different matter in relation to treaty-based international law:

> it does mean that the competence of a tribunal established under the OSPAR Convention was not intended to extend to obligations the Parties might have under other instruments (unless, of course, parts of the OSPAR Convention included a direct renvoi to such other instruments). Interpreting [the applicable law clause] otherwise would transform it into an unqualified and comprehensive jurisdictional regime, in which there would be no limit ratione materiae to the jurisdiction of a tribunal established under the OSPAR Convention.[46]

Based on this interpretation of applicable law and after considering arguments on "applicable international regulations" under Article 9(3)(d) of the OSPAR Convention, the tribunal determined that it could not accept Ireland's argument that the Aarhus Convention[47] applied.[48] Arbitrator Griffith dissented to this restrictive interpretation of applicable law and the majority's rejection "of the normative value of various international instruments invoked by Ireland".[49] Griffith argued, *inter alia*, first, that Article 38 of the ICJ Statute includes treaties and so the tribunal's mandate was not confined by the absence of specific reference to any other body of substantive conventional law. Secondly, the tribunal is guided by Article 31(3)(c) of the VCLT which refers to rules of international law corresponding to the catalogue of sources in Article 38(1) of the ICJ

44 Article 32(6)(a) of the OSPAR Convention provides that 'the arbitral tribunal shall decide according to the rules of international law and, in particular those of the OSPAR Convention': Convention for the Protection of the Marine Environment of the North-East Atlantic (Paris, 22 September 1992), 2354 UNTS 67.

45 *Access to Information under Article 9 of the OSPAR Convention (Ireland v United Kingdom)* (PCA Case No 2001–03), Final Award, 2 July 2003, (2003) 42 ILM 118 [84].

46 ibid [85]. This part of the tribunal's decision on the applicable law was supported by the majority, comprising Professor Reisman and Lord Mustill.

47 Convention on Access to Information, Public Participation in Decision-making and Access to Justice in Environmental Matters (25 June 1998), 38 ILM 517.

48 *Access to Information under Article 9 of the OSPAR Convention (Ireland v. United Kingdom)* (n 45) para 104.

49 ibid [1] (Dissenting Opinion of Gavan Griffith).

Statute.[50] Griffith considered it was common ground that reference to other international rules cannot extend the competence of the tribunal. However, Griffith determined that, although the Aarhus Convention was not binding international law under Article 31(3)(c) of the VCLT since it had not been ratified by the parties, the Aarhus Convention still has a "relevant normative and evidentiary value".[51] Arbitrator Griffith's dissenting opinion exemplifies a systemic approach to the jurisdiction and applicable law relationship, compared to the more consensual approach of the majority.

The tribunal in *Arctic Sunrise* also rejected an expansion of jurisdiction using Article 293(1) of UNCLOS to determine whether Russia had violated the ICCPR.[52] The tribunal expressly stated that the applicable law clause does not extend the jurisdiction of the tribunal and could not be used "to obtain a determination that some treaty other than the Convention has been violated".[53] However, in doing so, the tribunal attempted to distinguish *Guyana v Suriname* and similar cases:

> In the case of some broadly worded or general provisions, it may also be necessary to rely on primary rules of international law other than the Convention in order to interpret and apply particular provisions of the Convention. Both arbitral tribunals and ITLOS have interpreted the Convention as allowing for the application of relevant rules of international law. Article 293 of the Convention makes this possible. For instance, in *M/V "SAIGA" No. 2*, ITLOS took account of general international law rules on the use of force in considering the use of force for the arrest of a vessel.[54]

However, this fails to adequately address how the *Guyana v Suriname* and *M/V Saiga (No 2)*[55] cases actually used the other international law. The quotation from the tribunal does not indicate a determination of a claim under the

50 ibid [2] (Dissenting Opinion of Gavan Griffith).

51 Griffith relied on Article 18 of the VCLT and the ICJ's acceptance that unratified treaties may possess evidentiary value on the scope of the definition of environmental information: ibid [9–19] (Dissenting Opinion of Gavan Griffith).

52 The invoked provisions were Article 9 (right to liberty and security and prohibition against arbitrary arrest) and Article 12(2) (freedom to leave any country) of the International Covenant on Civil and Political Rights (19 December 1966), 999 UNTS 171.

53 *Arctic Sunrise* (*Netherlands v Russia*) (PCA Case No 2014–02), Award on the Merits, 14 August 2015 [192].

54 ibid [191].

55 *M/V Saiga* (*No 2*) (*St Vincent v Guinea*) (ITLOS Case No 2), Judgment, 1 July 1999.

"relevant rules of international law" but merely "took into account" the other law in the interpretation exercise of UNCLOS.[56]

In this way, the specialist tribunals of UNCLOS approach the question somewhat differently than the ICJ. The UNCLOS tribunals provide neat examples of the two different approaches to the jurisdiction and applicable law relationship, thereby demonstrating how the consensual approach to jurisdiction can conflict with a systemic view of applicable law.

1.1.1 Implications of This Murky Relationship

While the terms themselves should have some underlying meaning, even the more controversial issue of expanding jurisdiction through the applicable law clause is not consistently discussed within the jurisprudence. The inadequate discussion, combined with the diversity of jurisdictional and compromissory clauses, makes it difficult to come to a complete understanding of the relationship between these terms.

Some may argue that the lack of attention to the relationship between jurisdiction and applicable law is the result of the acceptance of the distinction between jurisdiction and applicable law, as identified in the ILC Fragmentation Report. This type of argument is in line with how international disputes are often argued before the tribunal. However, it is not this simple, as evidenced by the disagreement between majority and dissenting opinions.

The treatment of jurisdiction, applicable law and interpretation by a tribunal has a very clear impact on the applicability of other international law to particular disputes. Importantly for the purposes of this research, the differing treatment of these concepts can lead to fragmentation, albeit in a different way than imagined in the early days of the fragmentation crisis, namely the concerns of parallel litigation and forum shopping. Rather, as Forteau explains, "this 'fragmentation' rather gives birth to new questionings concerning above all the limits of contemporary international law and of the normative powers of international tribunals."[57] The exploration of an adjudicator's approach to these concepts seeks to understand some of these questions.

From the general discussion, the next section turns to the specific case studies of the WTO and investor-state tribunals. Chapter 2 examined the applicable

56 Tzeng also notes an additional problem with the tribunal's reasoning in that the tribunal failed to specify which 'broadly worded or general provision' was in issue in the *M/V Saiga* case: Tzeng (n 34) 254.

57 Mathias Forteau, 'The Diversity of Applicable Law Before International Tribunals as a Source of Forum Shopping and Fragmentation of International Law: An Assessment' in Rüdiger Wolfrum and Ina Gätzschmann (eds), *International Dispute Settlement: Room for Innovations?* (Springer Berlin Heidelberg 2013) 441.

law of these tribunals on the basis of their constitutive treaties, which illustrated the divergence between the constitutive treaties of the two tribunals. For the WTO, whether any law is applicable beyond the WTO covered agreements and the customary rules of interpretation is debatable. However, even on a liberal view of the applicable law in WTO disputes, it is still generally more restrictive than the applicable law of investor-state disputes. The next sections consider whether there is any difference in treatment of the jurisdiction-applicable law relationship based on the different treaty sources. In this way, the sections identify whether there is a general approach to the (inter)-relationship between jurisdiction and applicable law, despite terminological differences in constitutive treaties. The following sections discuss a collection of cases where the tribunal has specifically turned its mind to the jurisdiction-applicable law relationship when considering the application of other international law to the dispute.

1.2 *Treatment by WTO Panels and the Appellate Body*

The first panel and Appellate Body report to use the term "applicable law" gave us an insight into the approach to the relationship between applicable law and jurisdiction in WTO proceedings. In *Brazil – Desiccated Coconut*, the Appellate Body upheld the Panel's decision that Articles I, II and VI of the GATT 1994[58] were not part of the applicable law to the dispute due to a temporal jurisdictional limitation. The applicability of GATT was raised because the countervailing duty measure was imposed based on an investigation initiated prior to the entry into force of the WTO Agreement for Brazil. The Appellate Body referred to the new "integrated nature" of the WTO Agreement and the SCM Agreement in determining that parts of the GATT 1994 were not applicable law.[59] While the Appellate Body did not refer to jurisdictional limits on applicable law specifically, Brazil had argued before the Appellate Body that whether GATT 1994 applied to the substance of the dispute was "a fundamental jurisdictional issue".[60]

While there are limited references to the term "applicable law" after *Brazil – Desiccated Coconut*, the panels and Appellate Body use the concept of applicable law within their reasoning. In the proceeding decisions, we can identify

58 Article I concerns most-favored nation treatment, while Article II relates to the schedule of concessions and Article VI is anti-dumping and countervailing duties: General Agreement on Tariffs and Trade (30 October 1947), 55 UNTS 194.

59 *Brazil – Measures Affecting Desiccated Coconut* (*Report of the Appellate Body*) (21 February 1997), WT/DS22/AB/R 21.

60 ibid 7.

a common approach by these bodies in dealing with the relationship between jurisdiction and applicable law, namely the limited jurisdiction of the WTO panels also limits the applicable law. Given the debated scope of applicable law in WTO disputes, the narrow applicable law conclusion is not surprising. However, the link between jurisdiction and applicable law is of interest for any similarity with investor-state tribunals.

1.2.1 Peru – Agricultural Products

In *Peru – Agricultural Products*, the Panel was required to consider whether the complainant (Guatemala) had brought the proceedings in good faith, pursuant to Articles 3.7 and 3.10 of the DSU, which has been discussed in Chapter 4 (section 2.2).[61] The report of the Panel referred to the principle articulated in *US – Gasoline* that "a panel cannot read the texts of the agreements 'in clinical isolation from public international law'."[62] However, the Panel went on to refer specifically to the terms of reference in this case which were "to examine, in the light of the relevant provisions of the covered agreements cited by the parties to the dispute". On the basis of its terms of reference, the Panel concluded that it was:

> … only authorized to rule on the invocation of any rules of public international law applicable to the relations between the parties to the extent that the invocation of that rule of international law is based on a relevant provision of the covered agreements that has been invoked by one of the parties to the dispute.[63]

The Panel referred to its "authority to rule", which should be read as referring to its jurisdiction, on the applicable rules of public international law. In this way, the Panel implied that the applicable law is limited by the jurisdiction of the Panel. The Panel went on to refer to various public international law rules

61 These provisions largely concern bringing proceedings in good faith. Article 3.7 refers to the requirement that Members exercise their judgment as to whether dispute procedures would be fruitful while Article 3.10 requires Members to engage with dispute settlement procedures in good faith: Understanding on Rules and Procedures Governing the Settlement of Disputes, Marrakesh Agreement Establishing the World Trade Organization, Annex 2 (15 April 1994), 1869 UNTS 401.

62 *Peru – Additional Duty on Imports of Certain Agricultural Products* (*Report of the Panel*) (27 November 2014) WT/DS457/R [7.67]; referring to *United States – Standards for Reformulated and Conventional Gasoline* (*Report of the Appellate Body*) (29 April 1996), WT/DS2/AB/R 17.

63 *Peru – Agricultural Products* (n 62) para [7.69].

raised by Peru that could be used as evidence of a lack of good faith by Guatemala in bringing the proceedings. In particular, Peru argued that the proceedings defeated the object and purpose of the free trade agreement between the parties,[64] within the meaning of Article 18 of the VCLT.[65] However, the Panel rejected the argument that a violation of Article 18 of the VCLT with respect to a treaty that does not form part of the WTO covered agreements could constitute evidence of lack of good faith required by Articles 3.7 and 3.10.[66] Since the Panel analysed the arguments by Peru in the context of whether they meet the requirements of Articles 3.7 and 3.10, this suggests that the Panel was using these international legal rules as part of an interpretation of Article 3.7 and 3.10, rather than as part of the applicable law to the dispute.

Peru appealed the finding by the Panel that there was no evidence that Guatemala brought these proceedings in a manner contrary to its good faith obligations under Articles 3.7 and 3.10. In the appeal, the Appellate Body stuck quite strictly to determining good faith in relation to the rules and procedures of the DSU, rather than under any other international legal rules:

> … [waiver of WTO rights] should be ascertained on the basis of actions taken in relation to, or within the context of, the rules and procedures of the DSU. Thus, we proceed to examine in this dispute whether the participants clearly stipulated the relinquishment of their right to have recourse to WTO dispute settlement by means of a 'solution mutually acceptable to the parties' that is consistent with the covered agreements.[67]

In doing this compatibility exercise, the Appellate Body confined itself to determining whether the price range system under the free trade agreement constituted a solution mutually acceptable to both parties.[68] For the Appellate Body, the free trade agreement did not constitute a mutually acceptable solution within Article 3.7 of the DSU since the free trade agreement was negotiated before the initiation of the dispute and the agreement was not consistent with

64 Free Trade Agreement between Peru and the Republic of Guatemala (Tratado de libre comercio entre la República del Perú y la República de Guatemala), 6 December 2011.

65 *Peru – Agricultural Products* (n 62) para 7.89–7.92; Article 18 refers to the obligation not to defeat the object and purpose of a treaty prior to its entry into force: Vienna Convention on the Law of Treaties (Vienna, 23 May 1969), 1155 UNTS 331.

66 *Peru – Agricultural Products* (n 62) [7.92].

67 *Peru – Additional Duty on Imports of Certain Agricultural Products* (*Report of the Appellate Body*) (20 July 2015) WT/DS457/AB/R [5.25].

68 ibid [5.26].

the covered agreements.[69] Unlike the Panel, the Appellate Body did not refer to any other rules of public international law. However, the Appellate Body was required to consider whether the free trade agreement was consistent with obligations in the WTO Agreement on Agriculture. This exercise appears to fall within the area of general agreement in academic literature that panels and the Appellate Body may consider other international law norms where they are referred to by consent of the parties, for example, by specific incorporation in the agreements or through interpretation using customary rules of international law.[70] In this case, the reference to the free trade agreement should be read as being incorporated through the DSU's reference to "solution mutually acceptable", and thus still within the jurisdictional confines of the DSU. Both the Panel and the Appellate Body in this dispute stick strictly to the confines of the WTO covered agreements, in relation to both jurisdiction and applicable law, which indicates that the Panel and Appellate Body adopted the approach of linking jurisdiction and applicable law, thus limiting the possible applicable law in the dispute.

1.2.2 EC – Large Civil Aircraft

In *EC – Measures Affecting Trade in Large Civil Aircraft*, the Panel had to determine the relevance of the 1992 EC-US Agreement[71] to the proceedings. The EC argued that any alleged government support prior to the effective date of the 1992 EC-US Agreement should be excluded from the temporal scope of the proceedings on the basis that the 1992 EC-US Agreement was: (i) "applicable law"; (ii) a relevant rule of international law applicable to the interpretation of the SCM Agreement (a systemic integration argument); or (iii) as giving rise to an estoppel against the US.[72] The approach of panels and the Appellate Body to estoppel has already been discussed in Chapter 4, while the Article 31(3)(c) argument of the EC will be discussed in section 2.2 below. In relation to the applicable law argument, the Panel held that the 1992 EC-US Agreement was not a covered agreement within the terms of reference of the Panel nor

69 ibid.

70 See, for example, Trachtman (n 5) pp 136–7; Lorand Bartels, 'Applicable Law in WTO Dispute Settlement Proceedings' (2001) 35 Journal of World Trade 499, 519; Pauwelyn (n 6) 476; Andrew Mitchell, *Legal Principles in WTO Disputes* (Cambridge University Press 2008) 93.

71 Agreement between the European Economic Community and the Government of the United States of America concerning the application of the GATT on Trade in Civil Aircraft, Official Journal L 301 (17 October 1992).

72 *European Communities – Measures Affecting Trade in Large Civil Aircraft* (*Report of the Panel*) (30 June 2010) WT/DS316/R [7.70–7.76].

contained in the list of covered agreements in Appendix 1 to the DSU and so it did not have jurisdiction to determine the rights and obligations of the parties under the 1992 EC-US Agreement.[73] In the Panel's view, the EC was effectively asking it to find that the US agreed to waive its rights under the WTO agreements to challenge certain measures in WTO dispute settlement.[74] The primary reason for the rejection of the EC's argument that the 1992 EC-US Agreement was applicable law was that the 1992 EC-US Agreement preceded the SCM Agreement and there was no reference to the 1992 EC-US Agreement in the SCM Agreement nor did the EC make any reservations regarding the application or interpretation of the SCM Agreement in respect of the 1992 EC-US Agreement. The Panel considered it was not necessary to decide whether a waiver of a Member State's WTO rights was enforceable in WTO dispute settlement.[75]

Pursuant to the limited jurisdiction under the DSU, the Panel clearly limited the scope of its jurisdiction to the covered agreements and its terms of reference. However, what is interesting about the Panel's analysis is its reliance on the lack of any reference to the prior 1992 EC-US Agreement in the subsequent SCM Agreement in determining whether the 1992 EC-US Agreement could be part of the applicable law. In doing so, adopting a rather strict requirement of incorporation of other international law within WTO law. The Panel was influenced by jurisdictional limits in the determination of applicable law, supporting the second approach to jurisdiction and applicable law, that of the intimate connection between the two concepts.

It is also noteworthy that similar arguments to the reasoning of the Panel were made by Australia and Brazil when the 1992 EC-US Agreement was raised again in *US – Measures Affecting Trade in Large Civil Aircraft* (*Second Complaint*). Here, Brazil argued that the SCM Agreement was the applicable agreement as the 1992 EC-US Agreement was not a covered agreement and was outside the Panel's terms of reference. As such, Brazil considered that the Panel lacked jurisdiction to determine rights and obligations under the 1992 EC-US Agreement.[76] Similarly, Australia argued that the 1992 EC-US Agreement was not a covered agreement and so did not constitute applicable law in this dispute, referring to *Mexico – Soft Drinks* (discussed next) for the proposition that the DSU operates in relation to covered agreements only and that it

73 ibid [7.89].

74 ibid [7.91].

75 ibid [7.94]. The Panel's findings on the applicability of the 1992 EC-US Agreement in relation to the temporal scope of the proceedings were not subject to appeal to the Appellate Body.

76 *United States – Measures Affecting Trade in Large Civil Aircraft* (*Second Complaint*) (*Report of the Panel*) (31 March 2011), WT/DS353/R [7.1883].

is not the function of panels to seek to clarify the provisions in non-covered agreements.[77]

1.2.3 Mexico – Soft Drinks

The applicability of a free trade agreement between the disputing parties was also the subject of the Panel and Appellate Body decision in *Mexico – Tax Measures on Soft Drinks and Other Beverages*. Before the Panel, Mexico argued, first, that the Panel should decline to exercise jurisdiction to hear the case since the case linked to a broader dispute under the NAFTA.[78] Secondly, Mexico argued that its measures were necessary to secure US compliance with its obligations under the NAFTA, pursuant to Article XX(d) of the GATT.[79] Mexico was unsuccessful on both of these arguments and appealed the Panel decision.[80] In the appeal, the Appellate Body's analysis provides some indication of the jurisdiction and applicable law relationship. Mexico's final argument on whether the Panel should have declined to exercise jurisdiction related to the "applicability" of its WTO obligations in the circumstances where the subject measures were in response to the US's allegedly illegal act in refusing to select panellists for the inter-state NAFTA dispute. Mexico referred to the PCIJ's decision in the *Factory at Chorzów* case.[81] The Appellate Body rejected this argument:

> Mexico's arguments, as well as its reliance on the ruling in *Factory at Chorzów*, is misplaced. Even assuming, arguendo, that the legal principle reflected in the passage referred to by Mexico is applicable within the WTO dispute settlement system, we note that this would entail a determination whether the United States has acted consistently or inconsistently with its NAFTA obligations. We see no basis in the DSU for panels and the Appellate Body to adjudicate non-WTO disputes ... Accepting Mexico's interpretation would imply that the WTO dispute settlement system

---

77 ibid [7.1880].

78 *Mexico – Tax Measures on Soft Drinks and Other Beverages* (*Report of the Panel*) (7 October 2005) WT/DS308/R [7.1].

79 ibid [8.170]. Article XX(d) of the GATT is the general exception referring to measures "necessary to secure compliance with laws or regulations which are not inconsistent with the provisions of this Agreement ...".

80 *Mexico – Tax Measures on Soft Drinks and Other Beverages* (*Report of the Appellate Body*) (6 March 2006) WT/DS308/AB/R [6].

81 *Factory at Chorzów* (*Germany v Poland*), *Jurisdiction* [1927] PCIJ Rep Series A No 9 p 31, in which the PCIJ stated: '... one party cannot avail himself of the fact that the other has not fulfilled some obligation, or has not had recourse to some means of redress, if the former party has, by some illegal act, prevented the latter from fulfilling the obligation in question, or from having recourse to the tribunal which would have been open to him.'

could be used to determine rights and obligations outside the covered agreements.[82]

The Appellate Body's decision on this aspect of Mexico's appeal could be read as linking applicable law and jurisdiction. Essentially, the Appellate Body cautioned that if applicable law is left too wide, this could lead to requiring a broader jurisdiction in order to deal with all questions under that applicable law. The DSU clearly limits the jurisdiction of the WTO dispute settlement mechanism. The Appellate Body's cautioning against Mexico's argument could be read as suggesting that the distinction approach (based on systemic norms) could have this unwanted effect.

1.2.4 Conclusions on the WTO-Perspective of the Relationship between Jurisdiction and Applicable Law

While the WTO dispute settlement mechanism uses the term "applicable law" relatively infrequently, the panels and Appellate Body still undertake such an analysis, even without the terminological reference to applicable law. Despite limited assistance on jurisdiction and applicable law relationship in the DSU, the preceding analysis of these WTO cases indicates a similar approach: the cases share a similar jurisdictional trend in their approach to the relationship between jurisdiction and applicable law. The panels and Appellate Body have, in fact, considered there to be a link between jurisdiction and applicable law and thus, applicable law cannot be widened beyond the limited jurisdiction of the DSU. As this section only considered decisions that clearly discuss the relationship between jurisdiction and applicable law, the question becomes whether this is reflected in other areas of the dispute settlement mechanism's practice.

1.3 *Treatment of the Relationship by Investor-State Adjudicators*

While the jurisdiction and applicable law provisions differ between IIAs, we can still identify similar treatment of the relationship between jurisdiction and applicable law. The divergence of treaty language may explain some of the different approaches to the inclusion of other public international law; however, it does not seem to affect the tribunals' characterization of the relationship between jurisdiction and applicable law.

82 *Mexico – Soft Drinks (Appellate Body)* (n 80) para 56.

1.3.1 Tenaris v Venezuela (II)

In determining what constitutes a manifest excess of powers under Article 52(1)(b) of the ICSID Convention, the Annulment Committee in *Tenaris v Venezuela (II)* made pertinent comments on the jurisdiction-applicable law relationship. First, the Committee noted that a tribunal exceeds its powers when it exercises jurisdiction that it does not have, and when it fails to apply the proper law.[83] In doing so, the Committee relied strongly on consent as the cornerstone of the jurisdiction of an ICSID tribunal, with such consent also extending to the applicable law: "[a] tribunal that fails to apply the applicable law transgresses the boundaries of its mandate as expressed in the parties' consent *as much so as when it usurps jurisdiction*."[84] The Committee relevantly stated:

> These alternative expressions of excess of power are not simply juxtaposed but are substantively interconnected. According to Convention Article 41, the tribunal is the judge of its own competence. It has to exercise its judgment in applying and interpreting Convention Article 25 and any other agreements between the disputing parties (i.e. the provisions of a BIT, contract, investment law, etc.). Thus, an excess of powers made effective through the usurpation of competence is the result of the non-application of the applicable law.[85]

In applying this standard, the Committee found no manifest excess of powers in the application of the applicable law when establishing the tribunal's competence *ratione personae* or *ratione temporis*, and thereby the jurisdiction of ICSID. However, the comments of the Committee on the standard for manifest excess of powers are more pertinent to the jurisdiction-applicable law relationship than its ultimate finding that there was no manifest excess of powers.

1.3.2 Mamidoil Jetoil v Albania

In *Mamidoil Jetoil Greek Petroleum Products v Albania*, the tribunal had to consider whether the claimant could rely on the ECT[86] as an additional

83 *Tenaris SA & Talta v Venezuela (II)* (ICSID Case No ARB/12/23), Decision on Annulment, 28 December 2018 [65].

84 ibid [66–67] (emphasis added); the tribunal also referred to Professor Schreuer's statement that 'the provisions on applicable law are essential elements of the parties' agreement to arbitrate and constitute part of the parameters for the tribunal's activity': Christoph H Schreuer, *The ICSID Convention: A Commentary* (2nd edn, Cambridge University Press 2009) para 192.

85 *Tenaris II Annulment* (n 83) para 68.

86 The Energy Charter Treaty (Lisbon, 17 December 1994), 2080 UNTS 95.

instrument providing for Albania's consent to arbitration and the standards of protection.[87] At the time of the arbitration request, the claimant had only invoked jurisdiction under the IIA between Albania and Greece.[88] In order to circumvent the difficulty of relying on an instrument that was not invoked at the time the arbitration was started, the claimant argued that the ECT was applicable as substantive law.[89] However, the tribunal rejected the claimant's argument. The tribunal noted the distinction between "the applicability of a rule as a matter of substance" and whether an international treaty can be "the basis for a claim and establish a respondent State's consent to arbitration."[90] The tribunal went on to confirm that it was:

> … not convinced an investor can import the standards of protection of a different treaty (here, the ECT) by simply referring to that treaty as the 'law applicable' to the merits under another treaty (here, the BIT). The notion of applicable law would, in such a case, operate as a most-favoured nation clause with regard to both jurisdiction and merits, which it is not.[91]

The tribunal faced a relatively unusual situation of a claimant attempting to apply a completely different treaty as the basis of jurisdiction and applicable law. However, the tribunal's rejection of an applicable law clause overcoming jurisdictional limitations strongly suggests a link between the concepts of jurisdiction and applicable law. Ultimately, the tribunal did consider the ECT in addressing the investor and respondent's behavior on the basis that Albania did not object to the claimant's reliance on the ECT and both parties took positions as to the propriety of conduct under the ECT.[92] This is more likely a product of the adversarial nature of investment arbitration, the adherence to party agreement within ISDS and the different nature of general consent in the treaty compared to specific consent in the individual dispute, rather than general consideration of the jurisdiction and applicable law relationship.

---

87 *Mamidoil Jetoil Greek Petroleum Products Societe SA v Republic of Albania* (ICSID Case No ARB/11/24), Award, 30 March 2015 [274].

88 Article 10 of the Agreement between the Government of the Hellenic Republic and the Government of the Republic of Albania for the Encouragement and Reciprocal Protection of Investments (Tirana, 1 August 1991) provides for investor-state dispute settlement and contains the Contracting Parties' consent to arbitration.

89 *Mamidoil Jetoil v Albania* (n 87) para [268].

90 ibid [275].

91 ibid [276].

92 ibid [277–8].

1.3.3 Methanex v USA

Similarly, in *Methanex v USA*, the tribunal rejected an apparent attempt to adjudicate the respondent state's behavior under the GATT. The claimant referred to the applicable law clause of NAFTA which stated that the tribunal "shall decide the issues in dispute in accordance with this Agreement and applicable rules of international law".[93] The tribunal accepted that GATT jurisprudence could be relevant to interpreting the relevant NAFTA terminology on the basis of the applicable law clause of the NAFTA and Article 38(1) of the ICJ Statute.[94] However, the tribunal determined that to interpret the applicable law clause any further would "create a jurisdiction extending beyond Section A of Chapter 11" of the NAFTA, which was not the intention of the NAFTA parties.[95]

1.3.4 Conclusions on the ISDS-Perspective of the Relationship between Jurisdiction and Applicable Law

The cases of *Mamidoil* and *Methanex* present more extreme examples of claimants attempting to import other public international law into the investment dispute as a basis of the claim. Nevertheless, the cases demonstrate that general references to international law in the applicable law clause cannot override the terms of the more limited jurisdiction clause. These clear cases of arguments seeking to exceed jurisdiction support both the position of the prevailing nature of the jurisdiction clause at the jurisdictional stage as well as the influence of the limited jurisdiction over applicable law. While rather extreme arguments by claimants, such examples are clearer or more transparent as the tribunals are confronted head-on by the jurisdiction and applicable law relationship and must provide thorough reasons to avoid criticism of judicial overreach while also responding to one of the parties' central jurisdictional arguments.

When it comes to borderline cases in which the tribunal is not clearly being asked to determine a claim under a separate treaty regime, the answer becomes less certain or more difficult to draw out of tribunal reasoning: tribunals may hide beyond vague language, manage to avoid answering the question entirely or rely on normative values to determine the outcome. This is supported by the empirical results in Chapter 3 which illustrated the large proportion of decisions which incorporate other international law without stipulating the legal

---

93 North American Free Trade Agreement (17 December 1992), 32 ILM 289, Article 1131(1).

94 *Methanex Corporation v United States of America* (ad hoc, UNCITRAL), Final Award, 3 August 2005, II, Chapter B, [6].

95 ibid, II, Chapter B, [5]; referring *to Access to Information under Article 9 of the OSPAR Convention (Ireland v. United Kingdom)* (n 45), [1136].

basis or source of authority. Legal reasoning in this fashion does not meet a conscious and transparent standard. We should hold adjudicators to a standard by which they exhibit coherent judicial methodology to avoid unnecessary inconsistent outcomes.

1.4 *Implications: Divergent Treaty-Perspectives but a Common Tribunal Understanding?*

Drawing a conclusion from the treaties on the relationship between jurisdiction and applicable law is difficult. The treaties conferring jurisdiction on the investor-state and WTO dispute settlement mechanisms significantly diverge. The WTO DSU is different from most investment treaties in that the words "jurisdiction" and "applicable law" do not appear in its text. Additionally, the WTO agreements do not contain any applicable law clauses. The lack of clear jurisdiction and applicable law clauses in the DSU may explain the more restrained use of the terms "jurisdiction" and "applicable law" by the WTO dispute settlement bodies, instead often couching the use of such concepts in the language of authorization and the terms of reference of the dispute settlement mechanism. Comparatively, most investment agreements and the ICSID Convention include guidance on jurisdiction and applicable law for investor-state disputes. In many investment agreements and the ICSID Convention, jurisdiction and applicable law are set out in separate provisions, which could be read as suggesting that jurisdiction and applicable law are to be dealt with as distinct concepts. Yet, there is nothing else in the treaties to suggest such a reading. This is also not the picture that is painted by the jurisprudence. Instead, the surveyed cases suggest the lack of an applicable law clause does not change the analysis of the relationship between jurisdiction and applicable law and the jurisprudence suggests a predominant trend toward linking the concepts of jurisdiction and applicable law.

The surveyed cases demonstrate that where the tribunal turns its mind to the concept of jurisdiction and applicable law, the tribunal accepts a link between jurisdiction and applicable law. While some of these cases lack detailed reasoning on this issue, it is still noteworthy that we do not see a dismissal of a link between jurisdiction and applicable law. The acknowledgment of a link between jurisdiction and applicable law aligns quite closely with investment literature's analysis of a complex relationship between jurisdiction and applicable law.[96] The surveyed cases suggest a common thread of reasoning on the relationship between jurisdiction and applicable law in international trade

96 Waibel (n 7); Schreuer (n 8). See discussion in footnotes 7 and 8 above.

and investment disputes: applicable law cannot be read in isolation from the jurisdictional limits of the treaty. When the international trade and investment adjudicators turn their mind to these terms, they accept that a limited jurisdiction will limit the scope of the law applicable to the dispute. The surveyed tribunals are generally reluctant to open up the range of claims that may be brought before them, either as direct jurisdictional claims or indirectly through an enlarged scope of applicable law, based on their recognition of a link between jurisdiction and applicable law.

2 Resulting Inconsistency: Normativity and the Toolkit

While the previous section illustrates that adjudicators have defined the applicable law as clearly limited by jurisdiction, the problem certainly does not end there. The picture becomes murkier as these tribunals attempt to apply these concepts to complex jurisdictional and applicable law questions. This section explores two complications that emerge when we look deeper into the reasoning of the tribunals. First, whether this relationship between jurisdiction and applicable law, which is set out relatively clearly in the preceding analysis, is actually applied when the tribunals do not specifically turn their mind to the (inter)relationship between jurisdiction and applicable law. For this complication, the applicability of countermeasures in ISDS provides an example of inconsistent reasoning. Secondly, we see tribunals encountering difficulties in determining whether the other public international law relates to a question of applicable law or, rather, interpretation. For this second complication, the relationship between jurisdiction and the principle of systemic integration is analysed.

2.1 *Jurisdiction and Applicable Law: the Confusing Approach to Countermeasures*

An indication of the difficulties with applying these concepts can be seen in attempts to draw in general international law defences into investment disputes. As a result of a dispute between Mexico and the US under the NAFTA, we can directly compare two investment disputes discussing the application of countermeasures.[97]

97 A third award also dealt with countermeasures in the same context of the US-Mexico NAFTA dispute. However, the tribunal considered the argument in terms of whether the obligations were owed to nationals of a state and who holds the rights (the investor or their home state). The tribunal did not deal with the jurisdiction-applicable law

In *Corn Products v Mexico*,[98] the tribunal had to consider whether the countermeasures doctrine under international law was applicable to an investment dispute. Mexico raised the concept of countermeasures in defence to its alleged violation of the investment treaty, arguing that it had instituted the measures in response to the US's violation of the NAFTA.[99] The first question before the tribunal was whether the doctrine of countermeasures, devised in the context of legal relations between States, was applicable to a claim brought by a private investor under Chapter XI of the NAFTA (the investment chapter).[100] The tribunal held that the doctrine of countermeasures was not applicable to claims under the investment chapter of the NAFTA because of the nature of the rights of the investor: there was no room for a defence based upon the alleged wrongdoing of a State which was not a party to the proceedings.[101] While not explicitly referring to jurisdiction, this part of the analysis by the tribunal could be read as an application of the *Monetary Gold* principle,[102] and thus, provides little information on the jurisdiction and applicable law relationship.

However, the tribunal went on to comment on the effects of the limited jurisdiction of the tribunal upon the defence of countermeasures.[103] The tribunal noted that its jurisdiction was limited to violations of Chapter XI of the NAFTA, and it had no jurisdiction to determine whether there has been a breach of any other provision of the NAFTA.[104] The tribunal explained:

> It is immediately apparent that these jurisdictional limits give rise to serious difficulties in relation to the handling of Mexico's countermeasures

nexus: *Cargill v Poland* (ICSID Case No ARB(AF)/04/2), Award, 29 February 2008 [422 ff]. See, particularly [429], where the tribunal states that 'Respondent's argument that its actions were countermeasures cannot have the effect of precluding the wrongfulness of those actions in respect of a claim asserted under Chapter 11 by a national of the allegedly offending State. Given this conclusion, the Tribunal finds that it is unnecessary to decide upon Claimant's other objections to Respondent's countermeasures defense'.

98 *Corn Products International Inc v The United Mexican States* (ICSID Case No ARB(AF) /04/01), Decision on Responsibility, 15 January 2008.

99 ibid [59]. Mexico alleged that the US had acted in breach of the NAFTA by restricting the amount of Mexico's surplus sugar production which could be exported to the US and also that the US had frustrated the operation of the inter-state dispute settlement mechanism of NAFTA.

100 ibid [153].

101 ibid [161].

102 *Monetary Gold Removed from Rome in 1943* (*Italy v France, UK and USA*), Preliminary Question, Judgment [1954] ICJ Reports 19; see further, Christian Tomuschat, 'Article 36' in Andreas Zimmermann and others (eds), *The Statute of the International Court of Justice: A Commentary* (3rd edn, Oxford University Press 2019) 729 ff.

103 See *Corn Products v Mexico* (n 98) paras 180–192.

104 ibid [181].

> defence ... But the Tribunal does not have jurisdiction to determine whether these allegations against the United States are well-founded or not. The United States is not a party to these proceedings and the Tribunal does not have jurisdiction to determine whether any provision of the NAFTA falling outside Chapter XI has been violated. How, then, can the Tribunal determine whether the HFCS tax was a response to a prior violation of international law? And if it cannot determine that this requirement of a lawful countermeasure is satisfied, how can it uphold Mexico's countermeasures defence?[105]

Mexico attempted to get around this predicament by arguing that it was not necessary to establish that the US had violated the NAFTA, only that Mexico had a genuine belief that it had a reasonable prospect of succeeding in establishing that the US was in breach.[106] However, the tribunal rejected the argument on the basis that it was a fundamental prerequisite of countermeasures that an internationally wrongful act had been committed.[107] Consequently, the tribunal rejected Mexico's countermeasures defence, both on the basis that it was not applicable law and that, even if it were, Mexico could not establish one of the requirements of a countermeasure given the limited jurisdiction of the investment tribunal.[108] Like the decisions in the preceding section, the tribunal in *Corn Products v Mexico* accepted a link between jurisdiction and applicable law in determining that Mexico cannot rely on the doctrine of countermeasures.

An entirely different result on the application of countermeasures is found in *Archer Daniels Midland v Mexico*.[109] This case before a differently constituted ICSID tribunal involved the same tax measure imposed by Mexico and, again, Mexico raised the countermeasures defence. The tribunal in *Archer Daniels Midland* similarly considered that Mexico could not ultimately rely on the countermeasures defence, however, the tribunal's consideration of the jurisdiction and applicable law question reads quite differently. The tribunal determined that the customary international law defence of countermeasures was applicable to disputes under the investment chapter of NAFTA. While the investment chapter was *lex specialis* "in respect of its express content", customary international law applied in a residual way.[110] As the investment

105 ibid [182].

106 ibid [184].

107 ibid [185–187].

108 ibid [189].

109 *Archer Daniels Midland Company v The United Mexican States* (ICSID Case No ARB(AF)/04/05), Award, 21 November 2007.

110 ibid [119].

chapter did not prohibit the use of countermeasures, the tribunal considered "the question whether the countermeasures defence is available to the Respondent is not a question of *lex specialis*, but of customary international law".[111] As such, Mexico could raise the countermeasure defence under customary international law, which was law applicable to the dispute pursuant to the terms of NAFTA's governing law clause, thereby entering into a gap-filling exercise.[112]

While the applicability of the countermeasures defence is contrary to the decision reached in the *Corn Products* case, the tribunal still encountered the same jurisdictional conflict. The tribunal found that it had "no jurisdiction to decide whether the United States breached any of its international obligations" under other chapters of the NAFTA.[113] The treatment of jurisdiction and applicable law in relation to countermeasures by this tribunal raises an interesting question: how can a respondent rely on a defence for which the tribunal does not have jurisdiction to determine an essential element of the defence? The relationship between jurisdiction and applicable law was not explicitly considered by the tribunal in *Archer Daniels Midland*. Rather, it was only after the defence was found to be part of the applicable law to the dispute that the tribunal turned its mind to its jurisdiction. We can infer that based on this underlying problem with relying on the defence of countermeasures that the tribunal did not consider the link between jurisdiction and applicable law that was implicitly referred to by the tribunal in *Corn Products*.

If we simply looked at the results of the disputes, the inconsistency is not apparent: Mexico was unsuccessful in its countermeasures defence. However, there is substantive fragmentation as to whether the customary international law defence of countermeasures is applicable law to investor-state disputes.[114] The comparison between these two investor-state disputes highlights the difficulties that we encounter in defining the concepts of jurisdiction

111 ibid [120].

112 ibid [123]. Article 1131 of the NAFTA provides the governing law for an investment dispute, which includes, inter alia, 'applicable rules of international law'.

113 ibid [128]. As an alternative, Mexico had argued that the tribunal should stay the proceedings if it cannot make a determination of Mexico's customary international law rights: para 112. As such, the tribunal went on to address the other elements of countermeasures that it did have jurisdiction to address.

114 On countermeasures in the WTO, see *Mexico – Soft Drinks* (*Appellate Body*) (n 80). Although no WTO example was discussed in this section, the findings are arguably still applicable. The limitation of the analysis to investor-state dispute application of countermeasures was simply a result of the much smaller sample of relevant WTO decisions, thereby often limiting the examples of direct inconsistency that can be discussed.

and applicable law.[115] Furthermore, an adjudicator's view of the relationship between these two concepts affects the reasoning: a stricter definition of jurisdictional limits, through application of the limit of jurisdiction to applicable law, aligns more clearly with the normative goals of consent-based dispute settlement. In this way, the relationship between the opening (particularly applicable law and general principles) and closing tools available to adjudicators is murky, making it difficult to determine the appropriate judicial authority to apply other international law within the WTO and investor-state dispute settlement mechanisms.

2.2 *Jurisdiction and Interpretation: the Complexity of Systemic Integration*

The application of these terms in practice only becomes more difficult when we include interpretation powers and provisions into the mix. The interpretation and application of treaty obligations "can have far reaching implications" for the way that a tribunal deals with the dispute before it.[116] The interpretative techniques employed by international courts and tribunals plays an integral role in understanding the relationship between international laws, whether international law has a systemic nature or more individualized within regimes. On the systemic view of international law, the ILC Fragmentation Report explained:

> Legal interpretation, and thus legal reasoning, builds systemic relationships between rules and principles by envisaging them as parts of some human effort or purpose. Far from being merely an "academic" aspect of the legal craft, systemic thinking penetrates all legal reasoning, including the practice of law-application by judges and administrators. This results precisely from the "clustered" nature in which legal rules and principles appear. But it may also be rationalized in terms of a political obligation

115 It is not the purpose of this research to consider whether the tribunals reached the correct decision on the application of customary international law to investment disputes. The tribunals could have also framed the question of the applicability of countermeasures as a question of the identity of the parties, rather than a question of applicable law, thus potentially avoiding the pitfalls identified in the preceding analysis.

116 N Jansen Calamita, 'Countermeasures and Jurisdiction: Between Effectiveness and Fragmentation' (2010) 42 Georgetown Journal of International Law 233, 279; referring to *Oil Platforms (Islamic Republic of Iran v United States of America), Judgment* [2003] ICJ Reports 161.

> on law-appliers to make their decisions cohere with the preferences and expectations of the community whose law they administer.[117]

The choice of interpretation method and the justification for recourse to one rule instead of another can be the difference between harmonization of conflicting standards or prioritization of standards.[118] However, these rules of interpretation are often vague, leaving significant discretion in the hands of the arbitrator.[119]

As discussed in Chapter 4, uncertainty surrounds the application of systemic integration pursuant to Article 31(3)(c) of the VCLT. The existence of this uncertainty, particularly the questions "how widely" and "what does taking into account" mean, is highly pertinent for our enquiry on the relationship between consent and other public international law. The uncertainty could provide adequate wriggle room for adjudicators to argue for the application of Article 31(3)(c), thereby contributing to the systemic view of international law and defragmentation. On the other hand, the uncertainty could be used as an excuse not to apply the principle, potentially through taking a restrictive interpretation of the particular wording of Article 31(3)(c). Chapter 4 considered the role of systemic integration in system-building and creating coherence in international law, concluding with the variation between the focus on party intentions compared to systemic views on interpretation. This Chapter considers a different facet of systemic integration, namely the relationship with jurisdiction.

We can identify several similarities in the tribunals' reasoning to this question of interpretation. First, an inconsistent approach to Article 31(3)(c) transcends dispute settlement mechanisms, as illustrated in Chapter 4. As the tribunals delve into more complex applications of Article 31(3)(c), the tribunals

117 Koskenniemi (n 3) para 35.

118 In investor-state disputes, the choice of interpretation may also exhibit a pro-state or pro-investor approach. See the discussion in *Wintershall Aktiengesellschaft v Argentine Republic* (ICSID Case No ARB/04/14), Award, 8 December 2008 [89]; comparing the conclusions in *SGS Société Générale de Surveillance SA v Islamic Republic of Pakistan* (ICSID Case No ARB/01/13), Decision on Jurisdiction, 6 August 2003; and *SGS Société Générale de Surveillance SA v Republic of the Philippines* (ICSID Case No ARB/02/6), Decision of the Tribunal on Objections to Jurisdiction, 29 January 2004.

119 As French states, the indeterminate nature of treaty interpretation provides international arbitral tribunals with just the necessary degree of flexibility to fashion their own reasoning, 'hopefully without either exceeding jurisdictional limits or transgressing expectations of the adjudicative function': Duncan French, 'Treaty Interpretation and the Incorporation Of Extraneous Legal Rules' (2006) 55 International & Comparative Law Quarterly 281, 281–2.

begin to depart from their previous jurisprudence on the specific requirements of Article 31(3)(c), leading to inconsistency and uncertainty in the application of other law, as set out in Chapter 4 (section 3.3) above. Secondly, and most relevantly for the question of this Chapter, both dispute settlement mechanisms struggle with the relationship between jurisdiction and interpretation. Several decisions highlight the fine line between interpretation and application of "other" international law, linking back to the jurisdictional limits of the tribunal in the process. The way in which an adjudicator approaches the question of the relationship between jurisdiction and applicable law may affect the application of systemic integration to the dispute and, as a result, the possibility to consider non-economic issues within the dispute. The inconsistent approach to environmental agreements in the WTO (*US – Shrimp* compared to *EC – Biotech*) and the necessity defence in ISDS (the inconsistent cases on the Argentine financial crisis) explored in Chapter 4 (section 3.3), motivates us to consider whether other similarities exist, in particular, to what extent is there a similarity in their approach to the limits of Article 31(3)(c)?

2.2.1 Relationship between Jurisdiction and Article 31(3)(c): ISDS

Along with the Annulment Committee in *Mobil Exploration* on the necessity defence (see Chapter 4, section 3.3), the tribunal in *Eskosol* also exhibited the same reticence toward applying Article 31(3)(c) beyond what might be termed "clear" cases of interpretation. Article 31(3)(c) was invoked in the *Eskosol* proceedings as part of the intra-EU objection to the tribunal's jurisdiction under the ECT. After quoting the *Vattenfall* tribunal that "it is not the proper role of [Article 31(3)(c)] to rewrite the treaty being interpreted",[120] the tribunal rejected a role for Article 31(3)(c):

> And yet this would be the natural result of the Commission's arguments, by overriding as between some ECT Contracting Parties, but not others, the 'unconditional consent' to international arbitration clearly reflected in ECT Article 26(3). The Tribunal rejects the notion that VCLT Article 31(3)(c) can be used in this way.[121]

Here, the tribunal is making a clear comment on the relationship between Article 31(3)(c) and jurisdiction, maintaining the sanctity of the consensual

120 *Vattenfall AB and others v Federal Republic of Germany (II)* (ICSID Case No ARB/12/12), Decision on the Achmea Issue, 31 August 2018 [154].

121 *Eskosol S.pA in liquidazione v Italian Republic* (ICSID Case No ARB/15/50), Decision on Termination Request and Intra-EU Objection, 7 May 2019 [126].

nature of international jurisdiction. As such, different sources of international law must be treated with caution if it may affect the nature of consent to jurisdiction.[122] Although not directly criticizing the use of Article 31(3)(c), the number of ISDS tribunals avoiding the use of Article 31(3)(c) may also support this general concern with extending systemic integration.

The diverging treatment of systemic integration by investment tribunals in relation to the potential application of human rights norms to international investment law also provides us with an opportunity to consider the approach of those tribunals to the relationship between jurisdiction and applicable law. Importantly, we can see a distinction based on whether those human rights norms are applicable as a potential defence to the investment claim or as part of the state's obligation to the foreign investor. Article 31(3)(c) has played an important role in investor-state dispute settlement in bridging the gap between investment law and other normative frameworks. For example, in *Tulip Real Estate*, the tribunal referred to the right to fair trial in human rights treaties in the interpretation of the concept of a fundamental rule of procedure under the annulment procedure of the ICSID Convention.[123] *Urbaser* similarly accepted the possibility of taking into account human rights using Article 31(3)(c) in recognizing the human right to water, yet also demonstrates the limitation of this interpretative technique. While recognizing the right, the tribunal found it did not extend to incurring obligations on investors. This highlights the necessary distinction between *reading in* substantive obligations, which taps into the scope of the jurisdictional authority of a tribunal, compared to *interpreting* treaty obligations.[124]

122 The dissenting arbitrator in *Ambiente* made a similar argument in relation to Article 31(3)(c) and evolving interpretations: '[h]owever, in so far as "jurisdictional conventional obligations", evolving interpretation methods are unjustified unless expressly permitted or necessarily implied by the terms used by the text of the treaty or by general practice in its application, the reason being that the State's consent to jurisdiction rule is unfriendly to the validation of alleged "implied consents". Furthermore, in the present case it has not been plead, and still less proven, that the rule of State's consent to jurisdiction has evolved since the conclusion of the 1990 Argentina-Italy BIT. On the contrary, the rule has been confirmed in the most recent jurisprudence of the ICJ': *Ambiente Ufficio S.pA and others v Argentine Republic* (ICSID Case No ARB/08/9), Decision on Jurisdiction and Admissibility, 8 February 2013 [343].

123 *Tulip Real Estate v Turkey* (ICSID Case No ARB/11/28), Decision on Annulment, 30 December 2015 [86–92]. The Annulment Committee was careful to note that it was not adding in obligations extraneous to the ICSID Convention and was merely limiting itself to treaty interpretation.

124 *Urbaser SA v Argentine Republic* (ICSID Case No ARB/07/26), Award, 8 December 2016 [1200–1210]; similarly, see *The Rompetrol Group NV v Romania* (ICSID Case No ARB/06/3), Award, 6 May 2013 [169 ff] where the tribunal considered its limited jurisdiction meant it

A stricter approach to systemic integration can be found in *Grand River* and *South American Silver*, which emphasize the jurisdictional limitations of the tribunals. The tribunal in *Grand River* was encouraged to take a broad understanding of the scope of investment and to take into account other legal rules, urged by the claimant to bring into the process of interpretation human rights norms and customary rules relevant to indigenous peoples.[125] The tribunal referred to its limited jurisdiction and cautioned:

> The Tribunal understands the obligations 'to take into account' other rules of international law to require it to respect the Vienna Convention's rules governing treaty interpretation. However, the Tribunal does not understand this obligation to provide a license to import into NAFTA legal elements from other treaties, or to allow alteration of an interpretation established through the normal interpretive processes of the Vienna Convention. This is a Tribunal of limited jurisdiction; it has no mandate to decide claims based on treaties other than NAFTA.[126]

The tribunal ultimately avoided the difficult question to what extent a possible customary rule may affect the minimum standard of treatment under Article 1105 of NAFTA as the tribunal could dismiss the argument on the basis that the possible customary rules submitted by the claimant did not assist the individual investor in the dispute.[127] Here, pragmatism won out, allowing adjudicators to avoid questions of normative conflict that go to the heart of the legitimacy of international law.

In another decision concerning indigenous rights, *South American Silver Ltd v Bolivia*, the tribunal had to decide an investment dispute in which there was no applicable law clause, in either the relevant investment treaty or the arbitral institution's governing documents.[128] The claimant contended that the applicable law in an investment dispute is the investment treaty, as primary source of law and *lex specialis*, supplemented by general principles of

could not consider a breach of fair trial provisions in the ECHR but could interpret the BIT provisions in light of the ECHR fair trial standards. Although the tribunal did not provide a legal basis for its use of the ECHR in interpreting the BIT.

125 *Grand River Enterprises Six Nations Ltd v United States of America* (ad hoc, UNCITRAL), Award, 12 January 2011 [66].

126 ibid [71].

127 ibid [210–213].

128 The case was before the PCA, rather than under the ICSID Convention, and therefore there was no fall-back clause on the applicable law.

international law, as needed.[129] Bolivia argued that the tribunal was vested with broad discretion as to applicable law and that applicable law in this dispute should be interpreted in light of the sources of international and domestic law that guarantee protection of the rights of the indigenous communities affected by the investment project.[130] Bolivia specifically relied on systemic integration of the investment treaty based on Article 31(3)(c) of the VCLT. The tribunal cautioned against relying on the ICJ's decision in *Oil Platforms*,[131] as Bolivia had done, noting some difficulties arise from applying Article 31(3)(c) in matters of jurisdiction and normative conflict.[132] The tribunal instead noted that a court's jurisdiction cannot be extended to cover other treaties via Article 31(3)(c), nor could the treaties be brought through the "back door" if States have not consented to jurisdiction.[133] Additionally, the applicable law cannot be altered through rules of treaty interpretation.[134] As a result, the tribunal considered that the principle of systemic integration "must be applied in harmony with the rest of the provisions of the same articles and cautiously, in order to prevent the tribunal from exceeding its jurisdiction and applying rules to the dispute which the Parties have not agreed to."[135] The tribunal went on to reject Bolivia's argument that certain international rules on human rights protection and Bolivian national law were applicable.[136] In its decision, the tribunal emphasized the consent of the parties to both jurisdiction and the application of rules.[137] A strict approach is exemplified through the clear reasoning of the tribunal on the link with consent, although possibly at the expense of other legitimacy concerns, as discussed in the next Chapter.

---

129 *South American Silver Limited (Bermuda) v The Plurinational State of Bolivia* (PCA Case No 2013–15), Award, 22 November 2018 [186].

130 ibid [194].

131 *Oil Platforms* (n 116).

132 *South American Silver v Bolivia* (n 129) para 215.

133 ibid.

134 ibid [215].

135 ibid [216].

136 ibid [217–218].

137 The interplay of international economic law and human rights is further developed in Chapter 7, in discussing the normative legitimacy of the dispute settlement mechanisms from the perspective of global justice. The decision in *South American Silver* illustrates some of the legitimacy problems balancing "justice" and "legality" in cases touching upon *jus cogens* issues.

2.2.2 Relationship between Jurisdiction and Article 31(3)(c): WTO Disputes

Similarly, panels in WTO disputes have drawn comparable concerns on the fine line between interpretation and application, which we can link back to this concern on the relationship between jurisdiction and interpretation. In *Argentina – Poultry*, Argentina attempted to argue that MERCOSUR rulings were part of the normative framework to be taken into account by the panel.[138] The Panel rejected the relevance of MERCOSUR rulings under Article 31(3)(c). The Panel considered that Argentina had not relied on any statement or finding by the MERCOSUR Tribunal to suggest a particular interpretation of WTO agreements. Rather, the Panel determined that Argentina was arguing "that the earlier MERCOSUR Tribunal ruling requires [the panel] to rule in a particular way".[139] The Panel noted it was not bound to follow rulings in adopted WTO panels, let alone rulings of non-WTO dispute settlement bodies. By rejecting Argentina's argument in this way, the Panel chose not to reject the application of Article 31(3)(c) on the basis of the requirements of the provision, for example, the Panel could have considered that MERCOSUR rulings were not "applicable between the parties" of the WTO. Instead, the Panel takes a more principled approach on the nature of Article 31(3)(c) and its own judicial authority.

The Panel in *EC – Large Civil Aircraft* took an almost identical approach. This dispute (as set out in section 1.2 above) included a question on the relevance of a bilateral agreement between the EC and the US in relation to the temporal scope of the SCM Agreement. An alternative argument of the EC on the relevance of the 1992 EC-US Agreement was through the gateway of Article 31(3)(c). The Panel again criticized the so-called interpretation argument since the EC failed to indicate how the 1992 EC-US Agreement should influence interpretation of the actual terms of the SCM Agreement:

> In reality, this is an argument that a particular group of measures (i.e. support measures for large civil aircraft committed by either of the

138 *Argentina – Definitive Anti-Dumping Duties on Poultry from Brazil* (*Report of the Panel*) (22 April 2003), WT/DS241/R [7.18, 7.21]. Argentina also argued that Brazil's conduct in bringing the dispute in different fora was contrary to the principle of good faith, which warranted invocation of the principle of estoppel. Since Argentina does not invoke these principles through the lens of Article 31(3)(c), they have been analysed in other sections of the book.

139 ibid [7.41].

> parties prior to 17 July 1992) should be excluded from the disciplines of the SCM Agreement based on the 1992 Agreement, rather than an argument about the interpretation of provisions of the SCM Agreement, or of specific terms within those provisions.[140]

The panels in these WTO disputes do not go as far as the tribunal in the *Eskosol* award, with a clear emphasis on the importance of the consensual nature of international adjudication. Yet, we can read deeper into the panels' aversion to ruling in a particular way, suggesting the tension between consent and reference to "other" international law rules elucidated by Judge Buergenthal's separate opinion in *Oil Platforms* (see Chapter 4, section 3.1).

2.2.3 Implications

The preceding analysis only touches the surface of the use of systemic integration and Article 31(3)(c) in disputes before the WTO and investor-state dispute settlement mechanisms and should be read with the discussion in Chapter 4 in mind. Yet, the cases considered elucidate the remaining questions concerning how widely other law should be taken into account and what "taking into account" really means. The cases in which the claimant or respondent seeks to use Article 31(3)(c) to bring in other international agreements beyond interpretative assistance exemplify the limited jurisdiction of the tribunal. However, it is the borderline cases on interpretation or application of law where tribunals may find themselves in murky waters if we do not clearly delineate the impact of a limited jurisdiction on interpretation and applicable law powers, as illuminated by the *Mobil Exploration* and *El Paso* inconsistency. Combining these findings with the analysis in Chapter 4, the dichotomy of approaches to systemic integration, apology of party intentions and utopia of coherence, still play out, leading to confusion that begs for the legal reasoning of the adjudicators to provide much more clarity.

2.3 *Applicable Law and Interpretation*

If the jurisdiction and applicable law relationship is understood differently from one adjudicator to the next, the existence of a distinction between application and interpretation is also a question of important theoretical and practical relevance for fragmentation. This section is not intended to be an

---

140 *European Communities – Measures Affecting Trade in Large Civil Aircraft (Report of the Panel)* (n 72) para 7.99.

exhaustive account of how these terms may be used interchangeably or how it may be difficult to distinguish between them in practice.[141] Rather, from the attempts to understand jurisdiction's limitations on applicable law and interpretation, respectively, this section highlights that a liberal approach to interpretation can open the regime's applicable law up to the systemic nature of international law, sometimes in an unauthorized way. In this way, the role of interpretation may be overstated in regulating normative relationships, arguably based "on an understatement of the distinction between interpreting and applying international legal norms".[142] The distinction relates to what law tribunals are authorized to interpret (the applicable law) and what law is capable of being used in that interpretation (interpretation of the applicable law). The Appellate Body in *US – Definitive Anti-Dumping (China)* expressed this distinction succinctly as:

> the question is, whether, when interpreting the terms of [the WTO covered agreement], the relevant provisions of the ILC Articles may be taken into account as one among several interpretative elements. Thus, the treaty being applied is the SCM Agreement, and the attribution rules of the ILC Articles are to be taken into account in interpreting the meaning of the terms of that treaty.[143]

The inability to conceive of how jurisdiction interrelates with these concepts has similar flow-on effects for the function and scope of applicable law and interpretation. This is best exemplified in the WTO context in which there is, arguably, a more limited applicable law but interpretation is covered by the customary rules of interpretation.

---

141 For a more detailed consideration of this question, see Anastasios Gourgourinis, 'The Distinction between Interpretation and Application of Norms in International Adjudication' (2011) 2 Journal of International Dispute Settlement 31; Gleider I Hernández, 'Interpretative Authority and the International Judiciary' in Andrea Bianchi and Matthew Windsor (eds), *Interpretation in International Law* (Oxford University Press 2015) 175 ff.

142 As Gourgourinis argues, 'the international legal contours of the contemporary fragmentation analytics ... appear, unjustifiably I argue, limited to an overstatement of the role of interpretation in regulating normative relationships, based exactly on an understatement of the distinction between interpreting and applying international legal norms': Gourgourinis (n 141) 36.

143 *United States – Definitive Anti-Dumping and Countervailing Duties on Certain Products from China* (*Report of the Appellate Body*) (11 March 2011), WT/DS379/AB/R [316] (emphasis in original).

In the *Korea – Procurement* decision of a WTO Panel, the customary rules of interpretation played a fundamental role in the dispute, in a potentially questionable way, in relation to the applicable law.[144] The *Korea – Procurement* report (which was not appealed) was the first report which explained that the WTO dispute settlement mechanism could "fall back" on general international law.[145] The issue arising in that case was the basis for the non-violation claim made by the US under the Agreement on Government Procurement (GPA),[146] which differed from traditional non-violation claims as the "reasonable expectation of an entitlement to a benefit that had accrued pursuant to the *negotiation* rather than pursuant to a *concession*."[147] In determining that the US could bring such a non-violation claim, the Panel referred to Article 3.2 of the DSU, which sets out the power of the Panel to "clarify the existing provisions of the WTO agreements in accordance with customary rules of *interpretation* of public international law" (emphasis added). The Panel stated:

> However, the relationship of the WTO Agreements to customary international law is broader than this. Customary international law applies generally to the economic relations between the WTO Members. Such international law applies to the extent that the WTO treaty agreements do not "contract out" from it.[148]

As such, the Panel decided that it could review the claim of nullification or impairment raised by the US "within the framework of principles of international law which are generally applicable not only to performance of treaties but also to treaty negotiation."[149] In a footnote to this statement, the Panel appears to discount any potential limitation imposed by the Panel's limited jurisdiction (through referring to the terms of reference of a panel):

> We note that DSU Article 7.1 requires that the relevant covered agreement be cited in the request for a panel and reflected in the terms of reference of a panel. That is not a bar to a broader analysis of the type we are following here, for the GPA would be the referenced covered agreement and, in

144 *Korea – Measures Affecting Government Procurement* (*Report of the Panel*) (1 May 2000) WT/DS163/R.
145 Pauwelyn (n 6) 211.
146 Agreement on Government Procurement (Geneva, 12 April 1979), 1235 UNTS 258.
147 *Korea – Procurement* (n 144) para 7.87 (emphasis in original).
148 ibid [7.96].
149 ibid [7.101].

> our view, we are merely fully examining the issue of non-violation raised by the United States. We are merely doing it within the broader context of customary international law rather than limiting it to the traditional analysis that accords with the extended concept of pacta sunt servanda. The purpose of the terms of reference is to properly identify the claims of the party and therefore the scope of a panel's review. We do not see any basis for arguing that the terms of reference are meant to exclude reference to the broader rules of customary international law in interpreting a claim properly before the Panel.[150]

In this way, the Panel relies heavily on the scope of customary international law in interpretation of the WTO covered agreements to provide for an extension of the law applicable to the dispute beyond WTO law.[151]

While there was some criticism of the Panel's decision when it came before the DSB for adoption,[152] the Panel's statements have been cited numerous times by scholars and other panels in apparent support of its approach to the role of customary international law in WTO disputes.[153] Nonetheless, the decision

---

150 *Korea – Procurement* (n 144) fn 755 (para 7.101).

151 The role of customary international law identified by the Panel as applicable unless not contracted out from, may not be particularly controversial. However, the way in which the Panel applied the customary international law is where problems arise. As Bartels argued, '[t]his report was subject to a certain amount of criticism in the Dispute Settlement Body meeting following its adoption, but it is suggested here that, if anything, this criticism should be confined to the Panel's extension of the non-violation remedy, which is in any case a WTO-specific rule, to cases not involving schedules of concessions': Bartels (n 70) 517; see also, Pauwelyn (n 6) 482 ff.

152 'Minutes of Meeting on 19 June 2000 of the Dispute Settlement Body' (World Trade Organization 2000) WT/DSB/M/84 13–15. In particular, the Philippines drew attention to paragraph 7.93 of the Panel Report which read as follows: 'the non-violation remedy as it has developed in GATT/WTO jurisprudence should not be viewed in isolation from general principles of customary international law'. The Philippines was concerned about this statement because panels should interpret the rights and obligations of Members in a manner consistent with the covered agreements and in accordance with the general rules of interpretation of customary international law. There was a distinction between the rules of interpretation and the rights and obligations under customary international law. See further, the discussion in Chapter 7.

153 See, for example, *United States/Canada – Continued Suspension of Obligations in the EC-Hormones Dispute* (*Report of the Panel*) (31 March 2008), WT/DS320/AB/R ; WT/DS321/R [7.336]. The Appellate Body did not criticize the argument, merely mentioning it which may indicate an implicit approval: *United States/Canada – Continued Suspension of Obligations in the EC-Hormones Dispute* (*Report of the Appellate Body*) (16 October 2008), WT/DS320/AB/R ; WT/DS321/AB/R [278]; see further, Bartels (n 70) 517; Pauwelyn (n 6) 467.

illustrates some of the problems with a lack of understanding of the workings of the toolkit, in particular how the closing tool actually limits the opening tools. The difficulties faced in applying these terms can be seen in the Panel's extension of the non-violation claim, which is itself a WTO-specific rule. There does not appear to be any jurisdiction granted to panels to deal with claims in relation to error in treaty formation and so, the Panel should not have been able to decide upon this claim.[154] As such, this case demonstrates the difficulties for adjudicators in understanding the appropriate scope for other public international law to be applicable to international economic disputes in circumstances where tribunals do not consider how the closing tool of jurisdictional limitations may impact on applicable law.

2.4 *Conclusions and Implications*

The analysis in sections 1.2 and 1.3 indicated a tendency for trade and investment adjudicators to infer a relationship between the concepts of jurisdiction and applicable law. On this approach, jurisdictional limitations must necessarily limit the scope of applicable law. However, it is not always clearly followed through. The implications of different approaches to the relationship between jurisdiction and applicable law is neatly identified by the cases dealing with applicability of the customary international legal defence of countermeasures in trade and investment disputes. As the WTO agreements and most investment agreements do not appear to specifically refer to the customary international law defence of countermeasures, the availability of the defence will be affected by which approach to the relationship between jurisdiction and applicable law is taken. As considered in *Corn Products* and *Mexico – Soft Drinks*, understanding applicable law as limited by the tribunal's limited jurisdiction should result in the defence not being part of the applicable law. The reasoning behind the availability of the defence is that the tribunal cannot make findings in relation to certain elements of the defence for jurisdictional reasons and, as a result, rules out the applicability of the defence as a whole. However, as illustrated by *Archer Daniels*, if we distinguish between jurisdiction and applicable law, the defence is part of the law to be applied to the dispute but, for jurisdictional reasons, the tribunal cannot determine some elements of the defence. This may still leave the tribunal with room to dismiss the dispute on admissibility considerations. These complexities suggest we cannot simply rely on the concept

154 Pauwelyn (n 6) 483.

of state consent to define the applicability of other public international law in international economic disputes.

We are unlikely to be able to find the answers to these definitional questions in the jurisprudence. An over-reliance on adjudicators to resolve these questions underestimates the specific, limited factual situations raised in trade and investment disputes, which necessarily hamper sweeping, broad statements on international law by adjudicators.[155] The analysis in this Chapter demonstrated a general trend, yet it is difficult to draw an overarching rule, principle or theory from the available material. What this Chapter does identify is the importance of understanding the relationship between jurisdiction and applicable law and how divergence in approaches to this relationship can affect the outcome of the application of other international law and indeed the outcome of disputes.

State consent is not enough to fully understand the approach of adjudicators as other considerations of legitimacy are relied on by adjudicators to determine their power and authority to deal with questions of other international law. One such consideration is the international judicial function and the systematization of international law. As explored in Chapters 3 and 4, the responses to fragmentation rely on the international judicial function to explain the motivations or reasoning behind the attempts to address the indeterminacy of international law and the concept of jurisdiction. Yet, Chapter 4 illustrated that this approach does little more in explaining the approach of the tribunals to incorporating other public international law within the dispute settlement regimes.

Thus, these Chapters identify and explain how adjudicators end up consistently inconsistent, not only in relation to the outcome of the application of international law but also in their legal reasoning and normative goals. With a focus on the adjudicator's toolkit, these Chapters produce a general framework of the divergent approaches and how they have manifested in the WTO and investor-state dispute settlement regimes, summarized in Table 10 below.

155 As Crawford and Nevill note, there are limitations that law as a trade and profession imposes: 'it limits how much responsibility we might place on a tribunal or court for failing to satisfactorily resolve metaphysical and constitutional questions': Crawford and Nevill (n 31) 249.

TABLE 10 Overview of the consensual and systemic approaches in WTO and investor-state jurisprudence

	General principles of law	**Systemic integration**	**Applicable law**
Consensual Approach	Gap-filling role so long as principle is generally accepted and falls within the sources of law in applicable law clause	Interpretative role, connectivity required between rule and dispute	Limited by jurisdiction
	WTO: contested view of non liquet and whether any lacuna can be filled ISDS: Hulley – examination of whether applicable source of law in limited disputes	WTO: EC – Biotech ISDS: Mobil Exploration (Annulment Committee)	WTO: restricted by jurisdiction ISDS: Corn Products
Systemic/ coherence Approach	Gap-filling role based on the nature of general principles and role in creating determinacy in international law	Normative environment to be taken into account to create coherence in international law	Bridge to other international legal regimes Distinct from jurisdictional limits
	WTO: gap-filling through general principles ISDS: significant gap-filling by not only general principles but other sources of law	WTO: US – Shrimp ISDS: El Paso	ISDS: Archer Daniel Midland

CHAPTER 7

Legitimacy, Reform and the Adjudicator's Toolkit

The book has, so far, illustrated the difficulties with the use of the largely undefined tools available to adjudicators. The blurry edges of these concepts create space for adjudicators to expand or restrict their use. How these edges are utilized by adjudicators is potentially impacted by their view of their judicial function (whether that be the international judicial function or a more restrictive law-applying function), preconceptions of how international legal regimes interact and state sovereignty. This analysis focused on comparing adjudicators to each other to explain differing normative goals of the adjudicators. This Chapter turn to how the results play into different standards in assessing the legitimacy of international courts and tribunals. How do the different approaches compare when we assess them against other defined standards and perceptions of other actors? The Chapter then considers whether reforms could reduce the inconsistency inherent in the adjudicator's toolkit, even if we cannot address all legitimacy concerns.

1 Legitimacy

To assess and critique the work of the adjudicators, this section turns to how the approach of the adjudicators affects the legitimacy of their dispute settlement mechanisms. Given the herculean task of identifying and applying all the elements of legitimacy,[1] this section adopts the framework developed by Cohen et al[2] and isolates those standards of legitimacy most relevant to the use of the adjudicator's toolkit in trade and investment disputes.

1 To borrow Grossman's characterization of the task of identifying the different elements contributing to legitimacy: Nienke Grossman, 'The Normative Legitimacy of International Courts' (2013) 86 Temple Law Review 61, 65.

2 Harlan Grant Cohen and others, 'Legitimacy and International Courts – A Framework' in Andreas Follesdal and others (eds), *Legitimacy and International Courts* (Cambridge University Press 2018).

 | DOI:10.1163/9789004700932_008

1.1 *Legitimacy Framework*

In order to usefully apply the concept of legitimacy, concerns are often split into source-, process- and results-oriented factors.[3] The interplay between the adjudicator's opening and closing tools falls mostly under source-oriented and result-oriented factors.[4] Jurisdiction, our closing tool, naturally comprises part of the source legitimacy of any judicial decision since "consent to be bound is a powerful source-based justification of legitimacy".[5] Cohen et al also consider that the expectation that courts apply generally accepted methods of interpretation is another consideration of source-oriented factors.[6] In comparison, results-oriented factors concern the fulfilment of the functions of a tribunal, including, on the one hand, how well tribunals contribute to solving the specific problems they were created to solve, and on the other, how well tribunals perform functions beyond dispute settlement, such as providing guidance and serving as an integral part of the international regime.[7] Illustrating the difficult balance facing adjudicators when utilizing their toolkit, jurisdiction also plays a role in shaping results-oriented legitimacy. As noted by Shany:

> On the one hand, jurisdictional rules tend to limit the scope of judicial operations to those subject-matter areas and inter-actor relation, which the relevant international court is well situated to make a positive contribution to … On the other hand, the limits on judicial powers imposed by jurisdictional rules may lead to the promulgation of legal decisions regarded by outside observers as unfair or unjust.[8]

3 Rüdiger Wolfrum, 'Legitimacy of International Law from a Legal Perspective: Some Introductory Considerations' in Rüdiger Wolfrum and Volker Röben (eds), *Legitimacy in International Law* (Springer 2008) 6; Cohen and others (n 2) 5.

4 Process-oriented factors primarily concern the fairness and even-handedness of procedures of the adjudication. See: Thomas M Franck, *Fairness in International Law and Institutions* (Oxford University Press 1998) 6; JHH Weiler, 'The Rule of Lawyers and the Ethos of Diplomats: Reflections on the Internal and External Legitimacy of WTO Dispute Settlement' (2001) 35 Journal of World Trade 191, 204.

5 Cohen and others (n 2) 5; Yuval Shany, *Assessing the Effectiveness of International Courts: A Goal-Based Approach* (Oxford University Press 2014) 151; Allen Buchanan, 'The Legitimacy of International Law' in Samantha Besson and John Tasioulas (eds), *The Philosophy of International Law* (Oxford University Press 2010) 90; Allen Buchanan and Robert O Keohane, 'The Legitimacy of Global Governance Institutions' (2006) 20 Ethics & International Affairs 405, 412.

6 Cohen and others (n 2) 5.

7 ibid 6.

8 Shany (n 5) 151.

Legitimacy can be approached through a normative and sociological lens. Normative legitimacy refers to "the right to rule" according to a set of defined standards, whereas sociological legitimacy is more of an empirical concept, measuring the perception or beliefs of actors that the institution in question has a right to rule.[9] The distinction between approaches can be blurred in practice, particularly when taking into account the complementary and interdependent nature of the two approaches.[10] However, the approaches are different in terms of what they measure: the fulfilment of predefined standards compared to actual perceptions of external actors. Adopting this distinction between normative and sociological legitimacy, the Chapter will consider how the approach of the adjudicators addresses standards of normative legitimacy, in particular performance and justice standards. For sociological legitimacy, the Chapter measures the perceptions of State parties on the approach of the adjudicators.

The preceding Chapters of this book addressed the influence of design choices and normative goals of adjudicators on the outcomes of the application of international law within the trade and investment dispute settlement mechanisms. The complex ways in which these contextual elements may interact with each other can influence the mechanisms' respective legitimacy.[11] The different choices made in designing the WTO and investor-state dispute mechanisms had surprisingly little effect on the carrying out of the function of adjudicators when it came to questions of application of international law. Comparatively, the normative goals of the dispute settlement mechanisms, as envisioned by the adjudicators themselves, appear to have a larger impact on

9 Cohen and others (n 2); Robert Howse and others, 'Introduction' in Robert Howse and others (eds), *The Legitimacy of International Trade Courts and Tribunals* (Cambridge University Press 2018); Nienke Grossman, 'Solomonic Judgments and the Legitimacy of the International Court of Justice' in Andreas Follesdal and others (eds), *Legitimacy and International Courts* (Cambridge University Press 2018); Buchanan (n 5); Daniel Bodansky, 'The Concept of Legitimacy in International Law' in Rüdiger Wolfrum and Volker Röben (eds), *Legitimacy in International Law* (Springer 2008) 313.

10 As Land explains, '[the approaches] are complementary because normative and sociological legitimacy can be understood as different ways to measure justified authority. The concepts are interdependent because they depend on one another for meaning; we cannot understand beliefs about legitimate authority unless we also examine the normative grounds on which those beliefs are built. Finally, normative and sociological legitimacy are also mutually constitutive because acting in a normatively legitimate way can promote public perceptions of legitimacy': Molly K Land, 'Justice as Legitimacy in the European Court of Human Rights' in Andreas Follesdal and others (eds), *Legitimacy and International Courts* (Cambridge University Press 2018).

11 Cohen and others (n 2) 15 ff.

the outcomes, perhaps beyond what the original designer's may have intended. Now, this section asks how does the playing out of these contextual elements in practice align with, first, normative legitimacy standards and, secondly, the perception of States of the normative goals and influence of design choices?

1.2 *Normative Legitimacy*

Returning to the source-, process- and results-oriented factors of legitimacy, the adjudicator's toolkit plays a particular role in shaping source and outcome legitimacy. The difficulty with assessing source-oriented legitimacy, based on the traditional view of legitimacy founded on state consent,[12] is that the legal sources are indeterminate.[13] To use Thomas Franck's conception of the legitimacy of international law,[14] we could argue that any use of the adjudicator's toolkit is unjust due to its indeterminacy. For this reason, this section will not seek to answer whether the adjudicators have exceeded the scope of their authority in terms of source-oriented factors. Instead, the section will focus on the outcome and consider whether the decisions meet performance and justice standards.

1.2.1 Performance Standards

Performance standards link to results-oriented factors of legitimacy, addressing how well an international court performs its "functions". Cohen et al incorporate within their framework of performance factors the standard of how well a court performs its functions beyond dispute settlement, such as giving general guidance on interpretation.[15] In defining this standard, Thomas Franck's legitimacy indicator of coherence is often raised.[16] According to Franck, coherence

---

12 Democracy has also been raised as a basis for normative legitimacy: Buchanan (n 5) 93; Thomas Christiano, 'The Legitimacy of International Institutions' in Andrei Marmor (ed), *The Routledge Companion to Philosophy of Law* (Taylor & Francis 2012) 381. However, this is beyond the scope of this research.

13 As Bjorklund comments, this is where Franck's legitimacy criteria are most difficult to satisfy: 'there is at least some incoherence in the underlying rules, and a "regime" that is not designed to bring any coherence to them or, one might say, no "regime" at all': Andrea K Bjorklund, 'The Legitimacy of the International Center for Settlement of Investment Disputes' in Andreas Follesdal and others (eds), *Legitimacy and International Courts* (Cambridge University Press 2018) 273.

14 Franck, *Fairness in International Law and Institutions* (n 4) ch 2.

15 Cohen and others (n 2) 6.

16 See, for example, Grossman (n 9); Tullio Treves, 'Aspects of Legitimacy of Decisions of International Courts and Tribunals' in Rüdiger Wolfrum and Volker Röben (eds), *Legitimacy in International Law* (Springer 2008).

requires rules applied in like cases to be treated alike.[17] Coherency can legitimate rules because it "provides a reasonable connection between a rule, or the application of a rule, to 1) its own principled purpose, 2) principles previously employed to solve similar problems, and 3) a lattice of principles in use to resolve different problems".[18] According to Grossman:

> the point is that a court that muddies rules rather than clarifying them both weakens the compliance pull of the relevant rule and makes a poor case for its own authority as a law declaring body.[19]

The analysis of the use of the adjudicator's toolkit throughout this book calls into the question the adequacy of the decision-making of the adjudicators as part of the performance of the tribunals. It is clear that on an alarming number of occasions, adjudicators are not reaching a conscious and transparent standard of reasoning. The methodology of international adjudication applied is unclear and inconsistent, thereby detracting from the performance standard of the adjudicators.

As the cases of *Corn Products* and *Archer Daniels Midland* on countermeasures in Chapter 6 illustrate, the outcomes of the disputes are not necessarily affected by the incoherence of the application of the adjudicator's toolkit. However, the inadequate decision-making of the adjudicators regularly fails to meet the performance standards expected of international courts and tribunals, especially when it comes to issues of the environment and human rights, which are also relevant to assessing legitimacy under a justice standard in the next section.

Yet, it is not all doom and gloom for the legitimacy of trade and investment tribunals if we are looking to find coherency in the adjudicator's toolkit. The previous Chapters focused on the many examples of inconsistency to illustrate the irrelevance of design choices and the influence of different normative goals on the application of the toolkit. However, we can also see paths through to the light of consistency and coherence in certain, defined areas in the application of the toolkit in which the normative goals aligned. First, and relevantly to State consent as a source-oriented factor of legitimacy, opening tools are almost universally given a limited role in "reading in" jurisdictional obligations. Secondly, adjudicators agree that opening tools are necessary to fill gaps in the

17 Franck, *Fairness in International Law and Institutions* (n 4) 38.

18 Thomas M Franck, *The Power of Legitimacy among Nations* (Oxford University Press 1990) 147–8.

19 Grossman (n 9) 56.

procedural powers of tribunals, perhaps also enhancing the process-oriented legitimacy.

The agreement between adjudicators, and resulting coherence of decision-making, is most apparent in investor-state disputes, which grapple with the jurisdiction of tribunals more frequently than their WTO counterparts. Expanding jurisdiction, referring to attempts to imply consent of the tribunal or incorporate other substantive obligations within the treaty regime, is naturally considered within the strict confines of consent to jurisdiction.[20] For example, in *İçkale İnşaat Limited v Turkmenistan*, the claimant sought to rely on FET and non-discrimination protections as "international customary norms" as well as breaches of general principles of international law.[21] The tribunal's clear rejection of both attempts at expanding the tribunal's jurisdiction over causes of action not within the IIA illustrates the restrictive approach that should be taken to such questions of consent.[22] However, jurisdictional objections on the basis of customary and general principles of law enable a systemic approach to international law and also conforms to legal decisions standing on principle.

General principles have been applied to jurisdictional objections, both as a source of an objection and in relation to fulfilling conditions on jurisdiction. There is not necessarily a positive source of law for this inclusion within the treaties. Rather, it draws on the role of international courts and tribunals and the goal of the legal institutions they serve as well as the broader implication of tribunal decisions. In this way, while general principles may be applicable through applicable law or systemic integration, they are also necessary in the protection of the fabric of international dispute settlement, a key concern of the international judicial function as well as consensual approaches.

General principles and customary international law may also be used to legitimize a consensual approach to jurisdiction, thereby shielding the tribunal's maintenance of its jurisdiction where jurisdictional collisions occur.

---

20 Lauterpacht has also noted the judicial restraint exercised by the ICJ in relation to the question of its own jurisdiction: Hersch Lauterpacht, *The Development of International Law by the International Court* (Cambridge University Press 1982) ch 91.

21 *İçkale İnşaat Limited v Turkmenistan* (ICSID Case No ARB/10/24), Award, 8 March 2016 [341, 402].

22 It may be possible to point to inconsistent decisions to this, such as *Toto v Lebanon* (ICSID Case No ARB/07/12), Decision on Jurisdiction, 11 September 2009 [154] in which the tribunal considers the IIA sanctions not only breaches of specific provisions but also breaches of any rule of international law, including denial of justice under international law. In making this finding, the tribunal refers to the applicable law clause of the IIA. However, this decision arguably takes too broad a view of the role applicable law clauses and the relationship with jurisdiction and, as such, can be distinguished on that basis.

The tribunals are often cautious to cede their jurisdiction on the basis of other international law. The attempts by respondents before the WTO to rely on obligations (or breach of such obligations) under FTAs, such as the *Mexico – Soft Drinks*[23] and *Argentina – Poultry from Brazil*[24] as well as *Peru – Agricultural Products*[25] in Chapter 6 (section 1.2), supports such a conclusion. Each of these attempts were rejected on the basis of the consent to the jurisdiction of WTO panels, as a fundamental requirement.

This demonstrates agreement and areas of clear reasoning: tribunals are cautious to give up their jurisdiction on the basis of other law or other regimes.[26] In doing so, general international law is used to "legitimize" the exercise of the tribunal's jurisdiction. General international law may be used to interpret jurisdictional requirements or provide conflict rules in absence of such treaty rules. However, the line is drawn when other international law may expand jurisdiction or otherwise cede jurisdiction of a properly constituted tribunal. While this path between jurisdictional requirements may seem uncontroversial, it is important to acknowledge such examples. In doing so, we can bridge the gap between potentially competing approaches and narrow the perception of substantive fragmentation within regimes, thereby contributing to enhancing the source-oriented and resulted-oriented factors of legitimacy.

1.2.2 Justice Standards

Flowing from the insufficiency of state consent to ground claims of legitimacy in contemporary international law, scholars have turned to the concept of justice as a source-based factor of legitimacy.[27] This standard views protection of human rights as a necessary condition for the legitimacy of a political order.[28] Based on the standard as defined by Grossman, "courts cannot condone or facilitate the violation of a minimum core set of human rights and remain legitimate."[29]

23 *Mexico – Tax Measures on Soft Drinks and Other Beverages* (*Report of the Appellate Body*) (6 March 2006) WT/DS308/AB/R.

24 *Argentina – Definitive Anti-Dumping Duties on Poultry from Brazil* (*Report of the Panel*) (22 April 2003), WT/DS241/R.

25 *Peru – Additional Duty on Imports of Certain Agricultural Products* (*Report of the Appellate Body*) (20 July 2015) WT/DS457/AB/R.

26 The exception to this conclusion is fundamental rules of international law, such as *jus cogens*. However, such rules have not arisen in disputes before the WTO and investor-state dispute settlement mechanisms.

27 See, for example, Buchanan (n 5).

28 ibid 95.

29 Grossman (n 9) 97; Cohen and others (n 2) 7; Land (n 10).

Justice is a necessary but not sufficient condition as the presence of injustice may make an institution illegitimate, but doing justice may not always affirmatively promote the legitimacy of a court.[30] In the interpretation of vague terms of treaties, there may be a tension between "legal legitimacy" based on an interpretation of the treaty and justice-based legitimacy.[31] However, at a minimum, according to the conception of legitimacy founded on justice, courts cannot act in a manner that facilitates the violation of international law, especially those of high value like universal human rights, since such courts are established by States to apply international law.[32] In effect, this conception of legitimacy establishes a normative hierarchy of fundamental individual human rights above other rights, including trade and investment obligations under the specific treaty:

> The duty not to violate basic human rights is part of the world of law from which they draw, even if the case at issue concerns trade law, the law of the sea, or expropriation. Simply, there are some lines that international courts cannot cross and still retain their legitimacy.[33]

According to Grossman, this does not run counter to the object and purpose of international economic tribunals since all international rules are part of the same legal system and are not to be read "in clinical isolation" from each other.[34] This is where the tension between the inconsistent use of the adjudicator's toolkit based on the normative goals of the adjudicators becomes pertinent. Where aspects of the broader conflict between the parties that includes other moral or political values, such as human rights or the environment, falls outside the law applicable based on the limited jurisdiction of the tribunal, we find collision between justice and the "legitimacy of legality".[35]

---

30 Land (n 10) 87.

31 Cohen and others (n 2) 7.

32 Grossman (n 1) 100.

33 ibid 101.

34 ibid, adopting the terminology used by the Appellate Body in; *United States – Standards for Reformulated and Conventional Gasoline* (*Report of the Appellate Body*) (29 April 1996), WT/DS2/AB/R [45].

35 Treves (n 16) 178, who proceeds to explain: 'the claim that the judicial decision should address certain issues and values even when they are beyond the limits of the court's jurisdiction, or are unnecessary to solve the dispute, collides with the argument that a value, the moral or political weight of which is considered essential, is that courts and tribunals do not, in their decisions, go beyond what has been brought before them according to the applicable rules.'

WTO and ISDS adjudicators have consistently referred to broader international legal values to bring legitimacy to their decisions, even if they end up rejecting the applicability of a particular rule. These can be seen as "legitimizing statements" or "political *obiter dicta*" since the actual statement had no legal relevance to the ultimate decision. For example, noting that the regimes are not to be read in "clinical isolation" from international law and must respect peremptory norms of international law. The *Methanex* tribunal affirmed that "as a matter of international constitutional law a tribunal has an independent duty to apply imperative principles of law or *jus cogens* and not to give effect to parties' choices of law that are inconsistent with such principles".[36] On the one hand, although such legitimizing statements or incidental references are unnecessary to resolve the dispute, they contribute to the justice legitimacy of the tribunals. Such statements reaffirm the value of the international community and contribute to the harmonious development of international law.[37] On the other hand, such statements can also be delegitimising, from the perspective of those arguing in favor of the "legitimacy of legality", as undermining the proper exercise of the judicial function. For Treves, the reaction to such legitimizing statements reveals the subjective character of legitimacy as to whether legitimacy of legality or justice should prevail, even if the same values are held by stakeholders.[38]

These statements cannot single-handedly resolve the legitimacy of the dispute settlement mechanisms from a justice perspective. As Figure 7 and Figure 8 illustrated, there was little to no (for the WTO) international law applied on the basis of its priority or *jus cogens* status. In none of the analysed disputes was there any actual allegation of a violation of a *jus cogens* rule nor an argument that the IIA was in breach of *jus cogens*. For the small number of ISDS

36 *Methanex Corporation v United States of America* (ad hoc, UNCITRAL), Final Award, 3 August 2005 [24].

37 See discussion in Valentina Vadi, *Cultural Heritage in International Economic Law* (Brill Nijhoff 2023) 378.

38 In reviewing ICJ decisions with such legitimizing statements, Treves refers to the separate or dissenting opinions arguing in favor of legitimacy of legality which consider 'these statements – independently of their legality, which in some cases is seen as doubtful – are unnecessary to support the decision and, especially, inopportune from the point of view of the proper exercise of the judicial function. These separate and dissenting opinions see the "legitimizing statements" included in the decisions with the purpose of connecting them with important legal and moral principles, as delegitimizing elements that subtract from the overall acceptability of judicial decisions. The subjective character of the idea of legitimacy of judicial decisions emerges clearly in this opposition of views, not because the values invoked are not broadly shared, but because of the difference as to which one should prevail': Treves (n 16) 17.

disputes in which the other international rule had priority status, the incorporation of the other international law was merely an interpretative tool to clarify the meaning of treaty provisions, rather than to resolve conflicts of norms.[39] Since the legitimizing statements and interpretative clarifications were not central to the resolution of the dispute, the question remains whether the interplay between international economic law and *jus cogens* or fundamental human rights can be adequately addressed through the adjudicator's international law toolkit.[40] Certainly, the results show positive signs of reference to justice concerns within the regimes. Nonetheless, three issues of inconsistency in the adjudicator's toolkit revealed in the earlier Chapters are relevant to this assessment of legitimacy: (1) the applicable law and necessity defence, (2) general principles relating to the legality of the investment, and (3) jurisdictional limits of disputes and systemic integration.

First, protection of human rights may arise as part of the necessity defence.[41] Tribunals have recognized the conflict between human rights and investment obligations. For example, the Annulment Committee in *Sempra v Argentina* recognized that the Argentine economic crisis "raises the complex relationship between investment treaties, emergency and the human rights of both citizens

39 For example, ISDS tribunals have noted that one of the relevant factors in evaluating fair and equitable treatment included that enactment of general legislative statements are 'subject to subsequent modification, and possibly to withdrawal and cancellation within the limits of respect of fundamental human rights and *jus cogens*': see, for example, *Continental Casualty v Argentina* (ICSID Case No ARB/03/9), Award, 5 September 2008 [261]; *PV Investors v Spain* (PCA Case No 2012–14), Final Award, 28 February 2020 [579].

40 There is a wealth of literature on the interplay between human rights and international economic law. This section is only a small snapshot of issues revealed through the use of the adjudicator's toolkit to apply or reject other international law. For more detailed discussion, see Pierre-Marie Dupuy, Ernst-Ulrich Petersmann and Francesco Francioni (eds), *Human Rights in International Investment Law and Arbitration* (Oxford University Press 2009); Crina Baltag and Ylli Dautaj, 'Promoting, Regulating, and Enforcing Human Rights through International Investment Law and ISDS' (2021) 45 Fordham International Law Journal 1; Kabir AN Duggal and Nicholas J Diamond, 'Human Rights and Investor–State Dispute Settlement Reform: Fitting a Square Peg into a Round Hole?' (2021) 12 Journal of International Dispute Settlement 291; Joost Pauwelyn, 'Human Rights in WTO Dispute Settlement' in Thomas Cottier, Joost Pauwelyn and Elisabeth Bürgi Bonanomi (eds), *Human Rights and International Trade* (Oxford University Press 2005); Holger Hestermeyer, 'International Human Rights Law and Dispute Settlement in the World Trade Organization' in Martin Scheinin (ed), *Human Rights Norms in 'Other' International Courts* (1st edn, Cambridge University Press 2019).

41 Eric De Brabandere, 'International Investment Law and Human Rights', *Elgar Encyclopedia of Human Rights* (Edward Elgar Publishing 2022) 273.

and property owners".[42] However, the inconsistent approach to the application of the ILC Articles on the state of necessity, discussed in Chapter 3 (section 2.4), presents issues. Whether the strict customary international law requirements under Article 25 of the ILC Articles should be read in to IIA defences is likely to limit the circumstances precluding wrongfulness extending to human rights.

Secondly, legality requirements are relevant to protecting human rights as they can bar the application of investment protection to investments made in breach of human rights. The survey of ISDS practice on good faith as a general principle concerning the conduct of the investor in Chapter 4 (section 2.3) illustrates that such a question is not entirely resolved. Whether the conduct of the investor during the investment (compared to the creation of the investment) is subject to such legality requirements is somewhat opaque. Where an IIA includes a legality requirement referring to compliance with domestic laws, violation of human rights by the investor would likely result in a denial of investment protection.[43] Even so, examples where human rights have actually been applied as part of the domestic legality requirement are rare,[44] and ultimately not the focus of the adjudicator's toolkit. Where the IIA does not include a legality requirement or such IIA provision only refers to domestic law, tribunals have read in legality requirements on the basis of good faith as a general principle of law.[45] It would be untenable to argue that a clear breach of *jus cogens* would not strip an investor of its protection under the treaty. As the tribunal in *Phoenix Action v Czech Republic* stated in its "political *obiter dicta*": "to take an extreme example, nobody would suggest that ICSID protection should be granted to investments made … in pursuance of torture or genocide or in support of slavery."[46] However, what is encompassed as illegal conduct under the general principle of good faith beyond clear *jus cogens* norms is unclear. The *Hulley* tribunal's reluctance to recognize unclean hands as an applicable general principle of law presents concern for which legality requirements could be applied as general principles and the scope of those general principles. Human rights could arguably form part of international public policy, which has been recognized by ISDS tribunals as a legality

42 *Sempra v Argentine Republic* (ICSID Case No ARB/02/16), Decision on the Argentine Republic's Application for Annulment of the Award, 29 June 2010 [332].

43 De Brabandere (n 41) 270.

44 ibid.

45 See *Churchill Mining PLC and Planet Mining Pty Ltd v Republic of Indonesia* (ICSID Case No ARB/12/14 and 12/40), Award, 6 December 2016 [488–508].

46 *Phoenix Action v Czech Republic* (ICSID Case No ARB/06/5), Award, 15 April 2009 [78]; see also, Zachary Douglas, 'The Plea of Illegality in Investment Treaty Arbitration' (2014) 29 ICSID Review – Foreign Investment Law Journal 155, 181.

requirement.[47] Narrow interpretations of what constitutes illegal conduct under general principles may limit the scope of alleged violations of human rights that may be regulated. Further, the requirement that alleged violations must go to the "essence of the investment" also limits the situations in which the legality requirement can protect human rights.[48] The jurisdictional limits of the tribunal to determine whether a breach of human rights has been committed by the investor may also limit the capacity of the legality requirement to protect human rights.

This brings us to the final inconsistency in the adjudicator's toolkit: jurisdictional limits and systemic integration. The decisions in *South American Silver* and *Grand River* illustrate the normative legitimacy problems in balancing legality (the limited jurisdiction of the tribunals) and justice (coherence with human rights law). The decisions concerned indigenous rights, which have been argued to be *jus cogens* or *erga omnes* obligations, stemming from the self-determination rights of the indigenous peoples.[49] These decisions highlighted that trade and investment dispute settlement mechanisms are tribunals of limited jurisdiction and cannot adjudicate the actual violations of international human rights law.[50] However, the extent to which this limited jurisdiction results in a "compartmentalization" of human rights and international economic law[51] through unclear reasoning on the application of the

47 Pierre-Marie Dupuy and Jorge Vinuales, 'Human Rights and Investment Disciplines: Integration in Progress' in Marc Bungenberg and others (eds), *International Investment Law: A Handbook* (Hart Publishing 2015) 1765; Vadi (n 37) 395. Vadi further argues that international public policy protects *jus cogens* and that an emerging norm of peremptory character protects indigenous cultural heritage.

48 See, for example, *Fraport AG Frankfurt Airport Services Worldwide v Republic of the Philippines (II)* (ICSID Case No ARB/11/12), Award, 12 December 2014 [332].

49 See Valentina Vadi, *Cultural Heritage in International Investment Law and Arbitration* (Cambridge University Press 2014) 219 and references therein; on the interplay between indigenous rights and international economic law more generally, see Sergio Puig, *At the Margins of Globalization: Indigenous Peoples and International Economic Law* (Cambridge University Press 2021); John Borrows and Risa Schwartz (eds), *Indigenous Peoples and International Trade: Building Equitable and Inclusive International Trade and Investment Agreements* (Cambridge University Press 2020).

50 See also De Brabandere (n 41) 269–70; referring to the decisions in *Bernhard von Pezold v Republic of Zimbabwe* (ICSID Case No ARB/10/15), Award, 28 July 2015; *The Rompetrol Group NV v Romania* (ICSID Case No ARB/06/3), Award, 6 May 2013; and Vadi (n 49) 230; referring to *Glamis Gold Ltd v United States of America* (ad hoc, UNCITRAL), Final Award, 9 June 2009.

51 See Vadi (n 37) 358: "excessive compartmentalization impedes coherence; it emphasizes the particular over the universal; it may defeat important policy objectives of the international community by leading to competition and clashes between regimes'.

principle of systemic integration could be a delegitimizing factor. As argued in Chapter 6, clearer reasoning is required. Whether this reasoning leans more to consensual or justice-based concerns will depend on the normative goals. However, it is ultimately necessary to see these goals expressed in the reasoning, rather than having to search between the lines for parochial understandings of law.

For ISDS, the justice standard can be assessed through the (non)application of human rights law, but, for WTO adjudicators, the intersection with the environment has evolved as more of a concern. Protection of the environment does not form part of Grossman's conception of justice legitimacy, nor is it easily defined as a peremptory norm of international law. Yet, particularly considering the climate crisis, protection of the environment is an important value of the international community and possibly one of *erga omnes* character.[52] As the Appellate Body stated in *US – Shrimp*, the WTO agreements recognize "the importance and legitimacy of environmental protection as a goal of national and international policy" and so must be read "in light of contemporary concerns of the community of nations".[53] The use of systemic integration may have a legitimacy enhancing effect given both its source legitimacy as a customary international norm of interpretation[54] as well as through allowing the WTO's practice to evolve to "reflect shifting conceptions of legitimate international order".[55] Yet, as Chapter 4 revealed, there has been inconsistent treatment on Article 31(3)(c) and systemic integration in addressing these environmental concerns. While some balancing of trade and environment has been undertaken in disputes like *US – Shrimp*, balancing has been done in a limited way,

52 On the potential human rights impacts of the right to environment, see Malgosia Fitzmaurice, 'Human Right to Clean Environment and the Rights of Nature in the Anthropocene' (2022) 42 Polish Yearbook of International Law 155; on the *erga omnes* character of the protection of the environment, see Vice-President's Weeramantry's separate opinion in *Gabčíkovo-Nagymaros Project (Hungary v Slovakia), Judgment* [1997] ICJ Rep 7, 118; see also Nicola Strain, 'Regulating Collective Resources under Multilateral Treaties: The Decision in Whaling in the Antarctic (Australia v Japan)' (2019) 20 Melbourne Journal of International Law 572.

53 *United States – Import Prohibition of Certain Shrimp and Shrimp Products (Report of the Appellate Body)* (12 October 1998), WT/DS58/AB/R [129].

54 Shany (n 5) 206.

55 Ruth Teitel and Robert Howse, 'Cross-Judging: Tribunalization in a Fragmented but Interconnected Global Order Symposium – The Normalizing of Adjudication In Complex International Governance Regimes: Patterns, Possibilities, and Problems' (2008) 41 New York University Journal of International Law and Politics 959, 984–5.

respecting the nature of the WTO dispute settlement system.[56] The narrow approach to systemic interpretation, requiring legal rules to be applicable to *all* WTO members, provides worrying signs for the legitimacy of the WTO, from an environmental justice perspective.

1.3 *Sociological Legitimacy: States' Perceptions*

If the tribunals do *not* possess normative legitimacy (which the preceding section suggests is the case, based either on performance or justice standards), can we simply assume that sociological legitimacy is also lacking? The interplay between normative and sociological legitimacy is not so simple. For example, factors that contribute to sociological legitimacy may differ from those necessary for normative legitimacy or different actors may stress different standards of normative legitimacy.[57]

Sociological legitimacy is an empirical exercise, which is beyond the ambitions of this section. The following section is not intended to be an exhaustive account of critical reactions to these dispute settlement mechanisms (or the wider institutions behind them)[58] nor an evaluation of whether the tribunals have responded to these criticisms.[59] Rather, the section highlights some key criticisms relevant to the balance between consent and the international judicial function. What this section demonstrates, most importantly, is inconsistency between states themselves as to the normative goals of the dispute settlement mechanisms and whether aspects of the adjudicator's toolkit are appropriate in these international economic tribunals. Some state's

---

56 Reto Malacrida and Gabrielle Marceau, 'The WTO Adjudicating Bodies' in Robert Howse and others (eds), *The Legitimacy of International Trade Courts and Tribunals* (1st edn, Cambridge University Press 2018) 65; this, however, does likely contribute to the second substantive condition of legitimacy that courts promote the purposes of the normative regimes they are charged with interpreting and applying: Grossman (n 1) 103 ff.

57 Bjorklund (n 13) 236; Cohen and others (n 2) 10; Land (n 10) 85.

58 See, for example, Campbell McLachlan, 'The Assault on International Adjudication and the Limits of Withdrawal' (2019) 68 International & Comparative Law Quarterly 499; Michael Waibel and others (eds), *The Backlash Against Investment Arbitration: Perceptions and Reality* (Kluwer Law International 2010); Ernst-Ulrich Petersmann, 'The 'Crown Jewel of the WTO Has Been Stolen by US Trade Diplomats – and They Have No Intention of Giving It Back' in Denise Prévost, Iveta Alexovicova and Jens Hillebrand Pohl (eds), *Restoring Trust in Trade: Liber Amicorum in Honour of Peter Van den Bossche* (Hart 2019); Robert McDougall, 'The Crisis in WTO Dispute Settlement: Fixing Birth Defects to Restore Balance' (2018) 52 Journal of World Trade 867.

59 See, for example, Malcolm Langford, Cosette D Creamer and Daniel Behn, 'Regime Responsiveness in International Economic Disputes' in Szilárd Gáspár-Szilágyi, Daniel Behn and Malcolm Langford (eds), *Adjudicating Trade and Investment Disputes: Convergence or Divergence?* (Cambridge University Press 2020).

perception of the legitimacy of the dispute settlement mechanisms of the WTO and investment law is eroding as a result of aspects of the international judicial function while other states seek to strengthen the trends in judicial lawmaking.

The current trend to rely on the cooperation of the international judiciary to resolve conflict and fragmentation concerns requires trust in the international judicial system.[60] Such trust differs from domestic courts where the legislator may step in to provide guidance and legislative changes in response to jurisprudential trends.[61] However, the line between permissible judicial lawmaking and the negative connotation of judicial activism within the WTO and investor-state dispute settlement mechanisms has remained very fine. As with adjudicators, states' conceptions of the legitimacy of international law and judicial institutions are subjective and may evolve over time.[62]

To assess the sociological legitimacy of the tribunals, this section focuses on the statements made to reform bodies or political organs relevant to the dispute settlement mechanisms. The section does not include the arguments made by States in the course of legal proceedings, including during appeal procedures. Certainly, States may express their frustration or agreement with the approach of the adjudicators in appeal proceedings. However, it is not always clear the extent to which such statements may simply be part of a litigation strategy,[63] rather than concerns with the overall functioning of the system.[64]

---

60 Ralph Alexander Lorz, 'Fragmentation, Consolidation and the Future Relationship between International Investment Law and General International Law' in Freya Baetens (ed), *Investment Law within International Law* (Cambridge University Press 2013) 488.

61 While this might be slightly different for domestic constitutional courts, there are still methods by which a domestic legislator may change the constitution. Further, the domestic legislator usually has more control over the appointment of judges than at the international level.

62 Johann Robert Basedow, 'Why De-Judicialize? Explaining State Preferences on Judicialization in World Trade Organization Dispute Settlement Body and Investor-to-State Dispute Settlement Reforms' [2021] Regulation & Governance 4.

63 New research on compliance with ISDS decisions shows that Respondent States initiate annulment or set-aside proceedings against almost 70% of their losing awards: Nicola Strain and others, 'Compliance Politics and International Investment Disputes: A New Dataset' (2024) 27 Journal of International Economic Law 70, 89.

64 In addition, ISDS presents a particular issue with reviewing appeal proceedings since annulment of awards that are outside of the ICSID framework can occur in different domestic jurisdictions, and States may also seek to set-aside upon an investor seeking to enforce the award. Standards of the enforcing or set-aside court may be different. For example, in *Aboukhalil v Senegal*, Senegal argued before the Paris Court of Appeal that citations to the ECtHR were inappropriate: *Ibrahim Aboukhalil v Senegal* (*UNCITRAL, ad hoc*), *Judgement of the Paris Court of Appeal, 12 October 2021* (*N° RG 19/21625 – N° Portalis 35L7-VB7D-CBBL2*) [145 ff]. This case is not included in the doctrinal analysis since

Instead, the Appellate Body's or ICSID Annulment Committees' assessment of specific statements on appeal are included in the assessment in the previous Chapters.

1.3.1 WTO

As Chapter 2 and Chapter 3 revealed, the question has never been whether international law has been applied in disputes, either directly or through interpretative means. Rather, the question is whether this trend is in fact authorized by WTO law. Clearly, other international law is trickling into the system, albeit in smaller steps than its investment counterpart. What should we make of WTO Members response, or more accurately, lack of response to this development of WTO law?[65] Could this imply consent to the judicial practices of panels and Appellate Body when it comes to other international law? If it were not for the outstanding objections of the US and other states of this international judicial function role for panels and the Appellate Body, the sociological legitimacy of panels and the Appellate Body might have been easily assessed.

Within the WTO, concerns of judicial activism are not new. Early in the tenure of the WTO dispute settlement system, three Director-Generals raised concerns that dispute settlement was heading in a dangerous direction: gap-filling WTO law.[66] The Director-Generals considered that there was an excessive resort to litigation as a substitute for negotiation, particularly concerning in light of public perceptions of the "over-secret and over-powerful" process of dispute settlement in the WTO. In 2005, the US suggested amendments to the DSU to provide additional guidance for WTO adjudicative bodies, on the basis that "the reasoning and findings of reports may at times go beyond what the parties consider to be necessary to resolve the dispute".[67] The US pointed to

---

the Final Award is not publicly available and the domestic proceedings fall outside the methodological scope.

65 In a reproach of doctrinal discussion, Flett refers to such discussion potentially overlooking the steady trickle of international law into the WTO acquis "apparently without any of the WTO Members taking particular exception": James Flett, 'Importing Other International Regimes into World Trade Organization Litigation' in Margaret A Young (ed), *Regime Interaction in International Law: Facing Fragmentation* (Cambridge University Press 2012) 282.

66 Arthur Dunkel, Peter Sutherland and Renato Ruggiero, 'Joint Statement on the Multilateral Trading System' (*World Trade Organization*, 1 February 2001) <https://www.wto.org/english/news_e/news01_e/jointstatdavos_jan01_e.htm> accessed 17 December 2020.

67 'Negotiations on Improvements and Clarifications of the Dispute Settlement Understanding, Further Contribution of the United States on Improving Flexibility and Member Control in WTO Dispute Settlement – Communication from the United States' (World Trade Organization, Dispute Settlement Body 2005) TN/DS/W/82 1.

some specific areas that could have benefited from additional discussion by member governments, including:

> (a) situations where the relevant WTO text does not address an issue, leading to concerns over whether an adjudicative body might 'fill the gap' and consequently add to or diminish rights and obligations under the relevant agreement instead of clarifying those rights and obligations;
> – Gaps may reflect a situation where there was a limit upon what negotiators were able to agree. Alternatively, gaps may reflect an absence of any consideration by negotiators of the particular detail at issue.
> (b) situations in which legal concepts outside the WTO texts have been applied in a WTO dispute settlement proceeding, including asserted principles of international law other than customary international law rules of interpretation.[68]

The US noted there are only three areas in which public international law plays a role in WTO dispute settlement: the Marrakesh Agreement is public international law; the customary rules of interpretation of public international law in Article 31 to 33 of the VCLT pursuant to Article 3.2 of the DSU; and, covered agreements may expressly refer to other public international law.[69] The US suggested draft parameters for a proper interpretive approach to use in WTO dispute settlement, which reflected the fact that members "have not agreed to delegate to WTO adjudicative bodies the task of filling in gaps in the covered agreements".[70] While the empirical results in *Figure* 5 indicate that there was a downward trend after a peak in 2009, we certainly cannot conclude that the application of international law decreased as a result of these criticisms and suggestions. Rather, following the completion of high profile and complex disputes that deal with a range of international law, a tipping point in

---

68 ibid 2; this concern was also shared by Chile: 'Negotiations on Improvements and Clarifications of the Dispute Settlement Understanding on Improving Flexibility and Member Control in WTO Dispute Settlement – Contribution by Chile and the United States' (World Trade Organization, Dispute Settlement Body 2002) TN/DS/W/28 2.

69 'Negotiations on Improvements and Clarifications of the Dispute Settlement Understanding, Further Contribution of the United States on Improving Flexibility and Member Control in WTO Dispute Settlement – Communication from the United States' (n 67) 5–6.

70 'Negotiations on Improvements and Clarifications of the Dispute Settlement Understanding, Further Contribution of the United States on Improving Flexibility and Member Control in WTO Dispute Settlement – Communication from the United States' (n 67), Add. 1.

the development of the WTO's own jurisprudence on various international law issues may have been reached.

These concerns have been re-iterated in the US's more recent objections to the Appellate Body, arguing that, *inter alia*, the Appellate Body was erroneously claiming its reports are entitled to be treated as precedent and that the Appellate Body was also adding to or diminishing the rights and obligations of WTO members in various disputes.[71] The US pointed to Article 3.7 of the DSU to support the view that the negotiating members wanted "a dispute settlement system that would simply help to resolve disputes, not make law".[72] The criticisms of the US toward the WTO dispute settlement body reflects the US's conception of the legitimacy of international law and institutions, rooted in the language of the WTO Agreements and supposed intent of members.[73] For example, Petersmann referred to the US trade diplomats' insistence on the contractual nature of WTO market access and the denial of "constitutional" (e.g. judicial) dimensions of WTO law, their disregard for the dynamic evolution of multilateral treaties and judicial practices that clarify and develop WTO rules and principles.[74] More generally, in the US's view, albeit within margins over time and governments, international law should be state-centric and, as such, cannot evolve or expand authority without losing some of their legitimacy.[75] In this way, the US expects WTO adjudicators to act as dispute-settlers, and even possibly in an even more reduced role, rather than rule or regime developers.

Most other Members of the WTO have reacted critically to the US's approach, with many supporting the work of the Appellate Body as a central feature of the WTO system.[76] Notably, the EU has led a multilateral initiative

71 '2018 Trade Policy Agenda and 2017 Annual Report of the President of the United States on the Trade Agreements Program' (United States Trade Representative 2018) 23, 28.

72 'Report on the Appellate Body of the World Trade Organization' (United States Trade Representative 2020) 24.

73 Cohen also argues that while the arguments are facially positivistic, it is impossible to ignore the overlap between the US's positive assessment and self-interest: Harlan Grant Cohen, 'Culture Clash: The Sociology of WTO Precedent' in Amalie Frese and Julius Schumann (eds), *Precedents as Rules and Practice: New Approaches and Methodologies in Studies of Legal Precedents* (1st Edition, Nomos 2021) 113.

74 Ernst-Ulrich Petersmann, 'How Should WTO Members React to Their WTO Crises?' (2019) 18 World Trade Review 503, 510.

75 Basedow (n 62) 5.

76 For example, Mexico referred to 'a common concern with the current situation in the Appellate Body that was seriously affecting its workings and the overall dispute settlement system against the best interest of its Members. WTO Members had a responsibility to safeguard and preserve the Appellate Body, the dispute settlement system and the

to temporarily replace the appellate function of the DSB with the Multi-Party Interim Arrangement (MPIA).[77] Although noting some of the inefficiencies in the WTO system, the EU has defended one of the basic tenets of the WTO in "delivering the most effective and developed dispute settlement mechanism of any multilateral organization" and in doing so have focused their reform negotiation efforts on strengthening the independence of the Appellate Body and the rule of law.[78]

Turning to criticism of specific reports, all reports of the panels or Appellate Body have been adopted by the DSB. No reverse consensus has ever been reached in the DSB. This does not imply, however, that "consent" exists. Consensus confirms the primacy of state consent in the WTO and arguably lends democratic legitimacy. However, reverse consensus may not actually legitimize the decision, but rather should be seen as the loss of the institutional checks and balances against the Appellate Body's de facto judicial finality in the dispute settlement process.[79]

Instead, we can point to discussions in the DSB when reports come up for adoption that raise concerns of overreach or lawmaking by the panels and the Appellate Body. Even if reverse consensus was not reached, such discussions illustrate the varying concerns stemming from sociological legitimacy.[80] For example, the *Korea – Procurement* decision, important in setting up the fundamental role of customary rules of interpretation in WTO disputes, was criticized when it came before the DSB for adoption. In particular, the Philippines drew attention to paragraph 7.93 of the Panel Report, which read: "the non-violation remedy as it has developed in GATT/WTO jurisprudence should not be viewed in isolation from general principles of customary international law". The Philippines was concerned about this statement because panels

---

multilateral trading system': 'Minutes of Meeting on 28 January 2019 of the Dispute Settlement Body' (World Trade Organization 2019) WT/DSB/M/425 16.

77 European Commission, 'The WTO Multi-Party Interim Appeal Arrangement Gets Operational' (*Trade – European Commission*, 3 August 2020) <https://trade.ec.europa.eu/doclib/press/index.cfm?id=2176> accessed 10 August 2021.

78 European Commission, 'Concept Paper: WTO Modernization, 18 September 2018' 1, 15 <https://trade.ec.europa.eu/doclib/docs/2018/september/tradoc_157331.pdf> accessed 4 December 2018; see, further, Basedow (n 62) 12.

79 Wenwei Guan, 'Consensus Yet Not Consented: A Critique of the WTO Decision-Making by Consensus' (2014) 17 Journal of International Economic Law 77.

80 When interviewing state representatives in the DSB, Creamer and Godzimirska found that report statements had 'a systemic value for the legitimacy of the institution': Cosette D Creamer and Zuzanna Godzimirska, 'Deliberative Engagement within the World Trade Organization: A Functional Substitute for Authoritative Interpretations' (2015) 48 New York University Journal of International Law and Politics 413, 447.

should interpret the rights and obligations of Members in a manner consistent with the covered agreements and in accordance with the general rules of interpretation of customary international law. There was a distinction to be drawn between the rules of interpretation and the rights and obligations under customary international law, in the view of the Philippines.[81]

The concerns with judicial lawmaking in specific cases has not been universal. The EU has generally criticized the failure by the panels and the Appellate Body to consider other international law. For example, the EU regretted the panel's finding of actionable subsidies, "despite the fact that the EU had always meticulously complied with its bilateral 1992 agreement", an agreement which the Panel had found not to be applicable law in *EC – Large Civil Aircraft*.[82] Similarly, the EU disagreed with the jurisdiction-applicable law nexus that was drawn in *Mexico – Soft Drinks* in which the Appellate Body ruled out the possibility of determining whether a member acted consistently or inconsistently with non-WTO international obligations. The EU was critical of the Appellate Body's argument that this would mean adjudicating non-WTO disputes:

> Of course, Panels and the Appellate Body did not have the function to 'adjudicate' non-WTO disputes. But interpreting and applying non-WTO law and ruling on non-WTO obligations, where this was legally relevant for deciding a WTO dispute, did not mean 'adjudicating' a non-WTO dispute. It could even be required, as WTO law and dispute settlement practice showed, for example in relation to the Vienna Convention, the Lomé Convention, the UN Charter and IMF Understandings. The EC would therefore caution against a broad reading of the Appellate Body's statement regarding the permissibility to 'adjudicate non-WTO disputes.'[83]

Together with its support for strengthening the independence of the Appellate Body in reform efforts, the EU's criticisms of the more restrictive approach to other international law reflects a "quasi-constitutional" order for international law and institutions whereby institutions are in part independent of states and may evolve and expand without state consent.[84] As such, these States push for regime development as part of the normative goals of adjudicators.

81 'Minutes of Meeting on 19 June 2000 of the Dispute Settlement Body' (World Trade Organization 2000) WT/DSB/M/84 13–15.

82 'Minutes of Meeting on 1 June 2011 of the Dispute Settlement Body' (World Trade Organization 2011) WT/DSB/M/297 para 7.

83 'Minutes of Meeting on 24 March 2006 of the Dispute Settlement Body' (World Trade Organization 2006) WT/DSB/M/208 para 7.

84 Basedow (n 62) 5.

1.3.2 ISDS

International investment law, and its dispute settlement system, has been no stranger to criticism. The denunciation of the ICSID Convention beginning with Bolivia in 2007,[85] were high-profile signs of discontent and the emerging "legitimacy crisis" of investment arbitration.[86] The legitimacy crisis in ISDS is not one-dimensional. Criticisms of substantive issues include expansive interpretation of the rights of investors, negative effects on the policy space of public authorities to regulate environmental policy, and state's freedom to act in economic crises.[87] Amongst the criticisms is a concern with "the lack of coherence of a system based on decisions made by tribunals constituted to hear a specific case".[88] As such, one of the purposes of the reform discussions has been to consider how to avoid substantive fragmentation within international investment law.[89]

---

85 See discussion in Mélida N Hodgson, 'Reform and Adaptation: The Experience of the Americas with International Investment Law' (2020) 21 The Journal of World Investment & Trade 140; Bolivia denounced the ICSID Convention by written notice to the World Bank on 2 May 2007, Ecuador on 6 July 2009 and Venezuela on 24 January 2012: 'Denunciation of ICSID Convention' (*ICSID News Releases*, 16 May 2007) <https://icsid.worldbank.org/news-and-events/news-releases/denunciation-icsid-convention> accessed 12 April 2021; 'Denunciation of the ICSID Convention by Ecuador' (*ICSID News Releases*, 7 September 2009) <https://icsid.worldbank.org/news-and-events/news-releases/denunciation-icsid-convention-ecuador> accessed 12 April 2021; 'Venezuela Submits a Notice under Article 71 of the ICSID Convention' (*ICSID News Releases*, 26 January 2012) <https://icsid.worldbank.org/news-and-events/news-releases/venezuela-submits-notice-under-article-71-icsid-convention> accessed 12 April 2021.

86 Susan D Franck, 'The Legitimacy Crisis in Investment Treaty Arbitration: Privatizing Public International Law through Inconsistent Decisions' (2004) 73 Fordham Law Review 1521; Langford and Behn describe the discourse of 'legitimacy crisis' emerging in 2004 and 2005, following a building crisis in the early 2000s: Malcolm Langford and Daniel Behn, 'Managing Backlash: The Evolving Investment Treaty Arbitrator?' (2018) 29 European Journal of International Law 551, 554–6.

87 See, for example, Daniel Behn, Ole Kristian Fauchald and Malcolm Langford, 'The International Investment Regime and Its Discontents' in Daniel Behn, Ole Kristian Fauchald and Malcolm Langford (eds), *The Legitimacy of Investment Arbitration* (1st edn, Cambridge University Press 2022) s 2.4, which charts the legitimacy discourse in academic literature from both a quantitative and qualitative perspective.

88 'Possible Future Work in the Field of Dispute Settlement: Reforms of Investor-State Dispute Settlement (ISDS)' (United Nations Commission on International Trade Law 2017) A/CN.9/917 para 11; On whether these concerns are justified, see the empirical study of Daniel Behn, Malcolm Langford and Laura Létourneau-Tremblay, 'Empirical Perspectives on Investment Arbitration: What Do We Know? Does It Matter?' (2020) 21 The Journal of World Investment & Trade 188, 222–3, which concludes that inconsistency is 'a mixed picture'.

89 'Possible Future Work in the Field of Dispute Settlement: Reforms of Investor-State Dispute Settlement (ISDS)' (n 88) para 68.

The broader systemic coherence with international law has been little discussed in reform proposals. Much like the World Bank's approach in the 1960s,[90] reform of international investment law has focused on reform of ISDS, rather than the substantive rules of investment protection, as a first and "more likely successful" step of reform.[91] Nonetheless, the reform discussions shed light on the sociological legitimacy of design choices, such as the effect of decisions as precedential, and normative goals of rule and regime development, which are relevant to the use of the adjudicator's toolkit.

In this ongoing process, there is no single approach to reform.[92] Roberts has identified three different state approaches to reform: incremental, systemic and paradigmatic.[93] Systemic reform options closely link with the systemic view of international law and international judicial functions as seeking to bring more judicialization to the investor-state dispute settlement process. The systemic reforms have been popularized by the EU, with the EU seeking to build an investment court system (ICS) into its new investment agreements and a multilateral investment court (MIC) before the UNCITRAL reform process (which are discussed in detail in the next section). Legitimacy considerations play an important role in the EU's reform options. The EU points to establishment of permanent judicial (or quasi-judicial) bodies as models for similar public law disputes under "generally worded constitutional-like clauses" applied in regulating the sovereign actions of states.[94] Such judicialization efforts are consistent with the EU's approach to WTO reform and the EU's general quasi-constitutional view of international law, as discussed in the preceding section.[95]

In quite a different direction than criticisms against the WTO dispute settlement mechanism, some criticisms of ISDS highlight the lack of a permanent

---

90 See the analysis of Taylor St John, *The Rise of Investor-State Arbitration: Politics, Law, and Unintended Consequences* (Oxford University Press 2018).

91 'Possible Future Work in the Field of Dispute Settlement: Reforms of Investor-State Dispute Settlement (ISDS)' (n 88) para 14.

92 See Malcolm Langford and others, 'Special Issue: UNCITRAL and Investment Arbitration Reform: Matching Concerns and Solutions: An Introduction' (2020) 21 The Journal of World Investment & Trade 167; Yu refers to this as a lack of 'shared understanding' in a constructivist approach to the reform of international investment law: Chen Yu, *Dispute Settlement and the Reform of International Investment Law: Legalization through Adjudication* (Edward Elgar Publishing 2023) 158 ff.

93 Anthea Roberts, 'Incremental, Systemic, and Paradigmatic Reform of Investor-State Arbitration' (2018) 112 American Journal of International Law 410.

94 ibid 416.

95 Basedow (n 62) 14.

dispute settlement body or an appellate body, which "would bring more coherence as compared to the current system of ad hoc arbitral tribunals":[96]

> The setting up of an international investment court would constitute a departure from the current ISDS regime. In short, an international investment court would bring key features of domestic and international courts to the settlement of investment disputes. A multilateral process to set up such a court would aim at ensuring coherence of the reform efforts, and address the fragmentation of the current regime.[97]

Some States in the reform process have pointed to the need for consistency and coherence in decisions, contributing to predictability and correctness, values that support the rule of law.[98] The UNCITRAL Secretariat noted the Working Group on ISDS reform:

> may wish to consider whether the very nature of investment law and the fact that investment law and investment protection standards are fragmented in different sources of law, including numerous investment treaties and domestic regimes, mean that the method of resolving investment disputes must play a central role in the development of consistent legal standards.[99]

The Secretariat noted that arbitral tribunals operate as part "of a large adjudicatory system with public relevance" such that states should consider whether "arbitrators are under a general duty toward an international system of justice, to act in the public interest ... and if so, how to implement such duty".[100]

However, this is certainly not the view of all states in the reform process, evidenced by the states pushing for incremental and paradigmatic reforms within

96 'Possible Future Work in the Field of Dispute Settlement: Reforms of Investor-State Dispute Settlement (ISDS)' (n 88) para 15.

97 ibid 30.

98 See, for example, 'Possible Reform of Investor-State Dispute Settlement (ISDS): Submission from the European Union' (United Nations Commission on International Trade Law 2017) A/CN.9/WG.III/WP.145; 'Possible Reform of Investor-State Dispute Settlement (ISDS): Submission from the Government of China' (United Nations Commission on International Trade law 2019) A/CN.9/WG.III/WP.177.

99 'Possible Reform of Investor-State Dispute Settlement (ISDS): Consistency and Related Matters' (United Nations Commission on International Trade Law 2018) A/CN.9/WG.III/WP.150 para 30.

100 ibid 41.

the UNCITRAL process. Paradigmatic reform options outright reject the legitimacy and utility of investor-state dispute settlement at the international level while incrementalists typically suggest targeted reforms, rather than systemic changes.[101] After reviewing the divergent opinions amongst states during the UNCITRAL reform process, Yu concludes that "the actual and required level of shared understanding is so vast that flexibility is inevitably needed to uphold the legitimacy of the regime."[102]

Beyond the ISDS reform process in UNCITRAL, some states have also taken similar approaches to the US's arguments on the Appellate Body within their own investment treaties. For example, including specific provisions on the duties of arbitrators, which require arbitrators to "limit their analysis to the issues arising from the proceedings and that are required to issue a decision".[103]

1.4 *Implications*

Critiquing the use of the adjudicator's toolkit through the lens of legitimacy ends up as a mixed bag, reflecting the complex interplay of the contextual elements of design choices and normative goals. Reviewing the criticisms of states toward the tribunals' decisions leads to two conclusions. First, states are as inconsistent in their response to issues of other international law in trade and investment disputes as the adjudicators themselves. As the recent work of Basedow explains, these inconsistencies between states depend on their conception of legitimate international law and institutions:

> Some states see international law and institutions as interstate contracts, whose legitimacy primarily flows from state consent and satisfaction. … Other states understand international law as quasi-constitutional cosmopolitan order. International law is not merely a state-serving instrument but a governance system, whose legitimacy flows from broad societal consent, satisfaction, transparent, and accountable institutions.[104]

This is an inconsistency similar to the inconsistency from one adjudicator to the next, demonstrated in the previous Chapter. This makes it difficult to answer the proper exercise of the tribunal's jurisdictional authority on the

101 See the summary of positions in Roberts (n 93) 415–7.
102 Yu (n 92) 162.
103 Article 36 of the Agreement for the Reciprocal Promotion and Protection of Investments between the Argentine Republic and the United Arab Emirates (Abu Dhabi, 16 April 2018).
104 Basedow (n 62) 2.

basis of sociological legitimacy. How are we to interpret consent when states disagree on what they consented to?

If we throw in the mixed messages on normative legitimacy, we see how the actors are "talking past each other", to support Bjorklund's discussion of legitimacy in ICSID,[105] and muddying the waters of legitimacy. This makes the possible reform options to enhance the legitimacy of the dispute settlement mechanisms in the next section difficult to assess.

2 Reform Options

Based on the preceding understanding of the legitimacy problems facing the use of the adjudicator's toolkit, what can be done to fix these problems? Aligning the normative goals of adjudicators is likely to prove difficult, given the disagreement on the sociological legitimacy of the dispute settlement mechanisms. Instead, this section turns to reforms that could address the unjustified inconsistency revealed in the previous Chapters that undermines the normative legitimacy of the performance-based factors of the tribunals. Such reform options may reduce the areas of judicial discretion or give more guidance on the scope and function of dispute settlement within the regimes. The focus of the reforms, both in the Appellate Body crisis and ISDS, surround the institutional and procedural design of dispute settlement. Treaty reforms on the substance of trade and investment law have been set to the side. Not only are such reforms unlikely in the current negotiating climate, but treaty interpretation space will always exist.[106] Usually by the intention of States, treaties leave sufficient wriggle-room to adapt to future legal conditions.[107] Consequently, it is particularly important to consider the procedural design choices of the institutions tasked with interpreting these treaties.

105 Bjorklund (n 13).

106 On how international legal principles could be added to an IIA, in particular principles of international environmental law, see Kyla Tienhaara, *The Expropriation of Environmental Governance: Protecting Foreign Investors at the Expense of Public Policy* (University Press 2009) 290.

107 See, for example, Anne van Aaken, 'International Investment Law between Commitment and Flexibility: A Contract Theory Analysis' (2009) 12 Journal of International Economic Law 507; Joost Pauwelyn and Manfred Elsig, 'The Politics of Treaty Interpretation: Variations and Explanations Across International Tribunals' in Jeffrey L Dunoff and Mark Pollack (eds), *Interdisciplinary Perspectives on International Law and International Relations: The State of the Art* (Cambridge University Press 2012).

The section surveys the costs and benefits of three design choices that could be enhanced or introduced into the dispute settlement mechanisms in a search for consistency, and to some degree, correctness: formal mechanisms of communication between States and tribunals (in particular, binding authoritative treaty interpretation), clarifying and strengthening the role of precedent in the regimes, and greater institutionalization (appellate courts and standing courts). These are reform options raised throughout the UNCITRAL Working Group III process, although primarily to address the consistency and predictability of ISDS across the 3000 IIAs.[108] As such, this section draws heavily on reform discussion in ISDS, with the WTO acting as an example of whether such reform choices will benefit consistency on the application of other international law. By learning from the experience of the WTO, in particular the further institutionalization of dispute settlement, the section illustrates how design choices and normative goals must be aligned. Changing design without considering the underlying normative goals is not sufficient. It is important to note before examining the reforms that other legitimacy concerns may be created or needed to be assessed when designing the reforms,[109] however, this is beyond the scope of this book.

2.1 *Strengthening Interpretation and Communication Mechanisms of States*

States have adopted a number of mechanisms in both WTO and ISDS to assert their authoritative interpretation of the law of the regimes as well as provide guidance to the tribunals. These mechanisms could certainly strengthen and

---

108 See Julian Arato, Chester Brown and Federico Ortino, 'Parsing and Managing Inconsistency in Investor-State Dispute Settlement' (2020) 21 The Journal of World Investment & Trade 336; Stephan W Schill and Geraldo Vidigal, 'Designing Investment Dispute Settlement à La Carte: Insights from Comparative Institutional Design Analysis' (2020) 18 The Law & Practice of International Courts and Tribunals 314, 318; Anna De Luca and others, 'Responding to Incorrect Decision-Making in Investor-State Dispute Settlement: Policy Options' (2020) 21 The Journal of World Investment & Trade 374.

109 See, discussion on other costs and benefits of the reforms in Lisa Diependaele, Ferdi De Ville and Sigrid Sterckx, 'Assessing the Normative Legitimacy of Investment Arbitration: The EU's Investment Court System' (2019) 24 New Political Economy 37; Jeffrey Kucik and Sergio Puig, 'Toward an Effective Appellate Mechanism for ISDS Tribunals' (2023) 22 World Trade Review 562; Freya Baetens, 'The European Union's Proposed Investment Court System: Addressing Criticisms of Investor-State Arbitration While Raising New Challenges Investor Protection and Enforcement' (2016) 43 Legal Issues of Economic Integration 367; Marc Bungenberg and August Reinisch, *From Bilateral Arbitral Tribunals and Investment Courts to a Multilateral Investment Court: Options Regarding the Institutionalization of Investor-State Dispute Settlement* (2nd edn, Springer Berlin Heidelberg 2020).

revive state consent as an indicator of legitimacy, both from the normative and sociological perspective. By agreeing on an authoritative interpretation, areas of judicial discretion in interpretation are naturally reduced in favor of stronger political direction.[110] Perhaps even more drastically, binding interpretations by State parties could discourage judicial lawmaking as a normative goal of adjudicators. Can these mechanisms also help enhance the consistency of outcomes on the application of international law?

For the WTO, the state control over dispute settlement is quite clear in the text of the DSU and the WTO covered agreements more broadly. The ultimate binding decision is left to the DSB with panels and the Appellate Body merely providing recommendations, albeit that the significance of those recommendations has increased significantly with the inclusion of reverse consensus in WTO dispute settlement, as discussed in Chapter 5 (section 1.2). In addition, authoritative interpretation is left clearly in the hands of states, with the Ministerial Conference and the General Council having "the exclusive authority to adopt interpretations" under Article IX:2 of the Marrakesh Agreement.[111] The Appellate Body has referred to this provision as supporting the view that dispute settlement proceedings do not "make law"[112] as well as evidence of subsequent agreement under Article 31(3)(a) of the VCLT.[113]

The difficulty of reaching consensus or three-fourths majority in the WTO political bodies has meant that no authoritative interpretations under Article

110 Monika Polzin, 'Authentic Interpretations and International Courts: Like Calvin and Hobbes or Tom and Jerry' (2018) 33 Temple International & Comparative Law Journal 247, 272; Anthea Roberts, 'Power and Persuasion in Investment Treaty Interpretation: The Dual Role of States' (2010) 104 American Journal of International Law 179, 196.

111 The Article provides that authoritative interpretations are to be adopted by three-fourths majority of Members but that such interpretations 'shall not be used in a manner that would undermine the amendment provisions': Marrakesh Agreement Establishing the World Trade Organization (15 April 1994), 1867 UNTS 154.

112 The Appellate Body referred to the explicit aim of dispute settlement that meant Article 3.2 of the DSU is not meant to encourage either panels or the Appellate Body to 'make law' and referred to Article IX having the 'exclusive authority' to adopt interpretations of the WTO agreements: *United States – Wool Shirts and Blouses* (*Report of the Appellate Body*) (25 April 1997), WT/DS33/AB/R 19–20.

113 The Appellate Body has referred to the 'different functions and different legal effects' under WTO law of Article 31(3)(a) of the VCLT and authoritative interpretations under Article IX:2, but noted that authoritative interpretations 'are most akin' to subsequent agreements within Article 31(3)(a) of the VCLT: *United States – Measures Affecting the Production and Sale of Clove Cigarettes* (*Report of the Appellate Body*) (4 April 2012), WT/DS406/AB/R [257–259].

IX of the Marrakesh Agreement have been finalized.[114] However, this certainly does not suggest the agreement of WTO members with the interpretation by panels and the Appellate Body. Rather, it can be seen as the failure of the institutional checks and balances in the original design choices of the WTO dispute settlement mechanism. The ease of the quasi-automatic adoption of reports, an important element in the judicialization and legalization of the WTO dispute settlement mechanism, compared to the burdensome Article IX procedure arguably has led to an imbalance between adjudicatory interpretations and authoritative interpretation by states.[115]

Although no authoritative interpretation has been issued by the WTO members, the DSB can act as an informal mechanism to communicate WTO members' concerns with the functioning of the panels and Appellate Body.[116] Such an example of informal influence over dispute settlement procedure can be seen in the *amicus curiae* debate following *US – Shrimp*. The Appellate Body held that panels had the discretionary authority to seek information, which could include accepting information that had not been requested from a non-governmental source.[117] Later, in *EC – Asbestos*, the Appellate Body issued a communication with a procedure for non-state actor amicus briefs. These working procedures were heavily criticized at a special meeting of WTO members.[118] A wide range of WTO members showed a collective intention to send a message to the Appellate Body on the relationship between the political and adjudicatory bodies of the WTO.[119] For example, New Zealand noted "the importance of familiarizing the Appellate Body with the climate of opinion among Members". The Chairman of the DSB undertook to communicate these

114 See 'WTO Analytical Index: Guide to the WTO Law and Practice' (World Trade Organization 2020), WTO Agreement – Article IX (Practice).

115 See the discussion in Creamer and Godzimirska (n 80) 431; Guan (n 79) 90: 'this imbalanced tension between "judicial interpretation" vs. "authoritative interpretation" means that decisions from panels and the Appellate Body gain the 'de facto finality as interpretations of the law, even if they lack de jure finality. The lost balance between "judicial interpretation" vs. "authoritative interpretation" challenges and questions the legitimacy of panels and the Appellate Body's judicial activism arising out of reverse consensus'.

116 Or, to use Paine's conclusion, that the WTO DSB can act as a 'voice mechanism': Joshua Paine, 'The WTO's Dispute Settlement Body as a Voice Mechanism' (2019) 20 The Journal of World Investment & Trade 820.

117 *US – Shrimp* (n 53) paras 101–110.

118 The Chairman of the meeting noted that the Appellate Body should 'exercise extreme caution' but at that point in time, it was not appropriate to draw a conclusion on principle: 'Minutes of Meeting of the General Council on 22 November 2000' (World Trade Organization 2001) WT/GC/M/60.

119 ibid [86].

points to the Appellate Body and noted that "the Appellate Body should exercise extreme caution in future cases until Members had considered what rules were needed".[120] Without engaging with the criticism of members, the Appellate Body denied each of the requests to file briefs in those proceedings.[121] Since then, the Appellate Body has retained its view that it has the ability to seek information but has, in practice, not accepted any *amicus curiae* briefs that were not submitted by one of the parties to the dispute.[122]

In responding to the US blocking of Appellate Body appointments, proposals have been raised to institutionalize the communication by creating an annual meeting between the DSB and the Appellate Body. At such meetings, a WTO member could "express its views on adopted Appellate Body reports", beyond the current discussions at the time of adoption. This meeting would allow for concerns with the Appellate Body's approach in some areas, systemic issues or trends in jurisprudence to be voiced.[123] The *amicus curiae* episode demonstrates the potential for the Appellate Body to quietly adopt the results of such dialogue with member states, albeit while maintaining its own view of its power to do so. If such proposals result in the WTO dispute settlement mechanism more closely adhering to the opinions on gap-filling, the sociological legitimacy could be strengthened.[124] The consistency of responses to the application of international law within WTO disputes may be enhanced, although possibly at the expense of defragmentation depending on which

120 ibid [120].

121 *European Communities – Measures Affecting Asbestos and Products Containing Asbestos* (*Report of the Appellate Body*) (12 March 2001), WT/DS135/AB/R [53–57].

122 See, Squatrito's empirical analysis of amicus submissions up until the end of 2014: Theresa Squatrito, 'Amicus Curiae Briefs in the WTO DSM: Good or Bad News for Non-State Actor Involvement?' (2018) 17 World Trade Review 65, 79–81; See also Jeffrey L Dunoff, 'The Politics of International Constitutions: The Curious Case of the World Trade Organization' in Jeffrey L Dunoff and Joel P Trachtman (eds), *Ruling the World? Constitutionalism, International Law, and Global Governance* (Cambridge University Press 2009) 191–192.

123 'Communication from the European Union, China, Canada, India, Norway, New Zealand, Switzerland, Australia, Republic of Korea, Iceland, Singapore, Mexico, Costa Rica And Montenegro' (World Trade Organization, Dispute Settlement Body 2018) WT/GC/W/752/Rev.2 2.

124 See also, Langford, Behn and Creamer's empirical study of regime responsiveness, which concluded that WTO panels and Appellate Body members were responsive to political pressures, such as statements in the DSB: Langford, Creamer and Behn (n 59) 258–267; Kucik and Puig also conclude, following their empirical study of WTO Appellate Body precedent, that the Appellate Body changes and adapts its precedent following non-compliance by States: Jeffrey Kucik and Sergio Puig, 'The Appellate Body's Judicial Pathway: Precedent, Resistance and Adaptation' in Nico Krisch and Ezgi Yildiz (eds), *The Many Paths of Change in International Law* (1st edn, Oxford University Press 2023).

State's views win out in the process. However, a new legitimacy concern arises: the proposals present a tightrope in maintaining political support from members[125] while not threatening judicial independence.[126]

In ISDS, a number of mechanisms exist for a state to assert their interpretation or other methods of control over tribunals. This could include, for example, provisions enabling binding interpretations, institutionalized cooperation for treaty interpretation and consultations.[127] For example, the Uzbekistan-Korea IIA enables the Contracting Parties to "issue interpretations … if a dispute between the Contracting Parties or between a Contracting Party and an investor of the other Contracting Party concerning the interpretation of this Agreement arises". Such interpretations "shall be binding" on tribunals established under the investor-state settlement provisions.[128] Leaving aside the issue of the bilateralization of such mechanisms and therefore the difficulty of addressing systemic coherency in ISDS,[129] such mechanisms could be used to bring clarity to the interpretative approach under IIAs.

---

125 Creamer and Godzimirska's empirical study of statements in the DSB's adoption of report procedures illustrates the different levels of interaction by member states. Certain states are much more active, which could limit the democratic legitimacy of such proposals: Creamer and Godzimirska (n 80).

126 See the analysis in Paine (n 116) 843, 851: 'The amicus episode demonstrated starkly how the DSB's voice function could threaten the AB's judicial independence, with numerous members taking the position that the AB should have refrained from accepting amicus briefs given the widespread disapproval communicated by the WTO membership'; see also Yu (n 92) 93.

127 'Possible Reform of Investor-State Dispute Settlement (ISDS): Interpretation of Investment Treaties by Treaty Parties' (United Nations Commission on International Trade Law 2020) A/CN.9/WG.III/WP.191 paras 36–41. States may also clarify content through the interpretative rules of the VCLT, in particular Article 31(3)(a) and (b) concerning subsequent agreement and subsequent practice. However, since such a process relies on the tribunal applying these interpretative rules, this practice is not considered as a reform option to strengthen interpretative control by states.

128 Agreement between the Government of the Republic of Uzbekistan and the Government of the Republic of Korea for the Reciprocal Promotion and Protection of Investments (Tashkent, 19 April 2019), Article 15; See further examples in Relja Radović, 'The Dejudicialization of International Economic Law' in Jelena Bäumler and others (eds), *European Yearbook of International Economic Law 2021* (Springer International Publishing 2022) 328.

129 This concern has been noted in the Working Group III discussion: 'it was suggested that while these approaches were useful for the interpretation of a specific treaty, they did not constitute solutions for interpreting similar treaty provisions in different treaties. The importance of addressing these matters at a multilateral level was underlined. Therefore, it was said that there would be merit in discussing the options at UNCITRAL' in 'Report of Working Group III (Investor-State Dispute Settlement Reform) on the Work of Its Thirty-Sixth Session' (United Nations Commission on International Trade Law 2018) A/CN.9/964 para 38.

While the practice of including binding interpretation provisions has been increasing,[130] historically, treaty parties in ISDS have rarely included such mechanisms to ensure "correct" treaty interpretation. Less than 5% of IIAs expressly allow binding interpretations, and less than 2% contain institutional arrangements in the form of interpretative committees or commissions.[131] In practice, what we find is a rather infrequent use of such mechanisms.[132] Roberts suggests two factors that affect the ability of states to make use of such mechanisms in their interactions with tribunals: first, their capacity to know, assess and respond to the field's jurisprudence, and second, the ability of the States to agree with each other.[133] Consequently, discretion almost always remains in the hands of tribunals to deal with the indeterminacy and uncertainty of the IIAs on the application of international law.

Even when such treaty mechanisms of interpretation are utilized by the contracting ISDS states, two further issues arise. First, whether such official interpretations, particularly when issued in relation to pending disputes, are compatible with principles of fair procedure.[134] Secondly, are these interpretations binding and do tribunals actually follow such interpretations? Both of these issues have been played out in the relationship between NAFTA investor-state tribunals and the NAFTA Free Trade Commission, which was tasked with supervising the implementation of NAFTA and helping resolve disputes arising from its interpretation.[135] The Free Trade Commission notably issued a "Notes of Interpretation" purporting to restrict the minimum standard of treatment to the requirements of customary international law,[136] following

---

130 'Possible Reform of Investor-State Dispute Settlement (ISDS): Interpretation of Investment Treaties by Treaty Parties' (n 127) para 37 citing: 'World Investment Report 2019' (United Nations Conference on Trade and Development 2019) UNCTAD/WIR/2019 109–110.

131 United Nations Commission on International Trade Law, 'Possible Reform of Investor-State Dispute Settlement (ISDS): Interpretation of Investment Treaties by Treaty Parties' (n 127) para 38.

132 ibid [17], citing the paper by the OECD: Kathryn Gordon and Joachim Pohl, 'Investment Treaties over Time – Treaty Practice and Interpretation in a Changing World' (OECD Publishing 2015) 2015/02 13.

133 Roberts (n 110) 195.

134 Christoph H Schreuer, 'Diversity And Harmonization Of Treaty Interpretation In Investment Arbitration' in Malgosia Fitzmaurice, Olufemi Elias and Panos Merkouris (eds), *Treaty Interpretation and the Vienna Convention on the Law of Treaties: 30 Years On* (Brill Nijhoff 2010) 148; Franck, 'The Legitimacy Crisis in Investment Treaty Arbitration' (n 86) 1605.

135 North American Free Trade Agreement (17 December 1992), 32 ILM 289, Article 2001.

136 NAFTA Free Trade Commission, 'Notes of Interpretation of Certain Chapter 11 Provisions' (31 July 2001), paragraph B.

a string of inconsistent decisions on evaluating claims under the FET obligation of NAFTA.[137] As to the first issue on the timing and procedure of adoption of such interpretations, the interpretation was drafted in favor of respondent states generally. Ultimately, this enables one party to a dispute to influence the outcome of judicial proceedings to the detriment of the other party, which Schreuer argued was incompatible with principles of fair procedure and thus "undesirable".[138] This is a particular problem in ISDS in which only one party to the dispute is a treaty party, creating a tension between roles as treaty parties and respondents.[139] Comparatively, in fora like WTO dispute settlement, both complainant and respondent are represented in treaty-based interpretative negotiations.

Secondly, the extent to which this interpretation was binding or whether the tribunals could examine the legality of the interpretation was the subject of inconsistent treatment by tribunals. In considering whether the Note was a disguised amendment or a valid interpretative note, the tribunal in *Pope & Talbot* held that tribunals "had a duty to consider and decide" whether the Note is in fact an interpretation for the purposes of the relevant NAFTA Article.[140] Although the determination was ultimately not required, the tribunal considered that it would characterize the Note as an amendment, rather than a valid interpretation under the relevant Article.[141] Comparatively, the tribunal in *ADF v USA* considered that there was "no more authentic and authoritative source of instruction" and there was nothing in NAFTA to suggest a tribunal could determine for itself whether a document was an interpretation or an amendment. In addition, the tribunal stressed that there was "a systemic need" for such mechanisms for correcting interpretative errors or addressing consistency and continuity of interpretation across multiple ad hoc tribunals.[142] Further, the interpretation did not necessarily change the tribunals' approach to the minimum standard of treatment in NAFTA. Following the issuance of this Note, many awards concurred with the direct incorporation of free-standing treaty obligations, but, at the same time, "quietly ignored and, thus, tacitly rejected"

137 NAFTA, Article 1105(1), which refers to 'minimum standard of treatment', compared to other FET provisions which refer to providing 'fair and equitable treatment' (for example, Article 10[1] of the ECT).

138 Schreuer (n 134) 148.

139 See discussion in Roberts (n 110).

140 *Pope & Talbot v Canada* (UNCITRAL, ad hoc, Award in Respect of Damages, 31 May 2002) [23].

141 ibid [47].

142 *ADF Group Inc v United States of America* (ICSID Case No ARB(AF)/00/1), Award, 9 January 2003 [177]; See discussion in Polzin (n 110) 252 ff.

the exclusion of general principles of law from the minimum standard of treatment.[143] Rightly or wrongly (a question beyond the scope of this research), the authoritative interpretation of NAFTA, a potentially legislative act of treaty parties, was not fully influential in judicial legislative practices.

Albeit a short survey of treaty mechanisms to control dispute settlement, this survey evidences both a limited appetite or ability of states to implement such mechanisms. At the same time, there is potential for tribunals to continue in a lawmaking function in spite of such mechanisms.[144] If such mechanisms become more popular amongst States, the unwillingness of tribunals to follow the States' expressed intentions is likely to further undermine both the normative and sociological legitimacy of the dispute settlement mechanisms.

2.2 *Strengthening Precedent*

As a counterproposal to strengthening State interpretation mechanisms, the judicialization of the dispute settlement mechanisms could be strengthened through granting interpretations precedential value. Chapter 2 discussed the conflict between the harmonious development of international law and the limited role of adjudicators, thereby leading to an unofficial version of precedent in ISDS and WTO disputes. There is no positive law guidance on the weight of precedent in international law, rather the practice develops from international courts themselves in an effort to provide legal certainty and avoiding arbitrariness.[145] International law recognizes the *res judicata* effect of decisions (at least between the parties to the dispute, as discussed in Chapter 4 (section 2.2) and reflected in Article 59 of the ICJ Statute), but the extent of precedent and lawmaking effect of courts is much more controversial. Both regimes seem to lack legitimate authority for such lawmaking. The ISDS lacks authority in the sense that individual tribunals are constituted under different treaties for a single dispute.[146] For the WTO, the limitation of dispute

143 See the analysis in Charles H Brower, 'Why the FTC Notes of Interpretation Constitute a Partial Amendment of NAFTA Article 1105' (2005) 46 Virginia Journal of International Law 347, 356 ff.

144 As Langford, Behn and Creamer's analysis finds, WTO adjudicators are more likely to respond to legitimacy concerns of members than their ISDS counterparts: Langford, Creamer and Behn (n 59); This conclusion is also supported by Alschner's findings on the limited impact of treaty innovations on outcomes in investment arbitration, due to the entrenchment of old precedents: Wolfgang Alschner, *Investment Arbitration and State-Driven Reform: New Treaties, Old Outcomes* (Oxford University Press 2022).

145 On the particular motivations for precedent in WTO disputes, see Cohen (n 73).

146 See, for example Tullio Treves, 'Judicial Lawmaking in an Era of Proliferation of International Courts and Tribunals: Development or Fragmentation of International Law?' in

settlement to clarifying existing provisions and the balancing between judicial and political roles is delicate, with final decision-making left with the DSB and political bodies.[147]

Rather than dwelling on the current normative legitimacy of precedent in the dispute settlement regimes, this section asks whether including rule/regime development through precedential decision-making powers would actually assist the coherence and consistency of the use of the adjudicator's toolkit. Based on the normative goals of States addressed in the previous section, there is likely to be significant resistance from States to such proposals, particularly in the WTO. However, strengthening precedent has been discussed in the Working Group III negotiations as part of a systemic solution to consistency and coherence issues.[148]

By overturning some panel decisions on the application or rejection of other international law, the Appellate Body, and the "cogent reasons" approach to following Appellate Body decisions, has settled some of the indeterminacy of the applicable law and openness of WTO law. The de facto system of precedent established through this "cogent reasons" approach promotes the "security and predictability" of the multilateral regime, but also may enhance the persuasive authority of adjudicators' decisions.[149]

An example is the determination by the Appellate Body in *US – Definitive Anti-Dumping (China)* on the relevance of the ILC Articles on attribution. The Panel had rejected China's argument that "public body" in the SCM Agreement should be interpreted in a manner analogous to Article 5 of the ILC Articles.[150] The Panel determined that the ILC Articles were not "relevant rules" under

---

Rüdiger Wolfrum and Volker Röben (eds), *Developments of International Law in Treaty Making* (Springer 2005) 590.

147 See, for example, Andrew Lang, 'Twenty Years of the WTO Appellate Body's "Fragmentation Jurisprudence"' (2015) 14 Journal of International Trade Law and Policy 116, 123; or, the discussion on the requirement of referring indeterminate questions to political bodies in Joel P Trachtman, 'The Domain of WTO Dispute Resolution' (1999) 40 Harvard International Law Journal 333.

148 'Possible Reform of Investor-State Dispute Settlement (ISDS): Consistency and Related Matters' (n 99) paras 37–41.

149 Shany (n 5) 198, referring to; Peter Sutherland and others, 'The Future of the WTO: Assessing Institutional Challenges in the New Millenium' (World Trade Organization 2004) 52.

150 Article 1.1.(a)(1) refers to 'public body' in relation to the definition of a subsidy, namely 'there is a financial contribution by a government or any public body within the territory of a Member …': Agreement on Subsidies and Countervailing Measures, Marrakesh Agreement Establishing the World Trade Organization, Annex 1B (15 April 1994), 1869 UNTS 14; Article 5 of the ILC Articles refers to conduct of persons or entities exercising elements of governmental authority: Responsibility of States for Internationally Wrongful Acts (adopted by the International Law Commission at its fifty-third session, 2001).

Article 31(3)(c) of the VCLT that must be taken into account in the interpretation of the SCM Agreement.[151] The Appellate Body disagreed with this conclusion. By stepping through the provisions of Article 31(3)(c), the Appellate Body identified how the ILC Articles were in fact "relevant rules of international law applicable in the relations between the parties".[152] In doing so, the Appellate Body first considered whether Article 5 provided guidance for the interpretation of "public body". The Appellate Body considered that its interpretation "coincides with the essence of Article 5" and, thereby, Article 5 lent further support to its interpretation conclusion.[153] The Appellate Body did not then find it necessary to determine whether Article 5 of the ILC Articles was customary law, in light of US objections to such status[154] and the fact that the analysis "did not turn on Article 5".[155] However, the Appellate Body did note that prior WTO decisions had taken the ILC Articles into account.[156] In this way, the ILC Articles were not the primary or sole method of interpretation of "public body" but supported the Appellate Body's interpretation, thereby potentially enhancing the legitimacy of the decision as well as the coherence with general international law. The Appellate Body's decision on the interpretation of "public body", supported by the ILC Articles, has since been referred to and followed in a number of panel reports.[157]

Annulment Committee decisions do have some similar authoritative status, particularly when it comes to the interpretation of the ICSID Convention. This is exhibited in the development of the jurisprudence on the role of Article 42(1) of the ICSID Convention by two Annulment Committees, being the merely

151 *United States – Definitive Anti-Dumping and Countervailing Duties on Certain Products from China (Report of the Panel)* (22 October 2010), WT/DS379/R [8.87–91].

152 *United States – Definitive Anti-Dumping and Countervailing Duties on Certain Products from China (Report of the Appellate Body)* (11 March 2011), WT/DS379/AB/R [308–16].

153 ibid [310–11].

154 The US contended that the ILC Articles were not a subsequent agreement nor had the relevant Articles attained customary status. The US considered the 'level of detail and fine-line distinctions' means it remained an open and contested question whether all of the details and distinctions in Article 5 had risen to the status of customary international law: ibid [306].

155 ibid [311].

156 ibid [313].

157 *United States – Countervailing Duty Measures on Certain Products from China – Recourse to Article 21.5 of the DSU by China (Final Report of the Panel)* (21 March 2018), WT/DS437/RW [7.17]; *United States – Countervailing Measures on Certain Hot-Rolled Carbon Steel Flat Products from India (Report of the Appellate Body)* (8 December 2014), WT/DS/436/AB/R [4.17]; *United States – Countervailing Duty Measures on Certain Products from China (Report of the Panel)* (14 July 2014), WT/DS437/R [7.65]; each later decision referring to *US – Definitive Anti-Dumping (China) (Appellate Body)* (n 152) para 310.

corrective function of international law described in the *Klöckner* case[158] to the more expansive role found in *Wena Hotels*[159] (which has already been discussed in Chapter 2). On the other hand, the diversity of IIAs, combined with the limited role of, and ad hoc constitution of, Annulment Committees, makes it difficult for the same perception of precedent to flow through investor-state dispute settlement. Although application of the ILC Articles on attribution are relatively uncontroversial, the annulment procedure on the relevance of Article 25 of the ILC Articles to the IIA provision on necessity provides the counterpoint to the WTO example. A comparison of the decisions of the separate Annulment Committees in *Enron* and *Sempra*, set out in Chapter 3, on whether an annullable error occurred in relation to the application of customary law in interpreting the treaty exception illustrates this difficulty in ISDS.

This discussion highlights the potential for the resolution of the inconsistency uncovered in earlier Chapters through an enhanced precedential effect of decisions. Nonetheless, there are several limitations of this design choice. First, precedential effect is limited in its effectiveness without a standing appellate mechanism with broad powers to deal with questions of law, which is discussed in the next subsection. The mere existence of an appellate mechanism is not necessarily enough. The precedential effect must also be recognized by the lower courts. The inconsistency between the Appellate Body in *US – Shrimp* and the panel in *EC – Biotech* in relation to the application of environmental agreements through the prism of Article 31(3)(c) clearly illustrates this issue.

Secondly, the approach does not overcome the uncertainty of interpretation choices and the normative goals that may be taken into account in applying other international law. While the appellate mechanism, supported by precedential authority, may limit the interpretation choices of later ad hoc panels, the interpretation choice of the appellate mechanism when the issue of other international law is first raised still exists. The appellate mechanism's interpretation choice at this point could swing either way based on their choices on how the positive law should be interpreted. In addition, enhancing judicial lawmaking may not solve the sociological legitimacy critiques, particularly if such precedents attempt to do away with the consent doctrine. International law is a creation of states and international courts cannot survive without state support. The blocking of appointments to the Appellate Body reignited proposals

158 *Klöckner Industrie-Anlagen GmbH and others v United Republic of Cameroon and Société Camerounaise des Engrais* (ICSID Case No ARB/81/2), Ad Hoc Committee Decision on Annulment, 3 May 1985 [69].

159 *Wena Hotels Limited v Arab Republic of Egypt* (ICSID Case No ARB/94/4), Decision on the Application by the Arab Republic of Egypt for Annulment, 5 February 2002 [39–41].

to limit judicial lawmaking. Some WTO members suggested abolishing the de facto precedential effect, enabling panels "to adopt an interpretation of a WTO provision that is different from the one developed by the Appellate Body."[160]

Finally, precedential effect may exacerbate errors in interpretation, thereby embedding "bad" decisions on the application of international law within the regime. As Alschner's computational study of developments in the substantive law of ISDS revealed, mistakes are perpetuated through precedent and following prior cases led to rolling back innovation in new-generation treaties.[161] Further, the confidentiality issues in ISDS (see discussion in the Introduction) and the number of cases across arbitral institutions, with no central organizing mechanism, means it can be hard to access and assess the developments in investment treaty jurisprudence. New seminal awards may be lost amongst the published decisions without a neat hierarchy or structure.[162]

2.3 *Strengthening Adjudicatory Institutions and Appeal Mechanisms*

Standing institutions and appeal mechanisms could further the development of coherent and consistent reasoning through a stable membership, correcting legal errors of interpretation and thereby establishing a clear and coherent body of law.[163] In the Working Group III discussion, the primary objective of a multilateral court system or standalone permanent appellate mechanism is to promote the coherence of arbitral decisions.[164] The creation of multilateral

160 'Informal Process on Matters Related to the Functioning of the Appellate Body: Communication from Japan, Australia and Chile' (World Trade Organization, Dispute Settlement Body 2019) WT/GC/W/768/Rev.1 2; discussed in Paine (n 116).

161 Alschner (n 144) ch 6.

162 This is similar to Roberts' finding on the difficulty for States to stay abreast of developments in order to make use of their treaty interpretation powers: Roberts (n 110) 195.

163 Such proposals pre-date the current reform negotiations at UNCITRAL: Franck, 'The Legitimacy Crisis in Investment Treaty Arbitration' (n 86) 1606, 1617; Gus Van Harten, *Investment Treaty Arbitration and Public Law* (Oxford University Press 2008) ch 7; Tienhaara (n 106) 283; Langford and others (n 92) 184–5.

164 On the multilateral court system, see 'Possible Reform of Investor-State Dispute Settlement (ISDS): Submission from the European Union and Its Member States' (United Nations Commission on International Trade Law 2019) A/CN.9/WG.III/WP.159/Add.1 para 41 ('Predictability and consistency can only be effectively developed through the establishment of a standing mechanism with permanent, full-time adjudicators'); On the appellate mechanism, see 'Possible Reform of Investor-State Dispute Settlement (ISDS): Submission from the Government of China' (n 98) 4 ('an important factor in promoting application of the rule of law to the settlement of disputes'); 'Possible Reform of Investor-State Dispute Settlement (ISDS): Appellate and Multilateral Court Mechanisms' (United Nations Commission on International Trade Law 2019) A/CN.9/WG.III/WP.185 para 7: 'The objective would be that, over time, the dispute settlement process would be more

institutions offers a regime, particularly one as bilateralized as ISDS, centripetal force as multilateral institutions can provide a single authoritative judicial voice.[165] Such a voice arguably leads to greater consistency in interpretation since it can provide a more definitive interpretation. Enhanced appellate mechanisms may also create incentives for first instance adjudicators to be more diligent in their legal reasoning.[166]

To assess the impact that standing multilateral institutions and appeal mechanisms may have on improving consistency and coherence, we can consider the role of the Appellate Body of the WTO. From a theoretical design choice perspective, the Appellate Body of the WTO dispute settlement mechanism is a feature that could have provided a clarifying role to the application of other international law. The Appellate Body has a purely legal function, limited to appeals on "issues of law",[167] a "rule-oriented substitute" for the political consensus in the GATT procedures.[168] Together with the broad public functions of the WTO dispute settlement system in "providing security and predictability to the multilateral trading system" and "clarifying the existing provisions",[169] the Appellate Body has effectively functioned as a "court" with many of the inherent powers that courts are authorized to apply.[170] Legalization was further

---

accountable, and a body of legally authoritative general principles and interpretations could be developed so as to increase the coherence and predictability of the investment regime'.

165 Arato, Brown and Ortino (n 108); see also Luca and others (n 108); and Andrea K Bjorklund, 'The Road(s) Not Taken – the Past, Present, and Future of International Investment Law Reform' (2023) 39 Arbitration International 455, 467, who considers that a body with 'final' say would command sufficient respect.

166 Irene M Ten Cate, 'International Arbitration and the Ends of Appellate Review' (2011) 44 New York University Journal of International Law and Politics 1109, 1143.

167 Article 17.6, Understanding on Rules and Procedures Governing the Settlement of Disputes, Marrakesh Agreement Establishing the World Trade Organization, Annex 2 (15 April 1994), 1869 UNTS 401; Although the Appellate Body is ostensibly limited to issues of law under Article 17.6, there has been debate around the extent to which the Appellate Body has effectively reviewed factual findings of panels and has also 'completed the analysis' in the face of the lack of remand power: David Palmeter and Petros C Mavroidis, *Dispute Settlement in the World Trade Organization: Practice and Procedure* (2nd edn, Cambridge University Press 2004) 45 ff, 221, 227 ff.

168 Ernst-Ulrich Petersmann, *The GATT/WTO Dispute Settlement System: International Law, International Organizations and Dispute Settlement* (Kluwer Law International 1997) 186.

169 Article 3.2 DSU.

170 Ridhi Kabra, 'Inherent Powers of the WTO Appellate Body and ICSID Tribunals – A Tale of Cautious Convergence' in Daniel Behn, Malcolm Langford and Szilárd Gáspár-Szilágyi (eds), *Adjudicating Trade and Investment Disputes: Convergence or Divergence?* (Cambridge University Press 2020) 183; Chester Brown, 'The Inherent Powers of International Courts and Tribunals' (2006) 76 British Yearbook of International Law 195, 228 ff.

enhanced through the introduction of membership guidelines of Appellate Body members.[171] This standing institutional appellate mechanism should offer greater guidance and determinacy on the role of international law in the WTO dispute settlement mechanism. In this way, we would expect from the design choice that the decisions of the Appellate Body would overcome some of the inconsistencies seen in investor-state disputes that are not related to the different wording of the IIAs.

The creation of two levels of adjudication contributes to greater guidance and determinacy on the application of other international law. The creation of the WTO Appellate Body embedded a hierarchization of the WTO dispute settlement mechanism. This is reflected in the Appellate Body's decision in *US – Stainless Steel*, where the Appellate Body noted the "hierarchical structure" of the DSU and the "distinct roles" to be played by the panels and the Appellate Body, observing that a panel's failure to take into account prior Appellate Body interpretations "undermines the development of a coherent and predictable body" of jurisprudence.[172] As de Andrade concluded, based on interviews with panellists and other trade dispute settlement lawyers, there is a perceived natural difference in following reports of the Appellate Body compared to panel reports:

> There is a (perhaps psychologically motivated) feeling that [Appellate Body] reports are more authoritative than panel reports. It is difficult to ignore the fact that findings emanating from a permanent (quasi-) judicial body with the power to overturn 'wrong' legal findings, and which was conceived for the very purpose of ensuring legal correctness, have a different status than those issued by ad hoc panels.[173]

---

171 Pursuant to Article 17.6, an appeal is to be limited to issues of law and legal interpretations by the panel. In addition, Appellate Body members are to be 'persons of recognized authority, with demonstrated expertise in law, international trade and the subject matter of the covered agreements' (Article 17.3), while panellists are to be 'well-qualified governmental and/or non-governmental individuals' (Article 8.1): DSU; on how this may impact the composition of the Appellate Body, see Joost Pauwelyn, 'Who Decides Matters: The Legitimacy Capital of WTO Adjudicators versus ICSID Arbitrators' in Andreas Follesdal and others (eds), *Legitimacy and International Courts* (Cambridge University Press 2018).

172 *United States – Final Anti-Dumping Measures on Stainless Steel from Mexico (Report of the Appellate Body)* (30 April 2008), WT/DS344/AB/R [161].

173 Mariana Clara de Andrade, 'Precedent in the WTO: Retrospective Reflections for a Prospective Dispute Settlement Mechanism' (2020) 11 Journal of International Dispute Settlement 262, 275. de Andrade also refers to Weiler, writing in 2001, who noted that 'one cannot overestimate the importance of the mere existence of the Appellate Body to a shift

We can assess whether this is occurring by analysing the legal reasoning of an appellate mechanism in setting out the basis for the application of the other international law. The greater incidence of incorporation of other law on the basis of "established practice" within the WTO dispute settlement mechanism, compared to investor-state tribunals (see *Figure* 10 above), is evidence of the "cogent reasons" approach to precedents in WTO disputes and potentially indicative of a more authoritative role for the Appellate Body. As one Appellate Body member has put it:

> In matters of adjudication, there must be an end to every great debate. The Appellate Body exists to clarify the meaning of the covered agreements. On the question of zeroing it has spoken definitively. … The range of meanings that may constitute a permissible interpretation does not encompass meanings of such wide variability, and even contradiction, so as to accommodate the two rival interpretations. One must prevail. The Appellate Body has decided the matter. At a point in every debate, there comes a time when it is more important for a system of dispute resolution to have a definitive outcome, than further to pick over the entrails of battles past.[174]

The different role of a standing appellate mechanism may also come with expectations for a more conscious and transparent method of reasoning. Chapter 3 (section 1.2.3) showed the high tendency of the WTO and investor-state adjudicators to fail to clearly stipulate a legal or other basis for the application of other international law. Has the Appellate Body provided more conscious and transparent reasoning when incorporating other international law than WTO panels? To answer simply, no. The Appellate Body did not clearly explain its method of reasoning in more instances (37% of instances) compared to panels failing to provide a basis for their decision on other international law in 34% of decisions.

When compared to ISDS decisions, the Appellate Body fares even worse: ISDS tribunals only failed to provide clear reasoning on the incorporation of other international law in 28% of relevant decisions. While the Appellate Body may encourage panels to be more diligent than itself in providing clear reasoning through threat of appeal, ISDS adjudicators may instead have to ground

---

in organization legal culture. The Appellate Body, in style, content and self-understanding is a high court': Weiler (n 4) 199.

174 *United States – Continued Existence and Application of Zeroing Methodology* (*Report of the Appellate Body*) (4 February 2009), WT/DS350/AB/R [312].

their persuasiveness through their expertise and reasoning. As Sacerdoti explains:

> ... while the authority of WTO decisions is based on the quality of the institution and the predictability of a stable body of case law, within ISDS respect for ad hoc awards is grounded in the persuasiveness of the reasoning underpinning the award. Since international investment law is rooted in customary international law principles and the rather general terms of bilateral investment treaties, more robust knowledge and familiarity with international law at large, both substantive and procedural, is required than from panels applying specific WTO agreements under the ultimate control of the Appellate Body.[175]

However, the Appellate Body decisions are themselves a source of reduction in references to other international law, through quasi-precedent and the embedded hierarchization. By clarifying the role of other international law in the WTO *acquis*, the Appellate Body decision can be used as authority for an interpretation of the WTO Agreements in line with that other international law. Later cases may then refer to the Appellate Body's interpretation of the WTO provision without reference to the relevance of other international law within that interpretation. In *US – Definitive Anti-Dumping* (*China*), the Appellate Body's interpretation of "public body", which was supported by the ILC Articles, is what was then adopted and applied by later panels, without such panels needing to refer to the supportive guidance of the ILC Articles.[176] A clarifying role of this sort would not be as appropriate in the heterogeneous network of IIAs, lacking a hierarchical structure. While investor-state tribunals routinely refer to the reasoning and interpretation in earlier decisions, investment awards would lose some "persuasiveness of the reasoning underpinning the award" if the source of other international law was not also referred to.

---

175 Giorgio Sacerdoti, 'Panelists, Arbitrators, Judges: A Response to Joost Pauwelyn' (2015) 109 AJIL Unbound 283, 287.

176 *United States – Countervailing Duty Measures on Certain Products from China – Recourse to Article 21.5 of the DSU by China* (*Final Report of the Panel*) (n 157) para 7.17; *United States – Countervailing Measures on Certain Hot-Rolled Carbon Steel Flat Products from India* (*Report of the Appellate Body*) (n 157) para 4.17; *United States – Countervailing Duty Measures on Certain Products from China* (*Report of the Panel*) (n 157) para 7.65; each later decision referring to *US – Definitive Anti-Dumping* (*China*) (*Appellate Body*) (n 152) para 310.

The Appellate Body's role in reviewing issues of law and legal interpretations developed by a panel is far removed from the role of ICSID Annulment Committees. First, the scope of appeals. Appellate mechanisms are only effective in bringing consistency, coherence and correctness if the design includes a relatively wide scope of appeal. For the Appellate Body, the review of errors of law is much broader than ICSID Annulment Committees or domestic set-aside proceedings. Such proceedings are primarily limited to reigning in overt mistakes in procedure and manifest excesses of power. Legal interpretations and findings, on the other hand, are not the proper scope of annulment procedures.[177] This design choice represents the prioritization of finality over correctness through the annulment process, rather than appeal.[178] Importantly, the current draft provisions for an appellate mechanism in Working Group III includes "an error in the application or interpretation of the law".[179] While the draft also includes the current grounds of review of the ICSID and New York Convention, the inclusion of errors in application or interpretation of law opens the possibility to appeal (non)application of public international law, whether incorrectly applied or without sound interpretative methodology.[180] Secondly, the lack of a standing appellate mechanism. Ad hoc appellate tribunals are more likely to come to inconsistent decisions about existing inconsistent decisions,[181] exhibited in the difficulty with ending the great debate on the necessity defence in ISDS.[182] This is only exacerbated outside the ICSID

177 See further Luca and others (n 108) 383–6, setting out how the different grounds of annulment under the ICSID Convention are limited in their capacity to address the correctness of decisions.

178 Bjorklund (n 13) 275. Bjorklund notes that such a change from annulment 'involves a fundamental decision about the nature of dispute resolution for investment treaties'.

179 'Report of Working Group III (Investor-State Dispute Settlement Reform) on the Work of Its Fortieth Session' (United Nations Commission on International Trade law 2021) A/CN.9/1050 para 66: 'appellate mechanism would aim at correcting errors in the application or interpretation of applicable law'; 'Possible Reform of Investor-State Dispute Settlement (ISDS): Appellate Mechanism' (United Nations Commission on International Trade law 2022) A/CN.9/WG.III/WP.224 3–4: 'Subparagraph 1(a) reflects the wording found in recent international investment agreements and refers to an error in the application or interpretation of the law. "Law" means the law applied by the first-tier tribunal in its decision, which could be a treaty providing for the protection of investments or investors, a domestic legislation governing foreign investment or a law governing the investment contract. Issues of law addressed by the first-tier tribunal in its decision as well as the interpretation thereof form the basis of an appeal.'

180 Kucik and Puig (n 109) 566.

181 Franck, 'The Legitimacy Crisis in Investment Treaty Arbitration' (n 86) 1609.

182 On inconsistency in other standards, see Dohyun Kim, 'The Annulment Committee's Role in Multiplying Inconsistency in ICSID Arbitration: The Need to Move Away from an Annulment-Based System' (2011) 86 NYU Law Review 242.

context, where domestic courts apply different standards on appropriate arbitral decision-making under the New York Convention.

The EU's multilateral investment court proposal has an innovation that makes it difficult to fully compare with the WTO dispute settlement mechanism: the inclusion of a standing first instance adjudicatory body.[183] The WTO constitutes a mixture of standing and ad hoc mechanisms: WTO panels are appointed ad hoc, only once a dispute has emerged, with the Appellate Body as a standing institution with predetermined composition.[184] Not only will this suggestion do away with the party-appointed adjudicators deciding disputes on public law and policy,[185] but also the inconsistent composition of tribunal benches that may be contributing to the inconsistency of decisions.[186] However, this proposal requires careful consideration of the composition of the standing bodies, both in terms of diversity[187] but also expertise and authority. The EU's proposal suggests adjudicators should possess extensive knowledge and experience with public international law, somewhat similar to DSU's requirement that Appellate Body members be "persons of recognized authority". Yet, the EU's proposal is likely to further embed judicialization in ISDS, a difficult step with the current state of international economic adjudication from a sociological legitimacy perspective.

While there is certainly hope that multilateral institutions and standing appellate mechanisms can bring greater consistency and coherence to a dispute settlement regime on the application of international law, such an outcome is only likely if combined with a strengthened precedential effect. The institutional design of a two-level adjudicatory mechanism goes hand-in-hand with a different perception of precedent, to grant "a more authoritative status" to decisions of an appellate body.[188] Precedents from a hierarchical two-level system constrain the tribunal's discretion, arising from a normative expectation that similar cases should be decided in similar ways.[189] To realize its goal

183 'Possible Reform of Investor-State Dispute Settlement (ISDS): Submission from the European Union and Its Member States' (n 164) s 3; 'Possible Reform of Investor-State Dispute Settlement (ISDS): Appellate and Multilateral Court Mechanisms' (n 164) para 52.

184 Bungenberg and Reinisch (n 109) 24.

185 On possible biases of party-appointment, see Kucik and Puig (n 109) 567; 'Possible Reform of Investor-State Dispute Settlement (ISDS): Selection and Appointment of ISDS Tribunal Members' (United Nations Commission on International Trade law 2020) A/CN9/WGIII/WP203.

186 Bungenberg and Reinisch (n 109) 24.

187 See discussion in Diependaele, De Ville and Sterckx (n 109); Bjorklund (n 13); Andrea K Bjorklund and others, 'The Diversity Deficit in International Investment Arbitration' (2020) 21 The Journal of World Investment & Trade 410.

188 de Andrade (n 173) 275.

189 Yu (n 92) 53.

of predictability and consistency, the EU's proposal relies on "a sense of continuous collegiality" within a standing mechanism, compared to the lack of expectation that a ruling in one dispute will be followed by another ad hoc tribunal.[190] However, other States express strong reservations that decisions rendered through an appellate mechanism should not have precedential value.[191] Further, as discussed in the section above, predictability through precedent and standing appellate mechanisms risks embedding bad precedent.[192] This, in turn, may take away the flexibility that States originally intended in the system.[193]

2.4 *Implications*

Design choices to strengthen State control, or the judicialization of the dispute settlement mechanisms through precedent or multilateral institutions all demonstrate potential to limit discretion of individual adjudicators on the application of international law, thereby potentially turning the tide on the inconsistency and incoherence currently found in the utilization of the adjudicator's toolkit. Yet, such options, in themselves are imperfect alternatives.[194]

The primary imperfection of all these design choices is that States are required to agree, whether on the scope of the application of international law in their treaty interpretations or on the function of adjudicators as regime/rule building. Without such realignment of State preferences, differing normative goals will continue to play out in the use of the adjudicator's toolkit to address the defragmentation of international law. The further judicialization of the dispute settlement mechanisms presents a particular challenge since it may multiply the divergence between State and adjudicators, limiting the interaction

190 'Possible Reform of Investor-State Dispute Settlement (ISDS): Submission from the European Union and Its Member States' (n 164) para 41: 'Predictability and consistency can only be effectively developed through the establishment of a standing mechanism with permanent, full-time adjudicators. This is the key problem of the existing system. Under the current system, stakeholders cannot have reasonable expectations that a ruling in one dispute will be followed in another due to the ad hoc nature of the tribunals. In a standing mechanism a sense of "continuous collegiality" will build up.'

191 'Report of Working Group III (Investor-State Dispute Settlement Reform) on the Work of Its Fortieth Session' (n 179) para 60.

192 See further Kucik and Puig (n 109) 573.

193 See discussion in Schill and Vidigal (n 108).

194 To draw on Puig and Shaffer's comparative institutional design analysis: Sergio Puig and Gregory Shaffer, 'Imperfect Alternatives: Institutional Choice and the Reform of Investment Law' (2018) 112 American Journal of International Law 361.

between the actors and contributing to backlash against the system, quite clearly demonstrated in the US's stance in the Appellate Body crisis.[195]

Rather, a combination of all these reform options is likely required: States can clarify their treaty intentions before adjudicators that can incorporate these intentions in a single authoritative judicial voice, whether in a multilateral court or standing appellate mechanism.[196] It is not sufficient simply for adjudicators to fix the questions of the application of international law in a consistent and coherent way. Normative goals must be aligned through State guidance on interpretation, bringing coherence and correctness to the adjudicator's toolkit, while strengthened judicial features can ensure consistency through predictable application of precedent. As this is only a survey of issues related to the application of the adjudicator's toolkit on the force of international law, reform options still have a host of other legitimacy problems to contend with in international economic law.

195 See further Yu's analysis of the problems with legalization of ISDS without aligning state preferences: Yu (n 92).

196 See similar conclusions on design reforms in: ibid 169; Arato, Brown and Ortino (n 108).

CHAPTER 8

Conclusion

By taking the specialized tribunals of the WTO and investor-state dispute settlement as a case study, the extent of the openness of a dispute settlement mechanism to the force of international is shown to be influenced by an adjudicator's view of international law, whether from a systemic or a state-centric approach to international law. The tension is enabled through the indeterminacy of the treaty-texts on the jurisdiction and applicable law of the dispute settlement mechanisms, creating a space for adjudicative functions and interpretation choices by adjudicators to answer this problem. How adjudicators answer this problem not only affects the fragmentation of international law, but also the power balance between tribunals and their creator-states: to what extent have states delegated such normative questions of international law to adjudicators? The dispute settlement mechanisms of the WTO and international investment law demonstrate how these choices come into tension, not only in the legal reasoning of adjudicators but also in the backlash against the decisions of these tribunals. How limited jurisdiction tribunals, such as the WTO and investor-state tribunals, apply (or not) other international law is pertinent in the wake of critical responses of states to perceived judicial law-making and the focus on international tribunals as the key actors in integrating an otherwise fragmented international law. The book has contributed to our understanding of this complexity of law through an examination of normative goals and design choices.

The book illustrated the extent of the irrelevance of the design of dispute settlement mechanisms in relation to the force of international law. While other international law is frequently raised in both of these dispute settlement mechanisms, there appears to be little agreement on how such law should be treated. The "consistency in inconsistency" represents an important finding given the significant differences between the treaty-texts and historical development of these two dispute settlement systems. Despite an assumption that WTO adjudicators are likely to be more restrictive in relation to the application of other international law, based on the design choices, the book showed significant similarity with their investment law counterparts. The assumption that the WTO dispute settlement mechanism is more restrictive in relation to incorporating the broader international legal order primarily only extends to the initial process of integrating other international law, namely the parties bringing forward relevant other law. Due to more comprehensive agreements

 | DOI:10.1163/9789004700932_009

and more limited applicable law, less decisions of the WTO dispute settlement mechanism are faced with questions of other international law. However, once such law is before the WTO panel or Appellate Body, there is little difference from the approach of investor-state tribunals in how such other international law is included or excluded as well as the role that such law plays in the resolution of the dispute. In fact, there are even some surprising similarities in the method of application and reasoning of the dispute settlement mechanisms, such as the fact that more instances of treaties and general principles are actually taken into account by the WTO panels and the Appellate Body than the supposedly more "flexible" investor-state tribunals. Further, the similar extent of referrals to the applicable law as the legal basis for incorporation of international law is an unexpected underuse by investor-state adjudicators, indicating the limited relevance of simply including a broad applicable law clause in constitutive treaties as opening the mechanism up to other international law.

The adjudicator's toolkit should elucidate how adjudicators can open regimes to international law. However, the interaction between the opening and closing tools is ill-defined. How adjudicators seek to deal with such concepts demonstrates the tension between the systemic and consensualist choices, the two sides of the fragmentation debate, as summarized in Figure 17.

General principles of law, as an opening tool, are used in filling *lacunae* of international legal texts. Under the systemic view adopted by some WTO and investor-state adjudicators, and in line with an "international judicial function", general principles are integral mechanisms in gap-filling and avoiding the declaration of *non liquet*. Adopting a systemic view, adjudicators have applied general principles of law on the basis that they are a source of law pursuant to Article 38(1)(c) of the ICJ Statute. The empirical results indicated an almost even incorporation of general principles of law as well as treaty-law within

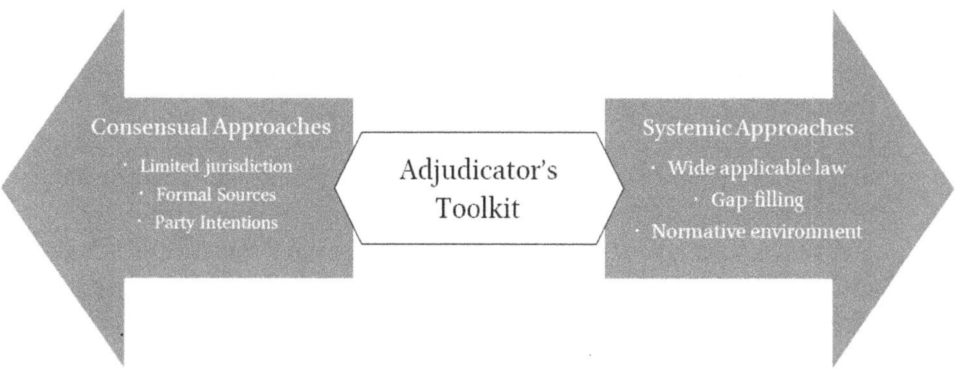

FIGURE 17 Framing the choices of adjudicators

the dispute settlement mechanisms, certainly a good omen for the defragmentation of international law. However, a consent-based examination has been undertaken by some adjudicators on whether some general principles were in fact a source of law applicable before that particular tribunal, leading to divergent results on the application of general principles in similar disputes.

Secondly, the principle of systemic integration, codified in Article 31(3)(c) of the VCLT, develops the coherency of international law. As such, systemic approaches to international law rely heavily on the principle in order for the broader normative environment to be considered within a subsystem of international law. As codified in legal rules of interpretation, consensualists in WTO and investor-state decisions have also relied on systemic integration to resolve indeterminacy of law. However, as with general principles, consensualists have been more concerned with the connection of the other law to the parties of the dispute. In addition, the principle should be merely an interpretative tool on a consensual approach and must be limited as such, avoiding displacing the applicable law through interpretation. The ambiguity of the principle of systemic integration, namely how widely other law is to be taken into account and what other law is relevant, has thus been treated quite differently on a consensual or systemic view of the question. From the empirical and doctrinal analysis of the WTO and investor-state treatment (or more accurately lack of treatment) of Article 31(3)(c), it is certainly possible that this indeterminacy could even be discouraging the utilization of this principle.

Thirdly, applicable law can be the gateway to other law, particularly where wide applicable law clauses, such as in many IIAs and Article 38(1) of the ICJ Statute, already exist in the treaty-conferring jurisdiction on the tribunal. However, consent to jurisdiction is a fundamental aspect of international dispute settlement. Such consent both empowers a tribunal with judicial functions and powers yet also delimits the scope of disputes that can be determined by the tribunal. Yet, the definition of jurisdiction is far from clear, particularly in regard to how jurisdiction interacts with the applicable law in the dispute. Are jurisdictional limits the final arbiter of the law applicable to the merits or is there an inherent distinction between jurisdiction and applicable law? When faced with clear and unequivocal attempts to expand jurisdiction on the basis of the wider applicable law, WTO and investor-state adjudicators unmistakably considered the jurisdictional limits as fundamental. However, the more borderline attempts of applicable law influencing the subject-matter jurisdiction of the tribunal have not been so lucidly handled, reflecting the need to better understand the relationship between jurisdiction and applicable law.

Although the approach of the WTO panels and the Appellate Body is somewhat more cautious in relation to these opening tools of international law than investor-state tribunals, the divergence is not as wide as we would expect from the design choices. Rather, by considering the language in the adjudicator's reasoning when considering each of these opening tools, the "consistency in inconsistency" results from the push and pull effect of different normative goals in both WTO and investor-state tribunal decisions.

The adjudicators do adopt an international judicial function to deal with the issues of other international law brought up within disputes. The WTO and investor-state dispute settlement mechanisms have made interesting comparisons of judicial lawmaking, in the sense of the international judicial function, both in relation to filling *lacunae* and creating coherency in international law. There is a wide-spread application of general principles to fill *lacunae* in the treaty-texts, not only by investor-state tribunals but also WTO panels for which it is less clear of their authority to do so. As such, it would be imprudent to argue that the WTO and investor-state adjudicators are *not* exercising most of the characteristics of the international judicial function. In this way, the studied adjudicators are not simply fulfilling a dispute settlement function but also undertake rule and lawmaking functions in both the development of the regimes and international law when they apply other international law.

Yet, the adjudicators are still restrained in their exercise of the international judicial function. The systemic approach is not always commensurate with positive law and the limited jurisdiction of the tribunals. The adjudicators' invocation of systemic integration on an ad hoc, rather than methodical basis, illustrates the limitations of the international judicial function to explain the approach to the application of other international law. Further, the undefined relationship between jurisdiction and applicable law requires a fine balance between the application of other international law, whether through applicable law or as interpretative material under Article 31(3)(c) of the VCLT. Such balance not always being clearly appreciated in the disputes, contributing to the "consistency in inconsistency".

Importantly, the analysis of the decisions of the investor-state and WTO tribunals illustrated the necessity of conscious and transparent standards of legal reasoning. Where normative goals of adjudicators are clouded in unclear legal reasoning, inconsistency of decisions can seem to be dire for the state of international law. Only when a adjudicator's views on the nature of international law are clear in the reasoning on legal norms can we clear a path through the inconsistency. In this way, a criticism of the judicial cooperation approaches to defragmentation that have dominated recent academic discussion of the topic is that they deal with the risks of fragmentation on substantive law, without fully addressing the institutional problems. Based on the analysis of the legal reasoning of WTO and investor-state tribunals in this book, it must be concluded that we are asking too much from tribunals based on the positive law and their limited jurisdiction to resolve the questions of fragmentation and the force of international law as a legal system.

Appendix

List of Relevant WTO Decisions

	Title	Symbol	Document date	Instances of other law
1	Saudi Arabia – Measures concerning the Protection of Intellectual Property Rights – Report of the Panel	WT/DS567/R	16.06.2020	3
2	India – Export Related Measures – Report of the Panel	WT/DS541/R	31.10.2019	1
3	Thailand – Customs and Fiscal Measures on Cigarettes from the Philippines – Second recourse to article 21.5 of the DSU by the Philippines – Report of the Panel	WT/DS371/RW2	12.07.2019	3
4	Russia – Measures Concerning Traffic in Transit – Report of the Panel	WT/DS512/R	05.04.2019	1
5	United States – Measures Concerning the Importation, Marketing and Sale of Tuna and Tuna Products – Recourse to article 21.5 of the DSU by the United States -- United States – Measures Concerning the Importation, Marketing and Sale of Tuna and Tuna Products – Second recourse to article 21.5 of the DSU by Mexico – AB-2017–9 – Report of the Appellate Body	WT/DS381/AB/RW/USA ; WT/DS381/AB/RW2	14.12.2018	1
6	Thailand – Customs and Fiscal Measures on Cigarettes from the Philippines – Recourse to article 21.5 of the DSU by the Philippines – Report of the Panel	WT/DS371/RW	12.11.2018	5

 | DOI:10.1163/9789004700932_010

	Title	Symbol	Document date	Instances of other law
7	Australia – Certain Measures Concerning Trademarks, Geographical Indications and Other Plain Packaging Requirements Applicable to Tobacco Products and Packaging – Report of the Panels	WT/DS435/R ; WT/DS441/R ; WT/DS458/R ; WT/DS467/R	28.06.2018	1
8	Korea – Import Bans, and Testing and Certification Requirements for Radionuclides – Report of the Panel	WT/DS495/R	22.02.2018	1
9	United States – Anti-Dumping and Countervailing Measures on Certain Coated Paper from Indonesia – Report of the Panel	WT/DS491/R	06.12.2017	2
10	United States – Measures Concerning the Importation, Marketing and Sale of Tuna and Tuna Products – Recourse to article 21.5 of the DSU by the United States – United States – Measures Concerning the Importation, Marketing and Sale of Tuna and Tuna Products – Second recourse to article 21.5 of the DSU by Mexico – Reports of the Panels	WT/DS381/ RW/USA ; WT/ DS381/RW2	26.10.2017	1
11	European Union – Measures Affecting Tariff Concessions on Certain Poultry Meat Products – Report of the Panel	WT/DS492/R	28.03.2017	1
12	United States – Certain Methodologies and Their Application to Anti-Dumping Proceedings Involving China – Report of the Panel	WT/DS471/R	19.10.2016	1

	Title	Symbol	Document date	Instances of other law
13	Colombia – Measures Relating to the Importation of Textiles, Apparel and Footwear – AB-2016–1 – Report of the Appellate Body	WT/DS461/AB/R	07.06.2016	2
14	Colombia – Measures Relating to the Importation of Textiles, Apparel and Footwear – Report of the Panel	WT/DS461/R	27.11.2015	3
15	Argentina – Measures Relating to Trade in Goods and Services – Report of the Panel	WT/DS453/R	30.09.2015	1
16	United States – Measures Affecting the Importation of Animals, Meat and Other Animal Products from Argentina – Report of the Panel	WT/DS447/R	24.07.2015	1
17	Peru – Additional Duty on Imports of Certain Agricultural Products – AB-2015–3 – Report of the Appellate Body	WT/DS457/AB/R	20.07.2015	3
18	United States – Countervailing Measures on Certain Hot-Rolled Carbon Steel Flat Products from India – AB-2014–7 – Report of the Appellate Body	WT/DS436/AB/R	08.12.2014	1
19	Peru – Additional Duty on Imports of Certain Agricultural Products – Report of the Panel	WT/DS457/R	27.11.2014	2
20	United States – Anti-Dumping Measures on Certain Shrimp from Viet Nam – Report of the Panel	WT/DS429/R	17.11.2014	1
21	Argentina – Measures Affecting the Importation of Goods – Reports of the Panel	WT/DS438/R ; WT/DS444/R ; WT/DS445/R	22.08.2014	1

	Title	Symbol	Document date	Instances of other law
22	United States – Countervailing and Anti-Dumping Measures on Certain Products from China – Report of the Panel	WT/DS449/R	27.03.2014	2
23	China – Measures Related to the Exportation of Rare Earths, Tungsten and Molybdenum – Reports of the Panel	WT/DS431/R ; WT/DS432/R ; WT/DS433/R	26.03.2014	4
24	Canada – Certain Measures Affecting the Renewable Energy Generation Sector – Canada – Measures Relating to the Feed-in Tariff Program – Reports of the Panels	WT/DS412/R ; WT/DS426/R	19.12.2012	1
25	China – Certain Measures Affecting Electronic Payment Services – Report of the Panel	WT/DS413/R	16.07.2012	2
26	Dominican Republic – Safeguard Measures on Imports of Polypropylene Bags and Tubular Fabric – Final report of the Panel	WT/DS415/R ; WT/DS416/R ; WT/DS417/R ; WT/DS418/R	31.01.2012	1
27	United States – Certain country of origin labeling (cool) requirements – Final reports of the Panel	WT/DS384/R ; WT/DS386/R	18.11.2011	2
28	United States – Anti-Dumping Measures on Certain Shrimp from Viet Nam – Report of the Panel	WT/DS404/R	11.07.2011	1
29	China – Measures Related to the Exportation of Various Raw Materials – Reports of the Panel	WT/DS394/R ; WT/DS395/R ; WT/DS398/R	05.07.2011	2
30	European Communities and Certain Member States – Measures Affecting Trade in Large Civil Aircraft – AB-2010–1 – Report of the Appellate Body	WT/DS316/AB/R	18.05.2011	3

	Title	Symbol	Document date	Instances of other law
31	United States – Measures Affecting Trade in Large Civil Aircraft (Second Complaint) – Report of the Panel	WT/DS353/R	31.03.2011	2
32	United States – Definitive Anti-Dumping and Countervailing Duties on Certain Products from China – AB-2010–3 – Report of the Appellate Body	WT/DS379/AB/R	11.03.2011	1
33	United States – Definitive Anti-Dumping and Countervailing Duties on Certain Products from China – Report of the Panel	WT/DS379/R	22.10.2010	1
34	European Communities and its Member States – Tariff Treatment of Certain Information Technology Products – Reports of the Panel	WT/DS375/R ; WT/DS376/R ; WT/DS377/R	16.08.2010	1
35	European Communities and Certain Member States – Measures Affecting Trade in Large Civil Aircraft – Report of the Panel	WT/DS316/R	30.06.2010	1
36	China – Measures Affecting Trading Rights and Distribution Services for Certain Publications and Audiovisual Entertainment Products – AB-2009–3 – Report of the Appellate Body	WT/DS363/AB/R	21.12.2009	1
37	United States – Measures Relating to Zeroing and Sunset Reviews – Recourse to Article 21.5 of the DSU by Japan – AB-2009–2 – Report of the Appellate Body	WT/DS322/AB/RW	18.08.2009	2
38	China – Measures Affecting Trading Rights and Distribution Services for Certain Publications and Audiovisual Entertainment Products – Report of the Panel	WT/DS363/R	12.08.2009	1

	Title	Symbol	Document date	Instances of other law
39	United States – Laws, Regulations and Methodology for Calculating Dumping Margins ("Zeroing") – Recourse to Article 21.5 of the DSU by the European Communities – AB-2009–1 – Report of the Appellate Body	WT/DS294/AB/RW	14.05.2009	1
40	China – Measures Affecting the Protection and Enforcement of Intellectual Property Rights – Report of the Panel	WT/DS362/R	26.01.2009	1
41	United States – Laws, Regulations and Methodology for Calculating Dumping Margins ("Zeroing") – Recourse to Article 21.5 of the DSU by the European Communities – Report of the Panel	WT/DS294/RW	17.12.2008	2
42	China – Measures Affecting Imports of Automobile Parts – AB-2008–10 – Report of the Appellate Body	WT/DS339/AB/R ; WT/DS340/AB/R ; WT/DS342/AB/R	15.12.2008	1
43	European Communities – Regime for the Importation, Sale and Distribution of Bananas – Second Recourse to Article 21.5 of the DSU by Ecuador – AB-2008–8 – European Communities – Regime for the Importation, Sale and Distribution of Bananas – Recourse to Article 21.5 of the DSU by the United States – AB-2008–9 – Reports of the Appellate Body	WT/DS27/AB/RW/USA ; WT/DS27/AB/RW2/ECU	26.11.2008	3

	Title	Symbol	Document date	Instances of other law
44	United States – Continued Suspension of Obligations in the EC – Hormones Dispute – AB-2008–5 – Report of the Appellate Body	WT/DS320/AB/R	16.10.2008	3
45	Canada – Continued Suspension of Obligations in the EC – Hormones Dispute – AB-2008–6 – Report of the Appellate Body	WT/DS321/AB/R	16.10.2008	3
46	China – Measures Affecting Imports of Automobile Parts – Reports of the Panel	WT/DS339/R ; WT/DS340/R ; WT/DS342/R	18.07.2008	1
47	European Communities – Regime for the Importation, Sale and Distribution of Bananas – Recourse to Article 21.5 of the DSU by the United States – Report of the Panel	WT/DS27/RW/USA	19.05.2008	1
48	United States – Final Anti-dumping Measures on Stainless Steel from Mexico – AB-2008–1 – Report of the Appellate Body	WT/DS344/AB/R	30.04.2008	1
49	European Communities – Regime for the Importation, Sale and Distribution of Bananas – Second Recourse to Article 21.5 of the DSU by Ecuador – Report of the Panel	WT/DS27/RW2/ECU	07.04.2008	1
50	United States – Continued Suspension of Obligations in the EC – Hormones Dispute – Report of the Panel	WT/DS320/R	31.03.2008	2
51	Canada – Continued Suspension of Obligations in the EC – Hormones Dispute – Report of the Panel	WT/DS321/R	31.03.2008	2
52	Brazil – Measures Affecting Imports of Retreaded Tyres – AB-2007–4 – Report of the Appellate Body	WT/DS332/AB/R	03.12.2007	1

	Title	Symbol	Document date	Instances of other law
53	Brazil – Measures Affecting Imports of Retreaded Tyres – Report of the Panel	WT/DS332/R	12.06.2007	2
54	European Communities – Measures Affecting the Approval and Marketing of Biotech Products – Reports of the Panel	WT/DS291/R ; WT/DS292/R ; WT/DS293/R	29.09.2006	2
55	Mexico – Tax Measures on Soft Drinks and Other Beverages – AB-2005-10 – Report of the Appellate Body	WT/DS308/AB/R	06.03.2006	2
56	United States – Laws, Regulations and Methodology for Calculating Dumping Margins ("Zeroing") – Report of the Panel	WT/DS294/R	31.10.2005	1
57	Mexico – Tax Measures on Soft Drinks and Other Beverages – Report of the Panel	WT/DS308/R	07.10.2005	1
58	European Communities – Customs Classification of Frozen Boneless Chicken Cuts – AB-2005-5 – Report of the Appellate Body	WT/DS269/AB/R ; WT/DS286/AB/R	12.09.2005	1
59	United States – Countervailing Duty Investigation on Dynamic Random Access Memory Semiconductors (DRAMS) from Korea – AB-2005-4 – Report of the Appellate Body	WT/DS296/AB/R	27.06.2005	1
60	European Communities – Customs Classification of Frozen Boneless Chicken Cuts – Complaint by Brazil – Report of the Panel	WT/DS269/R	30.05.2005	1
61	European Communities – Customs Classification of Frozen Boneless Chicken Cuts – Complaint by Thailand – Report of the Panel	WT/DS286/R	30.05.2005	1

	Title	Symbol	Document date	Instances of other law
62	European Communities – Export Subsidies on Sugar – AB-2005–2 – Report of the Appellate Body	WT/DS265/AB/R ; WT/DS266/AB/R ; WT/DS283/AB/R	28.04.2005	1
63	European Communities – Measures Affecting Trade in Commercial Vessels – Report of the Panel	WT/DS301/R	22.04.2005	1
64	European Communities – Protection of Trademarks and Geographical Indications for Agricultural Products and Foodstuffs – Complaint by the United States – Report of the Panel	WT/DS174/R	15.03.2005	1
65	European Communities – Protection of Trademarks and Geographical Indications for Agricultural Products and Foodstuffs – Complaint by Australia – Report of the Panel	WT/DS290/R	15.03.2005	1
66	Dominican Republic – Measures Affecting the Importation and Internal Sale of Cigarettes – Report of the Panel	WT/DS302/R	26.11.2004	1
67	United States – Measures Affecting the Cross-Border Supply of Gambling and Betting Services – Report of the Panel	WT/DS285/R	10.11.2004	1
68	European Communities – Export Subsidies on Sugar – Complaint by Australia – Report of the Panel	WT/DS265/R	15.10.2004	1
69	European Communities – Export Subsidies on Sugar – Complaint by Brazil – Report of the Panel	WT/DS266/R	15.10.2004	1
70	European Communities – Export Subsidies on Sugar – Complaint by Thailand – Report of the Panel	WT/DS283/R	15.10.2004	1

	Title	Symbol	Document date	Instances of other law
71	European Communities – Conditions for the Granting of Tariff Preferences to Developing Countries – AB-2004–1 – Report of the Appellate Body	WT/DS246/AB/R	07.04.2004	1
72	Japan – Measures Affecting the Importation of Apples – AB-2003–4 – Report of the Appellate Body	WT/DS245/AB/R	26.11.2003	1
73	Argentina – Definitive Anti-Dumping Duties on Poultry from Brazil – Report of the Panel	WT/DS241/R	22.04.2003	3
74	United States – Continued Dumping and Subsidy Offset Act of 2000 – AB-2002–7 – Report of the Appellate Body	WT/DS217/AB/R ; WT/DS234/AB/R	16.01.2003	1
75	European Communities – Anti-Dumping Duties on Imports of Cotton-Type Bed Linen from India – Recourse to Article 21.5 of the DSU by India – Report of the Panel	WT/DS141/RW	29.11.2002	2
76	European Communities – Trade Description of Sardines – AB-2002–3 – Report of the Appellate Body	WT/DS231/AB/R	26.09.2002	1
77	United States – Continued Dumping and Subsidy Offset Act of 2000 – Report of the Panel	WT/DS217/R ; WT/DS234/R	16.09.2002	1
78	United States – Anti-Dumping and Countervailing Measures on Steel Plate from India – Report of the Panel	WT/DS206/R	28.06.2002	1
79	European Communities – Trade Description of Sardines – Report of the Panel	WT/DS231/R	29.05.2002	1
80	Chile – Price Band System and Safeguard Measures Relating to Certain Agricultural Products – Report of the Panel	WT/DS207/R	03.05.2002	1

	Title	Symbol	Document date	Instances of other law
81	United States – Definitive Safeguard Measures on Imports of Circular Welded Carbon Quality Line Pipe from Korea – AB-2001–9 – Report of the Appellate Body	WT/DS202/AB/R	15.02.2002	1
82	United States – Tax Treatment for "Foreign Sales Corporations" – Recourse to Article 21.5 of the DSU by the European Communities – AB-2001–8 – Report of the Appellate Body	WT/DS108/AB/RW	14.01.2002	1
83	India – Measures Affecting the Automotive Sector – Report of the Panel	WT/DS146/R ; WT/DS175/R	21.12.2001	1
84	United States – Import Prohibition of Certain Shrimp and Shrimp Products – Recourse to Article 21.5 of the DSU by Malaysia – AB-2001–4 – Report of the Appellate Body	WT/DS58/AB/RW	22.10.2001	1
85	United States – Transitional Safeguard Measure on Combed Cotton Yarn from Pakistan – AB-2001–3 – Report of the Appellate Body	WT/DS192/AB/R	08.10.2001	2
86	United States – Tax Treatment for "Foreign Sales Corporations" – Recourse to Article 21.5 of the DSU by the European Communities – Report of the Panel	WT/DS108/RW	20.08.2001	1
87	United States – Section 211 Omnibus Appropriations Act of 1998 – Report of the Panel	WT/DS176/R	06.08.2001	1
88	United States – Anti-Dumping Measures on Certain Hot-Rolled Steel Products from Japan – AB-2001–2 – Report of the Appellate Body	WT/DS184/AB/R	24.07.2001	1

	Title	Symbol	Document date	Instances of other law
89	United States – Import Prohibition of Certain Shrimp and Shrimp Products – Recourse to Article 21.5 by Malaysia – Report of the Panel	WT/DS58/RW	15.06.2001	1
90	United States – Anti-Dumping Measures on Certain Hot-Rolled Steel Products from Japan – Report of the Panel	WT/DS184/R	28.02.2001	2
91	Argentina – Measures Affecting the Export of Bovine Hides and the Import of Finished Leather – Report of the Panel	WT/DS155/R	19.12.2000	2
92	European Communities – Anti-Dumping Duties on Imports of Cotton-Type Bed Linen from India – Report of the Panel	WT/DS141/R	30.10.2000	1
93	Guatemala – Definitive Anti-Dumping Measures on Grey Portland Cement from Mexico – Report of the Panel	WT/DS156/R	24.10.2000	2
94	European Communities – Measures Affecting Asbestos and Asbestos-Containing Products – Report of the Panel	WT/DS135/R	18.09.2000	1
95	Canada – Term of Patent Protection – AB-2000–7 – Report of the Appellate Body	WT/DS170/AB/R	18.09.2000	1
96	Korea – Measures Affecting Imports of Fresh, Chilled and Frozen Beef – Report of the Panel	WT/DS161/R ; WT/DS169/R	31.07.2000	1
97	United States – Import Measures on Certain Products from the European Communities – Report of the Panel	WT/DS165/R	17.07.2000	1
98	United States – Anti-Dumping Act of 1916 – Complaint by Japan – Report of the Panel	WT/DS162/R	29.05.2000	2

	Title	Symbol	Document date	Instances of other law
99	Brazil – Export Financing Programme for Aircraft – Recourse by Canada to Article 21.5 of the DSU – Report of the Panel	WT/DS46/RW	09.05.2000	1
100	Canada – Term of Patent Protection – Report of the Panel	WT/DS170/R	05.05.2000	1
101	Korea – Measures Affecting Government Procurement – Report of the Panel	WT/DS163/R	01.05.2000	2
102	United States – Anti-Dumping Act of 1916 – Complaint by the European Communities – Report of the Panel	WT/DS136/R	31.03.2000	1
103	United States – Tax Treatment for "Foreign Sales Corporations" – AB-1999–9 – Report of the Appellate Body	WT/DS108/AB/R	24.02.2000	1
104	Australia – Measures Affecting Importation of Salmon – Recourse to Article 21.5 by Canada – Report of the Panel	WT/DS18/RW	18.02.2000	2
105	United States – Sections 301–310 of the Trade Act of 1974 – Report of the Panel	WT/DS152/R	22.12.1999	2
106	Canada – Measures Affecting the Export of Civilian Aircraft – AB-1999–2 – Report of the Appellate Body	WT/DS70/AB/R	02.08.1999	1
107	Turkey – Restrictions on Imports of Textile and Clothing Products – Report of the Panel	WT/DS34/R	31.05.1999	3
108	Canada – Measures Affecting the Importation of Milk and the Exportation of Dairy Products – Report of the Panel	WT/DS103/R ; WT/DS113/R	17.05.1999	2
109	Japan – Measures Affecting Agricultural Products – AB-1998–8 – Report of the Appellate Body	WT/DS76/AB/R	22.02.1999	1

	Title	Symbol	Document date	Instances of other law
110	United States – Import Prohibition of Certain Shrimp and Shrimp Products – AB-1998–4 – Report of the Appellate Body	WT/DS58/AB/R	12.10.1998	2
111	Korea – Taxes on Alcoholic Beverages – Report of the Panel	WT/DS75/R ; WT/DS84/R	17.09.1998	1
112	Guatemala – Anti-Dumping Investigation Regarding Portland Cement from Mexico – Report of the Panel	WT/DS60/R	19.06.1998	1
113	European Communities – Customs Classification of Certain Computer Equipment – AB-1998–2 – Report of the Appellate Body	WT/DS62/AB/R ; WT/DS67/AB/R ; WT/DS68/AB/R	05.06.1998	1
114	United States – Import Prohibition of Certain Shrimp and Shrimp Products – Report of the Panel	WT/DS58/R	15.05.1998	2
115	European Communities – Measures Affecting Importation of Certain Poultry Products – Report of the Panel	WT/DS69/R	12.03.1998	1
116	European Communities – EC Measures Concerning Meat and Meat Products (Hormones) – AB-1997–4 – Report of the Appellate Body	WT/DS26/AB/R ; WT/DS48/AB/R	16.01.1998	2
117	India – Patent Protection for Pharmaceutical and Agricultural Chemical Products – AB-1997–5 – Report of the Appellate Body	WT/DS50/AB/R	19.12.1997	1
118	Argentina – Measures Affecting Imports of Footwear, Textiles, Apparel and other Items – Report of the Panel	WT/DS56/R	25.11.1997	1

	Title	Symbol	Document date	Instances of other law
119	European Communities – Regime for the Importation, Sale and Distribution of Bananas – AB-1997–3 – Report of the Appellate Body	WT/DS27/AB/R	09.09.1997	2
120	EC Measures Concerning Meat and Meat Products (Hormones) – Complaint by the United States – Report of the Panel	WT/DS26/R/USA	18.08.1997	2
121	EC Measures Concerning Meat and Meat Products (Hormones) – Complaint by Canada – Report of the Panel	WT/DS48/R/CAN	18.08.1997	2
122	European Communities – Regime for the Importation, Sale and Distribution of Bananas – Complaint by Ecuador – Report of the Panel	WT/DS27/R/ECU	22.05.1997	2
123	European Communities – Regime for the Importation, Sale and Distribution of Bananas – Complaint by Guatemala and Honduras – Report of the Panel	WT/DS27/R/GTM ; WT/DS27/R/HND	22.05.1997	2
124	European Communities – Regime for the Importation, Sale and Distribution of Bananas – Complaint by Mexico – Report of the Panel	WT/DS27/R/MEX	22.05.1997	2
125	European Communities – Regime for the Importation, Sale and Distribution of Bananas – Complaint by the United States – Report of the Panel	WT/DS27/R/USA	22.05.1997	2
126	United States – Measures Affecting Imports of Woven Wool Shirts and Blouses from India – AB-1991–1 – Report of the Appellate Body	WT/DS33/AB/R	25.04.1997	1
127	Brazil – Measures Affecting Desiccated Coconut – AB-1996–4 – Report of the Appellate Body	WT/DS22/AB/R	21.02.1997	1

	Title	Symbol	Document date	Instances of other law
128	Brazil – Measures Affecting Desiccated Coconut – Report of the Panel	WT/DS22/R	17.10.1996	1

List of Relevant ISDS Decisions

	Case name	Date	Phase of document	Instances of other law
1	Cairn Energy PLC and Cairn UK Holdings Limited (CUHL) v. Republic of India (PCA Case No. 2016–07)	21 December 2020	Award	8
2	RWE Innogy GmbH and RWE Innogy Aersa S.A.U. v. Kingdom of Spain (ICSID Case No. ARB/14/34)	18 December 2020	Award	1
3	STEAG GmbH v. Kingdom of Spain (ICSID Case No. ARB/15/4)	08 October 2020	Decision on Jurisdiction, Liability and Principles of Quantum	4
4	Raiffeisen Bank International AG and Raiffeisenbank Austria d.d. v. Republic of Croatia (ICSID Case No. ARB/17/34)	30 September 2020	Decision on Respondent Jurisdictional Objections	6

	Case name	Date	Phase of document	Instances of other law
5	Orascom TMT Investments S.à r.l. v. People's Democratic Republic of Algeria (ICSID Case No. ARB/12/35)	17 September 2020	Decision on Annulment	3
6	ESPF Beteiligungs GmbH, ESPF Nr. 2 Austria Beteiligungs GmbH and InfraClass Energie 5 GmbH & Co. KG v. Italian Republic (ICSID Case No. ARB/16/5)	14 September 2020	Award	6
7	Eskosol S.p.A. in liquidazione v. Italian Republic (ICSID Case No. ARB/15/50)	04 September 2020	Award	2
8	Cavalum SGPS, S.A. v. Kingdom of Spain (ICSID Case No. ARB/15/34)	31 August 2020	Decision on Jurisdiction, Liability and Directions on Quantum	3
9	Guris Construction and Engineering Inc. and others v. Arab Republic of Syria (ICA Case No. 21845/ZF/AYZ)	31 August 2020	Final Award	8
10	Iberdrola Energia S.A. v. Republic of Guatemala II (PCA Case No. 2017–41)	24 August 2020	Final Award	1
11	Michael Anthony Lee-Chin v. Dominican Republic (ICSID Case No. UNCT/18/3)	15 July 2020	Partial Award on Jurisdiction	2

	Case name	Date	Phase of document	Instances of other law
12	The Renco Group Inc v Republic of Peru (II) (PCA Case No. 2019–46)	30 June 2020	Decision on Expedited Preliminary Objections	3
13	Strabag SE v. State of Libya (ICSID Case No. ARB(AF)/15/1)	29 June 2020	Award	2
14	Addiko Bank v Croatia (ICSID Case No. ARB/17/37)	12 June 2020	Decision on Croatia's Jurisdictional Objection	4
15	Eiser and Energía Solar v Spain (ICSID Case No. ARB/13/36)	11 June 2020	Decision on Respondent Application for Annulment	1
16	Joshua Dean Nelson v. United Mexican States (ICSID Case No. UNCT/17/1)	05 June 2020	Final Award	1
17	Deutsche Telekom v. Republic of India (PCA Case No. 2014–10)	27 May 2020	Final Award	2
18	TECO Guatemala Holdings, LLC v. Republic of Guatemala (ICSID Case No. ARB/10/23)	13 May 2020	Resubmission Award	1
19	AMF v Czech Republic (PCA Case No. 2017–15)	11 May 2020	Final Award	6
20	Ortiz Construcciones y Proyectos S.A. v. People's Democratic Republic of Algeria (ICSID Case No. ARB/17/1)	29 April 2020	Award	1
21	GPF GP S.à.r.l v. Republic of Poland (SCC Case No. V2014/168)	29 April 2020	Final Award	3

	Case name	Date	Phase of document	Instances of other law
22	(DS)2, S.A., Peter de Sutter and Kristof De Sutter v. Republic of Madagascar II (ICSID Case No. ARB/17/18)	17 April 2020	Award	7
23	Blusun v Italy (ICSID Case No. ARB/14/3)	13 April 2020	Decision on Annulment	1
24	SunReserve v Italy (SCC Case No. V2016/32)	25 March 2020	Final Award	1
25	Daniel W. Kappes and Kappes, Cassidy & Associates v Guatemala (ICSID Case No. ARB/18/43)	13 March 2020	Decision on Respondent's Preliminary Objections	1
26	Hydro Energy 1 v Spain (ICSID Case No. ARB/15/42)	09 March 2020	Decision on Jurisdiction, Liability and Directions on Quantum	3
27	Micula v Romania (II) (ICSID Case No. ARB/14/29)	05 March 2020	Award	2
28	Strabag SE, Raiffeisen Centrobank AG and Syrena Immobilien Holding AG v. Republic of Poland (ICSID Case No. ADHOC/15/1)	04 March 2020	Partial Award on Jurisdiction	5
29	Staur Eiendom AS, EBO Invest AS and Rox Holding AS v. Republic of Latvia (ICSID Case No. ARB/16/38)	28 February 2020	Award	2
30	PV Investors v Spain (PCA Case No. 2012–14)	28 February 2020	Final Award	5

	Case name	Date	Phase of document	Instances of other law
31	Thomas Gosling and others v. Republic of Mauritius (ICSID Case No. ARB/16/32)	18 February 2020	Award	4
32	Canepa Green Energy Opportunities v Spain (ICSID Case No. ARB/19/4)	10 February 2020	Decision on the Second Proposal to Disqualify Mr Peter Rees QC	1
33	Adamakopoulos v Cyprus (ICSID Case No. ARB/15/49)	07 February 2020	Decision on Jurisdiction	2
34	Watkins Holdings v Spain (ICSID Case No. ARB/15/44)	21 January 2020	Award	4
35	Víctor Pey Casado and President Allende Foundation v. Republic of Chile I (ICSID Case No. ARB/98/2)	08 January 2020	Decision on Annulment	1
36	RWE Innogy v Spain (ICSID Case No. ARB/14/34)	30 December 2019	Decision on Jurisdiction, Liability and Certain Issues of Quantum	7
37	Bahgat v The Arab Republic of Egypt I (PCA Case No. 2012–07)	23 December 2019	Final Award	2
38	Mason Capital L.P. and Mason Management LLC v. Republic of Korea (PCA Case No. 2018–55)	22 December 2019	Decision on Preliminary Objections	1

	Case name	Date	Phase of document	Instances of other law
39	Sunlodges Ltd (BVI) and Sunlodges (T) Limited v. United Republic of Tanzania (PCA Case No. 2018–09)	20 December 2019	Award	2
40	García Armas and others v. Venezuela (PCA Case No. 2016–08)	13 December 2019	Award on Jurisdiction	2
41	BayWa v Spain (ICSID Case No. ARB/15/16)	02 December 2019	Decision on Jurisdiction, Liability and Directions on Quantum	5
42	Stadtwerke München and others v. Spain (ICSID Case No. ARB/15/1)	02 December 2019	Award	2
43	Canepa Green Energy Opportunities v Spain (ICSID Case No. ARB/19/4)	19 November 2019	Decision on the Proposal to Disqualify Mr Peter Rees QC	1
44	Magyar Farming Company Ltd v Hungary (ICSID Case No. ARB/17/27)	13 November 2019	Award	5
45	Enrique Heemsen and Jorge Heemsen v. Bolivarian Republic of Venezuela (PCA Case No. 2017–18)	29 October 2019	Award	1
46	Besserglik v Mozambique (ICSID Case No. ARB(AF)/14/2)	28 October 2019	Award	2
47	CMC v Mozambique (ICSID Case No. ARB/17/23)	24 October 2019	Award	2
48	Perenco v Ecuador (ICSID Case No. ARB/08/6)	27 September 2019	Award	3
49	OperaFund v Spain (ICSID Case No. ARB/15/36)	06 September 2019	Award	4

	Case name	Date	Phase of document	Instances of other law
50	Ballantine v Dominican Republic (PCA Case No. 2016–17)	03 September 2019	Final Award	1
51	Glencore International A.G. and C.I. Prodeco S.A. v. Republic of Colombia (ICSID Case No. ARB/16/6)	27 August 2019	Award	4
52	Belenergia v Italy (ICSID Case No. ARB/15/40)	06 August 2019	Award	5
53	Lao Holdings v Laos (I) (ICSID Case No. ARB(AF)/12/6)	06 August 2019	Award	3
54	Sanum Investments v Laos (I) (PCA Case No. 2013–13)	06 August 2019	Award	3
55	InfraRed Environmental Infrastructure v Spain (ICSID Case No. ARB/14/12)	02 August 2019	Award	3
56	SolEs Badajoz v Spain (ICSID Case No. ARB/15/38)	31 July 2019	Award	3
57	B-Mex LLC v Mexico (ICSID Case No. ARB(AF)/16/3)	19 July 2019	Partial Award	1
58	Tethyan Copper v Pakistan (ICSID Case No. ARB/12/1)	12 July 2019	Award	1
59	Rockhopper v Italy (ICSID Case No. ARB/17/14)	26 June 2019	Decision on the Intra-EU Jurisdictional Objection	2
60	United Utilities v Estonia (ICSID Case No. ARB/14/24)	21 June 2019	Award	3
61	9REN Holding v Spain (ICSID Case No. ARB/15/15)	31 May 2019	Award	3

	Case name	Date	Phase of document	Instances of other law
62	Teinver v Argentina (ICSID Case No. ARB/09/1)	29 May 2019	Decision on Argentina's Application for Annulment	2
63	WA Investments-Europa Nova v The Czech Republic (PCA Case No. 2014–19)	15 May 2019	Award	1
64	ICW v Czech Republic (PCA Case No. 2014–22)	15 May 2019	Award	1
65	Photovoltaik Knopf Betriebs v. The Czech Republic (PCA Case No. 2014–21)	15 May 2019	Award	1
66	Voltaic Network v Czech Republic (PCA Case No. 2014–20)	15 May 2019	Award	1
67	Mobil Exploration and Development v Argentine Republic (ICSID Case No. ARB/04/16)	08 May 2019	Decision on Annulment	1
68	Eskosol v Italy (ICSID Case No. ARB/15/50)	07 May 2019	Decision on Termination Request and Intra-EU Objection	5
69	Nissan v India (PCA Case No. 2017–37)	29 April 2019	Decision on Jurisdiction	1
70	Hydro S.r.l. and others v. Republic of Albania (ICSID Case No. ARB/15/28)	24 April 2019	Award	5
71	B3 Croatian Courier Coöperatief U.A. v. Republic of Croatia (ICSID Case No. ARB/15/5)	05 April 2019	Excerpts of Award	4
72	Indian Metals & Ferro Alloys Ltd v Indonesia (PCA Case No. 2015–40)	29 March 2019	Award	1

	Case name	Date	Phase of document	Instances of other law
73	Churchill Mining and Planet Mining v Indonesia (ICSID Case No. ARB/12/14 and 12/40)	18 March 2019	Decision on Annulment	2
74	NextEra v Spain (ICSID Case No. ARB/14/11)	12 March 2019	Decision on Jurisdiction, Liability and Principles of Quantum	2
75	ConocoPhillips v Venezuela (ICSID Case No. ARB/07/30)	08 March 2019	Award	1
76	Landesbank Baden-Württemberg and others v. Spain (ICSID Case No. ARB/15/45)	25 February 2019	Decision on the "Intra-EU" Jurisdictional Objection	2
77	Cube Infrastructure v Spain (ICSID Case No. ARB/15/20)	19 February 2019	Decision on Jurisdiction, Liability and a Partial Decision on Quantum	4
78	Anglo American v Venezuela (ICSID Case No. ARB(AF)/14/1)	18 January 2019	Award	1
79	CEF Energia v Italy (SCC Case No. V2015/158)	16 January 2019	Award	4
80	William Ralph Clayton and others v. Government of Canada (PCA Case No. 2009–04)	10 January 2019	Award on Damages	4
81	Tenaris SA & Talta v Venezuela (II) (ICSID Case No. ARB12/23)	28 December 2018	Decision on Annulment	2
82	Greentech and Novenergia v Italy (SCC Case No. V 2015/095)	23 December 2018	Award	3

	Case name	Date	Phase of document	Instances of other law
83	Manchester Securities v Poland (PCA Case No. 2015–18)	07 December 2018	Award	2
84	OOO Manolium Processing v Republic of Belarus (PCA Case No. 2018–06)	07 December 2018	Decision on Claimant Interim Measures Request	1
85	Mera Investment v Serbia (ICSID Case No. ARB/17/2)	30 November 2018	Decision on Jurisdiction	2
86	RREEF v Spain (ICSID Case No. ARB/13/30)	30 November 2018	Decision on Responsibility and the Principles of Quantum	7
87	South American Silver v Bolivia (PCA Case No. 2013–15)	22 November 2018	Award	5
88	von Pezold v Zimbabwe (ICSID Case No. ARB/10/15)	21 November 2018	Decision on Annulment	1
89	Athena Investments (formerly Greentech) v Spain (SCC Case No. 2015/150)	14 November 2018	Final Award	3
90	Cengiz v Libya (ICA Case No. 21537/ZF/AYZ)	07 November 2018	Award	4
91	Cortec Mining v Kenya (ICSID Case No. ARB/15/29)	22 October 2018	Award	3
92	Álvarez y Marín v Panama (ICISD Case No. ARB/15/14)	12 October 2018	Award	1
93	UP and CD Holding v Hungary (ICSID Case No. ARB/13/35)	09 October 2018	Award	4
94	Aven v Costa Rica (ICSID Case No. UNCT/15/3)	18 September 2018	Final Award	5
95	LDA v India (PCA Case No. 2014–26)	11 September 2018	Award	2
96	Vattenfall v Germany (II) (ICSID Case No. ARB/12/12)	31 August 2018	Decision on the Achmea Issue	3

	Case name	Date	Phase of document	Instances of other law
97	Unión Fenosa Gas v Egypt (ICSID Case No. ARB/14/4)	31 August 2018	Award	5
98	Chevron and TexPet v Ecuador (II) (PCA Case No. 2009–23)	30 August 2018	Second Partial Award on Track II	8
99	Gavrilovic v Croatia (ICSID Case No. ARB/12/39)	26 July 2018	Award	3
100	Marfin v Cyprus (ICSID Case No. ARB/13/27)	26 July 2018	Award	8
101	Mobil Investments Canada Inc v Canada (ICSID Case No. ARB/15/6)	13 July 2018	Decision on Jurisdiction and Admissibility	3
102	Krederi v Ukraine (ICSID Case No. ARB/14/17)	02 July 2018	Award	2
103	Casinos Austria v Argentina (ICSID Case No. ARB/14/32)	29 June 2018	Decision on Jurisdiction	3
104	Antin v Spain (ICSID Case No. ARB/13/31)	15 June 2018	Award	5
105	Olin v Libya (ICA Case No. 20355/MCP)	25 May 2018	Final Award	1
106	Masdar Solar v Spain (ICSID Case No. ARB/14/1)	16 May 2018	Award	4
107	Salini Impregilo v Argentina (ICSID Case No. ARB/15/39)	23 February 2018	Decision on Jurisdiction and Admissibility	4
108	Novenergia II – Energy & Environment (SCA), SICAR v. Kingdom of Spain (SCC Case No. V2015/063)	15 February 2018	Final Award	2
109	Munshi v Mongolia (SCC Emergency Arbitration No. EA2018/007)	05 February 2018	Award on Emergency Measures	1
110	UAB v Latvia (ICSID Case No. ARB/12/33)	22 December 2017	Award	4

	Case name	Date	Phase of document	Instances of other law
111	Lao Holdings v Laos (I) (ICSID Case No. ARB(AF)/12/6)	15 December 2017	Decision on the Merits of Claimants' Second Material Breach Application	1
112	Deutsche Telekom v India (PCA Case No. 2014–10)	13 December 2017	Interim Award	2
113	Infinito Gold Ltd v Republic of Costa Rica (ICSID Case No. ARB/14/5)	04 December 2017	Decision on Jurisdiction	1
114	Bear Creek Mining v Peru (ICSID Case No. ARB/14/21)	20 November 2017	Award	2
115	Tethyan Copper v Pakistan (ICSID Case No. ARB/12/1)	10 November 2017	Decision on Jurisdiction and Liability	2
116	JSW Solar v Czech Republic (PCA Case No. 2014–03)	11 October 2017	Final Award	1
117	Karkey Karadeniz v Pakistan (ICSID Case No. ARB/13/1)	22 August 2017	Award	3
118	EuroGas v Slovakia (ICSID Case No. ARB/14/14)	18 August 2017	Award	2
119	Perenco v Ecuador (ICSID Case No. ARB/08/6)	18 August 2017	Decision on Claimant's Application for Dismissal of Ecuador's Counterclaims	1
120	Teinver v Argentina (ICSID Case No. ARB/09/1)	21 July 2017	Award	1
121	PL Holdings v Poland (SCC Case No. V 2014/163)	28 June 2017	Partial Award	2
122	Beijing Urban Construction v Yemen (ICSID Case No. ARB/14/30)	31 May 2017	Decision on Jurisdiction	1

	Case name	Date	Phase of document	Instances of other law
123	Orascom TMT Investments S.à.r.l. v People's Democratic Republic of Algeria (ICSID Case No. ARB/12/35)	31 May 2017	Award	2
124	Vivendi v Argentina (II) (ICSID Case No. ARB/03/19)	05 May 2017	Decision on Annulment	2
125	Eiser and Energía Solar v Spain (ICSID Case No. ARB/13/36)	04 May 2017	Award	2
126	Gavazzi v Romania (ICSID Case No. ARB/12/25)	18 April 2017	Award (Excerpts)	1
127	Eskosol v Italy (ICSID Case No. ARB/15/50)	20 March 2017	Decision on Respondent's Application under Rule 41(5)	1
128	Eli Lilly and Company v Canada (ICSID Case No. UNCT/14/2)	16 March 2017	Final Award	1
129	Anglia Auto v Czech Republic (SCC Case No. 2014/181)	10 March 2017	Final Award	1
130	Busta v Czech Republic (SCC Case No. V2015/014)	10 March 2017	Final Award	2
131	Mobil Corporation (now Venezuela Holdings BV) v Venezuela (ICSID Case No. ARB/07/27)	09 March 2017	Decision on Annulment	2
132	Kim v Uzbekistan (ICSID Case No. ARB/13/6)	08 March 2017	Decision on Jurisdiction	3
133	WNC Factoring v Czech Republic (PCA Case No. 2014–34)	22 February 2017	Award	1

	Case name	Date	Phase of document	Instances of other law
134	Ampal-American Israel Corporation v Arab Republic of Egypt (ICSID Case No ARB/12/11)	21 February 2017	Decision on Liability and Heads of Loss	1
135	Czescik v Cyprus (SCC Case No. V2014/169)	11 February 2017	Final Award	1
136	A11Y v Czech Republic (ICSID Case No. UNCT/15/1)	09 February 2017	Decision on Jurisdiction	1
137	Burlington Resources v Ecuador (ICSID Case No. ARB/08/5)	07 February 2017	Decision on Reconsideration and Award	2
138	Burlington Resources v Ecuador (ICSID Case No. ARB/08/5)	07 February 2017	Decision on Counterclaims	1
139	Blusun v Italy (ICSID Case No. ARB/14/3)	27 December 2016	Award	5
140	Urbaser SA v Argentine Republic (ICSID Case No. ARB/07/26)	08 December 2016	Award	3
141	Churchill Mining and Planet Mining v Indonesia (ICSID Case No. ARB/12/14 and 12/40)	06 December 2016	Award	2
142	Windstream Energy v Canada (PCA Case No. 2013–22)	27 September 2016	Award	1
143	Víctor Pey Casado and President Allende Foundation v. Republic of Chile I (ICSID Case No. ARB/98/2)	13 September 2016	Award II	4
144	Merck Sharpe & Dohme LLC v Ecuador (PCA Case No. 2012–10)	06 September 2016	Second Decision on Interim Measures	2

	Case name	Date	Phase of document	Instances of other law
145	Rusoro Mining v Venezuela (ICSID Case No. ARB(AF)/12/15)	22 August 2016	Award	3
146	Menzies Middle East and Africa SA and Aviation Handling Services International Ltd. v. Republic of Senegal (ICSID Case No. ARB / 15/21)	05 August 2016	Award	1
147	Central European Aluminium Company (CEAC) v Montenegro (ICSID Case No. ARB/14/8)	26 July 2016	Award	1
148	Devas v India (PCA Case No. 2013–09)	25 July 2016	Award on Jurisdiction and Merits	2
149	The Renco Group Inc v Republic of Peru (ICSID Case no. UNCT/13/1)	15 July 2016	Partial Award on Jurisdiction	4
150	Isolux v Spain (SCC Case No. V2013/153)	12 July 2016	Award	1
151	Philip Morris v Uruguay (ICSID Case No. ARB/10/7)	08 July 2016	Award	6
152	Dunkeld v Belize (I) (PCA Case NO. 2010–13)	28 June 2016	Award	1
153	Allard v Barbados (PCA Case No. 2012–06)	27 June 2016	Award	1
154	RREEF v Spain (ICSID Case No. ARB/13/30)	06 June 2016	Decision on Jurisdiction	3
155	Murphy v Ecuador (II) (PCA Case No. 2012–16)	06 May 2016	Partial Final Award	1
156	MNSS v Montenegro (ICSID Case No. ARB(AF)/12/8)	04 May 2016	Award	1

	Case name	Date	Phase of document	Instances of other law
157	Uzan v Turkey (SCC Case No. 2014/023)	20 April 2016	Award on Respondent's Bifucated Preliminary Objection	1
158	Vestey v Venezuela (ICSID Case No. ARB/06/4)	15 April 2016	Award	2
159	Crystallex v Venezuela (ICSID Case No. ARB(AF)/11/2)	04 April 2016	Award	3
160	Mesa Power Group LLC v. Government of Canada (PCA Case No. 2012–17)	24 March 2016	Award	5
161	İçkale İnşaat Limited v Turkmenistan (ICSID Case No. ARB/10/24)	08 March 2016	Award	3
162	UP and CD Holding v Hungary (ICSID Case No. ARB/13/35)	03 March 2016	Decision on Preliminary Issues of Jurisdiction	1
163	Micula v Romania (I) (ICSID Case No. ARB/05/20)	26 February 2016	Decision on Annulment	1
164	Copper Mesa Mining v Ecuador (PCA Case No. 2012–2)	15 February 2016	Award	3
165	EDF International v Argentina (ICSID Case No. ARB/03/23)	05 February 2016	Decision on Annulment	1
166	Total SA v Argentina (ICSID Case No. ARB/04/1)	01 February 2016	Decision on Annulment	1
167	Ampal-American Israel Corporation v Arab Republic of Egypt (ICSID Case No ARB/12/11)	01 February 2016	Decision on Jurisdiction	1
168	Charanne v Spain (SCC Case No. 062/2012)	21 January 2016	Award	3

	Case name	Date	Phase of document	Instances of other law
169	Tulip Real Estate v Turkey (ICSID Case No. ARB/11/28)	30 December 2015	Decision on Annulment	2
170	Oxus Gold v Uzbekistan (ad hoc)	17 December 2015	Final Award	2
171	Al Tamimi v Oman (ICSID Case No. ARB/11/33)	03 November 2015	Award	1
172	Occidental v Ecuador (ICSID Case No. ARB/06/11)	02 November 2015	Decision on Annulment of the Award	3
173	Quiborax v Bolivia (ICSID Case No. ARB/06/2)	16 September 2015	Award	3
174	von Pezold v Zimbabwe (ICSID Case No. ARB/10/15)	28 July 2015	Award	5
175	Kılıç v Turkmenistan (ICSID Case No. ARB/10/1)	14 July 2015	Decision on Annulment	1
176	Mobil Corporation (now Venezuela Holdings BV) v Venezuela (ICSID Case No. ARB/07/27)	12 June 2015	Decision on Revision	2
177	Ping An v Belgium (ICSID Case No. ARB/12/29)	30 April 2015	Award	3
178	Gavrilovic v Croatia (ICSID Case No. ARB/12/39)	30 April 2015	Decision on Provisional Measures	1
179	Gavazzi v Romania (ICSID Case No. ARB/12/25)	21 April 2015	Decision on Jurisdiction, Admissibility and Liability	1
180	Accession Mezzanine v Hungary (ICSID Case No. ARB/12/3)	17 April 2015	Award	1
181	Poštová banka, a.s. and ISTROKAPITAL SE v Hellenic Republic (ICSID Case No. ARB/13/8)	09 April 2015	Award	1

	Case name	Date	Phase of document	Instances of other law
182	Mamidoil Jetoil Greek Petroleum Products v Albania (ICSID Case No. ARB/11/24	30 March 2015	Award	3
183	William Ralph Clayton and others v. Government of Canada (PCA Case No. 2009–04)	17 March 2015	Award on Jurisdiction and Liability	2
184	OI European Group v Venezuela (ICSID Case No. ARB/11/25)	10 March 2015	Award	1
185	Awdi v Romania (ICSID Case No. ARB/10/13)	02 March 2015	Award	1
186	Hochtief v Argentina (ICSID Case No. ARB/07/31)	29 December 2014	Decision on Liability	1
187	British Caribbean Bank v Belize (PCA Case No. 2010–18)	19 December 2014	Award	2
188	Al-Warraq v Indonesia (ad hoc)	15 December 2014	Final Award	5
189	Fraport v Philippines (II) (ICSID Case No. ARB/11/12)	12 December 2014	Award	2
190	Alemanni v Argentina (ICSID Case No. ARB/07/8)	17 November 2014	Decision on Jurisdiction and Admissibility	1
191	Mobil v Venezuela (ICSID Case No. ARB/07/27)	09 October 2014	Award	2
192	Gold Reserve v Venezuela (ICSID Case No. ARB(AF)/09/1)	22 September 2014	Award	1
193	Perenco v Ecuador (ICSID Case No. ARB/08/6)	12 September 2014	Decision on Remaining Issues of Jurisdiction and on Liability	2

	Case name	Date	Phase of document	Instances of other law
194	Apotex Holdings v USA (ICSID Case No. ARB(AF)/12/1)	25 August 2014	Award	1
195	Tatneft v Ukraine (PCA Case No. 2008–8)	29 July 2014	Award	3
196	Hulley Enterprises v Russia (PCA Case No. 2005–03/AA226)	18 July 2014	Final Award	5
197	Veteran Petroleum v Russia (PCA Case No. 2005–05/AA28)	18 July 2014	Final Award	6
198	Yukos Universal v Russia (PCA Case No. 2005–04/AA227)	18 July 2014	Final Award	7
199	Lao Holdings v Laos (I) (ICSID Case No. ARB(AF)/12/6)	30 May 2014	Ruling on Motion to Amend the Provisional Measures Order	1
200	Achmea v Slovak Republic (II) (PCA Case No. 2013–12)	20 May 2014	Award on Jurisdiction and Admissibility	3
201	Minnotte and Lewis v Poland (ICSID Case No. ARB(AF)/10/1)	16 May 2014	Award	4
202	Enkev v Beheer v Poland (PCA Case No. 2013–01)	29 April 2014	First Partial Award	1
203	Emmis International v Hungary (ICSID Case No. ARB/12/2)	16 April 2014	Award	1
204	ConocoPhillips v Venezuela (ICSID Case No. ARB/07/30)	10 March 2014	Decision on Respondent Request for Reconsideration	1
205	Stati v Kazakhstan (SCC Case No. 116/2010)	19 December 2013	Award	2

	Case name	Date	Phase of document	Instances of other law
206	Burlington Resources v Ecuador (ICSID Case No. ARB/08/5)	13 December 2013	Decision on the Proposal for Disqualification of Professor Francisco Orrego Vicuna	1
207	Sanum Investments v Laos (I) (PCA Case No. 2013–13)	13 December 2013	Award on Jurisdiction	2
208	Micula v Romania (I) (ICSID Case No. ARB/05/20)	11 December 2013	Final Award	1
209	Total SA v Argentina (ICSID Case No. ARB/04/1)	27 November 2013	Award	1
210	Energoalians v Moldova (ad hoc)	23 October 2013	Award	4
211	KT Asia v Kazakhstan (ICSID Case No. ARB/09/8)	17 October 2013	Award	1
212	Metal-Tech v Uzebekistan (ICSID Case No. ARB/10/3)	04 October 2013	Award	4
213	ECE v Czech Republic (PCA Case No. 2010–05)	19 September 2013	Final Award	2
214	ConocoPhillips v Venezuela (ICSID Case No. ARB/07/30)	03 September 2013	Decision on Jurisdiction and Merits	2
215	Awdi v Romania (ICSID Case No. ARB/10/13)	26 July 2013	Decision on the Admissibility of the Third Objection to Jurisdiction and Admissibility	2
216	ST-AD v Bulgaria (PCA Case No. 2011–06)	18 July 2013	Award on Jurisdiction	3
217	Malicorp v Egypt (ICSID Case No. ARB/08/18)	03 July 2013	Decision on Annulment	1
218	Kılıç v Turkmenistan (ICSID Case No. ARB/10/1)	02 July 2013	Award	1

	Case name	Date	Phase of document	Instances of other law
219	Philip Morris v Uruguay (ICSID Case No. ARB/10/7)	02 July 2013	Decision on Jurisdiction	1
220	Convial Callao v Peru (ICSID Case No. ARB/10/2)	21 May 2013	Final Award	1
221	Bosca v Lithuania (PCA Case No. 2011–04)	17 May 2013	Award	2
222	Rompetrol v Romania (ICSID Case No. ARB/06/3)	06 May 2013	Award	5
223	Mobil Exploration and Development v Argentine Republic (ICSID Case No. ARB/04/16)	10 April 2013	Decision on Jurisdiction and Liability	2
224	Arif v Moldova (ICSID Case No. ARB/11/23)	08 April 2013	Award	3
225	Emmis International v Hungary (ICSID Case No. ARB/12/2)	11 March 2013	Decision on Respondent's Objection under ICSID Arbitration Rule 41(5)	1
226	Ambiente Ufficio v Argentina (ICSID Case No. ARB/08/9)	08 February 2013	Decision on Jurisdiction and Admissibility	1
227	Teinver v Argentina (ICSID Case No. ARB/09/1)	21 December 2012	Decision on Jurisdiction	2
228	Urbaser SA v Argentine Republic (ICSID Case No. ARB/07/26)	19 December 2012	Decision on Jurisdiction	2
229	Víctor Pey Casado and President Allende Foundation v. Republic of Chile I (ICSID Case No. ARB/98/2)	18 December 2012	Decision on the Application for Annulment of the Republic of Chile	1
230	Burlington Resources v Ecuador (ICSID Case No. ARB/08/5)	14 December 2012	Decision on Liability	1

	Case name	Date	Phase of document	Instances of other law
231	Achmea (formerly Eureko BV) v Slovak Republic (I) (PCA Case No. 2008–13)	07 December 2012	Final Award	3
232	Electrabel v Hungary (ICSID Case No. ARB/07/19)	30 November 2012	Decision on Jurisdiction, Applicable Law and Liability	1
233	Bosh v Ukraine (ICSID Case No. ARB/08/11)	25 October 2012	Award	2
234	EURAM Bank v Slovakia (PCA Case No. 2010–17)	22 October 2012	Award on Jurisdiction	2
235	Bureau Veritas v Paraguay (ICSID Case No. ARB/07/9)	09 October 2012	Further Decision on Objections to Jurisdiction	1
236	Occidental v Ecuador (ICSID Case No. ARB/06/11)	05 October 2012	Award	3
237	Daimler Financial v Argentina (ICSID Case No. ARB/05/1)	22 August 2012	Award	2
238	Quasar de Valors v Russia (SCC Case No. 24/2007)	20 July 2012	Award	2
239	Swisslion v Macedonia (ICSID Case No. ARB/09/16)	06 July 2012	Award	1
240	Al-Warraq v Indonesia (ad hoc)	21 June 2012	Award on Respondent's Preliminary Objections to Jurisdiction and Admissibility of the Claims	1
241	Goetz v Burundi (II) (ICSID Case No. ARB/01/2)	21 June 2012	Award	1
242	EDF International v Argentina (ICSID Case No. ARB/03/23)	11 June 2012	Award	3

	Case name	Date	Phase of document	Instances of other law
243	SAUR v Argentina (ICSID Case No. ARB/04/4)	06 June 2012	Decision on Jurisdiction and Liability	2
244	H&H v Egypt (ICSID Case No. ARB/09/15)	05 June 2012	Decision on Respondent's Objections to Jurisdiction	1
245	Pac Rim Cayman v El Salvador (ICSID Case No. ARB/09/12)	01 June 2012	Decision on Jurisdictional Objections	1
246	Oostergetel v Slovak Republic (ad hoc)	23 April 2012	Final Award	2
247	Chevron and TexPet v Ecuador (II) (PCA Case No. 2009–23)	27 February 2012	Third Interim Award on Jurisdiction and Admissibility	3
248	ICS v Argentina (I) (PCA Case No. 2010–9)	10 February 2012	Award on Jurisdiction	2
249	Roussalis v Romania (ICSID Case No. ARB/06/1)	07 December 2011	Award	1
250	White Industries v India (ad hoc)	30 November 2011	Final Award	1
251	El Paso v Argentina (ICSID Case No. ARB/03/15)	31 October 2011	Award	4
252	Continental Casualty v Argentina (ICSID Case No. ARB/03/9)	16 September 2011	Decision on the Application for Partial Annulment	1
253	Libananco v Turkey (ICSID Case No. ARB/06/8)	02 September 2011	Award	2
254	Chevron and TexPet v Ecuador (I) (PCA Case No. 2007–02/AA277)	31 August 2011	Final Award	1
255	Abaclat v Argentina (ICSID Case No. ARB/07/5)	04 August 2011	Decision on Jurisdiction and Admissibility	2

	Case name	Date	Phase of document	Instances of other law
256	Impregilo v Argentina (I) (ICSID Case No. ARB/07/17)	21 June 2011	Award	1
257	HICEE v Slovakia (PCA Case No, 2009–11)	23 May 2011	Partial Award	1
258	Paushok v Mongolia (ad hoc)	28 April 2011	Award on Jurisdiction and Liability	1
259	Lemire v Ukraine (II) (ICSID Case No. ARB/06/18)	28 March 2011	Award	1
260	Fuchs v Georgia (ICSID Case No. ARB/07/15)	21 March 2011	Decision of the ad hoc Committee to Suspend the Annulment Proceeding	1
261	Kardassopoulos v Georgia (ICSID Case No. ARB/05/18)	21 March 2011	Decision of the ad hoc Committee to Suspend the Annulment Proceeding	1
262	Malicorp v Egypt (ICSID Case No. ARB/08/18)	07 February 2011	Award	2
263	Grand River v US (UNCITRAL)	12 January 2011	Award	2
264	Total SA v Argentina (ICSID Case No. ARB/04/1)	27 December 2010	Decision on Liability	2
265	Fraport v Philippines (I) (ICSID Case No. ARB/03/25)	23 December 2010	Decision on the Application for Annulment	1
266	Murphy Exploration and Production Company International v Republic of Ecuador (I) (ICSID Case No. ARB/08/4)	15 December 2010	Award on Jurisdiction	1

	Case name	Date	Phase of document	Instances of other law
267	RSM v Grenada (ICSID Case No. ARB/10/6)	10 December 2010	Award	1
268	Frontier v Czech Republic (PCA Case No. 2008–09)	12 November 2010	Final Award	4
269	Achmea v Slovak Republic (I) (PCA Case No. 2008–13)	26 October 2010	Award on Jurisdiction, Arbitrability and Suspension	2
270	Tatneft v Ukraine (PCA Case No. 2008–8)	28 September 2010	Partial Award on Jurisdiction	3
271	RosInvest v Russia (SCC Case No. 079/2005)	12 September 2010	Final Award	1
272	Vivendi v Argentina (I) (ICSID Case No. ARB/97/3)	10 August 2010	Decision on the Argentine Republic's Application for Annulment of the Award	1
273	AWG Group Ltd v Argentina	30 July 2010	Decision on Liability	2
274	Suez v Argentina (ICSID Case No. ARB/03/17)	30 July 2010	Decision on Liability	2
275	Vivendi v Argentina (II) (ICSID Case No. ARB/03/19)	30 July 2010	Decision on Liability	2
276	Enron v Argentina (ICSID Case No. ARB/01/3)	30 July 2010	Decision on the Application for Annulment of the Argentine Republic	1
277	Sempra v Argentina (ICSID Case No. ARB/02/16)	29 June 2010	Decision on the Argentine Republic's Application for Annulment of the Award	1

	Case name	Date	Phase of document	Instances of other law
278	Liman Caspian Oil v Kazakhstan (ICSID Case No. ARB/07/14)	22 June 2010	Excerpts of Award	1
279	Hamester v Ghana (ICSID Case No. ARB/07/24)	18 June 2010	Award	1
280	Gemplus v Mexico (ICSID Case No. ARB(AF)/04/3)	16 June 2010	Award	2
281	Mobil v Venezuela (ICSID Case No. ARB/07/27)	10 June 2010	Decision on Jurisdiction	1
282	ATA Construction v Jordan (ICSID Case No. ARB/08/2)	18 May 2010	Award	4
283	Oostergetel v Slovak Republic (ad hoc)	30 April 2010	Decision on Jurisdiction	2
284	Nova Scotia v Venezuela (I) (PCA Case No. 2009–14)	22 April 2010	Award on Jurisdiction	1
285	Merrill & Ring v Canada (ICSID Case No. UNCT/07/1)	31 March 2010	Award	3
286	Chevron and TexPet v Ecuador (I) (PCA Case No. 2007–02/AA277)	30 March 2010	Partial Award on the Merits	2
287	Kardassopoulos v Georgia (ICSID Case No. ARB/05/18)	03 March 2010	Award	1
288	Hulley Enterprises v Russia (PCA Case No. 2005–03/ AA226)	30 November 2009	Interim Award on Jurisdiction and Admissibility	1
289	Veteran Petroleum v Russia (PCA Case No. 2005–05/ AA28)	30 November 2009	Interim Award on Jurisdiction and Admissibility	1
290	Yukos Universal v Russia (PCA Case No. 2005–04/ AA227)	30 November 2009	Interim Award on Jurisdiction and Admissibility	1
291	EDF (Services) v Romania (ICSID Case No. ARB/05/13)	08 October 2009	Award	2

	Case name	Date	Phase of document	Instances of other law
292	Cargill v Mexico (ICSID Case No. ARB(AF)/05/2)	18 September 2009	Award	1
293	Cementownia "Nowa Huta" v Turkey (ICSID Case No. ARB(AF)/06/2)	17 September 2009	Award	1
294	Toto v Lebanon (ICISD Case No. ARB/07/12)	11 September 2009	Decision on Jurisdiction	3
295	Al-Bahloul v Tajikstan (SCC Case No. 064/2008)	02 September 2009	Partial Award on Jurisdiction and Liability	2
296	Azurix v Argentina (I) (ICSID Case No. ARB/01/12)	01 September 2009	Decision on the Application for Annulment of the Argentine Republic	2
297	Europe Cement v Turkey (ICSID Case No. Arb(AF)/07/2)	13 August 2009	Award	1
298	European Media Ventures SA v Czech Republic (ad hoc arbitration)	08 July 2009	Partial Award on Liability	2
299	Bau v Thailand	01 July 2009	Award	1
300	Saipem v Bangladesh (ICSID Case No. ARB/05/7)	30 June 2009	Award	5
301	Tza Yap Shum v Republic of Peru (ICSID Case No. ARB / 07/6)	19 June 2009	Decision on Jurisdiction and Competence	2
302	Perenco v Ecuador (ICSID Case No. ARB/08/6)	08 May 2009	Decision on Provisional Measures	1
303	Funnekotter v Zimbabwe (ICSID Case No. ARB/05/6)	22 April 2009	Award	2
304	Phoenix Action v Czech Republic (ICSID Case No. ARB/06/5)	15 April 2009	Award	2

	Case name	Date	Phase of document	Instances of other law
305	TSA Spectrum v Argentina (ICSID Case No. ARB/05/5)	19 December 2008	Award	2
306	Nordzucker v Poland	10 December 2008	Partial Award (Jurisdiction)	3
307	Wintershall v Argentina (ICSID Case No. ARB/04/14)	08 December 2008	Award	8
308	Chevron and TexPet v Ecuador (I) (PCA Case No. 2007–02/AA277)	01 December 2008	Interim Award	6
309	LESI v Algeria (ICSID Case No. ARB/05/3)	12 November 2008	Award	1
310	Jan de Nul v Egypt (ICSID Case No. ARB/04/13)	06 November 2008	Award	3
311	National Grid v Argentina	03 November 2008	Award	2
312	Micula v Romania (I) (ICSID Case No. ARB/05/20)	24 September 2008	Decision on Jurisdiction and Admissibility	3
313	Société Générale v Dominican Republic (LCIA Case No. UN 7927)	19 September 2008	Preliminary Objections to Jurisdiction	3
314	Continental Casualty v Argentina (ICSID Case No. ARB/03/9)	05 September 2008	Award	8
315	Plama Consortium v Bulgaria (ICSID Case No. ARB/03/24)	27 August 2008	Award	2
316	Duke Energy v Ecuador (ICSID Case No. ARB/04/19)	18 August 2008	Award	2
317	Rumeli v Kazakhstan (ICSID Case No. ARB/05/16)	29 July 2008	Award	4

	Case name	Date	Phase of document	Instances of other law
318	Biwater Gauff v Tanzania (ICSID Case No. ARB/05/22)	24 July 2008	Award	5
319	Helnan v Egypt (ICSID Case No. ARB/05/19)	03 July 2008	Award	1
320	Trans-Global v Jordan (ICSID Case No. ARB/07/25)	12 May 2008	Decision on the Respondent's Objection Under Rule 41(5) of the ICSID Arbitration Rules	1
321	Víctor Pey Casado and President Allende Foundation v. Republic of Chile I (ICSID Case No. ARB/98/2)	08 May 2008	Award	7
322	Rompetrol v Romania (ICSID Case No. ARB/06/3)	18 April 2008	Decision on Respondent's Preliminary Objections on Jurisdiction and Admissibility	1
323	AMTO v Ukraine (SCC Case No. 080/2005)	26 March 2008	Final Award	2
324	Noble Energy v Ecuador (ICSID Case No. ARB/05/12)	05 March 2008	Decision on Jurisdiction	2
325	Cargill v Poland (ICSID Case No. ARB(AF)/04/2) / UNCITRAL	29 February 2008	Award	4
326	Desert Line v Yemen (ICSID Case No. ARB/05/17)	06 February 2008	Award	4
327	Corn Products v Mexico (ICSID Case No. ARB(AF)/04/1	15 January 2008	Decision on Responsibility	3

	Case name	Date	Phase of document	Instances of other law
328	BG v Argentina (ad hoc)	24 December 2007	Final Award	4
329	Archer Daniels Midland v Mexico (ICSID Case No. ARB(AF)/04/5)	21 November 2007	Award	1
330	RosInvest v Russia (SCC Case No. 079/2005)	01 October 2007	Award on Jurisdiction	1
331	Sempra v Argentina (ICSID Case No. ARB/02/16)	28 September 2007	Award	3
332	CMS Gas Transmission v Argentina (ICSID Case No. ARB/01/8)	25 September 2007	Decision of the ad hoc Committee on Argentina's Application for Annulment	1
333	Industria Nacional de Alimentos v Peru (ICSID Case No. ARB/03/4)	05 September 2007	Decision on Annulment	1
334	Fraport v Philippines (I) (ICSID Case No. ARB/03/25)	16 August 2007	Award	2
335	MCI Power v Ecuador (ICSID Case No. ARB/03/6)	31 July 2007	Award	2
336	Tokios Tokeles v Ukraine (ICSID Case No. ARB/02/18)	26 July 2007	Award	1
337	Kardassopoulos v Georgia (ICSID Case No. ARB/05/18)	06 July 2007	Decision on Jurisdiction	1
338	Binder v Czech Republic	06 June 2007	Award on Jurisdiction	1
339	Hussein Nauman Soufraki v United Arab Emirates (ICSID Case No. ARB/02/7)	05 June 2007	Decision of the Ad Hoc Committee on the Application for Annulment of Mr- Soufraki	1

	Case name	Date	Phase of document	Instances of other law
340	UPS v Canada (ICSID Case No. UNCT/02/1)	24 May 2007	Award on the Merits	1
341	Enron v Argentina (ICSID Case No. ARB/01/3)	22 May 2007	Award	1
342	Eastern Sugar v Czech Republic (SCC Case No. 088/2004)	27 March 2007	Partial Award	3
343	Saipem v Bangladesh (ICSID Case No. ARB/05/7)	21 March 2007	Decision on Jurisdiction and Recommendation on Provisional Measures	3
344	Siemens v Argentina (ICSID Case No. ARB/02/8)	06 February 2007	Award	3
345	PSEG v Turkey (ICSID Case No. ARB/02/5)	19 January 2007	Award	1
346	Champion Trading Company and Ameritrade International, Inc. v. Arab Republic of Egypt (ICSID Case No. ARB/02/9)	27 October 2006	Award	1
347	LG&E v Argentina (ICSID Case No. ARB/02/1)	03 October 2006	Decision on Liability	1
348	ADC v Hungary (ICSID Case No. ARB/03/16)	02 October 2006	Award	2
349	Inceysa v El Salvador (ICSID Case No. ARB/03/26)	02 August 2006	Award	6
350	Pan American Energy v Argentina; and BP v Argentina (ICSID Case No. ARB/03/13 & ARB/04/8)	27 July 2006	Decision on Preliminary Objections	3
351	Fireman's Fund Insurnace v Mexico (ICSID Case No. ARB(AF)/02/01)	17 July 2006	Award	1

	Case name	Date	Phase of document	Instances of other law
352	Azurix v Argentina (I) (ICSID Case No. ARB/01/12)	14 July 2006	Award	2
353	Canfor v USA	06 June 2006	Decision of Preliminary Question	2
354	Telefónica v Argentina (ICSID Case No. ARB/03/20)	25 May 2006	Decision on Jurisdiction	1
355	Berschader v Russia (SCC Case No. 080/2004)	21 April 2006	Award	1
356	Saluka v Czech Republic (PCA Case No. 2001–04)	17 March 2006	Partial Award	2
357	International Thunderbird Gaming Corporation v United Mexican States (ad hoc)	26 January 2006	Award	3
358	Vivendi v Argentina (I) (ICSID Case No. ARB/97/3)	14 November 2005	Decision on Jurisdiction	2
359	Aguas del Tunari v Bolivia (ICSID Case No. ARB/02/3)	21 October 2005	Decision on Respondent's Objections to Jurisdiction	1
360	Noble Ventures v Romania (ICSID Case No. ARB/01/11)	12 October 2005	Award	2
361	Canfor v USA	07 September 2005	Order of the Consolidation Tribunal	2
362	Methanex Corporation v USA	03 August 2005	Final Award	5
363	CMS Gas Transmission v Argentina (ICSID Case No. ARB/01/8)	12 May 2005	Award	4
364	Camuzzi International SA v Argentine Republic (I) (ICSID Case No. ARB/03/2)	11 May 2005	Decision on Objections to Jurisdiction	1
365	Sempra v Argentina (ICSID Case No. ARB/02/16)	11 May 2005	Decision on Objections to Jurisdiction	1

	Case name	Date	Phase of document	Instances of other law
366	AES Corporation v Argentine Republic (ICSID Case No. ARB/02/17)	26 April 2005	Decision on Jurisdiction	1
367	Impregilo v Pakistan (II) (ICSID Case No. ARB/03/3)	22 April 2005	Decision on Jurisdiction	4
368	Petrobart v Kyrgyz Republic (SCC Arbitration No. 126/2003)	29 March 2005	Award	2
369	L.E.S.I. v Algeria (ICSID Case No. ARB/03/8)	10 January 2005	Award	1
370	Occidental Exploration and Production Company v Republic of Ecuador (I), LCIA Case No. UN3467	01 July 2004	Award	5
371	PSEG v Turkey (ICSID Case No. ARB/02/5)	04 June 2004	Decision on Jurisdiction	1
372	Saluka v Czech Republic (PCA Case No. 2001–04)	07 May 2004	Decision on Jurisdiction over the Czech Republic's Counterclaim	1
373	LG&E v Argentina (ICSID Case No. ARB/02/1)	30 April 2004	Decision of the Arbitral Tribunal on Objections to Jurisdiction	1
374	Waste Management v Mexico (ICSID Case No. ARB(AF)/00/3	30 April 2004	Final Award	1
375	Tokios Tokeles v Ukraine (ICSID Case No. ARB/02/18)	29 April 2004	Decision on Jurisdiction	2
376	Mitchell v Congo (ICSID Case No. ARB/99/7)	09 February 2004	Final Award	2

	Case name	Date	Phase of document	Instances of other law
377	SGS v Philippines (ICSID Case No. ARB/02/6)	29 January 2004	Decision of the Tribunal on Objections to Jurisdiction	3
378	IBM v Ecuador (ICSID Case No. ARB/02/10)	22 December 2003	Decision on Jurisdiction	1
379	Generation Ukraine v Ukraine (ICSID Case No. ARB/00/9)	16 September 2003	Award	1
380	SGS v Pakistan (ICSID Case No. ARB/01/13)	06 August 2003	Decision on Jurisdiction	3
381	Loewen v USA (ICSID Case No. ARB(AF)/98/3)	26 June 2003	Final Award	1
382	Tecmed v Mexico (ICSID Case No. ARB(AF)/00/2)	29 May 2003	Award	3
383	Yaung Chi v Myanmar (ASEAN ID Case No. ARB/01/1)	31 March 2003	Award	1
384	CME Czech Republic BV v Czech Republic	14 March 2003	Final Award	2
385	ADF v USA (ICSID Case No. ARB(AF)/00/1)	09 January 2003	Award	1
386	Feldman v Mexico (ICSID Case No. ARB(AF)/99/1	16 December 2002	Award	4
387	UPS v Canada (ICSID Case No. UNCT/02/1)	22 November 2002	Award on Jurisdiction	1
388	Mondev International Ltd v United States of America (ICSID Case No. ARB(AF)/99/2)	11 October 2002	Final Award	2
389	Methanex Corporation v USA	07 August 2002	Partial Award	3
390	Vivendi v Argentina (I) (ICSID Case No. ARB/97/3)	03 July 2002	Decision on Annulment	1

	Case name	Date	Phase of document	Instances of other law
391	Waste Management v Mexico (ICSID Case No. ARB(AF)/00/3	26 June 2002	Decision on Mexico's Preliminary Objection concerning the Previous Proceedings	2
392	Middle East Cement Shipping and Handling Co SA v Arab Republic of Egypt (ICSID Case No. ARB/99/6)	12 April 2002	Award	2
393	Wena Hotelas Limited v Arab Republic of Egypt (ICSID Case No. ARB/98/4)	05 February 2002	Annulment Proceeding	1
394	Lauder v Czech Republic (ad hoc)	03 September 2001	Final Award	2
395	Genin v Estonia (ICSID Case No. ARB/99/2)	25 June 2001	Award	1
396	Pope & Talbot v Canada	10 April 2001	Award on the Merits of Phase 2	1
397	Wena Hotelas Limited v Arab Republic of Egypt (ICSID Case No. ARB/98/4)	08 December 2000	Award	2
398	Feldman v Mexico (ICSID Case No. ARB(AF)/99/1	06 December 2000	Decision on Jurisdiction	2
399	Gruslin v Malaysia (II) (ICSID Case No. ARB/99/3)	27 November 2000	Final Award	1
400	S.D. Myers v Canda	13 November 2000	Partial Award	2
401	Metalclad v Mexico (ICSID Case No. ARB(AF)/97/1)	30 August 2000	Award	1
402	Pope & Talbot v Canada	26 June 2000	Interim Award	1

	Case name	Date	Phase of document	Instances of other law
403	CSOB v Slovak Republic (ICSID Case No. ARB/97/4)	24 May 1999	Decision of the Tribunal on Objections to Jurisdiction	2
404	Sedelmayer v Russia	07 July 1998	Arbitration Award	4
405	Ethyl Corporation v Canada (ad hoc)	24 June 1998	Award on Jurisdiction	2
406	AAPL v Sri Lanka (ICSID Case No. ARB/87/3)	27 June 1990	Award	2

References

Table of Cases

International Investment Tribunals

9REN Holding S.a.r.l v Kingdom of Spain (ICSID Case No ARB/15/15), Award, 31 May 2019

A11Y LTD v Czech Republic (ICSID Case No UNCT/15/1), Decision on Jurisdiction, 9 February 2017

Abaclat and Others vs Argentina (ICSID Case No ARB/07/5), Decision on Jurisdiction and Admissibility, 4 August 2011

Adamakopoulos v Cyprus (ICSID Case No ARB/15/49), Decision on Jurisdiction, 7 February 2020

ADF Group Inc v United States of America (ICSID Case No ARB(AF)/00/1, Award, 9 January 2003

Ambiente Ufficio S.pA and others v Argentine Republic (ICSID Case No ARB/08/9), Decision on Jurisdiction and Admissibility, 8 February 2013

Amco Asia Corporation and others v Republic of Indonesia (ICSID Case No ARB/81/1), Decision on the Application for Annulment, 16 May 1986

AMF Aircraftleasing Meier & Fischer GmbH & Co v The Czech Republic (PCA Case No 2017–15), Final Award, 11 May 2020

Ampal-American Israel Corporation v Arab Republic of Egypt (ICSID Case No ARB/12/11), Award, 1 February 2016

AMTO v Ukraine (SCC Case No 080/2005), Final Award, 26 March 2008

Anglia Auto Accessories Ltd v Czech Republic (SCC Case No 2014/181), Final Award, 10 March 2017

Anglo American v Venezuela (ICSID Case No ARB(AF)/14/1), Award, 18 January 2019

Archer Daniels Midland Company v The United Mexican States (ICSID Case No ARB(AF)/04/05), Award, 21 November 2007

Asian Agricultural Products Ltd v Republic of Sri Lanka (ICSID Case No ARB/87/3), Award, 27 June 1990

Austrian Airlines v The Slovak Republic (ad hoc, UNCITRAL), Final Award, 9 October 2009

Azurix v Argentina (I) (ICSID Case No ARB/01/12), Decision on the Application for Annulment of the Argentine Republic, 1 September 2009

Belenergia SA v Italian Republic (ICSID Case No ARB/15/40), Award, 6 August 2019

Bernhard von Pezold v Republic of Zimbabwe (ICSID Case No ARB/10/15), Award, 28 July 2015

Berschader v Russia (SCC Case No 080/2004), Award, 21 April 2006

Besserglik v Mozambique (ICSID Case No ARB(AF)/14/2), Award, 28 October 2019
Blusun SA, Jean-Pierre Lecorcier and Michael Stein v Italian Republic (ICSID Case No ARB/14/3), Award, 27 December 2016
B-Mex, LLC and Others v United Mexican States (ICSID Case No ARB(AF)/16/3), Partial Award, 19 July 2019
Burlington Resources Inc v Republic of Ecuador (ICSID Case No ARB/08/5), Decision on Jurisdiction, 2 June 2010
Burlington Resources Inc v Republic of Ecuador (ICSID Case No ARB/08/5), Decision on Ecuador's Counterclaims, 7 February 2017
Cairn Energy PLC and Cairn UK Holdings Limited (CUHL) v Republic of India (PCA Case No 2016–07), Award, 21 December 2020
Canfor v USA (ad hoc), Order of the Consolidation Tribunal, 7 September 2005
Cargill v Poland (ICSID Case No ARB(AF)/04/2), Award, 29 February 2008
Casinos Austria v Argentina (ICSID Case No ARB/14/32), Decision on Jurisdiction, 29 June 2018
Ceskoslovenska Obchodni Banka, AS v The Slovak Republic (ICSID Case No ARB/97/4), Decision on Objections to Jurisdiction, 24 May 1999
Chevron and TexPet v Ecuador (I) (PCA Case No 2007–02/AA277), Interim Award, 1 December 2008
Chevron and TexPet v Ecuador (II) (PCA Case No 2009–23), Second Partial Award on Track II, 30 August 2018
Churchill Mining PLC and Planet Mining Pty Ltd v Republic of Indonesia (ICSID Case No ARB/12/14 and 12/40), Decision on Annulment, 18 March 2019
Churchill Mining PLC and Planet Mining Pty Ltd v Republic of Indonesia (ICSID Case No ARB/12/14 and 12/40), Award, 6 December 2016
CME Czech Republic BV v Czech Republic (ad hoc), Final Award, 14 March 2003
CMS Gas Transmission v Argentina (ICSID Case No ARB/01/8), Award, 12 May 2005
CMS Gas Transmission v Argentina (ICSID Case No ARB/01/8), Decision of the ad hoc Committee on Argentina's Application for Annulment, 25 September 2007
Continental Casualty v Argentina (ICSID Case No ARB/03/9), Award, 5 September 2008
Continental Casualty v Argentina (ICSID Case No ARB/03/9), Decision on the Application for Partial Annulment, 16 September 2011
Corn Products International Inc v The United Mexican States (ICSID Case No ARB(AF)/04/01), Decision on Responsibility, 15 January 2008
Cube Infrastructure Fund SICAV v Kingdom of Spain (ICSID Case No ARB/15/20), Decision on Jurisdiction, Liability and Partial Decision on Quantum, 19 February 2019
Daimler Financial v Argentina (ICSID Case No ARB/02/1), Award, 22 August 2012
Deutsche Telekom v India (PCA Case No 2014–10), Interim Award, 23 December 2017
Devas v India (PCA Case No 2013–09), Award on Jurisdiction and Merits, 25 July 2016
EDF International v Argentina (ICSID Case No ARB/03/23), Award, 11 June 2012

EDF (Services) v Romania (ICSID Case No ARB/05/13), Award, 8 October 2009
El Paso Energy International Company v The Argentine Republic (ICSID Case No ARB/03/15), Award, 31 October 2011
El Paso Energy International Company v The Argentine Republic (ICSID Case No ARB/03/15), Decision of the Ad Hoc Committee on the Application for Annulment of the Argentine Republic, 22 September 2014
Electrabel SA v Hungary (ICSID Case No ARB/07/19), Award, 25 November 2015
Electrabel SA v Hungary (ICSID Case No ARB/07/19), Decision on Jurisdiction, Applicable Law and Liability, 30 November 2012
Emmis International v Hungary (ICSID Case No ARB/12/2), Decision on Respondent's Objection under ICSID Arbitration Rule 41(5), 11 March 2013
Energoalians v Mongolia (ad hoc), Award, 23 October 2013
Enron Creditors Recovery Corp and Ponderosa Assets, LP v Argentine Republic (ICSID Case No ARB/01/3), Award, 22 May 2007
Enron Creditors Recovery Corp and Ponderosa Assets, LP v Argentine Republic (ICSID Case No ARB/01/3), Decision on the Application for the Annulment of the Argentine Republic, 30 July 2010
Eskosol S.pA in liquidazione v Italian Republic (ICSID Case No ARB/15/50), Decision on Respondent's Application Under Rule 41(5), 20 March 2017
Eskosol S.pA in liquidazione v Italian Republic (ICSID Case No ARB/15/50), Award, 4 September 2020
Eskosol S.pA in liquidazione v Italian Republic (ICSID Case No ARB/15/50), Decision on Termination Request and Intra-EU Objection, 7 May 2019
EuroGas Inc and Belmont Resources Inc v Slovak Republic (ICSID Case No ARB/14/14), Award, 18 August 2017
Europa Nova v The Czech Republic (PCA Case No 2014–19), Award, 15 May 2019
Fraport AG Frankfurt Airport Services Worldwide v Republic of the Philippines (II) (ICSID Case No ARB/11/12), Award, 12 December 2014
García Armas and others v Venezuela (PCA Case No 2016–08), Award on Jurisdiction, 13 December 2019
Glamis Gold Ltd v United States of America (ad hoc, UNCITRAL), Final Award, 9 June 2009
Grand River Enterprises Six Nations Ltd v United States of America (ad hoc, UNCITRAL), Award, 12 January 2011
Greentech Energy Systems A/S, NovEnergia II Energy & Environment (SCA) SICAR, and NovEnergia II Italian Portfolio SA v The Italian Republic (SCC Case No V 2015/095), Award, 23 December 2018
Guris Construction and Engineering Inc and others v Arab Republic of Syria (ICA Case No 21845/ZF/AYZ), Final Award, 31 August 2020
Hesham Talaat M Al-Warraq v The Republic of Indonesia (ad hoc, UNCITRAL), Final Award, 15 December 2014

HOCHTIEF Aktiengesellschaft v Argentine Republic (ICSID Case No ARB/07/31, Decision on Jurisdiction, 24 October 2011)

Hulley Enterprises v Russia (PCA Case No 2005–03/AA226), Final Award, 18 July 2014

Hulley Enterprises v Russia (PCA Case No 2005–03/AA26), Interim Award on Jurisdiction and Admissibility, 30 November 2009

Hydro S.r.l and others v Republic of Albania (ICSID Case No ARB/15/28), Award, 24 April 2019

Iberdrola Energía, SA v Republic of Guatemala (II) (PCA Case No 2017–41), Final Award, 24 August 2020

İçkale İnşaat Limited v Turkmenistan (ICSID Case No ARB/10/24), Award, 8 March 2016

ICW v Czech Republic (PCA Case No 2014–22), Award, 15 May 2019

Impregilo v Argentine Republic (I) (ICSID Case No ARB/07/17), Award, 21 June 2011

Impregilo v Pakistan (II) (ICSID Case No ARB/03/3), Decision on Jurisdiction, 22 April 2005

Inceysa Vallisoletana SL v Republic of El Salvador (ICSID Case No ARB/03/26), Award, 2 August 2006

InfraRed Environmental Infrastructure v Spain (ICSID Case No ARB/14/12), Award, 2 August 2019

Ivan Peter Busta and James Peter Busta v Czech Republic (SCC Case No V2015/014), Final Award, 10 March 2017

Karkey Karadeniz Elektrik Uretim AS v Islamic Republic of Pakistan (ICSID Case No ARB/13/1), Award, 22 August 2017

Kim v Republic of Uzbekistan (ICSID Case No ARB/13/6), Decision on Jurisdiction, 8 March 2017

Klöckner Industrie-Anlagen GmbH and others v United Republic of Cameroon and Société Camerounaise des Engrais (ICSID Case No ARB/81/2), Ad Hoc Committee Decision on Annulment, 3 May 1985

Lauder v Czech Republic (ad hoc), Final Award, 5 September 2001

LG&E v Argentine Republic (ICSID Case No ARB/02/1), Decision on Liability, 3 October 2006

Louis Dreyfus Armateurs SAS v Republic of India (PCA Case No 2014–26), Award, 11 September 2018

Mamidoil Jetoil Greek Petroleum Products Societe SA v Republic of Albania (ICSID Case No ARB/11/24), Award, 30 March 2015

Mason Capital LP and Mason Management LLC v Republic of Korea (PCA Case No 2018–55), Decision on Preliminary Objections, 22 December 2019

Metal-Tech Ltd v Republic of Uzbekistan (ICSID Case No ARB/10/3), Award, 4 October 2013

Methanex Corporation v United States of America (ad hoc, UNCITRAL), Final Award, 3 August 2005

Micula v Romania (I) (ICSID Case No ARB/05/20), Decision on Annulment, 26 February 2016

Mobil Corporation (now Venezuela Holdings BV) v Venezuela (ICSID Case No ARB/07/27), Decision on Annulment, 9 March 2017

Mobil Exploration and Development v Argentine Republic (ICSID Case No ARB/04/16), Decision on Annulment, 8 May 2019

Mobil Exploration and Development v Argentine Republic (ICSID Case No ARB/04/16), Decision on Jurisdiction and Liability, 10 April 2013

National Grid PLC v The Argentine Republic (ad hoc, UNCITRAL), Award, 3 November 2008

Oxus Gold v Uzbekistan (ad hoc), Final Award, 17 December 2015

Oztas Construction v Libya (ICA Case No 21603/ZF/AYZ), Final Award, 14 June 2018

Pac Rim Cayman LLC v Republic of El Salvador (ICSID Case No ARB/09/12), Award, 14 October 2016)

Pan American Energy v Argentina; BP v Argentina (ICSID Case No ARB/03/13 and 04/8), Decision on Preliminary Objection, 27 July 2006

Perenco Ecuador Ltd v Republic of Ecuador and Empresa Estatal Petróleos del Ecuador (ICSID Case No ARB/08/6), Award, 27 September 2019

Perenco Ecuador Ltd v Republic of Ecuador and Empresa Estatal Petróleos del Ecuador (ICSID Case No ARB/08/6), Decision on Jurisdiction, 30 June 2011

Philip Morris Brands SARL v Oriental Republic of Uruguay (ICSID Case No ARB/10/7), Award, 8 July 2016

Phoenix Action v Czech Republic (ICSID Case No ARB/06/5), Award, 15 April 2009

Photovoltaik Knopf Betriebs v The Czech Republic (PCA Case No 2014–21), Award, 15 May 2019

Plama Consortium Limited v Republic of Bulgaria (ICSID Case No ARB/03/24), Award, 27 August 2008

Pope & Talbot v Canada (UNCITRAL, ad hoc, Award in Respect of Damages, 31 May 2002)

PV Investors v Spain (PCA Case No 2012–14), Final Award, 28 February 2020

Quasar de Valors v Russia (SCC Case No 24/2007), Award, 20 July 2012

Renco Group Inc v Republic of Peru (II) (PCA Case No 2019–46), Decision on Expedited Preliminary Objections, 30 June 2020

Romak SA v The Republic of Uzbekistan (PCA Case No 2007–07/AA280), Award, 26 November 2009

RosInvestCo UK Ltd v The Russian Federation (SCC Case No 079/2005), Final Award, 12 September 2010

RosInvestCo UK Ltd v The Russian Federation (SCC Case No V079/2005), Award on Jurisdiction, October 2007

RREEF v Spain (ICSID Case No ARB/13/30), Decision on Responsibility and the Principles of Quantum, 30 November 2018

RWE Innogy GmbH and RWE Innogy Aersa SAU v Kingdom of Spain (ICSID Case No ARB/14/34), Award, 18 December 2020

Saipem S.pA v The People's Republic of Bangladesh (ICSID Case No ARB/05/07), Decision on Jurisdiction and Provisional Measures, 21 March 2007

Salini Impregilo S.pA v Argentine Republic (ICSID Case No ARB/15/39), Decision on Jurisdiction and Admissibility, 23 February 2018

Sanum Investments v Laos (I) (PCA Case No 2013–13), Award, 6 August 2019

Sanum Investments v Laos (I) (PCA Case No 2013–13), Award on Jurisdiction, 13 December 2013

Sedelmayer v Russia (ad hoc), Arbitration Award, 7 July 1998

Sempra v Argentine Republic (ICSID Case No ARB/02/16), Award, 28 September 2007

Sempra v Argentine Republic (ICSID Case No ARB/02/16), Decision on the Argentine Republic's Application for Annulment of the Award, 29 June 2010

SGS Société Générale de Surveillance SA v Islamic Republic of Pakistan (ICSID Case No ARB/01/13), Decision on Jurisdiction, 6 August 2003

SGS Société Générale de Surveillance SA v Republic of the Philippines (ICSID Case No ARB/02/6), Decision of the Tribunal on Objections to Jurisdiction, 29 January 2004

Siemens AG v Argentine Republic (ICSID Case No ARB/02/8), Award, 6 February 2007

South American Silver Limited (Bermuda) v The Plurinational State of Bolivia (PCA Case No 2013–15), Award, 22 November 2018

Southern Pacific Properties (Middle East) Ltd v Arab Republic of Egypt (ICSID Case No ARB/84/3), Preliminary Objections to Jurisdiction, 14 April 1988

ST-AD v Bulgaria (PCA Case No 2001–06), Award on Jurisdiction, 18 July 2013

Standard Chartered Bank (Hong Kong) Limited v Tanzania Electric Supply Company Limited (ICSID Case No ARB/10/20), Decision on Annulment, 22 August 2018

Stati v Kazakhstan (SCC Case No 116/2010), Award, 19 December 2013

SunReserve Luxco Holdings SARL v The Italian Republic (SCC Arbitration V 2016/32), Final Award, 25 March 2020

Tatneft v Ukraine (PCA Case No 2008–8), Partial Award on Jurisdiction, 28 September 2010

Tenaris SA & Talta v Venezuela (II) (ICSID Case No ARB/12/23), Decision on Annulment, 28 December 2018

Tethyan Copper Company Pty Limited v Islamic Republic of Pakistan (ICSID Case No ARB/12/1), Decision on Jurisdiction and Liability, 10 November 2017

The Rompetrol Group NV v Romania (ICSID Case No ARB/06/3), Award, 6 May 2013

Thomas Gosling and others v Republic of Mauritius (ICSID Case No ARB/16/32), Award, 18 February 2020

Toto v Lebanon (ICSID Case No ARB/07/12), Decision on Jurisdiction, 11 September 2009

Tulip Real Estate v Turkey (ICSID Case No ARB/11/28), Decision on Annulment, 30 December 2015
UAB E energija (Lithuania) v Republic of Latvia (ICSID Case No ARB/12/33), Award, 22 December 2017
Unión Fenosa Gas v Egypt (ICSID Case No ARB/14/4), Award, 31 August 2018
Urbaser SA v Argentine Republic (ICSID Case No ARB/07/26), Decision on Jurisdiction, 19 December 2012
Urbaser SA v Argentine Republic (ICSID Case No ARB/07/26), Award, 8 December 2016
Vattenfall AB and others v Federal Republic of Germany (II) (ICSID Case No ARB/12/12), Decision on the Achmea Issue, 31 August 2018
Veteran Petroleum Limited v The Russian Federation (PCA Case No 2005–05/AA28), Final Award, 18 July 2014
Veteran Petroleum Limited v The Russian Federation (PCA Case No 2005–05/AA28), Interim Award on Jurisdiction and Admissibility, 30 November 2009
Víctor Pey Casado and President Allende Foundation v Republic of Chile (I) (ICSID Case No ARB/98/2), Award, 8 May 2008
Voltaic Network v Czech Republic (PCA Case No 2014–20), Award, 15 May 2019
Wena Hotels Limited v Arab Republic of Egypt (ICSID Case No ARB/94/4), Decision on the Application by the Arab Republic of Egypt for Annulment, 5 February 2002
Windstream Energy v Canada (PCA Case No 2013–22), Award, 27 September 2016
Wintershall Aktiengesellschaft v Argentine Republic (ICSID Case No ARB/04/14), Award, 8 December 2008
WNC Factoring Limited v The Czech Republic (PCA Case No 2014–34), Award, 22 February 2017
Yukos Universal Limited (Isle of Man) v The Russian Federation (PCA Case No 2005–04/AA27), Final Award, 18 July 2014
Yukos Universal Limited (Isle of Man) v The Russian Federation (PCA Case No 2005–04/AA27), Interim Award on Jurisdiction and Admissibility, 30 November 2009

World Trade Organization

Argentina – Definitive Anti-Dumping Duties on Poultry from Brazil (Report of the Panel) (22 April 2003), WT/DS241/R
Australia – Certain Measures Concerning Trademarks, Geographical Indications and Other Plain Packaging Requirements Applicable to Tobacco Products and Packaging (Reports of the Appellate Body) (9 June 2020), WT/DS435/AB/R ; WT/DS441/AB/R
Australia – Measures Affecting the Importation of Apples from New Zealand (Report of the Panel) (9 August 2010), WT/DS367/R
Australia – Measures Affecting the Importation of Salmon (Report of the Appellate Body) (6 November 1998), WT/DS18/AB/R

Brazil – Measures Affecting Desiccated Coconut (Report of the Appellate Body) (21 February 1997), WT/DS22/AB/R

China – Measures Imposing Anti-Dumping Duties on High-Performance Stainless Steel Seamless Tubes (HP-SSST) from Japan / China – Measures Imposing Anti-Dumping Duties on High-Performance Stainless Steel Seamless Tubes (HP-SSST) from the European Union (Report of the Appellate Body) (14 October 2015), WT/DS454/AB/R; WT/DS460/AB/R

China – Measures Related to the Exportation of Various Raw Materials (Reports of the Panel) (5 July 2011), WT/DS394/R; WT/DS395/R; WT/DS398/R

European Communities – Anti-Dumping Duties on Imports of Cotton-Type Bed Linen from India – Recourse to Article 21.5 of the DSU by India (Report of the Panel) (29 November 2002), WT/DS141/RW

European Communities – Customs Classification of Frozen Boneless Chicken Cuts – Complaint by Brazil (Report of the Panel) (30 May 2005), WT/DS269/R

European Communities – Customs Classification of Frozen Boneless Chicken Cuts – Complaint by Thailand (Report of the Panel) (30 May 2005), WT/DS286/R

European Communities – Customs Classification of Frozen Boneless Chicken Cuts (Report of the Appellate Body) (12 September 2005), WT/DS269/AB/R ; WT/DS286/AB/R

European Communities – Export Subsidies on Sugar (Report of the Appellate Body) (28 April 2005), WT/DS265/AB/R ; WT/DS266/AB/R ; WT/DS283/AB/R

European Communities – Measures Affecting Asbestos and Products Containing Asbestos (Report of the Appellate Body) (12 March 2001), WT/DS135/AB/R

European Communities – Measures Affecting the Approval and Marketing of Biotech Products (Report of the Panel) (29 September 2006), WT/DS291/R; WT/DS292/R; WT/DS293/R

European Communities – Measures Affecting Trade in Large Civil Aircraft (Report of the Panel) (30 June 2010) WT/DS316/R

European Communities – Measures Concerning Meat and Meat Products (Hormones) (Report of the Appellate Body) (16 January 1998), WT/DS26/AB/R ; WT/DS48/AB/R

European Communities – Regime for the Importation, Sale and Distribution of Bananas – Recourse to Article 21.5 of the DSU by the United States (Report of the Panel) (19 May 2008), WT/DS27/RW/USA

European Communities – Regime for the Importation, Sale and Distribution of Bananas – Second Recourse to Article 21.5 (Report of the Appellate Body) (26 November 2008), WT/DS27/AB/RW/USA ; WT/DS27/AB/RW2/ECU

European Communities – Regime for the Importation, Sale and Distribution of Bananas (Report of the Appellate Body) (9 September 1997) WT/DS27/AB/R

European Communities – Regime for the Importation, Sale and Distribution of Bananas – Complaint by the United States (Report of the Panel) (22 May 1997), WT/DS27/R/USA

European Union – Cost Adjustment Methodologies and Certain Anti-Dumping Measures on Imports from Russia (Second Complaint) (Report of the Panel) (24 July 2020), WT/DS494/R

European Union – Measures Affecting Tariff Concessions on Certain Poultry Meat Products (Report of the Panel) (28 March 2017), WT/DS492/R

Guatemala – Definitive Anti-Dumping Measures on Grey Portland Cement from Mexico (Report of the Panel) (24 October 2000), WT/DS156/R

India – Certain Measures Relating to Solar Cells and Solar Modules (Report of the Appellate Body) (24 February 2016), WT/DS456/AB/R

India – Measures Affecting the Automotive Sector (Report of the Panel) (21 December 2001), WT/DS146/R ; WT/DS175/R

India – Patent Protection for Pharmaceutical and Agricultural Chemical Products (Report of the Appellate Body) (19 December 1997), WT/DS50/AB/R

India – Quantitative Restrictions on Imports of Agricultural, Textile and Industrial Products (Report of the Appellate Body) (23 August 1999), WT/DS90/AB/R

Japan – Taxes on Alcoholic Beverages (Report of the Appellate Body) (4 October 1996), WT/DS8/AB/R; WT/DS10/AB/R; WT/DS11/AB/R

Korea – Measures Affecting Government Procurement (Report of the Panel) (1 May 2000) WT/DS163/R

Korea – Sunset Review of Anti-Dumping Duties on Stainless Steel Bars (Report of the Panel) (30 November 2020), WT/DS553/R

Mexico – Anti-Dumping Investigation of High Fructose Corn Syrup (HFCS) from the United States – Recourse to Article 21.5 of the DSU by the United States (Report of the Appellate Body) (22 October 2001) WT/DS132/AB/RW

Mexico – Tax Measures on Soft Drinks and Other Beverages (Report of the Appellate Body) (6 March 2006) WT/DS308/AB/R

Mexico – Tax Measures on Soft Drinks and Other Beverages (Report of the Panel) (7 October 2005) WT/DS308/R

Peru – Additional Duty on Imports of Certain Agricultural Products (Report of the Appellate Body) (20 July 2015) WT/DS457/AB/R

Peru – Additional Duty on Imports of Certain Agricultural Products (Report of the Panel) (27 November 2014) WT/DS457/R

Philippines – Taxes on Distilled Spirits (Report of the Panel) (15 August 2011), WT/DS396/R ; WT/DS403/R

Russia – Measures Concerning Traffic in Transit (Report of the Panel) (5 April 2019), WT/DS512/R

Saudi Arabia – Measures concerning the Protection of Intellectual Property Rights (Report of the Panel) (16 June 2020), WT/DS/567/R

Thailand – Customs and Fiscal Measures on Cigarettes from the Philippines – Recourse to article 21.5 of the DSU by the Philippines (Report of the Panel) (12 November 2018), WT/DS371/RW

Thailand – Customs and Fiscal Measures on Cigarettes from the Philippines – Second recourse to article 21.5 of the DSU by the Philippines (Report of the Panel) (12 July 2019), WT/DS371/R.W2

Ukraine – Anti-Dumping Measures on Ammonium Nitrate (Report of the Appellate Body) (12 September 2019), WT/DS493/AB/R

United States – Anti-Dumping Act of 1916 – Complaint by Japan (Report of the Panel) (29 May 2000), WT/DS162/R

United States – Anti-Dumping Act of 1916 – Complaint by the European Communities (Report of the Panel) (31 March 2000), WT/DS136/R

United States – Anti-Dumping Act of 1916 (Report of the Appellate Body) (28 August 2000) WT/DS136/AB/R ; WT/DS/162/AB/R

United States – Anti-Dumping and Countervailing Measures on Certain Coated Paper from Indonesia (Report of the Panel) (6 December 2017), WT/DS491/R

United States – Anti-Dumping Measures on Certain Hot-Rolled Steel Products from Japan (Report of the Appellate Body) (24 July 2001), WT/DS184/AB/R

United States – Certain Methodologies and their Application to Anti-Dumping Proceedings Involving China (Report of the Panel) (19 October 2016), WT/DS471/R

United States – Continued Existence and Application of Zeroing Methodology (Report of the Appellate Body) (4 February 2009), WT/DS350/AB/R

United States – Countervailing and Anti-Dumping Measures on Certain Products from China (Report of the Panel) (27 March 2014), WT/DS449/R

United States – Countervailing Duties on Certain Corrosion-Resistant Carbon Steel Flat Products from Germany (Report of the Appellate Body) (28 November 2002), WT/DS213/AB/R

United States – Countervailing Duty Measures on Certain Products from China – Recourse to Article 21.5 of the DSU by China (Final Report of the Panel) (21 March 2018), WT/DS437/RW

United States – Countervailing Duty Measures on Certain Products from China (Report of the Panel) (14 July 2014), WT/DS437/R

United States – Countervailing Measures on Certain Hot-Rolled Carbon Steel Flat Products from India (Report of the Appellate Body) (8 December 2014), WT/DS/436/AB/R

United States – Definitive Anti-Dumping and Countervailing Duties on Certain Products from China (Report of the Appellate Body) (11 March 2011), WT/DS379/AB/R

United States – Definitive Anti-Dumping and Countervailing Duties on Certain Products from China (Report of the Panel) (22 October 2010), WT/DS379/R

United States – Definitive Safeguard Measures on Imports of Circular Welded Carbon Quality Line Pipe from Korea (Report of the Appellate Body) (15 February 2002), WT/DS202/AB/R

United States – Final Anti-Dumping Measures on Stainless Steel from Mexico (Report of the Appellate Body) (30 April 2008), WT/DS344/AB/R

United States – Import Measures on Certain Products from the European Communities (Report of the Panel) (17 July 2000), WT/DS165/R

United States – Import Prohibition of Certain Shrimp and Shrimp Products – Recourse to Article 21.5 by Malaysia (Report of the Panel) (15 June 2001), WT/DS58/RW

United States – Import Prohibition of Certain Shrimp and Shrimp Products (Report of the Appellate Body) (12 October 1998), WT/DS58/AB/R

United States – Measures Affecting the Production and Sale of Clove Cigarettes (Report of the Appellate Body) (4 April 2012), WT/DS406/AB/R

United States – Measures Affecting Trade in Large Civil Aircraft (Second Complaint) – Recourse to Article 21.5 of the DSU by the European Union (Report of the Panel) (9 June 2017), WT/DS353/RW

United States – Measures Affecting Trade in Large Civil Aircraft (Second Complaint) (Report of the Panel) (31 March 2011), WT/DS353/R

United States – Section 110(5) of the US Copyright Act (Report of the Panel) (15 June 2000), WT/DS160/R

United States – Sections 301–310 of the Trade Act of 1974 (Report of the Panel) (22 December 1999), WT/DS152/R

United States – Standards for Reformulated and Conventional Gasoline (Report of the Appellate Body) (29 April 1996), WT/DS2/AB/R

United States – Standards for Reformulated and Conventional Gasoline (Report of the Panel) (29 January 1996), WT/DS2/R

United States – Tariff Measures on Certain Goods from China (Report of the Panel) (15 September 2020), WT/DS543/R

United States – Transitional Safeguard Measure on Combed Cotton Yarn from Pakistan (Report of the Appellate Body) (8 October 2001) WT/DS192/AB/R

United States – Wool Shirts and Blouses (Report of the Appellate Body) (25 April 1997), WT/DS33/AB/R

United States/Canada – Continued Suspension of Obligations in the EC-Hormones Dispute (Report of the Appellate Body) (16 October 2008), WT/DS320/AB/R; WT/DS321/AB/R

United States/Canada – Continued Suspension of Obligations in the EC-Hormones Dispute (Report of the Panel) (31 March 2008), WT/DS320/AB/R; WT/DS321/R

International Court of Justice

Ahmadou Sadio Diallo (Republic Guinea v Democratic Republic of the Congo), Judgment [2012] ICJ Reports 324

Ambatielos Case (Greece v United Kingdom), Judgment [1953] ICJ Reports 10

Application of the Convention on the Prevention and Punishment of the Crime of Genocide (Bosnia and Herzegovina v Serbia and Montenegro), Judgment [2007] ICJ Reports 43

Application of the Convention on the Prevention and Punishment of the Crime of Genocide (Croatia v Serbia), Judgment [2015] ICJ Reports 3

Application of the Convention on the Prevention and Punishment of the Crime of Genocide (Croatia v Serbia), Preliminary Objection, Judgment [2008] ICJ Reports 412

Application of the International Convention for the Suppression of the Financing of Terrorism and of the International Convention on the Elimination of all Forms of Racial Discrimination (Ukraine v Russian Federation), Preliminary Objection [2019] ICJ Reports 558

Application of the International Convention on the Elimination of All Forms of Racial Discrimination (Georgia v Russian Federation), Preliminary Objections, Judgment of 1 April 2011 [2011] ICJ Reports 70

Corfu Channel Case (United Kingdom v Albania), Preliminary Objection [1948] ICJ Reports 15

Delimitation of the Maritime Boundary in the Gulf of Maine Area (Canada v United States of America), Judgment [1984] ICJ Reports 246

Effect of Awards of Compensation made by the United Nations Administrative Tribunal, Advisory Opinion [1954] ICJ Reports 47

Elettronica Sicula S.pA (ELSI) (United States of America v Italy), Judgment [1989] ICJ Reports 15

Factory at Chorzów (Germany v Poland), Jurisdiction [1927] PCIJ Rep Series A No 9

Gabčíkovo-Nagymaros Project (Hungary v Slovakia), Judgment [1997] ICJ Rep 7

Interpretation of the Greco-Turkish Agreement of December 1st, 1926, Advisory Opinion [1928] PCIJ Rep B No 16

Judgments of the Administrative Tribunal of the ILO upon complaints made against the UNESCO, Advisory Opinion [1956] ICJ Reports 77

Judgments of the Courts of Danzig, Advisory Opinion [1928] PCIJ Report Series B No 15

Kasikili/Sedudu Island (Botswana v Namibia), Judgment [1999] ICJ Reports 1045

Legal Consequences of the Construction of a Wall in the Occupied Palestinian Territory, Advisory Opinion [2004] ICJ Reports 38

Legality of the Threat or Use of Nuclear Weapons, Advisory Opinion [1996] ICJ Reports 226

Legality of the Use of Force (Serbia and Montenegro v Belgium), Preliminary Objections [2004] ICJ Reports 279

Military and Paramilitary Activities in and Against Nicaragua (Nicaragua v United States of America), Judgment [1986] ICJ Reports 14

Military and Paramilitary Activities in and Against Nicaragua (Nicaragua v United States of America), Jurisdiction and Admissibility [1984] ICJ Reports 392

Monetary Gold Removed from Rome in 1943 (Italy v France, UK and USA), Preliminary Question, Judgment [1954] ICJ Reports 19

North Sea Continental Shelf (Federal Republic of Germany v Denmark), Judgment [1969] ICJ Reports 3

Northern Cameroons (Cameroon v United Kingdom), Preliminary Objections [1963] ICJ Reports 14

Nottebohm (Liechtenstein v Guatemala), Preliminary Objections [1953] ICJ Reports 111

Nuclear Tests (Australia v France), Merits, Judgment [1974] ICJ Reports 253

Obligation to Negotiate Access to the Pacific Ocean (Bolivia v Chile), Judgment [2018] ICJ Reports 507

Oil Platforms (Islamic Republic of Iran v United States of America), Judgment [2003] ICJ Reports 161

Oil Platforms (Islamic Republic of Iran v United States of America), Preliminary Objection, Judgment [1996] ICJ Reports 803

Pulp Mills on the River Uruguay (Argentina v Uruguay), Judgment [2010] ICJ Reports 14

Request for Interpretation of the Judgment of 15 June 1962 in the Case Concerning the Temple of Preah Vihear (Cambodia v Thailand) (Cambodia v Thailand), Judgment [2013] ICJ Reports 281

Rights of Minorities in Upper Silesia (Minority Schools) (Germany v Poland), Judgment [1928] PCIJ Rep Series A No 15

SS Lotus (France v Turkey), Judgment [1927] PCIJ Series A No 10

Status of Eastern Carelia, Advisory Opinion [1923] PCIJ Report Series B No 5

The Barcelona Traction, Light and Power Company Limited (New Application: 1962) (Belgium v Spain), Second Phase, Judgment [1970] ICJ Reports 3

The Mavrommatis Palestine Concessions (Greece v United Kingdom), Objection to Jurisdiction [1924] PCIJ Rep Series A No 2

Others

Access to Information under Article 9 of the OSPAR Convention (Ireland v United Kingdom) (PCA Case No 2001–03), Final Award, 2 July 2003, (2003) 42 ILM 118

Amoco International Finance Corporation v The Government of the Islamic Republic of Iran and others (1987) 15 Iran-US CTR 189

Arctic Sunrise (Netherlands v Russia) (PCA Case No 2014–02), Award on the Merits, 14 August 2015

Cases of Dual Nationality – Decision No 22 (Anglo-Italian Conciliation Commission) (1954) 14 UNRIAA 27

Genie Lantman Elton (USA) v United Mexican States (Mexico-United States, General Claims Commission, 13 May 1929) (1929) IV UNRIAA 529

Guyana v Suriname (PCA Case No 2004–04), Award of the Arbitral Tribunal, 17 September 2007, (2007) 47 ILM 166

Ibrahim Aboukhalil v Senegal (UNCITRAL, ad hoc), Judgement of the Paris Court of Appeal, 12 October 2021 (N° RG 19/21625 – N° Portalis 35L7-VB7D-CBBL2)

Islamic Republic of Iran v United States (IUSCT Case No A/1), Decision (DEC8-A1-FT), 17 May 1982, (1982) 1 Iran-US CTR 144

M/V Saiga (No 2) (St Vincent v Guinea) (ITLOS Case No 2), Judgment, 1 July 1999

Prosecutor v Tadić (ICTY Case No IT-94–1-A), Judgment of the Appeals Chamber, 15 July 1999

Southern Bluefin Tuna (New Zealand v Japan, Australia v Japan), Award on Jurisdiction and Admissibility, 4 August 2000, XXIII UNRIAA 1

The MOX Plant Case (Ireland v United Kingdom) (PCA 2002–01), Suspension of Proceedings on Jurisdiction and Merits, Order of 24 June 2003

The MOX Plant Case (Ireland v United Kingdom) (PCA 2002–01), Counter-Memorial of the United Kingdom, 9 January 2003

The MOX Plant Case (Ireland v United Kingdom), Provisional Measures, Order of 3 December 2001, ITLOS Reports 95

Table of Treaties and Other Instruments

1907 Convention for the Pacific Settlement of International Disputes (The Hague, concluded 18 October 1907), 1 Bevans 577

Agreement between the Argentine Republic and the Italian Republic on Investment Promotion and Protection (Buenos Aires, 22 May 1990)

Agreement between the European Economic Community and the Government of the United States of America concerning the application of the GATT on Trade in Civil Aircraft, Official Journal L 301 (17 October 1992)

Agreement between the Government of the Hellenic Republic and the Government of the Republic of Albania for the Encouragement and Reciprocal Protection of Investments (Tirana, 1 August 1991)

Agreement between the Government of the People's Republic of China and the Government of the Lao People's Democratic Republic concerning the Encouragement and Reciprocal Protection of Investments (Vientiane, 31 January 1993)

Agreement between the Government of the Republic of Uzbekistan and the Government of the Republic of Korea for the Reciprocal Promotion and Protection of Investments (Tashkent, 19 April 2019)

Agreement between the Government of the United Kingdom and Northern Ireland and the Government of the Republic of Argentina for the Promotion and Protection of Investments (London, 11 December 1990)

Agreement between the Government of the United Kingdom of Great Britain and Northern Ireland and the Government of the Czech and Slovak Federal Republic for the Promotion and Protection of Investments (Prague, 10 July 1990)

Agreement between the Kingdom of Spain and the Republic of El Salvador on the Reciprocal Promotion and Protection of Investments (San Salvador, 14 February 1995)

Agreement between the Republic of Zimbabwe and the Federal Republic of Germany concerning the Encouragement and Reciprocal Protection of Investments (Harare, 29 September 1995)

Agreement between the Swiss Confederation and the Republic of Zimbabwe on the Protection of Investments (Harare, 15 August 1996)

Agreement for the Promotion and Reciprocal Protection of Investments between the Kingdom of Spain and the Republic of Argentina (Buenos Aires, 3 October 1991), 1699 UNTS 203

Agreement for the Reciprocal Promotion and Protection of Investments between the Argentine Republic and the United Arab Emirates (Abu Dhabi, 16 April 2018)

Agreement for the Reciprocal Promotion and Protection of Investments between the Kingdom of Spain and the Republic of Egypt (Madrid, 3 November 1992)

Agreement on Government Procurement (Geneva, 12 April 1979), 1235 UNTS 258

Agreement on Safeguards, Marrakesh Agreement Establishing the World Trade Organization, Annex 1A (15 April 1994), 1869 UNTS 154

Agreement on Subsidies and Countervailing Measures, Marrakesh Agreement Establishing the World Trade Organization, Annex 1B (15 April 1994), 1869 UNTS 14

Agreement on Textiles and Clothing, Marrakesh Agreement Establishing the World Trade Organization, Annex 1A (15 April 1994, terminated 1 January 2005), 1868 UNTS 14

Agreement on the Application of Sanitary and Phytosanitary Measures, Marrakesh Agreement Establishing the World Trade Organization, Annex 1A (15 April 1994), 1867 UNTS 493

Charter of the United Nations (San Francisco, 24 October 1945), 1 UNTS XVI

Convention for the Promotion and Reciprocal Protection of Investments between Spain and the Russian Federation (Madrid, 26 October 1990)

Convention for the Protection of the Marine Environment of the North-East Atlantic (Paris, 22 September 1992), 2354 UNTS 67

Convention on Access to Information, Public Participation in Decision-making and Access to Justice in Environmental Matters (25 June 1998), 38 ILM 517

Convention on Biological Diversity (Rio de Janeiro, 5 June 1992), 1760 UNTS 79

Convention on the Prevention and Punishment of the Crime of Genocide (9 December 1948), 78 UNTS 277

Convention on the Recognition and Enforcement of Foreign Arbitral Awards (New York, 10 June 1958), 330 UNTS 3

Convention on the Settlement of Investment Disputes Between States and Nationals of Other States (Washington, 18 March 1965), 575 UNTS 159

European Convention for the Protection of Human Rights and Fundamental Freedoms (4 November 1950, as amended by Protocols No. 11 and 14), ETS 5

Final Act of the Conference to Conclude a Convention on the Conservation of Migratory Species of Wild Animals (Bonn, 23 June 1979), 19 ILM 11

Free Trade Agreement between Peru and the Republic of Guatemala (Tratado de libre comercio entre la República del Perú y la República de Guatemala), 6 December 2011

General Agreement on Tariffs and Trade (30 October 1947), 55 UNTS 194

ICSID Additional Facility Rules (effective as of 27 September 1978)

ICSID Arbitration Rules (effective as of 10 April 2006)

International Court of Arbitration of the International Chamber of Commerce, Arbitration Rules (in force as from 1 March 2017)

International Covenant on Civil and Political Rights (19 December 1966), 999 UNTS 171

Marrakesh Agreement Establishing the World Trade Organization (15 April 1994), 1867 UNTS 154

North American Free Trade Agreement (17 December 1992), 32 ILM 289

Permanent Court of Arbitration Optional Rules for Arbitrating Disputes Between Two Parties of Which Only One Is a State (effective 6 July 1993)

Responsibility of States for Internationally Wrongful Acts (adopted by the International Law Commission at its fifty-third session, 2001)

Rome Statute of the International Criminal Court (adopted 17 July 1998), 2187 UNTS 90

Statute of the International Court of Justice (San Francisco, concluded 26 June 1945), 3 Bevans 1179

Statute of the Permanent Court of International Justice (16 December 1920, as amended by Protocol of 14 September 1929)

Statute of the River Uruguay, a treaty signed by Argentina and Uruguay (26 February 1975), 1295 UNTS 340

The Energy Charter Treaty (Lisbon, 17 December 1994), 2080 UNTS 95

Treaty between United States of America and The Argentine Republic concerning the Reciprocal Encouragement and Protection of Investment (Washington, 14 November 1991)

Treaty of Amity, Economic Relations and Consular Rights between the United States and Iran (Tehran, signed 15 August 1955)

Treaty of Friendship, Commerce and Navigation between the United States of America and the Republic of Nicaragua (Managua, 21 January 1956), 3567 UNTS 3

UNCITRAL Arbitration Rules (with new article 1, paragraph 4, as adopted in 2013)

Understanding on Rules and Procedures Governing the Settlement of Disputes, Marrakesh Agreement Establishing the World Trade Organization, Annex 2 (15 April 1994), 1869 UNTS 401

United Nations Convention on the Law of the Sea (Montego Bay, 10 December 1982), 1833 UNTS 397

Universal Declaration of Human Rights (adopted 10 December 1948), UNGA Res 217 A(III)

Vienna Convention on Consular Relations (Vienna, 24 April 1963), 596 UNTS 261

Vienna Convention on Diplomatic Relations (Vienna, 18 April 1961), 500 UNTS 95

Vienna Convention on the Law of Treaties (Vienna, 23 May 1969), 1155 UNTS 331

Table of Reports and Documents

Agenda 21, adopted by the United Nations Conference on Environment and Development, 14 June 1992, UN Doc. A/CONF.151/26/Rev.1

Council of Australian Law Deans, 'Statement on the Nature of Legal Research' <https://cald.asn.au/wp-content/uploads/2017/11/cald-statement-on-the-nature-of-legal-research-20051.pdf> accessed 8 December 2023

General Agreement on Tariffs and Trade, 'Understanding Regarding Notification, Consultation, Dispute Settlement and Surveillance: Adopted on 28 November 1979, GATT Doc No. L/4907.' <https://exhibits.stanford.edu/gatt/catalog/kb635pf3561> accessed 15 October 2019

International Center for Settlement of Investment Disputes, '2020 ICSID Annual Report' (2020)

International Center for Settlement of Investment Disputes, 'Denunciation of ICSID Convention' (*ICSID News Releases*, 16 May 2007) <https://icsid.worldbank.org/news-and-events/news-releases/denunciation-icsid-convention> accessed 12 April 2021

International Center for Settlement of Investment Disputes, 'Denunciation of the ICSID Convention by Ecuador' (*ICSID News Releases*, 7 September 2009) <https://icsid.worldbank.org/news-and-events/news-releases/denunciation-icsid-convention-ecuador> accessed 12 April 2021

International Center for Settlement of Investment Disputes, The History of the ICSID Convention: Documents Concerning the Origin and the Formulation of the Convention on the Settlement of Investment Disputes between States and Nationals of Other States, vol II (1970)

International Center for Settlement of Investment Disputes, 'The ICSID Caseload – Statistics' (International Center for Settlement of Investment Disputes 2020) Issue 2021–1

International Center for Settlement of Investment Disputes, 'Venezuela Submits a Notice under Article 71 of the ICSID Convention' (*ICSID News Releases*, 26 January 2012) <https://icsid.worldbank.org/news-and-events/news-releases/venezuela-submits-notice-under-article-71-icsid-convention> accessed 12 April 2021

Dunkel A, Sutherland P and Ruggiero R, 'Joint Statement on the Multilateral Trading System' (*World Trade Organization*, 1 February 2001) <https://www.wto.org/english/news_e/news01_e/jointstatdavos_jan01_e.htm> accessed 17 December 2020

European Commission, 'Concept Paper: WTO Modernization, 18 September 2018' <https://trade.ec.europa.eu/doclib/docs/2018/september/tradoc_157331.pdf> accessed 4 December 2018

European Commission, 'The WTO Multi-Party Interim Appeal Arrangement Gets Operational' (*Trade – European Commission*, 3 August 2020) <https://trade.ec.europa.eu/doclib/press/index.cfm?id=2176> accessed 10 August 2021

Hafner G, 'Risks Ensuing from Fragmentation of International Law' (International Law Commission 2000) ILC (LII)/WG/LT.1/Add.1

International Bank for Reconstruction and Development, 'Report of the Executive Directors on the Convention on the Settlement of Investment Disputes between States and Nationals of Other States' (International Bank for Reconstruction and Development 1965)

International Court of Justice, 'Statement of H.E. Mr. Abdulqawi Ahmed Yusuf, President of the International Court of Justice before the Sixth Committee of the General Assembly, New York', 1 November 2009

International Court of Justice, 'The Proliferation of International Judicial Bodies: The Outlook for the International Legal Order, Speech by H.E Judge Gilbert Guillaume, President of the International Court of Justice, to the Sixth Committee of the General Assembly of the United Nations, 27 October 2000' <https://www.icj-cij.org/public/files/press-releases/1/3001.pdf> accessed 10 December 2020

International Law Commission, 'Report of the International Law Commission on the Work of Its Seventy-Second Session' (International Law Commission 2021) A/76/10

Koskenniemi M, 'Fragmentation of International Law: Difficulties Arising from the Diversification and Expansion of International Law, Report of the Study Group of the International Law Commission' (International Law Commission 2006) A/CN.4/L.682

NAFTA Free Trade Commission, 'Notes of Interpretation of Certain Chapter 11 Provisions' (31 July 2001)

Sutherland P and others, 'The Future of the WTO: Assessing Institutional Challenges in the New Millenium' (World Trade Organization 2004)

United Nations Commission on International Trade Law, 'Possible Future Work in the Field of Dispute Settlement: Concurrent Proceedings in International Arbitration' (United Nations Commission on International Trade law 2017) A/CN.9/915

United Nations Commission on International Trade Law, 'Possible Future Work in the Field of Dispute Settlement: Reforms of Investor-State Dispute Settlement (ISDS)' (United Nations Commission on International Trade law 2017) A/CN.9/917

United Nations Commission on International Trade Law, 'Possible Reform of Investor-State Dispute Settlement (ISDS): Appellate and Multilateral Court Mechanisms' (United Nations Commission on International Trade law 2019) A/CN.9/WG.III/WP.185

United Nations Commission on International Trade Law, 'Possible Reform of Investor-State Dispute Settlement (ISDS): Appellate Mechanism' (United Nations Commission on International Trade law 2022) A/CN.9/WG.III/WP.224

United Nations Commission on International Trade Law, 'Possible Reform of Investor-State Dispute Settlement (ISDS): Consistency and Related Matters' (United Nations Commission on International Trade law 2018) A/CN.9/WG.III/WP.150

United Nations Commission on International Trade Law, 'Possible Reform of Investor-State Dispute Settlement (ISDS): Interpretation of Investment Treaties by Treaty Parties' (United Nations Commission on International Trade law 2020) A/CN.9/WG.III/WP.191

United Nations Commission on International Trade Law, 'Possible Reform of Investor-State Dispute Settlement (ISDS): Selection and Appointment of ISDS Tribunal Members' (United Nations Commission on International Trade law 2020) A/CN9/WGIII/WP203

United Nations Commission on International Trade Law, 'Possible Reform of Investor-State Dispute Settlement (ISDS): Submission from the European Union' (United Nations Commission on International Trade law 2017) A/CN.9/WG.III/WP.145

United Nations Commission on International Trade Law, 'Possible Reform of Investor-State Dispute Settlement (ISDS): Submission from the European Union and Its Member States' (United Nations Commission on International Trade law 2019) A/CN.9/WG.III/WP.159/Add.1

United Nations Commission on International Trade Law, 'Possible Reform of Investor-State Dispute Settlement (ISDS): Submission from the Government of China' (United Nations Commission on International Trade law 2019) A/CN.9/WG.III/WP.177

United Nations Commission on International Trade Law, 'Report of Working Group III (Investor-State Dispute Settlement Reform) on the Work of Its Fortieth Session' (United Nations Commission on International Trade law 2021) A/CN.9/1050

United Nations Commission on International Trade Law, 'Report of Working Group III (Investor-State Dispute Settlement Reform) on the Work of Its Thirty-Sixth Session' (United Nations Commission on International Trade law 2018) A/CN.9/964

United Nations Conference on Trade and Development, 'Bilateral Investment Treaties 1995–2006: Trends in Investment Rulemaking' (United Nations 2007) UNCTAD/ITE/IIT/2006/5

United Nations Conference on Trade and Development, 'World Investment Report 2019' (United Nations Conference on Trade and Development 2019) UNCTAD/WIR/2019

United Nations Conference on Trade and Development, 'International Investment Agreements Navigator' (*UNCTAD Investment Policy Hub*) <https://investmentpolicy.unctad.org/international-investment-agreements> accessed 27 April 2021

United States Trade Representative, '2018 Trade Policy Agenda and 2017 Annual Report of the President of the United States on the Trade Agreements Program' (United States Trade Representative 2018)

United States Trade Representative, 'Report on the Appellate Body of the World Trade Organization' (United States Trade Representative 2020)

Vázquez-Bermúdez M, 'Second Report on General Principles of Law' (International Law Commission 2020) A/CN.4/741

Vázquez-Bermúdez M, 'Third Report on General Principles of Law by Marcelo Vázquez-Bermúdez, Special Rapporteur' (International Law Commission 2022) A/CN.4/753

World Trade Organization, 'Communication from the European Union, China, Canada, India, Norway, New Zealand, Switzerland, Australia, Republic of Korea, Iceland, Singapore, Mexico, Costa Rica And Montenegro' (World Trade Organization, Dispute Settlement Body 2018) WT/GC/W/752/Rev.2

World Trade Organization, 'Informal Process on Matters Related to the Functioning of the Appellate Body: Communication from Japan, Australia and Chile' (World Trade Organization, Dispute Settlement Body 2019) WT/GC/W/768/Rev.1

World Trade Organization, 'Minutes of Meeting of the General Council on 22 November 2000' (World Trade Organization 2001) WT/GC/M/60

World Trade Organization, 'Minutes of Meeting on 1 June 2011 of the Dispute Settlement Body' (World Trade Organization 2011) WT/DSB/M/297

World Trade Organization, 'Minutes of Meeting on 19 June 2000 of the Dispute Settlement Body' (World Trade Organization 2000) WT/DSB/M/84

World Trade Organization, 'Minutes of Meeting on 24 March 2006 of the Dispute Settlement Body' (World Trade Organization 2006) WT/DSB/M/208

World Trade Organization, 'Minutes of Meeting on 28 January 2019 of the Dispute Settlement Body' (World Trade Organization 2019) WT/DSB/M/425

World Trade Organization, 'Negotiations on Improvements and Clarifications of the Dispute Settlement Understanding, Further Contribution of the United States on Improving Flexibility and Member Control in WTO Dispute Settlement – Communication from the United States' (World Trade Organization, Dispute Settlement Body 2005) TN/DS/W/82

World Trade Organization, 'Negotiations on Improvements and Clarifications of the Dispute Settlement Understanding on Improving Flexibility and Member Control in WTO Dispute Settlement – Contribution by Chile and the United States' (World Trade Organization, Dispute Settlement Body 2002) TN/DS/W/28

World Trade Organization, 'WTO Documents Online' <https://docs.wto.org/dol2fe/Pages/FE_Search/FE_S_S005.aspx> accessed 29 March 2021

World Trade Organization, 'WTO Analytical Index: Guide to the WTO Law and Practice' (World Trade Organization 2020)

Bibliography

Adams M, Husa J and Oderkerk M, 'Method and Methodology of Comparative Law: Introductory Remarks' in Maurice Adams, Jaakko Husa and Marieke Oderkerk (eds), *Comparative Law Methodology*, vol 1 (Edward Elgar Publishing 2017)

Allen S and others, 'Introduction: Defining State Jurisdiction and Jurisdiction in International Law' in Stephen Allen and others (eds), *The Oxford Handbook of Jurisdiction in International Law* (Oxford University Press 2019)

Alschner W, 'The Impact of Investment Arbitration on Investment Treaty Design: Myths versus Reality' (2017) 42 Yale Journal of International Law 1

Alschner W, Investment Arbitration and State-Driven Reform: New Treaties, Old Outcomes (Oxford University Press 2022)

Alvarez JE, The Public International Law Regime Governing International Investment (Brill Nijhoff 2011)

Alvarez JE, The Boundaries of Investment Arbitration: The Use of Trade and European Human Rights Law in Investor-State Disputes (JurisNet 2018)

Alvarez JE, 'Epilogue: "Convergence" Is a Many-Splendored Thing' in Szilárd Gáspár-Szilágyi, Daniel Behn and Malcolm Langford (eds), *Adjudicating Trade and Investment Disputes: Convergence or Divergence?* (Cambridge University Press 2020)

Ambrus M, 'Constitutionalization through Fragmented Adjudication?' in Andrzej Jakubowski and Karolina Wierczyńska (eds), *Fragmentation vs the Constitutionalization of International Law: A Practical Inquiry* (Routledge 2016)

Amerasinghe CF, *Jurisdiction of International Tribunals* (Kluwer Law International 2003)

Amerasinghe CF, Jurisdiction of Specific International Tribunals (Martinus Nijhoff 2008)

Amerasinghe CF, International Arbitral Jurisdiction (Brill Nijhoff 2011)

Andenas M, 'Reassertion and Transformation: From Fragmentation to Convergence in International Law' (2014) 46 Georgetown Journal of International Law 685

Andenas M and Bjorge E, 'Introduction: From Fragmentation to Convergence in International Law' in Eirik Bjorge and Mads Andenas (eds), *A Farewell to Fragmentation: Reassertion and Convergence in International Law* (Cambridge University Press 2015)

Andenas M and Chiussi L, 'Cohesion, Convergence and Coherence of International Law' in Mads Andenas and others (eds), *General Principles and the Coherence of International Law* (Brill Nijhoff 2019)

Andenas M and Leiss JR, 'The Systemic Relevance of "Judicial Decisions" in Article 38 of the ICJ Statute' (2017) 77 Heidelberg Journal of International Law 907

Arato J, Brown C and Ortino F, 'Parsing and Managing Inconsistency in Investor-State Dispute Settlement' (2020) 21 The Journal of World Investment & Trade 336

Atanasova D, 'Applicable Law Provisions in Investment Treaties: Forever Midnight Clauses?' (2019) 10 Journal of International Dispute Settlement 396

Baetens F, 'Muddling the Waters of Treaty Interpretation? Relevant Rules of International Law in the MOX Plant OSPAR Arbitration and EC – Biotech Case' (2008) 77 Nordic Journal of International Law 197

Baetens F, 'The European Union's Proposed Investment Court System: Addressing Criticisms of Investor-State Arbitration While Raising New Challenges Investor Protection and Enforcement' (2016) 43 Legal Issues of Economic Integration 367

Baetens F, 'Invoking Human Rights: A Useful Line of Attack or a Defence Tool for States in Investor-State Dispute Settlement?' in Martin Scheinin (ed), *Human Rights Norms in 'Other' International Courts* (Cambridge University Press 2019)

Baetens F, 'Unseen Actors in International Courts and Tribunals: Challenging the Legitimacy of International Adjudication' in Freya Baetens (ed), *Legitimacy of Unseen Actors in International Adjudication* (Cambridge University Press 2019)

Baetens F (ed), Identity and Diversity on the International Bench: Who Is the Judge? (Oxford University Press 2020)

Baltag C, 'Applicable Law under Article 26(6) the Energy Charter Treaty and Environmental Protection: Promoting Sustainable Development in the Energy Field' (2019) 16 Transnational Dispute Management (TDM)

Baltag C and Dautaj Y, 'Promoting, Regulating, and Enforcing Human Rights through International Investment Law and ISDS' (2021) 45 Fordham International Law Journal 1

Banifatemi Y, 'The Law Applicable in Investment Treaty Arbitration' in Katia Yannaca-Small (ed), *Arbitration under International Investment Agreements: A Guide to the Key Issues* (Oxford University Press 2010)

Banifatemi Y and Edson E, 'Jurisdiction of the Center' in Julien Fouret, Rémy Gerbay and Gloria Alvarez (eds), *The ICSID Convention, Regulations and Rules: A Practical Commentary* (Edward Elgar Publishing 2019)

Bartels L, 'Applicable Law in WTO Dispute Settlement Proceedings' (2001) 35 Journal of World Trade 499

Bartels L, 'The Separation of Powers in the WTO: How to Avoid Judicial Activism' (2004) 53 International and Comparative Law Quarterly 861

Bartels L, 'The Appellate Body and Public International Law' in Federico Ortino and Sergey Ripinsky (eds), *WTO Law and Process: The Proceedings of the 2005 and 2006 Annual WTO Conferences* (British Institute of International and Comparative Law 2007)

Bartels L, 'Jurisdiction and Applicable Law Clauses: Where Does a Tribunal Find the Principal Norms Applicable to the Case before It?' in Tomer Broude and Yuval Shany (eds), *Multi-Sourced Equivalent Norms in International Law* (Hart Publishing 2011)

Basedow JR, 'Why De-Judicialize? Explaining State Preferences on Judicialization in World Trade Organization Dispute Settlement Body and Investor-to-State Dispute Settlement Reforms' [2021] Regulation & Governance

Baylis E, 'The Transformative Potential of Rigorous Empirical Research Empirical Approaches to International Law' (2010) 104 American Society of International Law Proceedings 31

Beaulac S, 'The Lotus Case in Context: Sovereignty, Westphalia, Vattel, and Positivism' in Stephen Allen and others (eds), *The Oxford Handbook of Jurisdiction in International Law* (Oxford University Press 2019)

Beckerle S, 'Stare Decisis in the WTO Dispute Settlement Procedure: A Response to the Trump Administration's Criticism' (2019) 14 Global Trade and Customs Journal 513

Behn D, Fauchald OK and Langford M, 'The International Investment Regime and Its Discontents' in Daniel Behn, Ole Kristian Fauchald and Malcolm Langford (eds), *The Legitimacy of Investment Arbitration* (1st edn, Cambridge University Press 2022)

Behn D, Langford M and Létourneau-Tremblay L, 'Empirical Perspectives on Investment Arbitration: What Do We Know? Does It Matter?' (2020) 21 The Journal of World Investment & Trade 188

Benvenisti E and Downs GW, 'The Empire's New Clothes: Political Economy and the Fragmentation of International Law' (2007) 60 Stanford Law Review 595

Benvenisti E and Downs GW, Between Fragmentation and Democracy: The Role of National and International Courts (Cambridge University Press 2017)

Besson S and d'Aspremont J, 'The Sources of International Law. An Introduction' in Samantha Besson and Jean d'Aspremont (eds), *The Oxford Handbook on the Sources of International Law* (Oxford University Press 2017)

Bianchi A, *Constitutionalism and Global Governance* (Oxford University Press 2016)

Bílková V, 'The Threads (or Threats?) Of a Managerial Approach: Afterword to Laurence Boisson de Chazournes' Foreword' (2017) 28 European Journal of International Law 1259

Bjorge E, 'The Convergence of the Methods of Treaty Interpretation: Different Regimes, Different Methods of Interpretation?' in Mads Andenas and Eirik Bjorge (eds), *A Farewell to Fragmentation* (Cambridge University Press 2015)

Bjorklund AK, 'Assessing the Effectiveness of Soft Law Instruments in International Investment Law' in Andrea K Bjorklund and August Reinisch (eds), *International Investment Law and Soft Law* (Edward Elgar Publishing 2012)

Bjorklund AK, 'Applicable Law in International Investment Disputes' in Chiara Giorgetti (ed), *Litigating International Investment Arbitration Disputes* (Brill Nijhoff 2014)

Bjorklund AK, 'The Legitimacy of the International Center for Settlement of Investment Disputes' in Andreas Follesdal and others (eds), *Legitimacy and International Courts* (Cambridge University Press 2018)

Bjorklund AK, 'The Road(s) Not Taken – the Past, Present, and Future of International Investment Law Reform' (2023) 39 Arbitration International 455

Bjorklund AK and others, 'The Diversity Deficit in International Investment Arbitration' (2020) 21 The Journal of World Investment & Trade 410

Bodansky D, 'Non Liquet and the Incompleteness of International Law' in Laurence Boisson de Chazournes and Philippe Sands (eds), *International Law, the International Court of Justice and Nuclear Weapons* (Cambridge University Press 1999)

Bodansky D, 'The Concept of Legitimacy in International Law' in Rüdiger Wolfrum and Volker Röben (eds), *Legitimacy in International Law* (Springer 2008)

Bodansky D and Lawrence JC, 'Trade and Environment' in Daniel Bethlehem and others (eds), *The Oxford Handbook of International Trade Law* (Oxford University Press 2009)

Boisson de Chazournes L, 'Plurality in the Fabric of International Courts and Tribunals: The Threads of a Managerial Approach' (2017) 28 European Journal of International Law 13

Boisson de Chazournes L, 'Variations around the Notion of Consent in Investment Arbitration' in Samantha Besson (ed), *Consenting to International Law* (1st edn, Cambridge University Press 2023)

Born G, Morris D and Forrest S, 'A Margin of Appreciation: Appreciating Its Irrelevance in International Law' (2020) 61 Harvard International Law Journal 65

Borrows J and Schwartz R (eds), Indigenous Peoples and International Trade: Building Equitable and Inclusive International Trade and Investment Agreements (Cambridge University Press 2020)

Bottini G and Bräutigam EM, 'Investment Claims against Latin American States: Environmental Protection and the Applicable Law' in Kate Miles (ed), *Research Handbook on Environment and Investment Law* (Edward Elgar Publishing 2019)

Broches A, 'Convention on the Settlement of Investment Disputes: Some Observations on Jurisdiction' (1966) 5 Columbia Journal of Transnational Law 263

Brower CH, 'Why the FTC Notes of Interpretation Constitute a Partial Amendment of NAFTA Article 1105' (2005) 46 Virginia Journal of International Law 347

Brown C, 'The Inherent Powers of International Courts and Tribunals' (2006) 76 British Yearbook of International Law 195

Brown C, A Common Law of International Adjudication (Oxford University Press 2007)

Buchanan A, 'The Legitimacy of International Law' in Samantha Besson and John Tasioulas (eds), *The Philosophy of International Law* (Oxford University Press 2010)

Buchanan A and Keohane RO, 'The Legitimacy of Global Governance Institutions' (2006) 20 Ethics & International Affairs 405

Bungenberg M and Reinisch A, From Bilateral Arbitral Tribunals and Investment Courts to a Multilateral Investment Court: Options Regarding the Institutionalization of Investor-State Dispute Settlement (2nd edn, Springer Berlin Heidelberg 2020)

Bungenberg M and Titi C, 'Precedents in International Investment Law' in Marc Bungenberg and others (eds), *International Investment Law: A Handbook* (Hart Publishing 2015)

Butler W, 'Comparative Approaches to International Law' (1985) 190 Collected Courses of the Hague Academy of International Law 9

Calamita NJ, 'Countermeasures and Jurisdiction: Between Effectiveness and Fragmentation' (2010) 42 Georgetown Journal of International Law 233

Cate IMT, 'International Arbitration and the Ends of Appellate Review' (2011) 44 New York University Journal of International Law and Politics 1109

Charlotin D, 'The Place of Investment Awards and WTO Decisions in International Law: A Citation Analysis' (2017) 20 Journal of International Economic Law 279

Charney J, 'Is International Law Threatened by Multiple International Tribunals?' (1998) 271 Collected Courses of the Hague Academy of International Law 101

Cheng B, General Principles of Law as Applied by International Courts and Tribunals (reprint 2006, Steven & Sons 1953)

Christiano T, 'The Legitimacy of International Institutions' in Andrei Marmor (ed), *The Routledge Companion to Philosophy of Law* (Taylor & Francis 2012)

Cohen HG, 'Theorizing Precedent in International Law' in Andrea Bianchi and Matthew Windsor (eds), *Interpretation in International Law* (Oxford University Press 2015)

Cohen HG, 'Culture Clash: The Sociology of WTO Precedent' in Amalie Frese and Julius Schumann (eds), *Precedents as Rules and Practice: New Approaches and Methodologies in Studies of Legal Precedents* (1st Edition, Nomos 2021)

Cohen HG, 'Legitimacy and International Courts – A Framework' in Andreas Follesdal and others (eds), *Legitimacy and International Courts* (Cambridge University Press 2018)

Cook G, A Digest of WTO Jurisprudence on Public International Law Concepts and Principles (Cambridge University Press 2015)

Cook G, 'The Illusion of "Evolutionary Interpretation" in WTO Dispute Settlement' in Georges Abi-Saab, Gabrielle Marceau and Clément Marquet (eds), *Evolutionary Interpretation and International Law* (Hart 2019)

Costelloe D, 'Conceptions of State Jurisdiction in the Jurisprudence of the International Court of Justice and the Permanent Court of International Justice' in Stephen Allen and others (eds), *The Oxford Handbook of Jurisdiction in International Law* (Oxford University Press 2019)

Crawford J, 'Investment Arbitration and the ILC Articles on State Responsibility' (2010) 25 ICSID Review 127

Crawford J, *State Responsibility: The General Part* (Cambridge University Press 2013)

Crawford J, *Brownlie's Principles of International Law* (9th edn, Oxford University Press 2019)

Crawford J and Nevill P, 'Relations between International Courts and Tribunals: The "Regime Problem"' in Margaret A Young (ed), *Regime Interaction in International Law: Facing Fragmentation* (Cambridge University Press 2012)

Creamer CD and Godzimirska Z, 'Deliberative Engagement within the World Trade Organization: A Functional Substitute for Authoritative Interpretations' (2015) 48 New York University Journal of International Law and Politics 413

d'Aspremont J, 'Comparativism and Colonizing Thinking in International Law' (2020) 57 Canadian Yearbook of International Law/Annuaire canadien de droit international 89

de Andrade MC, 'General Principles of Procedural Law in the Practice of the WTO Appellate Body' (2021) 24 International Community Law Review 444

de Andrade MC, 'Precedent in the WTO: Retrospective Reflections for a Prospective Dispute Settlement Mechanism' (2020) 11 Journal of International Dispute Settlement 262

De Brabandere E, Investment Treaty Arbitration as Public International Law: Procedural Aspects and Implications (Cambridge University Press 2014)

De Brabandere E, 'International Investment Law and Human Rights', *Elgar Encyclopedia of Human Rights* (Edward Elgar Publishing 2022)

De Wet E, 'Sources and the Hierarchy of International Law: The Place of Peremptory Norms and Article 103 of the UN Charter within the Sources of International Law' in Samantha Besson and Jean D'Aspremont (eds), *The Oxford Handbook on the Sources of International Law* (Oxford University Press 2017)

Desta MG, 'Soft Law in International Law: An Overview' in Andrea K Bjorklund and August Reinisch (eds), *International Investment Law and Soft Law* (Edward Elgar Publishing 2012)

Di Benedetto S, International Investment Law and the Environment (Edward Elgar Publishing 2013)

Diependaele L, De Ville F and Sterckx S, 'Assessing the Normative Legitimacy of Investment Arbitration: The EU's Investment Court System' (2019) 24 New Political Economy 37

Dolzer R and Schreuer C, *Principles of International Investment Law* (2nd edn, Oxford University Press 2012)

Đorđeska M, General Principles of Law Recognized by Civilized Nations (1922–2018): The Evolution of the Third Source of International Law Through the Jurisprudence of the Permanent Court of International Justice and the International Court of Justice (Brill Nijhoff 2020)

Dörr O, 'Article 31: General Rule of Interpretation' in Oliver Dörr and Kirsten Schmalenbach (eds), *Vienna Convention on the Law of Treaties: A Commentary* (2nd edn, Springer Berlin Heidelberg 2018)

Douglas Z, *The International Law of Investment Claims* (Cambridge University Press 2009)

Douglas Z, 'The Plea of Illegality in Investment Treaty Arbitration' (2014) 29 ICSID Review – Foreign Investment Law Journal 155

Duggal KAN and Diamond NJ, 'Human Rights and Investor–State Dispute Settlement Reform: Fitting a Square Peg into a Round Hole?' (2021) 12 Journal of International Dispute Settlement 291

Dumberry P, The Formation and Identification of Rules of Customary International Law in International Investment Law (Cambridge University Press 2016)

Dumberry P, A Guide to General Principles of Law in International Investment Arbitration (Oxford University Press 2020)

Dunoff JL, 'The Politics of International Constitutions: The Curious Case of the World Trade Organization' in Jeffrey L Dunoff and Joel P Trachtman (eds), *Ruling the World? Constitutionalism, International Law, and Global Governance* (Cambridge University Press 2009)

Dupuy P-M, Petersmann E-U and Francioni F (eds), *Human Rights in International Investment Law and Arbitration* (Oxford University Press 2009)

Dupuy P-M and Vinuales J, 'Human Rights and Investment Disciplines: Integration in Progress' in Marc Bungenberg and others (eds), *International Investment Law: A Handbook* (Hart Publishing 2015)

Edwards HT, 'The Effects of Collegiality on Judicial Decision Making' (2002) 151 University of Pennsylvania Law Review 1639

Fauchald OK, 'The Legal Reasoning of ICSID Tribunals – An Empirical Analysis' (2008) 19 European Journal of International Law 301

Fitzmaurice G, The General Principles of International Law: Considered from the Standpoint of the Rule of Law (Sitjhoff 1957)

Fitzmaurice G, 'The Future of Public International Law and of the International Legal System in the Circumstances of Today: Second and Final Part of an Abstract (Prepared by the Author) of a Special Report' (1976) 5 International Relations 949

Fitzmaurice G, The Law and Procedure of the International Court of Justice, vol 2 (Cambridge University Press 1993)

Fitzmaurice M, 'Human Right to Clean Environment and the Rights of Nature in the Anthropocene' (2022) 42 Polish Yearbook of International Law 155

Flett J, 'Importing Other International Regimes into World Trade Organization Litigation' in Margaret A Young (ed), *Regime Interaction in International Law: Facing Fragmentation* (Cambridge University Press 2012)

Forteau M, 'The Diversity of Applicable Law Before International Tribunals as a Source of Forum Shopping and Fragmentation of International Law: An Assessment' in Rüdiger Wolfrum and Ina Gätzschmann (eds), *International Dispute Settlement: Room for Innovations?* (Springer Berlin Heidelberg 2013)

Francioni F (ed), Environment, Human Rights and International Trade (Hart 2001)

Franck SD, 'Empirical Modalities: Lessons for the Future of International Investment Empirical Approaches to International Law' (2010) 104 American Society of International Law Proceedings 33

Franck SD, 'The Legitimacy Crisis in Investment Treaty Arbitration: Privatizing Public International Law through Inconsistent Decisions' (2004) 73 Fordham Law Review 1521

Franck TM, *The Power of Legitimacy among Nations* (Oxford University Press 1990)

Franck TM, Fairness in International Law and Institutions (Oxford University Press 1998)

French D, 'Treaty Interpretation and the Incorporation Of Extraneous Legal Rules' (2006) 55 International & Comparative Law Quarterly 281

Fumagalli L, 'Jura Novit Curia', *Max Planck Encyclopedia of International Procedural Law* (Oxford University Press 2018)

Gaillard E and Banifatemi Y, 'The Meaning of "and" in Article 42(1), Second Sentence, of the Washington Convention: The Role of International Law in the ICSID Choice of Law Process' (2003) 18 ICSID Review 375

Gaja G, 'General Principles of Law', *Max Planck Encyclopedia of Public International Law* (Oxford University Press 2020)

Gao RY, 'What Are We Talking About When We Talk About Deference in Investment Treaty Arbitration?' (2022) 13 Journal of International Dispute Settlement 472

Gardiner RK, *Treaty Interpretation* (2nd edn, Oxford University Press 2015)

Gattini A, Tanzi A and Fontanelli F, 'Under the Hood of Investment Arbitration: General Principles of Law' in Andrea Gattini, Attila Tanzi and Filippo Fontanelli (eds), *General Principles of Law and International Investment Arbitration* (Brill Nijhoff 2018)

Gattini A, (eds), General Principles of Law and International Investment Arbitration (Brill Nijhoff 2018)

Giorgetti C, 'Cross-Fertilization of Procedural Law Among International Courts and Tribunals: Methods and Meanings' in Arman Sarvarian and others (eds), *Procedural Fairness in International Courts and Tribunals* (British Institute of International and Comparative Law 2015)

Giorgetti C and Pollack M, 'Beyond Fragmentation: Cross-Fertilization, Cooperation, and Competition among International Courts and Tribunals' in Chiara Giorgetti and Mark Pollack (eds), *Beyond Fragmentation* (1st edn, Cambridge University Press 2022)

Gordon K and Pohl J, 'Investment Treaties over Time – Treaty Practice and Interpretation in a Changing World' (OECD Publishing 2015) 2015/02

Gourgourinis A, 'The Distinction between Interpretation and Application of Norms in International Adjudication' (2011) 2 Journal of International Dispute Settlement 31

Grossman N, 'The Normative Legitimacy of International Courts' (2013) 86 Temple Law Review 61

Grossman N, 'Solomonic Judgments and the Legitimacy of the International Court of Justice' in Andreas Follesdal and others (eds), *Legitimacy and International Courts* (Cambridge University Press 2018)

Guan W, 'Consensus Yet Not Consented: A Critique of the WTO Decision-Making by Consensus' (2014) 17 Journal of International Economic Law 77

Hanqin X, Jurisdiction of the International Court of Justice (Brill Nijhoff 2017)

Hart HLA, *The Concept of Law* (3rd edn, with a postscript edited by Penelope A Bullock and Joseph Raz, and an introduction and notes by Leslie Green, Oxford University Press 2012)

Hernández GI, 'Interpretation' in Jorg Kammerhofer and Jean D'Aspremont (eds), *International Legal Positivism in a Post-Modern World* (Cambridge University Press 2014)

Hernández GI, The International Court of Justice and the Judicial Function (Oxford University Press 2014)

Hernández GI, 'Interpretative Authority and the International Judiciary' in Andrea Bianchi and Matthew Windsor (eds), *Interpretation in International Law* (Oxford University Press 2015)

Hestermeyer H, 'International Human Rights Law and Dispute Settlement in the World Trade Organization' in Martin Scheinin (ed), *Human Rights Norms in 'Other' International Courts* (1st edn, Cambridge University Press 2019)

Higgins R, 'The ICJ, the ECJ, and the Integrity of International Law' (2003) 52 International and Comparative Law Quarterly 1

Higgins R, 'A Babel of Judicial Voices? Ruminations from the Bench' (2006) 55 International & Comparative Law Quarterly 791

Hilf M and Goettsche G, 'The Relation of Economic and Non-Economic Principles in International Law' in Stefan Griller (ed), *International Economic Governance and Non-Economic Concerns: New Challenges for the International Legal Order* (Springer-Verlag Wien 2003)

Hirsch M, 'Sources of International Investment Law' in Andrea K Bjorklund and August Reinisch (eds), *International Investment Law and Soft Law* (Edward Elgar Publishing 2012)

Hodgson MN, 'Reform and Adaptation: The Experience of the Americas with International Investment Law' (2020) 21 The Journal of World Investment & Trade 140

Holtermann JVH and Madsen MR, 'Toleration, Synthesis or Replacement? The "Empirical Turn" and Its Consequences for the Science of International Law' (2016) 29 Leiden Journal of International Law 1001

Howse R and others, 'Introduction' in Robert Howse and others (eds), *The Legitimacy of International Trade Courts and Tribunals* (Cambridge University Press 2018)

Howse R and Teitel R, 'Global Judicial Activism, Fragmentation, and the Limits of Constitutionalism in International Law' in Ulrich Fastenrath and others (eds), *From Bilateralism to Community Interest: Essays in Honour of Bruno Simma* (Oxford University Press 2011)

Hutchinson T and Duncan N, 'Defining and Describing What We Do: Doctrinal Legal Research' (2012) 17 Deakin Law Review 83

Janig P and Reinisch A, 'General Principles and the Coherence of International Investment Law: Of Res Judicata, Lis Pendens and the Value of Precedents' in Mads Andenas and others (eds), *General Principles and the Coherence of International Law* (Brill Nijhoff 2019)

Kabra R, 'Inherent Powers of the WTO Appellate Body and ICSID Tribunals – A Tale of Cautious Convergence' in Daniel Behn, Malcolm Langford and Szilárd Gáspár-Szilágyi (eds), *Adjudicating Trade and Investment Disputes: Convergence or Divergence?* (Cambridge University Press 2020)

Kammerhofer J, International Investment Law and Legal Theory: Expropriation and the Fragmentation of Sources (Cambridge University Press 2021)

Kim D, 'The Annulment Committee's Role in Multiplying Inconsistency in ICSID Arbitration: The Need to Move Away from an Annulment-Based System' (2011) 86 NYU Law Review 242

Kingsbury B, 'Foreword: Is the Proliferation of International Courts and Tribunals a Systemic Problem Symposium Issue: The Proliferation of International Tribunals: Piecing Together the Puzzle' (1998) 31 New York University Journal of International Law and Politics 679

Klabbers J, 'Reluctant Grundnormen: Articles 31(3)(c) and 42 of the Vienna Convention on the Law of Treaties and the Fragmentation of International Law' in Matthew

Craven, Malgosia Fitzmaurice and Maria Vogiatzi (eds), *Time, History and International Law* (Brill Nijhoff 2007)

Kleinlein T, 'Judicial Lawmaking by Judicial Restraint? The Potential of Balancing in International Economic Law' in Armin von Bogdandy and Ingo Venzke (eds), *International Judicial Lawmaking: On Public Authority and Democratic Legitimation in Global Governance* (Springer 2012)

Kolb R, 'General Principles of Procedural Law' in Andreas Zimmermann and others (eds), *The Statute of the International Court of Justice: A Commentary* (3rd edn, Oxford University Press 2019)

Koskenniemi M, From Apology to Utopia: The Structure of International Legal Argument (Cambridge University Press 2005)

Koskenniemi M, 'The Fate of Public International Law: Between Technique and Politics' (2007) 70 The Modern Law Review 1

Koskenniemi M, 'The Case for Comparative International Law' (2009) 20 Finnish Yearbook of International Law 1

Koskenniemi M, 'The Function of Law in the International Community: 75 Years After' (2009) 79 British Yearbook of International Law 353

Koskenniemi M, and Leino P, 'Fragmentation of International Law? Postmodern Anxieties' (2002) 15 Leiden Journal of International Law 553

Kotuby C and Sobota L, General Principles of Law and International Due Process: Principles and Norms Applicable in Transnational Disputes (Oxford University Press 2017)

Kube V and Petersmann E-U, 'Human Rights Law in International Investment Arbitration' in Andrea Gattini, Attila Tanzi and Filippo Fontanelli (eds), *General Principles of Law and International Investment Arbitration* (Brill Nijhoff 2018)

Kucik J and Puig S, 'The Appellate Body's Judicial Pathway: Precedent, Resistance and Adaptation' in Nico Krisch and Ezgi Yildiz (eds), *The Many Paths of Change in International Law* (1st edn, Oxford University Press 2023)

Kucik J and Puig S, 'Toward an Effective Appellate Mechanism for ISDS Tribunals' (2023) 22 World Trade Review 562

Kuijper P, 'A Legal Drafting Group for the Doha Round: A Modest Proposal' (2003) 37 Journal of World Trade 1031

Kurtz J, 'Adjudging the Exceptional at International Investment Law: Security, Public Order and Financial Crisis' (2010) 59 International & Comparative Law Quarterly 325

Kurtz J, 'The Paradoxical Treatment of the ILC Articles on State Responsibility in Investor-State Arbitration' (2010) 25 ICSID Review 200

Kurtz J, 'Building Legitimacy Through Interpretation in Investor-State Arbitration: On Consistency, Coherence, and the Identification of Applicable Law' in Zachary

Douglas, Joost Pauwelyn and Jorge Vinuales (eds), *The Foundations of International Investment Law: Bringing Theory Into Practice* (Oxford University Press 2014)

Land MK, 'Justice as Legitimacy in the European Court of Human Rights' in Andreas Follesdal and others (eds), *Legitimacy and International Courts* (Cambridge University Press 2018)

Lang A, 'The Role of the International Court of Justice in a Context of Fragmentation' (2013) 62 International and Comparative Law Quarterly 777

Lang A, 'Twenty Years of the WTO Appellate Body's "Fragmentation Jurisprudence"' (2015) 14 Journal of International Trade Law and Policy 116

Langford M and others, 'Special Issue: UNCITRAL and Investment Arbitration Reform: Matching Concerns and Solutions: An Introduction' (2020) 21 The Journal of World Investment & Trade 167

Langford M and Behn D, 'Managing Backlash: The Evolving Investment Treaty Arbitrator?' (2018) 29 European Journal of International Law 551

Langford M, Behn D and Lie RH, 'The Revolving Door in International Investment Arbitration' (2017) 20 Journal of International Economic Law 301

Langford M, Creamer CD and Behn D, 'Regime Responsiveness in International Economic Disputes' in Szilárd Gáspár-Szilágyi, Daniel Behn and Malcolm Langford (eds), *Adjudicating Trade and Investment Disputes: Convergence or Divergence?* (Cambridge University Press 2020)

Lauterpacht E, '"Partial" Judgments and the Inherent Jurisdiction of the International Court of Justice' in Vaughan Lowe and Malgosia Fitzmaurice (eds), *Fifty Years of the International Court of Justice* (Cambridge University Press 1996)

Lauterpacht E, 'Principles of Procedure in International Litigation' (2011) 345 Collected Courses of the Hague Academy of International Law 1

Lauterpacht H, 'The So-Called Anglo-American and Continental Schools of Thought in International Law' (1931) 12 British Year Book of International Law 31

Lauterpacht H, The Function of Law in the International Community (Oxford University Press 1933)

Lauterpacht H, *International Law: Being the Collected Papers of Hersch Lauterpacht*, vol 2: The Law of Peace (Elihu Lauterpacht ed, Cambridge University Press 1975)

Lauterpacht H, The Development of International Law by the International Court (Cambridge University Press 1982)

Lauterpacht H, The Function of Law in the International Community (Oxford University Press 2011)

Leeuw FL, 'Empirical Legal Research: The Gap between Facts and Values and Legal Academic Training' (2015) 11 Utrecht Law Review 19

Lentner GM, 'The Perils of Quantitative Research in International Law' in Rossana Deplano (ed), *Pluralizing International Legal Scholarship* (Edward Elgar 2019)

Leutwiler F (ed), Trade Policies for a Better Future: The 'Leutwiler Report', the GATT and the Uruguay Round (Martinus Nijhoff Publishers 1987)

Linderfalk U, 'General Principles as Principles of International Legal Pragmatics: The Relevance of Good Faith for the Application of Treaty Law' in Mads Andenas and others (eds), *General Principles and the Coherence of International Law* (Brill Nijhoff 2019)

Linos K and Carlson M, 'Qualitative Methods for Law Review Writing Symposium: Developing Best Practices for Legal Analysis' (2017) 84 University of Chicago Law Review 213

Lorz RA, 'Fragmentation, Consolidation and the Future Relationship between International Investment Law and General International Law' in Freya Baetens (ed), *Investment Law within International Law* (Cambridge University Press 2013)

Luca AD and others, 'Responding to Incorrect Decision-Making in Investor-State Dispute Settlement: Policy Options' (2020) 21 The Journal of World Investment & Trade 374

Maisley N, 'Better to See International Law This Other Way: The Case against International Normative Positivism' (2021) 12 Jurisprudence 151

Malacrida R and Marceau G, 'The WTO Adjudicating Bodies' in Robert Howse and others (eds), *The Legitimacy of International Trade Courts and Tribunals* (1st edn, Cambridge University Press 2018)

Mann FA, 'The Doctrine of Jurisdiction in International Law' (1964) 111 Collected Courses of the Hague Academy of International Law 1

Marceau G, 'A Call for Coherence in International Law: Praises for the Prohibition Against "Clinical Isolation" in WTO Dispute Settlement' (1999) 33 Journal of World Trade 87

Marceau G, 'Evolutive Interpretation by the WTO Adjudicator' (2018) 21 Journal of International Economic Law 791

McDougall R, 'The Crisis in WTO Dispute Settlement: Fixing Birth Defects to Restore Balance' (2018) 52 Journal of World Trade 867

McLachlan C, 'The Principle of Systemic Integration and Article 31(3)(c) of the Vienna Convention' (2005) 54 International & Comparative Law Quarterly 279

McLachlan C, 'Investment Treaties and General International Law' (2008) 57 International & Comparative Law Quarterly 361

McLachlan C, 'The Assault on International Adjudication and the Limits of Withdrawal' (2019) 68 International & Comparative Law Quarterly 499

McLachlan C, Shore L and Weiniger M, *International Investment Arbitration: Substantive Principles* (2nd edn, Oxford University Press 2017)

McNair AD, *The Law of Treaties* (Clarendon Press 1961)

Merkouris P, Article 31(3)(c) VCLT and the Principle of Systemic Integration: Normative Shadows in Plato's Cave (Brill Nijhoff 2015)

Michaels R and Pauwelyn J, 'Conflict of Norms and Conflict of Laws? Different Techniques in the Fragmentation of International Law' in Tomer Broude and Yuval Shany (eds), *Multi-Sourced Equivalent Norms in International Law* (Hart Publishing 2011)

Mitchell A, *Legal Principles in WTO Disputes* (Cambridge University Press 2008)

Murphy S, 'The Utility and Limits of Canons and Other Interpretative Principles in Public International Law' in Joseph Klingler, Yuri Parkhomenko and Constantinos Salonidis (eds), *Between the Lines of the Vienna Convention? Canons and Other Principles of Interpretation in Public International Law* (Kluwer Law International 2019)

Noll G, 'Theorizing Jurisdiction' in Anne Orford and Florian Hoffmann (eds), *The Oxford Handbook of the Theory of International Law*, vol 1 (Oxford University Press 2016)

Paine J, 'Standard of Review: Investment Arbitration', *Max Planck Encylopedia of International Procedural Law* (Oxford University Press 2018)

Paine J, 'The WTO's Dispute Settlement Body as a Voice Mechanism' (2019) 20 The Journal of World Investment & Trade 820

Palmeter D and Mavroidis PC, Dispute Settlement in the World Trade Organization: Practice and Procedure (2nd edn, Cambridge University Press 2004)

Paparinskis M, 'Equivalent Primary Rules and Differential Secondary Rules: Countermeasures in WTO and Investment Protection Law' in Tomer Broude and Yuval Shany (eds), *Multi-Sourced Equivalent Norms in International Law* (Bloomsbury Publishing 2011)

Pasquet L, 'De-Fragmentation Techniques', *Max Planck Encyclopedia of International Procedural Law* (Oxford University Press 2018)

Paulus A, 'International Adjudication' in Samantha Besson and John Tasioulas (eds), *The Philosophy of International Law* (Oxford University Press 2010)

Pauwelyn J, 'The Role of Public International Law in the WTO: How Far Can We Go?' (2001) 95 The American Journal of International Law 535

Pauwelyn J, Conflict of Norms in Public International Law: How WTO Law Relates to Other Rules of International Law (Cambridge University Press 2003)

Pauwelyn J, 'How to Win a World Trade Organization Dispute Based on Non-World Trade Organization Law' (2003) 37 Journal of World Trade 997

Pauwelyn J, 'Human Rights in WTO Dispute Settlement' in Thomas Cottier, Joost Pauwelyn and Elisabeth Bürgi Bonanomi (eds), *Human Rights and International Trade* (Oxford University Press 2005)

Pauwelyn J, 'The Rule of Law without the Rule of Lawyers? Why Investment Arbitrators Are from Mars, Trade Adjudicators from Venus' (2015) 109 American Journal of International Law 761

Pauwelyn J, 'Who Decides Matters: The Legitimacy Capital of WTO Adjudicators versus ICSID Arbitrators' in Andreas Follesdal and others (eds), *Legitimacy and International Courts* (Cambridge University Press 2018)

Pauwelyn J and Elsig M, 'The Politics of Treaty Interpretation: Variations and Explanations Across International Tribunals' in Jeffrey L Dunoff and Mark Pollack (eds), *Interdisciplinary Perspectives on International Law and International Relations: The State of the Art* (Cambridge University Press 2012)

Pauwelyn J and Pelc K, 'Who Writes the Rulings of the World Trade Organization? A Critical Assessment of the Role of the Secretariat in WTO Dispute Settlement' (Social Science Research Network 2019)

Pellet A, 'Should We (Still) Worry about Fragmentation?' in Andreas Follesdal and Geir Ulfstein (eds), *The Judicialization of International Law: A Mixed Blessing?* (Oxford University Press 2018)

Pellet A, 'Canons of Interpretation under the Vienna Convention' in Joseph Klingler, Yuri Parkhomenko and Constantinos Salonidis (eds), *Between the Lines of the Vienna Convention? Canons and Other Principles of Interpretation in Public International Law* (Kluwer Law International 2019)

Pellet A and Müller D, 'Article 38' in Andreas Zimmermann and others (eds), *The Statute of the International Court of Justice: a commentary* (3rd edn, Oxford University Press 2019)

Peters A, 'Fragmentation and Constitutionalization' in Anne Orford and Florian Hoffmann (eds), *The Oxford Handbook of the Theory of International Law* (Oxford University Press 2016)

Peters A, 'The Refinement of International Law: From Fragmentation to Regime Interaction and Politicization' (2017) 15 International Journal of Constitutional Law 671

Petersmann E-U, The GATT/WTO Dispute Settlement System: International Law, International Organizations and Dispute Settlement (Kluwer Law International 1997)

Petersmann E-U, 'Constitutional Theories of International Economic Adjudication and Investor-State Arbitration' in Pierre-Marie Dupuy, Ernst-Ulrich Petersmann and Francesco Francioni (eds), *Human Rights in International Investment Law and Arbitration* (Oxford University Press 2009)

Petersmann E-U, 'The 'Crown Jewel of the WTO Has Been Stolen by US Trade Diplomats – and They Have No Intention of Giving It Back' in Denise Prévost, Iveta Alexovicova and Jens Hillebrand Pohl (eds), *Restoring Trust in Trade: Liber Amicorum in Honour of Peter Van den Bossche* (Hart 2019)

Petersmann E-U, 'How Should WTO Members React to Their WTO Crises?' (2019) 18 World Trade Review 503

Polzin M, 'Authentic Interpretations and International Courts: Like Calvin and Hobbes or Tom and Jerry' (2018) 33 Temple International & Comparative Law Journal 247

Puerta S and Samples TR, 'Investment Law's Transparency Gap' (2022) 55 Cornell International Law Journal 9

Puig S, At the Margins of Globalization: Indigenous Peoples and International Economic Law (Cambridge University Press 2021)

Puig S and Shaffer G, 'Imperfect Alternatives: Institutional Choice and the Reform of Investment Law' (2018) 112 American Journal of International Law 361

Pulkowski D, 'Lex Specialis Derogat Legi Generali / Generalia Specialibus Non Derogant' in Joseph Klingler, Yuri Parkhomenko and Constantinos Salonidis (eds), *Between the Lines of the Vienna Convention? Canons and Other Principles of Interpretation in Public International Law* (Kluwer Law International 2018)

Qureshi AH, *Interpreting WTO Agreements: Problems and Perspectives* (2nd edn, Cambridge University Press 2015)

Radović R, Beyond Consent: Revisiting Jurisdiction in Investment Treaty Arbitration (Brill Nijhoff 2021)

Radović R, 'The Dejudicialization of International Economic Law' in Jelena Bäumler and others (eds), *European Yearbook of International Economic Law 2021* (Springer International Publishing 2022)

Reece R, Massot A and Bartoli M-H, 'Searching for the Applicable Law in WTO Litigation, Investment and Commercial Arbitration' in Jorge Huerta-Goldman, Antoine Romanetti and Franz Xaver Stinimann Fuentes (eds), *WTO Litigation, Investment Arbitration and Commercial Arbitration* (Kluwer Law International 2013)

Reinisch A, 'Necessity in International Investment Arbitration – An Unnecessary Split of Opinions in Recent ICSID Cases – Comments on CMS v. Argentina and LG&E v. Argentina' (2007) 8 Journal of World Investment & Trade 191

Reinisch A, 'The Interpretation of International Investment Agreements' in Marc Bungenberg and others (eds), *International Investment Law: A Handbook* (Hart Publishing 2015)

Reinisch A, 'Jurisdiction and Admissibility in International Investment Law' in Andrea Gattini, Attila Tanzi and Filippo Fontanelli (eds), *General Principles of Law and International Investment Arbitration* (Brill Nijhoff 2018)

Ridi N, 'The Shape and Structure of the "Usable Past": An Empirical Analysis of the Use of Precedent in International Adjudication' (2019) 10 Journal of International Dispute Settlement 200

Ridi N, 'Approaches to External Precedent: The Invocation of International Jurisprudence in Investment Arbitration and WTO Dispute Settlement' in Daniel Behn, Malcolm Langford and Szilárd Gáspár-Szilágyi (eds), *Adjudicating Trade and Investment Disputes: Convergence or Divergence?* (Cambridge University Press 2020)

Roberts A, 'Power and Persuasion in Investment Treaty Interpretation: The Dual Role of States' (2010) 104 American Journal of International Law 179

Roberts A, 'Incremental, Systemic, and Paradigmatic Reform of Investor-State Arbitration' (2018) 112 American Journal of International Law 410

Roberts A, 'Conceptualizing Comparative International Law' in Anthea Roberts and others (eds), *Comparative International Law* (Oxford University Press 2018)

Roessler F, 'Dispute Settlement in the WTO: From a Deliberately Designed to a Spontaneously Grown Order' in Bernard Hoekman, Joost Pauwelyn and Manfred Elsig (eds), *Assessing the World Trade Organization: Fit for Purpose?* (Cambridge University Press 2017)

Rosenne S, The International Court of Justice: An Essay in Political and Legal Theory (AW Sijthoff 1957)

Rosenne S, The Law and Practice of the International Court, 1920–2005 (4th edn, Brill Nijhoff 2006)

Ryngaert C, *Jurisdiction in International Law* (2nd edn, Oxford University Press 2015)

Sacerdoti G, 'Panelists, Arbitrators, Judges: A Response to Joost Pauwelyn' (2015) 109 AJIL Unbound 283

Sacerdoti G, 'The Authority of "Precedent" in International Adjudication: The Contentious Case of the WTO Appellate Body's Practice' (2020) 19 The Law & Practice of International Courts and Tribunals 497

Schill SW, The Multilateralization of International Investment Law (Cambridge University Press 2009)

Schill SW, 'The Multilateralization of International Investment Law: Emergence of a Multilateral System of Investment Protection on Bilateral Grounds' (2010) 2 Trade, Law and Development 59

Schill SW and Vidigal G, 'Designing Investment Dispute Settlement à La Carte: Insights from Comparative Institutional Design Analysis' (2020) 18 The Law & Practice of International Courts and Tribunals 314

Schreuer CH, *The ICSID Convention: A Commentary* (2nd edn, Cambridge University Press 2009)

Schreuer CH, 'Diversity And Harmonization Of Treaty Interpretation In Investment Arbitration' in Malgosia Fitzmaurice, Olufemi Elias and Panos Merkouris (eds), *Treaty Interpretation and the Vienna Convention on the Law of Treaties: 30 Years On* (Brill Nijhoff 2010)

Schreuer CH, 'Jurisdiction and Applicable Law in Investment Treaty Arbitration' (2014) 1 McGill Journal of Dispute Resolution 1

Schreuer CH, 'Multiple Proceedings' in Andrea Gattini, Attila Tanzi and Filippo Fontanelli (eds), *General Principles of Law and International Investment Arbitration* (Brill Nijhoff 2018)

Scobbie IGM, 'The Theorist as Judge: Hersch Lauterpacht's Concept of the International Judicial Function' (1997) 8 European Journal of International Law 264

Shaffer G and Ginsburg T, 'The Empirical Turn in International Legal Scholarship' (2012) 106 American Journal of International Law 1

Shany Y, The Competing Jurisdictions of International Courts and Tribunals (Oxford University Press 2004)

Shany Y, 'Jurisdiction and Admissibility' in Cesare Romano, Karen Alter and Yuval Shany (eds), *The Oxford Handbook of International Adjudication* (Oxford University Press 2013)

Shany Y, Assessing the Effectiveness of International Courts: A Goal-Based Approach (Oxford University Press 2014)

Shany Y, Questions of Jurisdiction and Admissibility before International Courts (Cambridge University Press 2015)

Shaw MN, Rosenne's Law and Practice of the International Court: 1920–2015, vol II (5th edn, Brill Nijhoff 2016)

Shirlow E and Gore KN, The Vienna Convention on the Law of Treaties in Investor-State Disputes: History, Evolution and Future (Wolters Kluwer 2022)

Simma B, 'Fragmentation in a Positive Light' (2003) 25 Michigan Journal of International Law 845

Simma B and Kill T, 'Harmonizing Investment Protection and International Human Rights: First Steps toward a Methodology' in Christina Binder and others (eds), *International Investment Law for the 21st Century* (Oxford University Press 2009)

Simma B and Paulus A, 'The Responsibility of Individuals for Human Rights Abuses in Internal Conflicts: A Positivist View' (1999) 93 American Journal of International Law 291

Simma B and Pulkowski D, 'Of Planets and the Universe: Self-Contained Regimes in International Law' (2006) 17 European Journal of International Law 483

Simma B and Pulkowski D, 'Two Worlds. but Not Apart: International Investment Law and General International Law' in Marc Bungenberg and others (eds), *International Investment Law: A Handbook* (Hart Publishing 2015)

Smits JM, 'What Is Legal Doctrine? On The Aims and Methods of Legal-Dogmatic Research' in Edward L Rubin, Hans-W Micklitz and Rob van Gestel (eds), *Rethinking Legal Scholarship: A Transatlantic Dialogue* (Cambridge University Press 2017)

Sornarajah M, Resistance and Change in the International Law on Foreign Investment (Cambridge University Press 2015)

Spak G and Kapterian G, 'The World Trade Organization' in Chiara Giorgetti (ed), *The Rules, Practice and Jurisprudence of International Courts and Tribunals* (Martinus Nijhoff Publishers 2012)

Spiermann O, 'Investment Arbitration: Applicable Law' in Marc Bungenberg and others (eds), *International Investment Law: A Handbook* (Hart Publishing 2015)

Squatrito T, 'Amicus Curiae Briefs in the WTO DSM: Good or Bad News for Non-State Actor Involvement?' (2018) 17 World Trade Review 65

St John T, The Rise of Investor-State Arbitration: Politics, Law, and Unintended Consequences (Oxford University Press 2018)

Steger D, 'The Jurisdiction of the WTO' (2004) 98 American Society of International Law Proceedings 142

Stewart TP, *The GATT Uruguay Round: A Negotiating History (1986–1992)*, vol 2 (Kluwer Law and Taxation Publishers 1993)

Strain N, 'Invoking Systemic Ideals or Systemic Rules? Jurisdiction in WTO and Investor-State Dispute Settlement' (2022) 82 Zeitschrift für ausländisches öffentliches Recht und Völkerrecht / Heidelberg Journal of International Law 401

Strain N, 'Regulating Collective Resources under Multilateral Treaties: The Decision in Whaling in the Antarctic (Australia v Japan)' (2019) 20 Melbourne Journal of International Law 572

Strain N, 'Jurisdiction and Applicable Law in Investor-State and WTO Dispute Settlement: Comparing Consent and Inconsistency in the Application of Other International Law' (University of Oslo, Faculty of Law 2022)

Strain N, 'Methodological Consistency in the Interpretation of International Treaties in Investor-State Arbitration: An Empirical Study' in Guiditta Cordero-Moss and Diego P Fernández Arroyo (eds), *Applicable Law Issues in International Arbitration / Questions de droit applicable dans l'arbitrage international*, vol 25 (Brill Nijhoff 2022)

Strain N and others, 'Compliance Politics and International Investment Disputes: A New Dataset' (2024) 27 Journal of International Economic Law 70

Subedi SP, International Investment Law: Reconciling Policy and Principle (3rd edn, Hart Publishing 2016)

Tams CJ, 'Controlling Consent: Insights from Binding Dispute Settlement' in Samantha Besson (ed), *Consenting to International Law* (1st edn, Cambridge University Press 2023)

Tanzi A, 'The Relevance of the Foreign Investor's Good Faith' in Andrea Gattini, Attila Tanzi and Filippo Fontanelli (eds), *General Principles of Law and International Investment Arbitration* (Brill Nijhoff 2018)

Teitel R and Howse R, 'Cross-Judging: Tribunalization in a Fragmented but Interconnected Global Order Symposium – The Normalizing of Adjudication In Complex International Governance Regimes: Patterns, Possibilities, and Problems' (2008) 41 New York University Journal of International Law and Politics 959

Thin S, 'Guardians of Legality? The International Judicial Function in an Era of Community Interest' (2023) 92 Nordic Journal of International Law 499

Thirlway HWA, 'The Law and Procedure of the International Court of Justice 1960–1989: Part Nine' (1999) 69 British Yearbook of International Law 1

Thirlway HWA, 'The Drafting of ICJ Decisions: Some Personal Recollections and Observations Agora: The International Court of Justice at 60 (Part I)' (2006) 5 Chinese Journal of International Law 15

Tienhaara K, The Expropriation of Environmental Governance: Protecting Foreign Investors at the Expense of Public Policy (University Press 2009)

Tomuschat C, 'Article 36' in Andreas Zimmermann and others (eds), *The Statute of the International Court of Justice: A Commentary* (3rd edn, Oxford University Press 2019)

Trachtman JP, 'The Domain of WTO Dispute Resolution' (1999) 40 Harvard International Law Journal 333

Trachtman JP, 'Review of Conflict of Norms in Public International Law: How WTO Law Relates to Other Rules of International Law' (2004) 98 The American Journal of International Law 855

Trachtman JP, 'The Jurisdiction of the WTO' (2004) 98 American Society of International Law Proceedings 139

Trachtman JP, 'Jurisdiction in WTO Dispute Settlement' in Bruce Wilson and Rufus Yerxa (eds), *Key Issues in WTO Dispute Settlement: The First Ten Years* (Cambridge University Press 2005)

Trachtman JP, 'WTO Trade and Environment Jurisprudence: Avoiding Environmental Catastrophe' (2017) 58 Harvard International Law Journal 273

Treves T, 'Judicial Lawmaking in an Era of Proliferation of International Courts and Tribunals: Development or Fragmentation of International Law?' in Rüdiger Wolfrum and Volker Röben (eds), *Developments of International Law in Treaty Making* (Springer 2005)

Treves T, 'Aspects of Legitimacy of Decisions of International Courts and Tribunals' in Rüdiger Wolfrum and Volker Röben (eds), *Legitimacy in International Law* (Springer 2008)

Tzeng P, 'Jurisdiction and Applicable Law Under UNCLOS' (2016) 126 The Yale Law Journal 242

Vadi V, Cultural Heritage in International Investment Law and Arbitration (Cambridge University Press 2014)

Vadi V, Analogies in International Investment Law and Arbitration (Cambridge University Press 2015)

Vadi V, Cultural Heritage in International Economic Law (Brill Nijhoff 2023)

van Aaken A, 'International Investment Law between Commitment and Flexibility: A Contract Theory Analysis' (2009) 12 Journal of International Economic Law 507

Van Damme I, Treaty Interpretation by the WTO Appellate Body (Oxford University Press 2009)

Van Damme I, 'Jurisdiction, Applicable Law, and Interpretation' in Daniel Bethlehem and others (eds), *The Oxford Handbook of International Trade Law* (Oxford University Press 2012)

Van Damme I, 'Understanding the Choice for Evolutionary Interpretation' in Georges Abi-Saab, Gabrielle Marceau and Clément Marquet (eds), *Evolutionary Interpretation and International Law* (Hart 2019)

Van den Bossche P and Zdouc W, The Law and Policy of the World Trade Organization: Text, Cases and Materials (Cambridge University Press 2017)

Van Harten G, *Investment Treaty Arbitration and Public Law* (Oxford University Press 2008)

Villalpando SM, 'Attribution of Conduct to the State: How the Rules of State Responsibility May Be Applied Within the WTO Dispute Settlement System' (2002) 5 Journal of International Economic Law 393

von Bogdandy A and Venzke I, 'Beyond Dispute: International Judicial Institutions as Lawmakers' in Armin von Bogdandy and Ingo Venzke (eds), *International Judicial Lawmaking: On Public Authority and Democratic Legitimation in Global Governance* (Springer 2012)

von Bogdandy A and Venzke I, 'In Whose Name? An Investigation of International Courts' Public Authority and Its Democratic Justification' (2012) 23 European Journal of International Law 7

von der Decken K, 'Article 30: Application of Successive Treaties Relating to the Same Subject Matter', *Vienna Convention on the Law of Treaties: A Commentary* (2nd edn, Springer Berlin Heidelberg 2018)

Vranken JBM, 'Methodology of Legal Doctrinal Research' in Mark Van Hoecke (ed), *Methodologies of Legal Research: Which Kind of Method for What Kind of Discipline* (Hart Publishing 2011)

Waibel M, 'Investment Arbitration: Jurisdiction and Admissibility' in Marc Bungenberg and others (eds), *International Investment Law* (Beck Nomos Hart 2015)

Waibel M (eds), The Backlash Against Investment Arbitration: Perceptions and Reality (Kluwer Law International 2010)

Webb P, International Judicial Integration and Fragmentation (Oxford University Press 2013)

Weeramantry JR, *Treaty Interpretation in Investment Arbitration* (Oxford University Press 2012)

Weil P, '"The Court Cannot Conclude Definitively" ... Non Liquet Revisited' (1998) 36 Columbia Journal of Transnational Law 109

Weiler JHH, 'The Rule of Lawyers and the Ethos of Diplomats: Reflections on the Internal and External Legitimacy of WTO Dispute Settlement' (2001) 35 Journal of World Trade 191

Weiss F, 'Inherent Powers of National and International Courts' in Federico Ortino and Ernst-Ulrich Petersmann (eds), *The WTO Dispute Settlement System 1995–2003* (Kluwer 2003)

Wolfrum R, 'Legitimacy of International Law from a Legal Perspective: Some Introductory Considerations' in Rüdiger Wolfrum and Volker Röben (eds), *Legitimacy in International Law* (Springer 2008)

Wouters J and others, 'General Principles and the Coherence of International Law: Setting the Scene' in Mads Andenas and others (eds), *General Principles and the Coherence of International Law* (Brill Nijhoff 2019)

Yee S, 'Article 38 of the ICJ Statute and Applicable Law: Selected Issues in Recent Cases' (2016) 7 Journal of International Dispute Settlement 472

Yu C, Dispute Settlement and the Reform of International Investment Law: Legalization through Adjudication (Edward Elgar Publishing 2023)

Zang MQ, Judicial Engagement of International Economic Courts and Tribunals (Edward Elgar Publishing 2020)

Zarbiyev F, 'Judicial Activism in International Law – A Conceptual Framework for Analysis' (2012) 3 Journal of International Dispute Settlement 247

Index

www.ingramcontent.com/pod-product-compliance
Lightning Source LLC
LaVergne TN
LVHW022359021026
849161LV00021B/675